You're Reading in the Wrong Direction!!

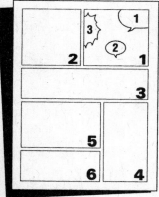

Whoops! Guess what? You're starting at the wrong end of the comic!

…It's true! In keeping with the original Japanese format, **One Piece** is meant to be read from right to left, starting in the upper-right corner.

Unlike English, which is read from left to right, Japanese is read from right to left, meaning that action, sound effects and word-balloon order are completely reversed…something which can make readers unfamiliar with Japanese feel pretty backwards themselves. For this reason, manga or Japanese comics published in the U.S. in English have sometimes been published "flopped"— that is, printed in exact reverse order, as though seen from the other side of a mirror.

By flopping pages, U.S. publishers can avoid confusing readers, but the compromise is not without its downside. For one thing, a character in a flopped manga series who once wore in the original Japanese version a T-shirt emblazoned with "M A Y" (as in "the merry month of") now wears one which reads "Y A M"! Additionally, many manga creators in Japan are themselves unhappy with the process, as some feel the mirror-imaging of their art skews their original intentions.

We are proud to bring you Eiichiro Oda's **One Piece** in the original unflopped format. For now, though, turn to the other side of the book and let the journey begin…!

—Editor

FEB -- 2011

NARUTO

Story and Art by
Masashi Kishimoto

Naruto is determined to become the greatest ninja ever!

Twelve years ago the Village Hidden in the Leaves was attacked by a fearsome threat. A nine-tailed fox spirit claimed the life of the village leader, the Hokage, and many others. Today, the village is at peace and a troublemaking kid named Naruto is struggling to graduate from Ninja Academy. His goal may be to become the next Hokage, but his true destiny will be much more complicated. The adventure begins now!

WORLD'S BEST SELLING MANG

www.shonenjump.com   www.vi

SHONEN JUMP MANGA

ONE PIECE

Vol. 78
CHAMPION OF EVIL

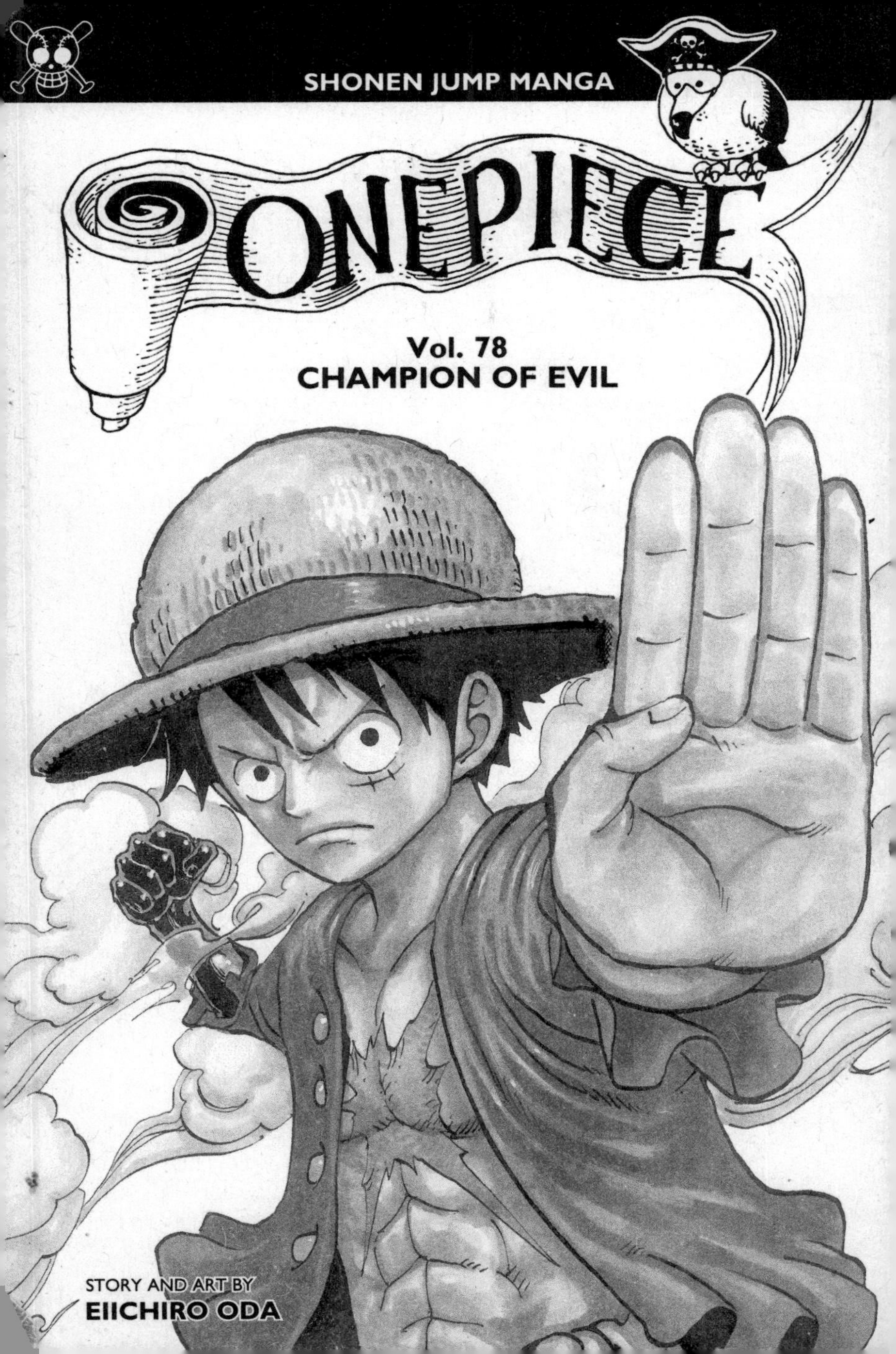

STORY AND ART BY
EIICHIRO ODA

The Straw Hat Crew

Monkey D. Luffy

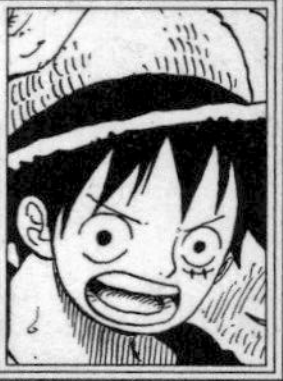

A young man who dreams of becoming the Pirate King. After training with Rayleigh, he and his crew head for the New World!

Captain, Bounty: 400 million berries

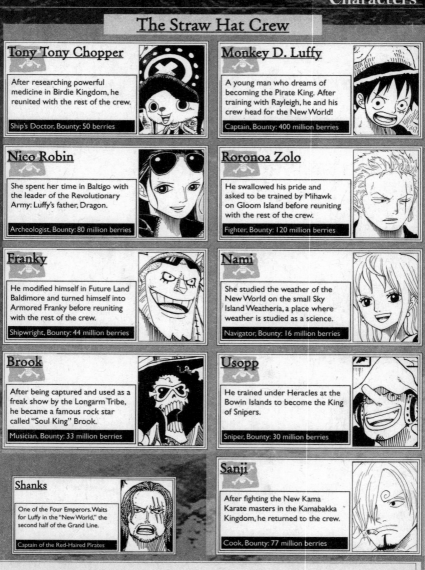

Tony Tony Chopper

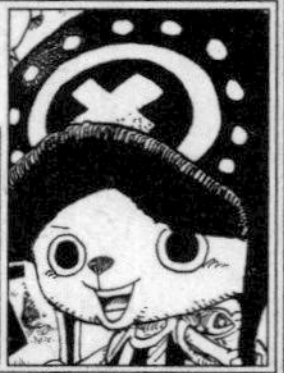

After researching powerful medicine in Birdie Kingdom, he reunited with the rest of the crew.

Ship's Doctor, Bounty: 50 berries

Roronoa Zolo

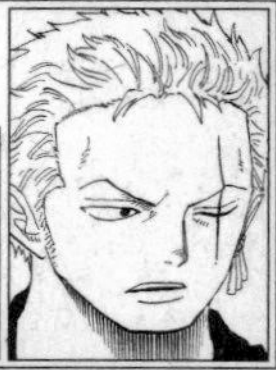

He swallowed his pride and asked to be trained by Mihawk on Gloom Island before reuniting with the rest of the crew.

Fighter, Bounty: 120 million berries

Nico Robin

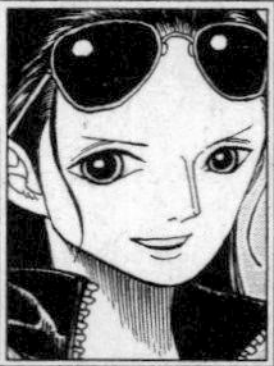

She spent her time in Baltigo with the leader of the Revolutionary Army: Luffy's father, Dragon.

Archeologist, Bounty: 80 million berries

Nami

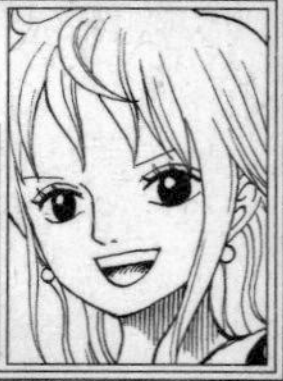

She studied the weather of the New World on the small Sky Island Weatheria, a place where weather is studied as a science.

Navigator, Bounty: 16 million berries

Franky

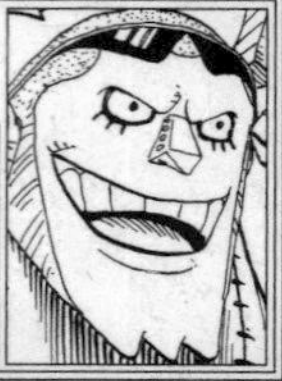

He modified himself in Future Land Baldimore and turned himself into Armored Franky before reuniting with the rest of the crew.

Shipwright, Bounty: 44 million berries

Usopp

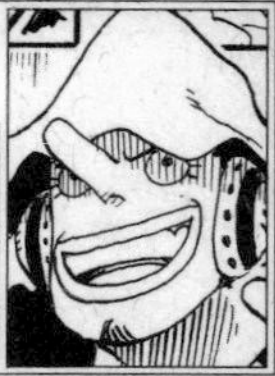

He trained under Heracles at the Bowin Islands to become the King of Snipers.

Sniper, Bounty: 30 million berries

Brook

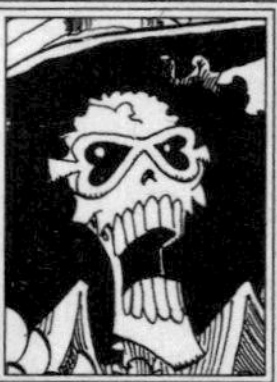

After being captured and used as a freak show by the Longarm Tribe, he became a famous rock star called "Soul King" Brook.

Musician, Bounty: 33 million berries

Sanji

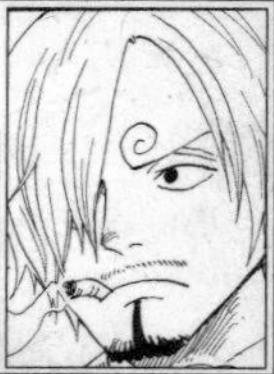

After fighting the New Kama Karate masters in the Kamabakka Kingdom, he returned to the crew.

Cook, Bounty: 77 million berries

Shanks

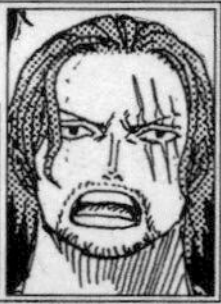

One of the Four Emperors. Waits for Luffy in the "New World," the second half of the Grand Line.

Captain of the Red-Haired Pirates

one-legged toy soldier who informs them of the nation's hidden darkness, and they decide to help the little Tontattas in their fight for freedom. As their companions hold off the Don Quixote Family, Luffy and Law face off in direct battle against Doflamingo!! There, the past that ties Law, Corazon and Doflamingo together is revealed. Law fights back against Doflamingo to fulfill Corazon's wishes—but his arm gets chopped off! Meanwhile, the forces of Luffy's army emerge triumphant, one by one!! Only a few foes remain...

The story of ONE PIECE 1»78

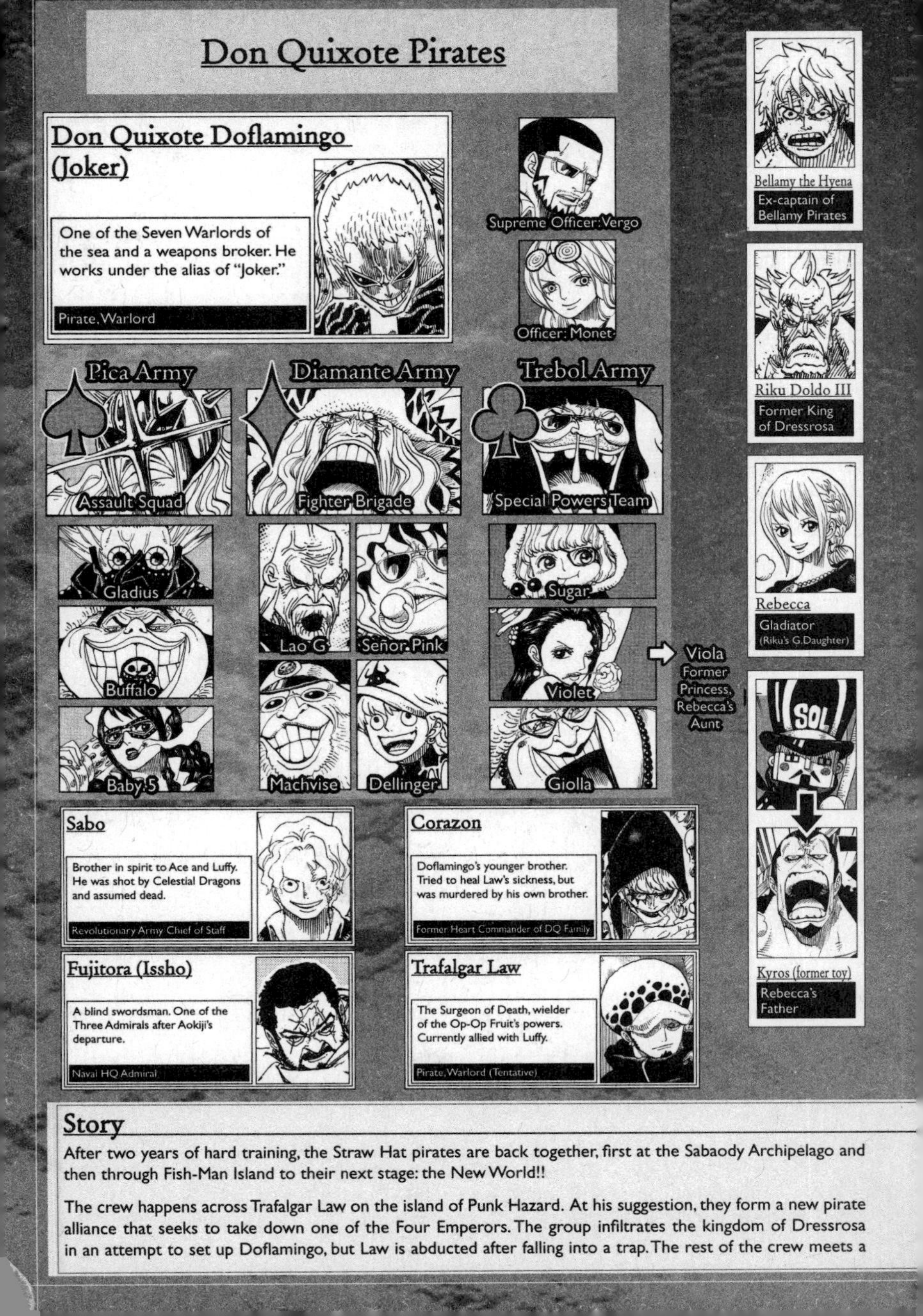

Don Quixote Pirates
Don Quixote Doflamingo (Joker)
One of the Seven Warlords of the sea and a weapons broker. He works under the alias of "Joker."
Pirate, Warlord
Supreme Officer: Vergo
Officer: Monet
Pica Army
Assault Squad
Gladius
Buffalo
Baby 5
Diamante Army
Fighter Brigade
Lao G
Señor Pink
Machvise
Dellinger
Trebol Army
Special Powers Team
Sugar
Violet
Giolla
Viola
Former Princess, Rebecca's Aunt
Bellamy the Hyena
Ex-captain of Bellamy Pirates
Riku Doldo III
Former King of Dressrosa
Rebecca
Gladiator
(Riku's G.Daughter)
SOL
Kyros (former toy)
Rebecca's Father
Sabo
Brother in spirit to Ace and Luffy. He was shot by Celestial Dragons and assumed dead.
Revolutionary Army Chief of Staff
Corazon
Doflamingo's younger brother. Tried to heal Law's sickness, but was murdered by his own brother.
Former Heart Commander of DQ Family
Fujitora (Issho)
A blind swordsman. One of the Three Admirals after Aokiji's departure.
Naval HQ Admiral
Trafalgar Law
The Surgeon of Death, wielder of the Op-Op Fruit's powers. Currently allied with Luffy.
Pirate, Warlord (Tentative)

Story

After two years of hard training, the Straw Hat pirates are back together, first at the Sabaody Archipelago and then through Fish-Man Island to their next stage: the New World!!

The crew happens across Trafalgar Law on the island of Punk Hazard. At his suggestion, they form a new pirate alliance that seeks to take down one of the Four Emperors. The group infiltrates the kingdom of Dressrosa in an attempt to set up Doflamingo, but Law is abducted after falling into a trap. The rest of the crew meets a

NEW WORLD ONE PIECE

Vol. 78
CHAMPION OF EVIL

CONTENTS

Chapter 776:

HERO OF THE COLISEUM

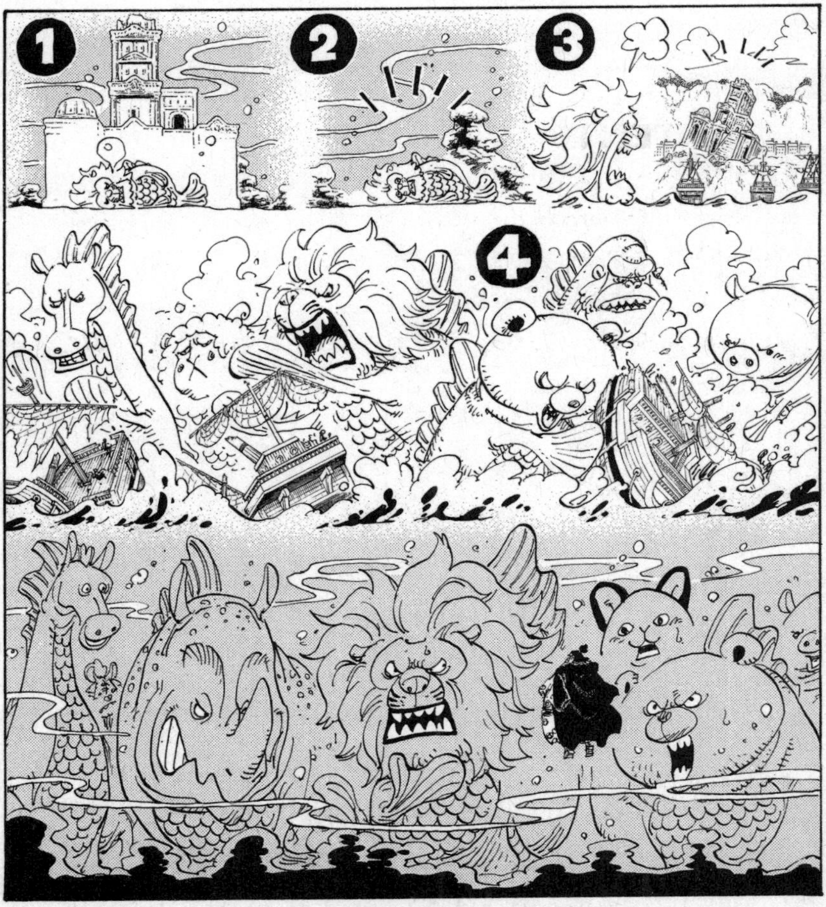
1
2
3
4

THE SOLITARY JOURNEY OF JIMBEI, FIRST SON OF THE SEA, VOL. 21: "THE SEA BEASTS' MISUNDERSTANDING"

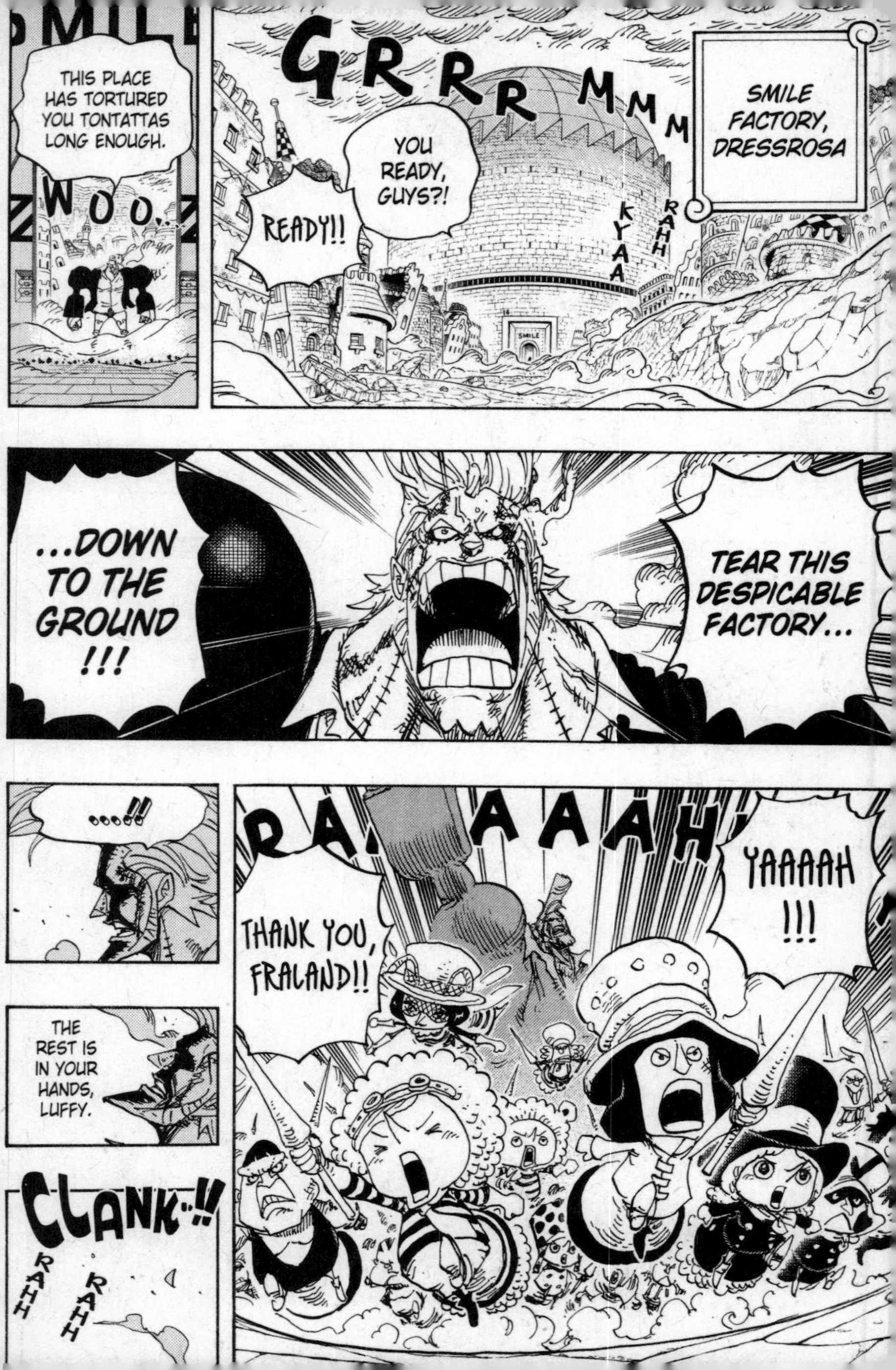
SMILE FACTORY, DRESSROSA
GRRRMMMM
YOU READY, GUYS?!
READY!!
KYAA
RAHH
THIS PLACE HAS TORTURED YOU TONTATTAS LONG ENOUGH.
WOO..
TEAR THIS DESPICABLE FACTORY...
...DOWN TO THE GROUND!!!
RAAAAAH
YAAAAH!!!
THANK YOU, FRALAND!!
....!!
THE REST IS IN YOUR HANDS, LUFFY.
CLANK!!
RAHH
RAHH

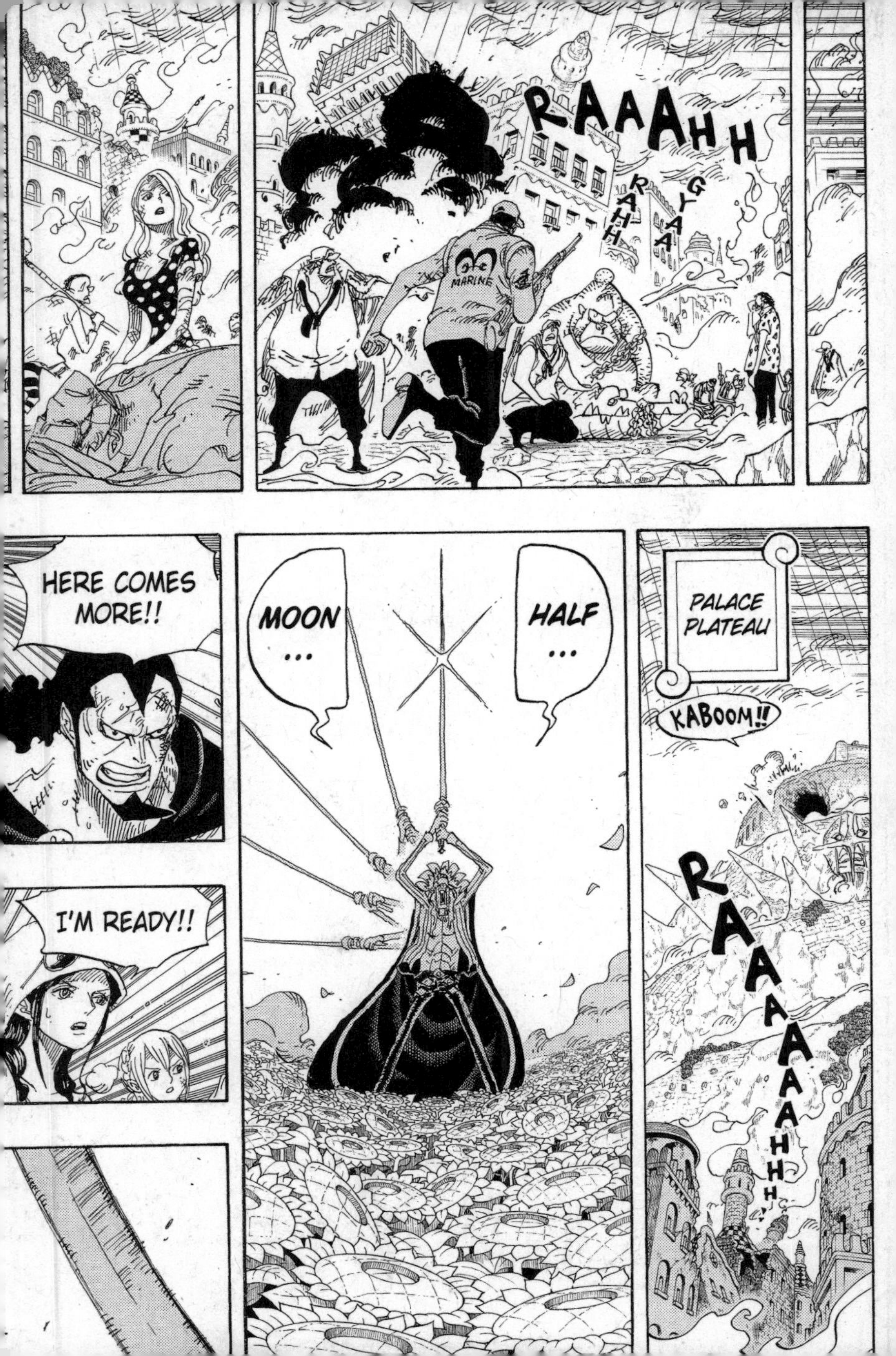
RAAAHH
GYAA
RAHH
PALACE PLATEAU
KABOOM!!
RAAAAAAAHH
HALF ...
MOON ...
HERE COMES MORE!!
I'M READY!!

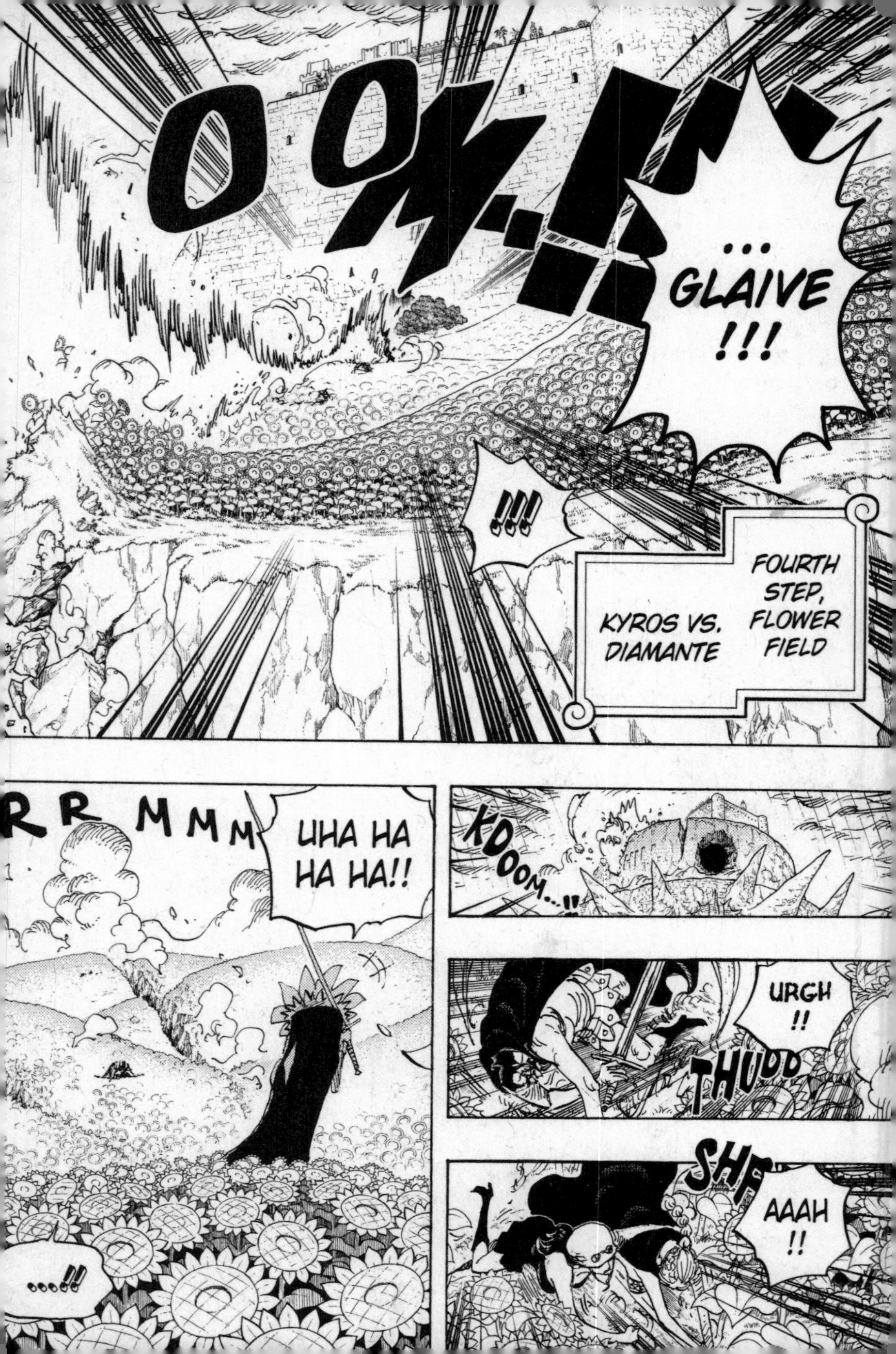

... GLAIVE !!!
!!!
FOURTH STEP, FLOWER FIELD
KYROS VS. DIAMANTE
KDOOOM...!!
URGH !!
THUDD
SHF
AAAH !!
RRRMMM
UHA HA HA HA!!
...!!

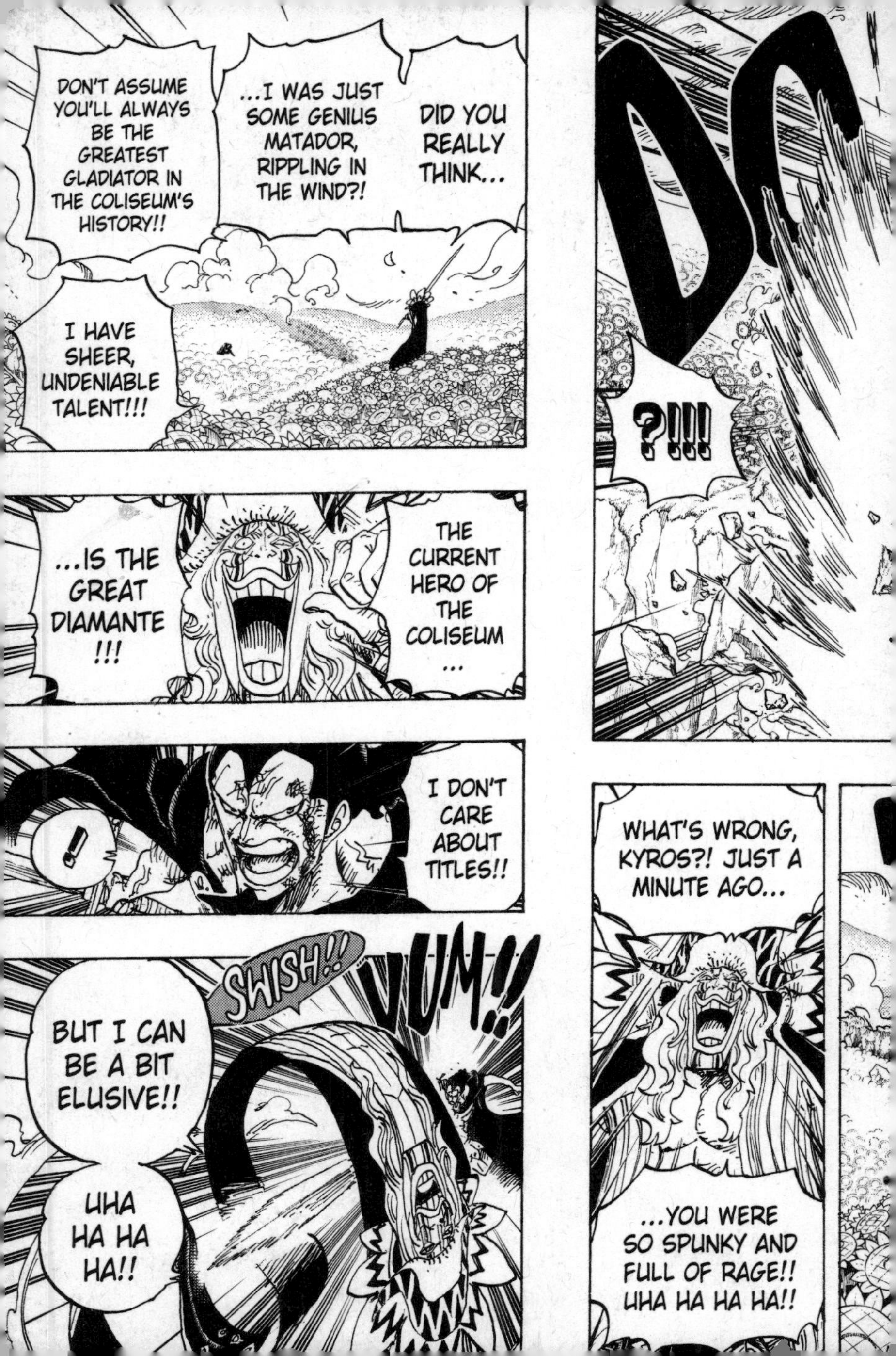
DO
?!!!
DID YOU REALLY THINK...
...I WAS JUST SOME GENIUS MATADOR, RIPPLING IN THE WIND?!
DON'T ASSUME YOU'LL ALWAYS BE THE GREATEST GLADIATOR IN THE COLISEUM'S HISTORY!!
I HAVE SHEER, UNDENIABLE TALENT!!!
THE CURRENT HERO OF THE COLISEUM...
...IS THE GREAT DIAMANTE!!!
WHAT'S WRONG, KYROS?! JUST A MINUTE AGO...
...YOU WERE SO SPUNKY AND FULL OF RAGE!! UHA HA HA HA!!
I DON'T CARE ABOUT TITLES!!
!
VUM!!
SWISH!!
BUT I CAN BE A BIT ELUSIVE!!
UHA HA HA HA!!

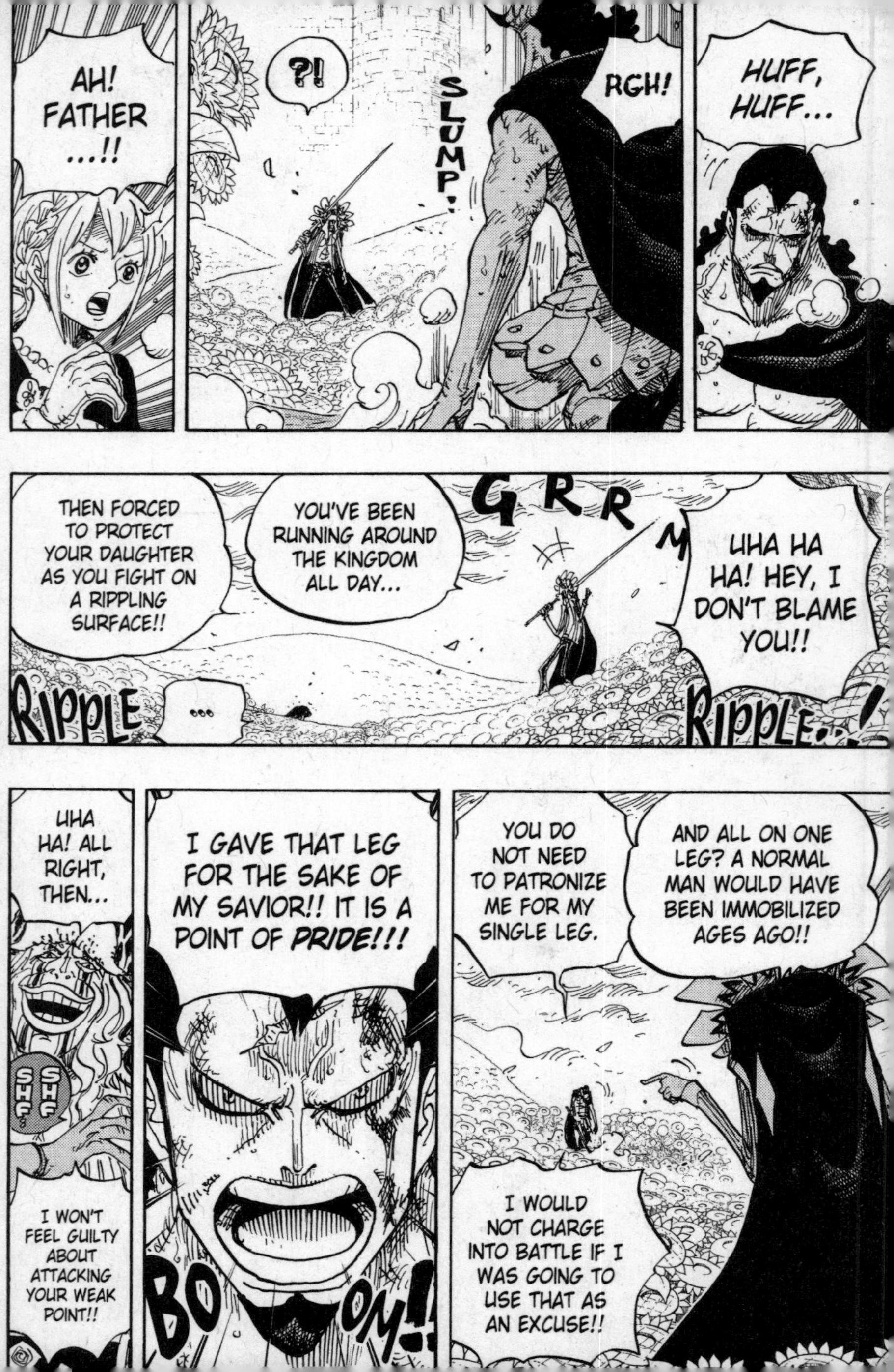
HUFF, HUFF...
RGH!
SLUMP
?!
AH! FATHER ...!!
UHA HA HA! HEY, I DON'T BLAME YOU!!
RIPPLE...
GRRRM
YOU'VE BEEN RUNNING AROUND THE KINGDOM ALL DAY...
THEN FORCED TO PROTECT YOUR DAUGHTER AS YOU FIGHT ON A RIPPLING SURFACE!!
...
RIPPLE
AND ALL ON ONE LEG? A NORMAL MAN WOULD HAVE BEEN IMMOBILIZED AGES AGO!!
YOU DO NOT NEED TO PATRONIZE ME FOR MY SINGLE LEG.
I WOULD NOT CHARGE INTO BATTLE IF I WAS GOING TO USE THAT AS AN EXCUSE!!
I GAVE THAT LEG FOR THE SAKE OF MY SAVIOR!! IT IS A POINT OF *PRIDE*!!!
BOOM!!
UHA HA! ALL RIGHT, THEN...
SHF SHF
I WON'T FEEL GUILTY ABOUT ATTACKING YOUR WEAK POINT!!

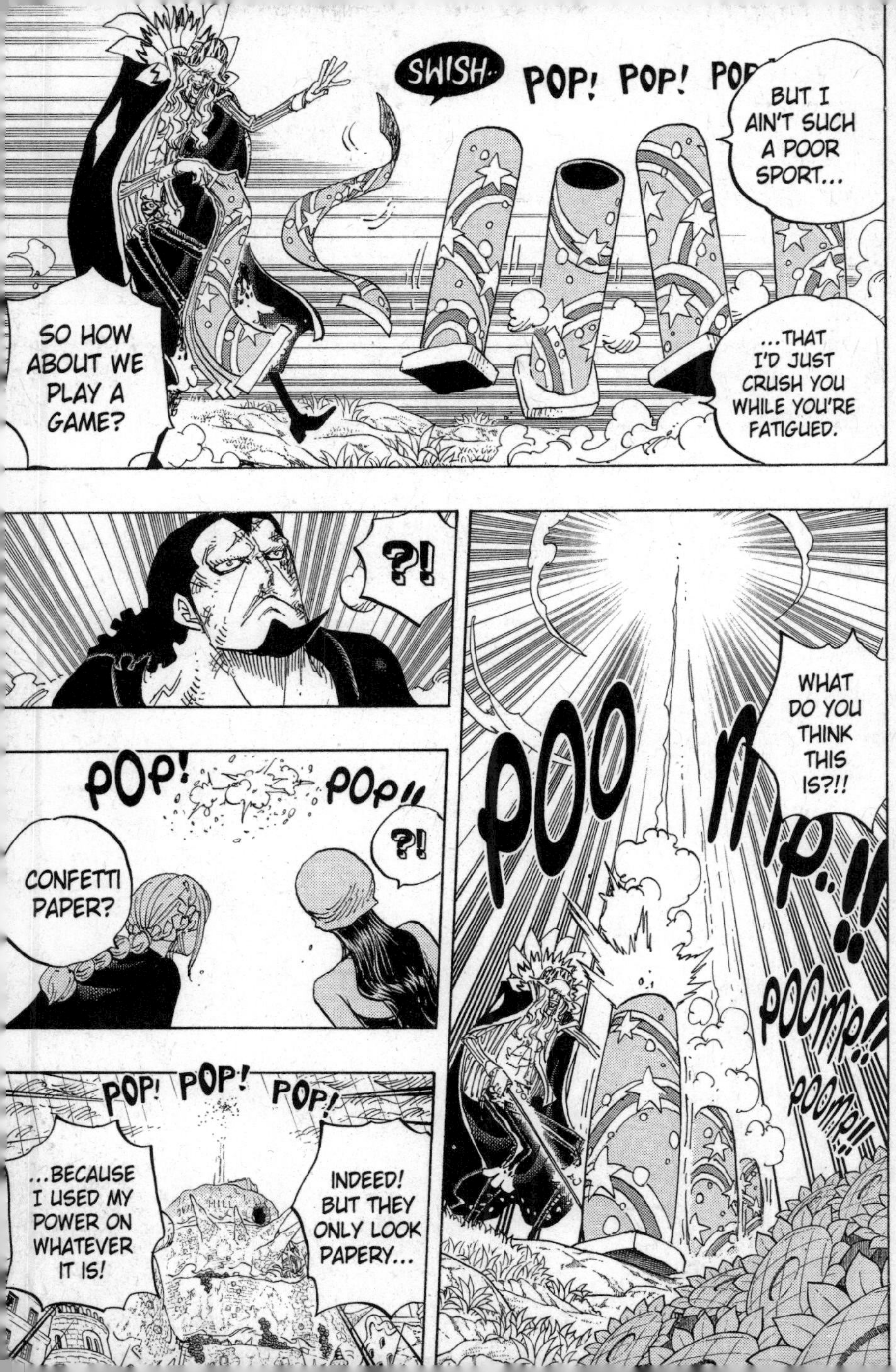
BUT I AIN'T SUCH A POOR SPORT...
POP! POP! POP
SWISH..
...THAT I'D JUST CRUSH YOU WHILE YOU'RE FATIGUED.
SO HOW ABOUT WE PLAY A GAME?
WHAT DO YOU THINK THIS IS?!!
POOOMP..!!
POOMP!!
POOMP!!
?!
POP!
POP!!
?!
CONFETTI PAPER?
POP! POP! POP!
INDEED! BUT THEY ONLY LOOK PAPERY...
...BECAUSE I USED MY POWER ON WHATEVER IT IS!

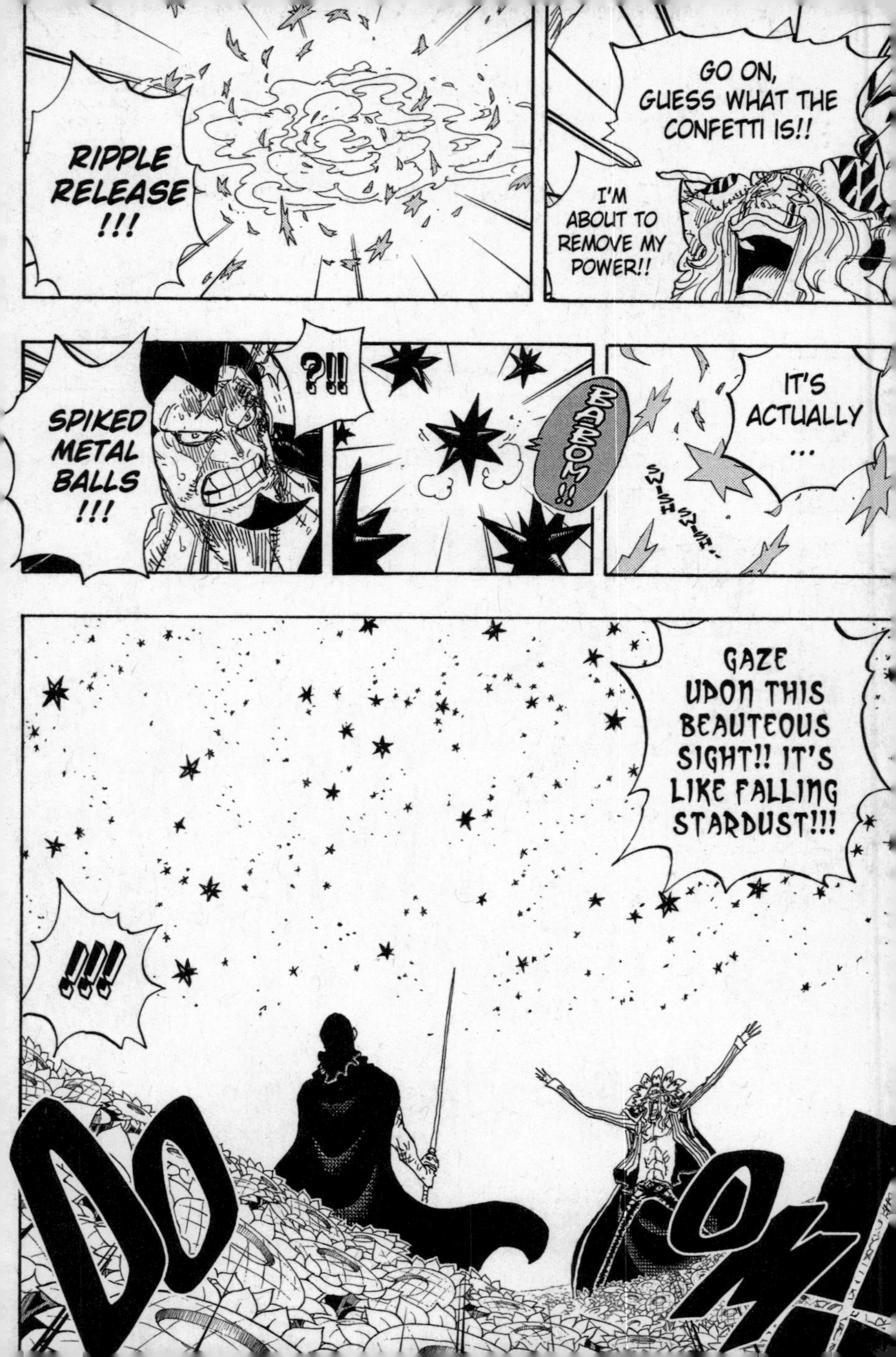
GO ON, GUESS WHAT THE CONFETTI IS!!
I'M ABOUT TO REMOVE MY POWER!!
RIPPLE RELEASE!!!
IT'S ACTUALLY...
SWISH SWISH
BABOOM!!
?!!
SPIKED METAL BALLS!!!
GAZE UPON THIS BEAUTEOUS SIGHT!! IT'S LIKE FALLING STARDUST!!!
!!!
DOON!

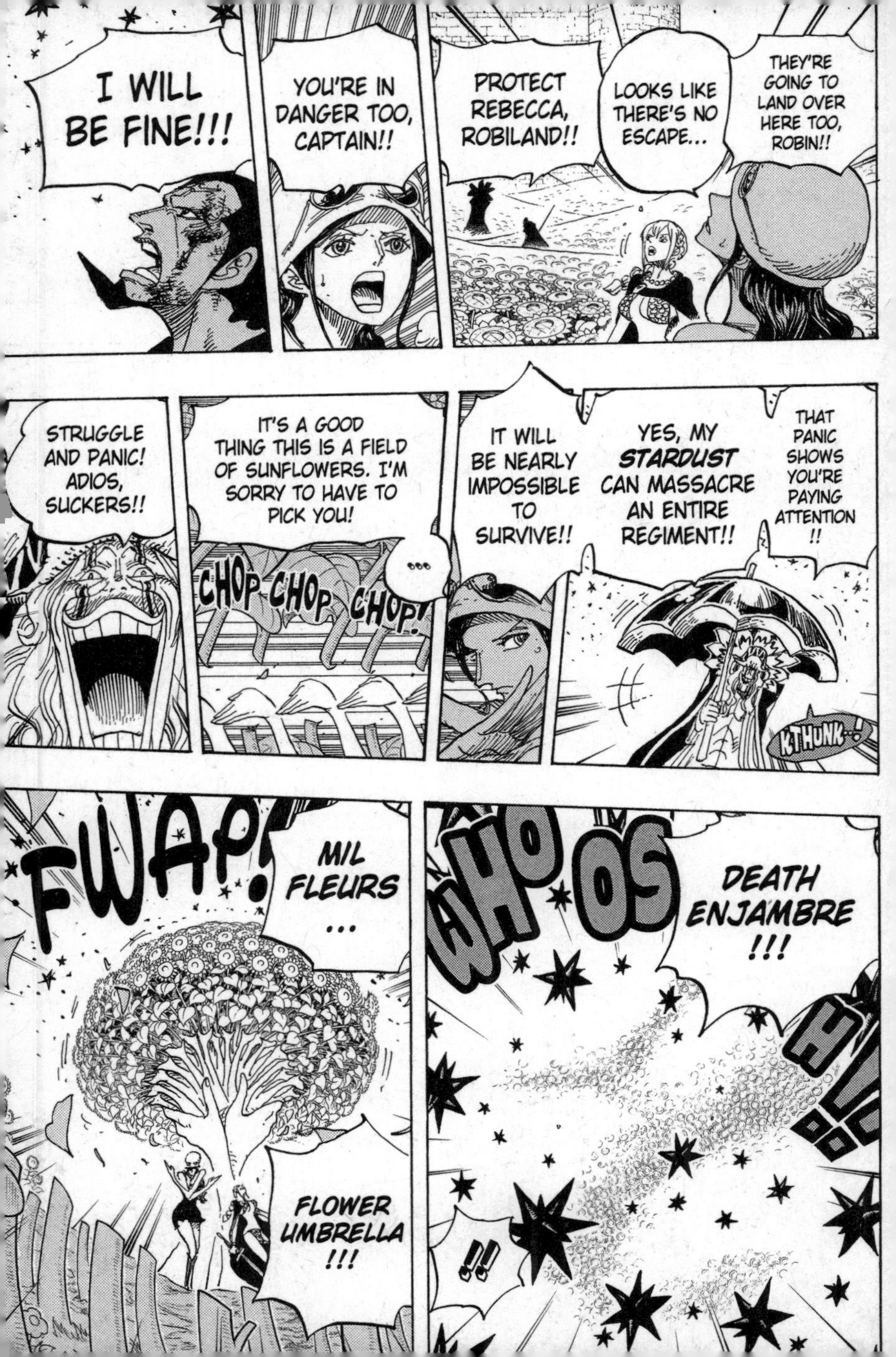
THEY'RE GOING TO LAND OVER HERE TOO, ROBIN!!
LOOKS LIKE THERE'S NO ESCAPE...
PROTECT REBECCA, ROBILAND!!
YOU'RE IN DANGER TOO, CAPTAIN!!
I WILL BE FINE!!!
THAT PANIC SHOWS YOU'RE PAYING ATTENTION !!
YES, MY STARDUST CAN MASSACRE AN ENTIRE REGIMENT!!
IT WILL BE NEARLY IMPOSSIBLE TO SURVIVE!!
K'THUNK
...
IT'S A GOOD THING THIS IS A FIELD OF SUNFLOWERS. I'M SORRY TO HAVE TO PICK YOU!
CHOP CHOP CHOP!
STRUGGLE AND PANIC! ADIOS, SUCKERS!!
DEATH ENJAMBRE !!!
WHOOS
!!
MIL FLEURS ...
FWAP!
FLOWER UMBRELLA !!!

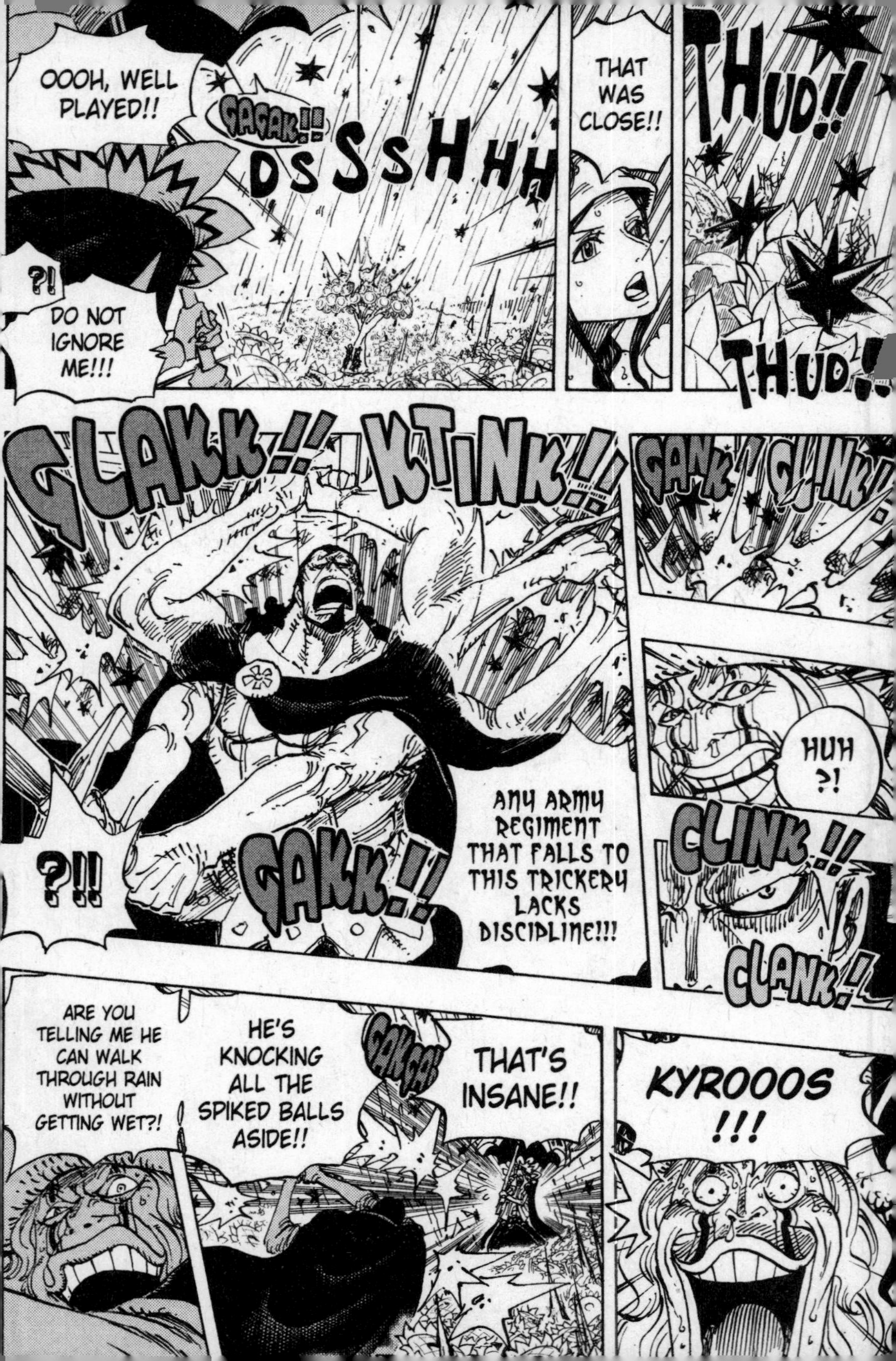
THUD!!
THUD!!
THAT WAS CLOSE!!
GAGAK!!
DSSSHHH
OOOH, WELL PLAYED!!
?!
DO NOT IGNORE ME!!!
GANK CLINK!!
HUH ?!
CLINK!!
CLANK!!
KTINK!!
GLAKK!!
ANY ARMY REGIMENT THAT FALLS TO THIS TRICKERY LACKS DISCIPLINE!!!
GAKK!!
?!!
KYROOOS !!!
THAT'S INSANE!!
HE'S KNOCKING ALL THE SPIKED BALLS ASIDE!!
ARE YOU TELLING ME HE CAN WALK THROUGH RAIN WITHOUT GETTING WET?!

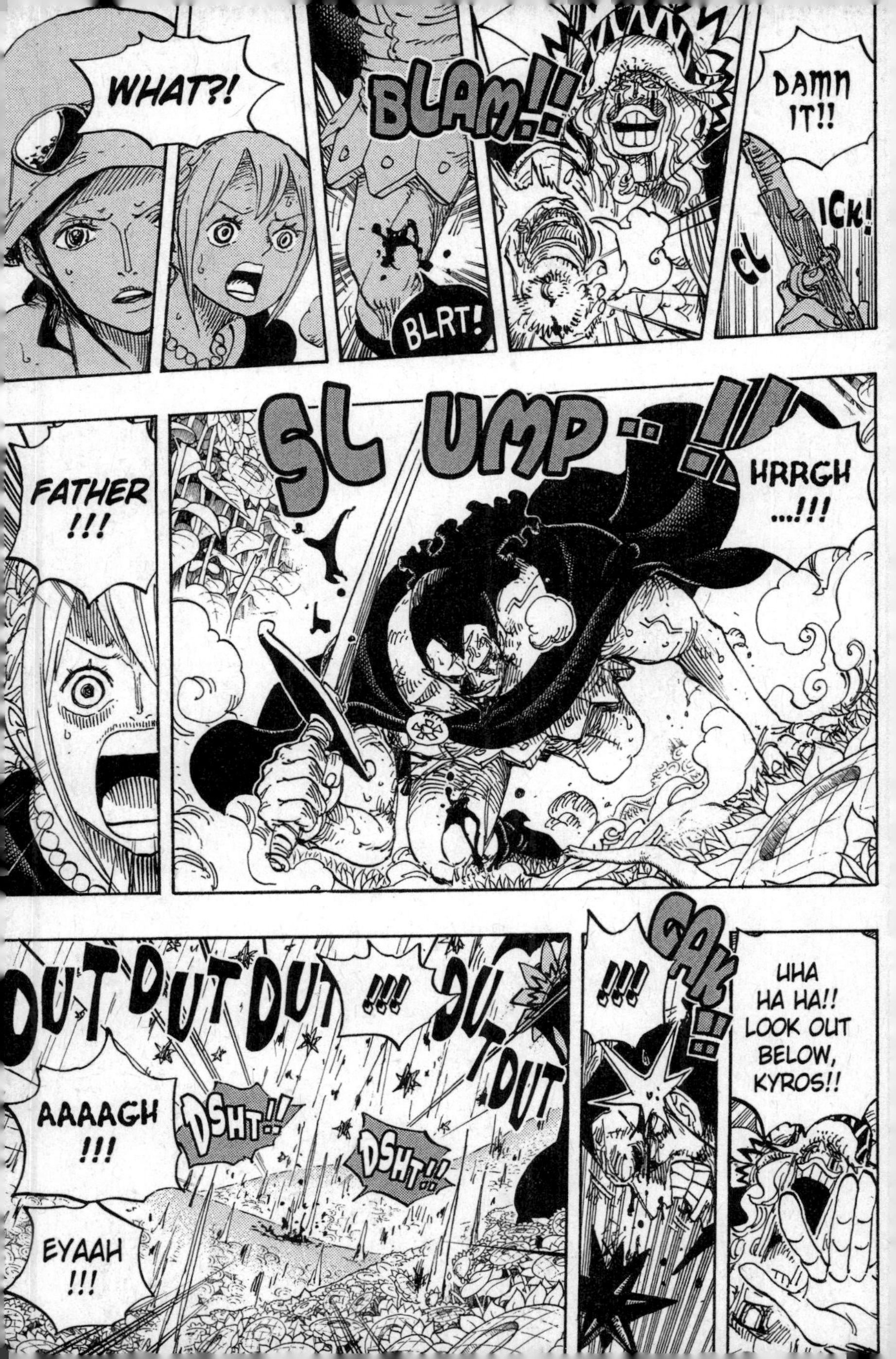
DAMN IT!!
CLICK!
BLAM!!
BLRT!
WHAT?!
SLUMP..!!
HRRGH ...!!!
FATHER !!!
UHA HA HA!! LOOK OUT BELOW, KYROS!!
GAK!!
!!!
DUT
DUT
!!!
DUT
DUT
DUT
DUT
DSHT!!
DSHT!!
AAAAGH !!!
EYAAH !!!

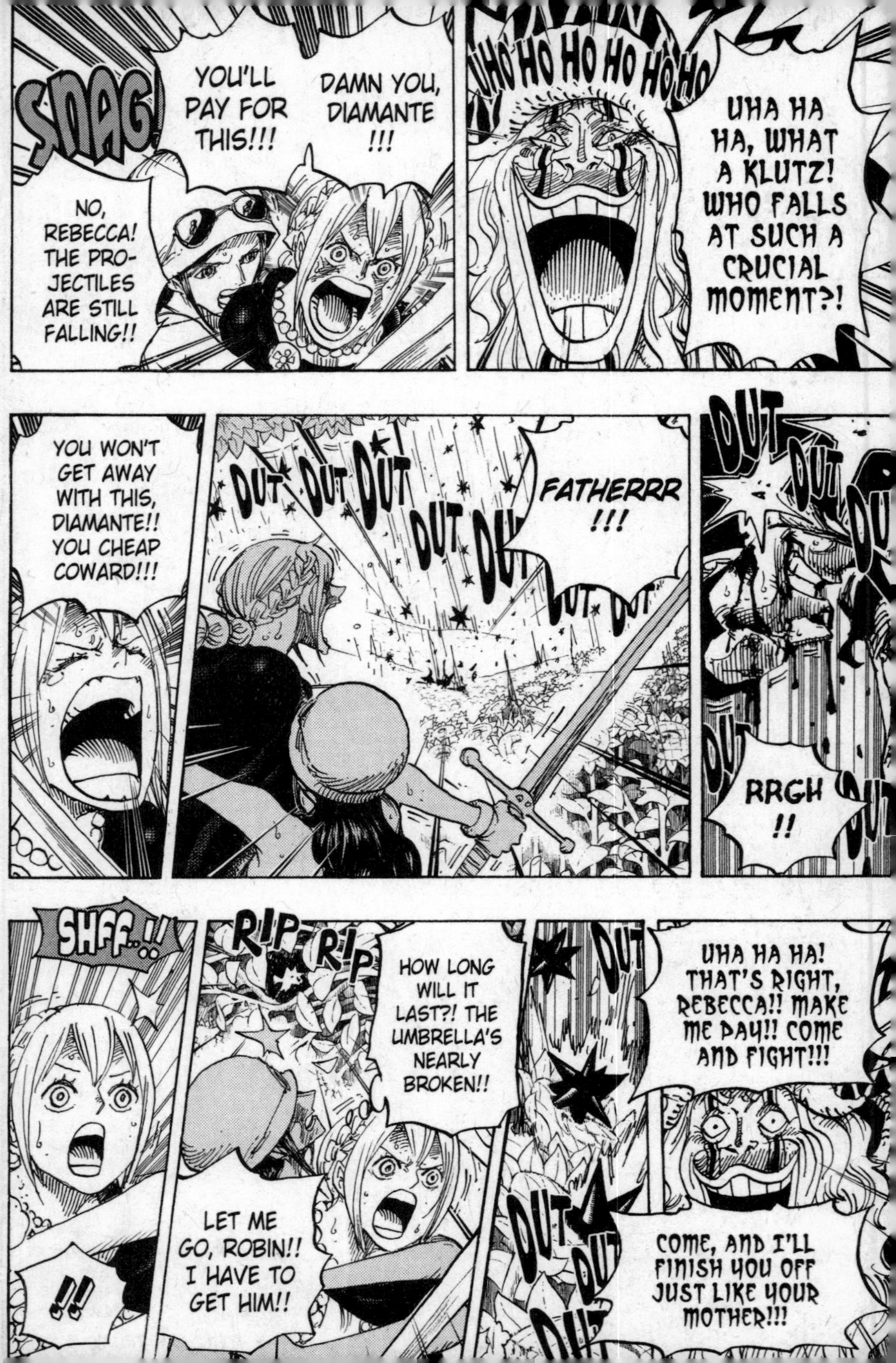
UHO HO HO HO HO HO HO
UHA HA HA, WHAT A KLUTZ! WHO FALLS AT SUCH A CRUCIAL MOMENT?!
DAMN YOU, DIAMANTE!!!
YOU'LL PAY FOR THIS!!!
SNAG
NO, REBECCA! THE PROJECTILES ARE STILL FALLING!!
DUT DUT DUT
RRGH!!
DUT
FATHERRR!!!
DUT DUT DUT DUT DU
DUT DUT
YOU WON'T GET AWAY WITH THIS, DIAMANTE!! YOU CHEAP COWARD!!!
UHA HA HA! THAT'S RIGHT, REBECCA!! MAKE ME PAY!! COME AND FIGHT!!!
COME, AND I'LL FINISH YOU OFF JUST LIKE YOUR MOTHER!!!
DUT
DUT DUT
RIP RIP
HOW LONG WILL IT LAST?! THE UMBRELLA'S NEARLY BROKEN!!
LET ME GO, ROBIN!! I HAVE TO GET HIM!!
SHFF..!!
!!

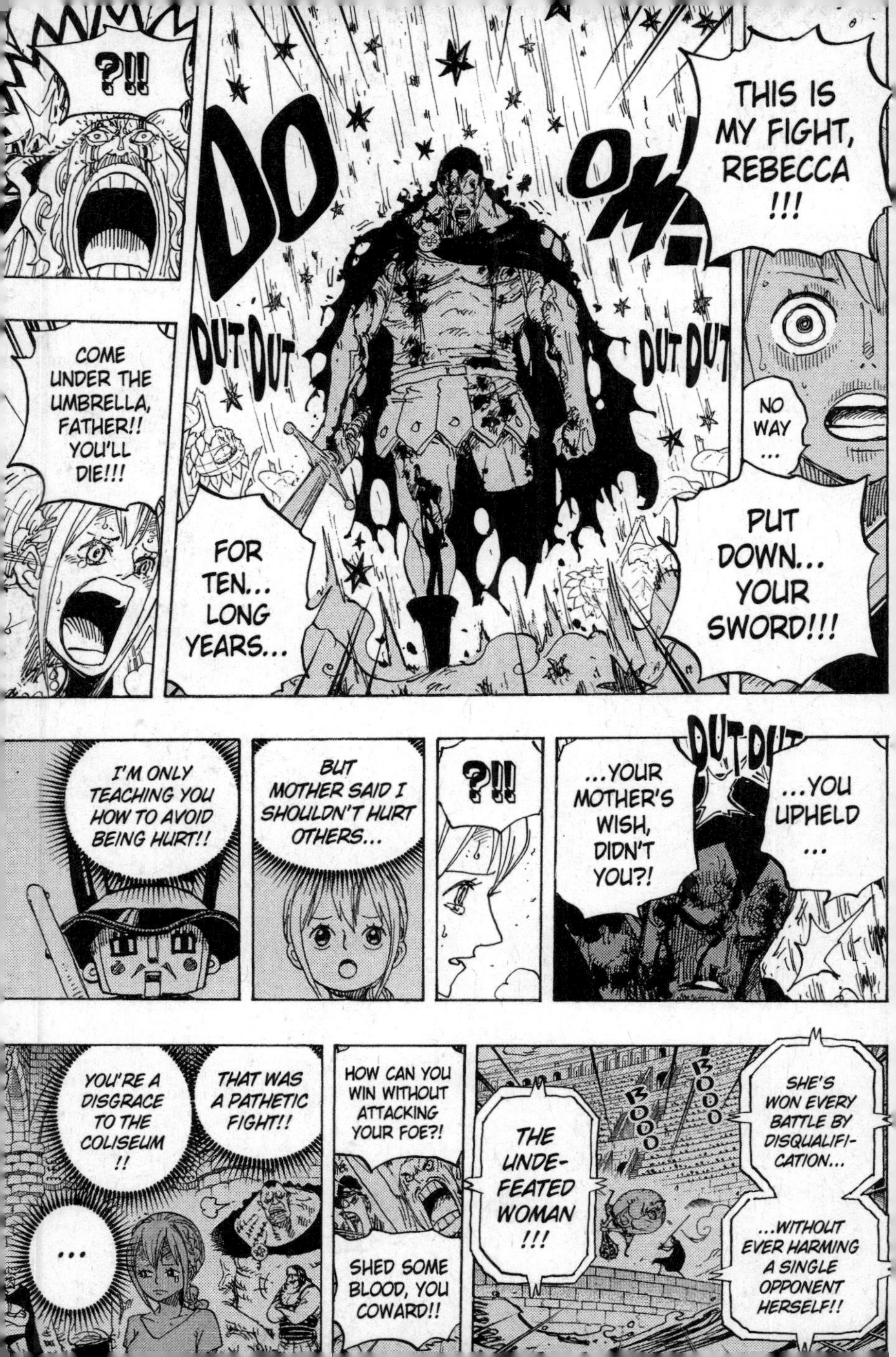
THIS IS MY FIGHT, REBECCA !!!
NO WAY ...
PUT DOWN... YOUR SWORD!!!
DOOM
DUT DUT
DUT DUT
FOR TEN... LONG YEARS...
?!!
COME UNDER THE UMBRELLA, FATHER!! YOU'LL DIE!!!
DUT DUT
...YOU UPHELD ...
...YOUR MOTHER'S WISH, DIDN'T YOU?!
?!!
BUT MOTHER SAID I SHOULDN'T HURT OTHERS...
I'M ONLY TEACHING YOU HOW TO AVOID BEING HURT!!
BOOO
BOOO
SHE'S WON EVERY BATTLE BY DISQUALIFI-CATION...
...WITHOUT EVER HARMING A SINGLE OPPONENT HERSELF!!
THE UNDE-FEATED WOMAN !!!
HOW CAN YOU WIN WITHOUT ATTACKING YOUR FOE?!
SHED SOME BLOOD, YOU COWARD!!
THAT WAS A PATHETIC FIGHT!!
YOU'RE A DISGRACE TO THE COLISEUM !!
...

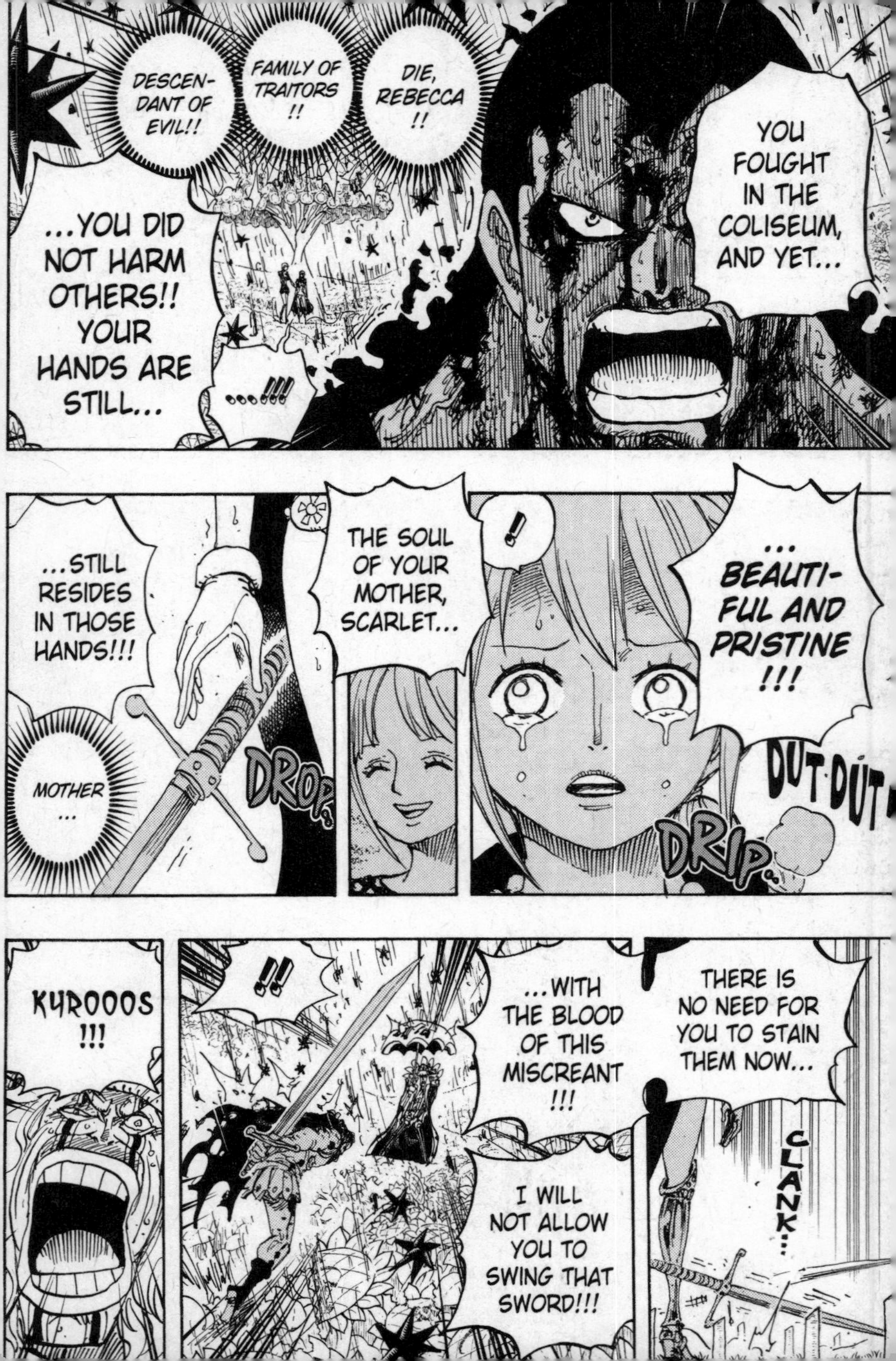
YOU FOUGHT IN THE COLISEUM, AND YET...
DIE, REBECCA!!
FAMILY OF TRAITORS!!
DESCENDANT OF EVIL!!
...YOU DID NOT HARM OTHERS!! YOUR HANDS ARE STILL...
...!!!
!
...BEAUTIFUL AND PRISTINE!!!
DUT DUT
DRIP
THE SOUL OF YOUR MOTHER, SCARLET...
...STILL RESIDES IN THOSE HANDS!!!
DROP
MOTHER...
THERE IS NO NEED FOR YOU TO STAIN THEM NOW...
CLANK...
...WITH THE BLOOD OF THIS MISCREANT!!!
!!
I WILL NOT ALLOW YOU TO SWING THAT SWORD!!!
KYROOOS!!!

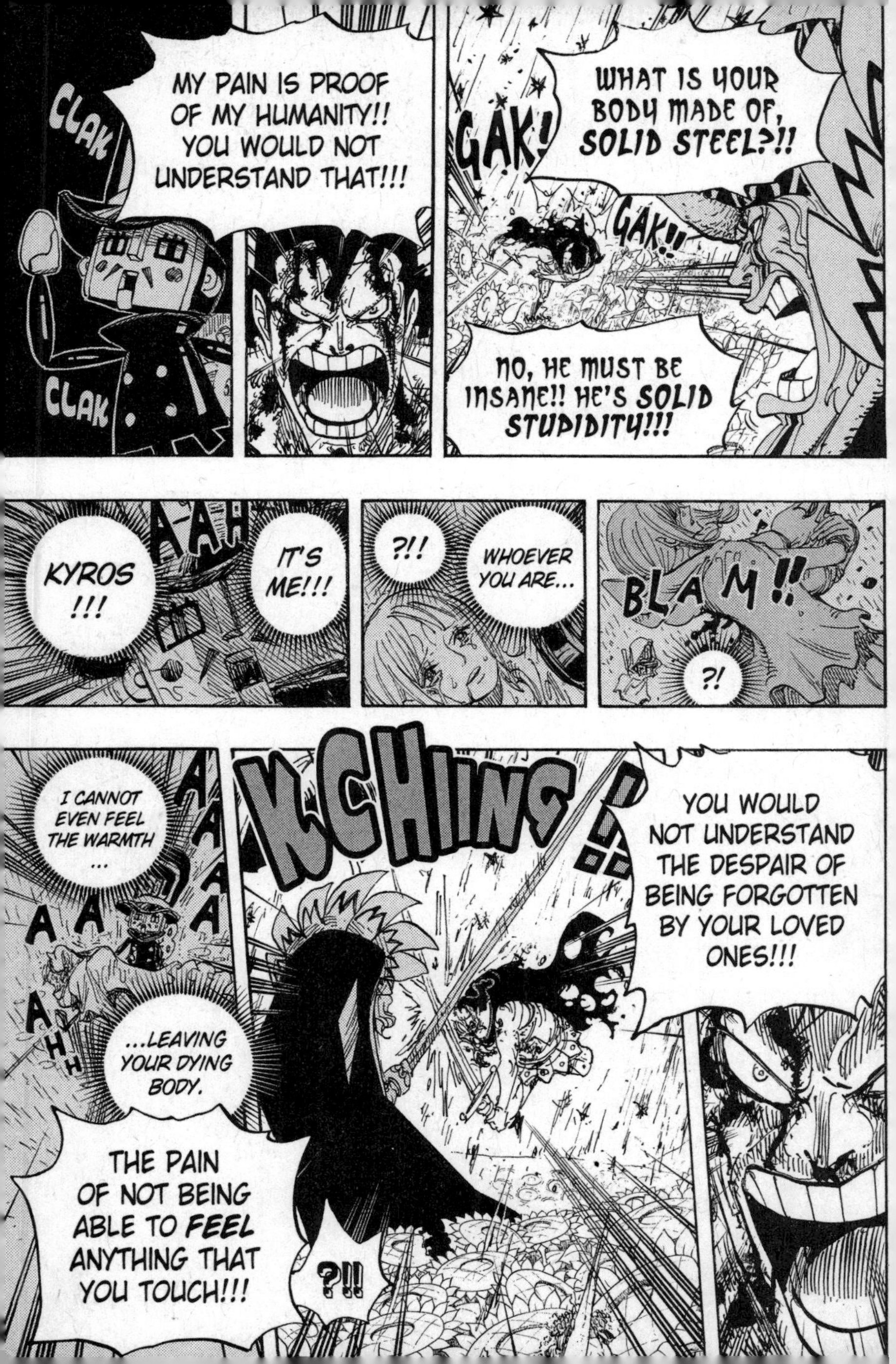
WHAT IS YOUR BODY MADE OF, SOLID STEEL?!!
GAK!
GAK!!
NO, HE MUST BE INSANE!! HE'S SOLID STUPIDITY!!!
MY PAIN IS PROOF OF MY HUMANITY!! YOU WOULD NOT UNDERSTAND THAT!!!
CLAK
CLAK
BLAM!!
?!
?!!
WHOEVER YOU ARE...
IT'S ME!!!
AAH
KYROS!!!
KCHIING!!
YOU WOULD NOT UNDERSTAND THE DESPAIR OF BEING FORGOTTEN BY YOUR LOVED ONES!!!
AAAAAAAAHH
I CANNOT EVEN FEEL THE WARMTH ...
...LEAVING YOUR DYING BODY.
THE PAIN OF NOT BEING ABLE TO FEEL ANYTHING THAT YOU TOUCH!!!
?!!

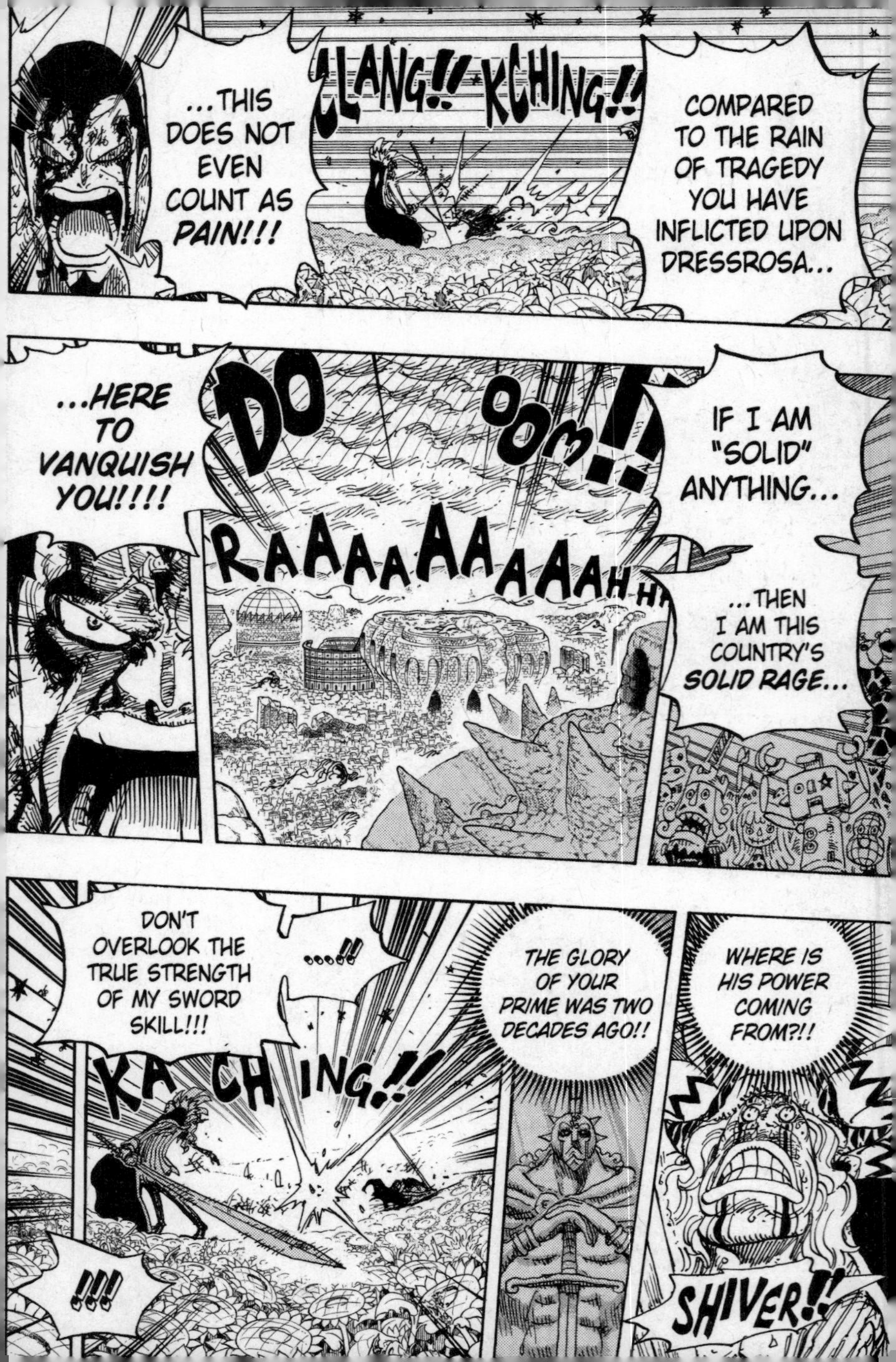
COMPARED TO THE RAIN OF TRAGEDY YOU HAVE INFLICTED UPON DRESSROSA...
CLANG!! KCHING!!
...THIS DOES NOT EVEN COUNT AS PAIN!!!
IF I AM "SOLID" ANYTHING...
...THEN I AM THIS COUNTRY'S SOLID RAGE...
DOOOM!!
RAAAAAAAAAAHH
...HERE TO VANQUISH YOU!!!!
WHERE IS HIS POWER COMING FROM?!!
SHIVER!!
THE GLORY OF YOUR PRIME WAS TWO DECADES AGO!!
DON'T OVERLOOK THE TRUE STRENGTH OF MY SWORD SKILL!!!
....!!
KA CHING!!!
!!!

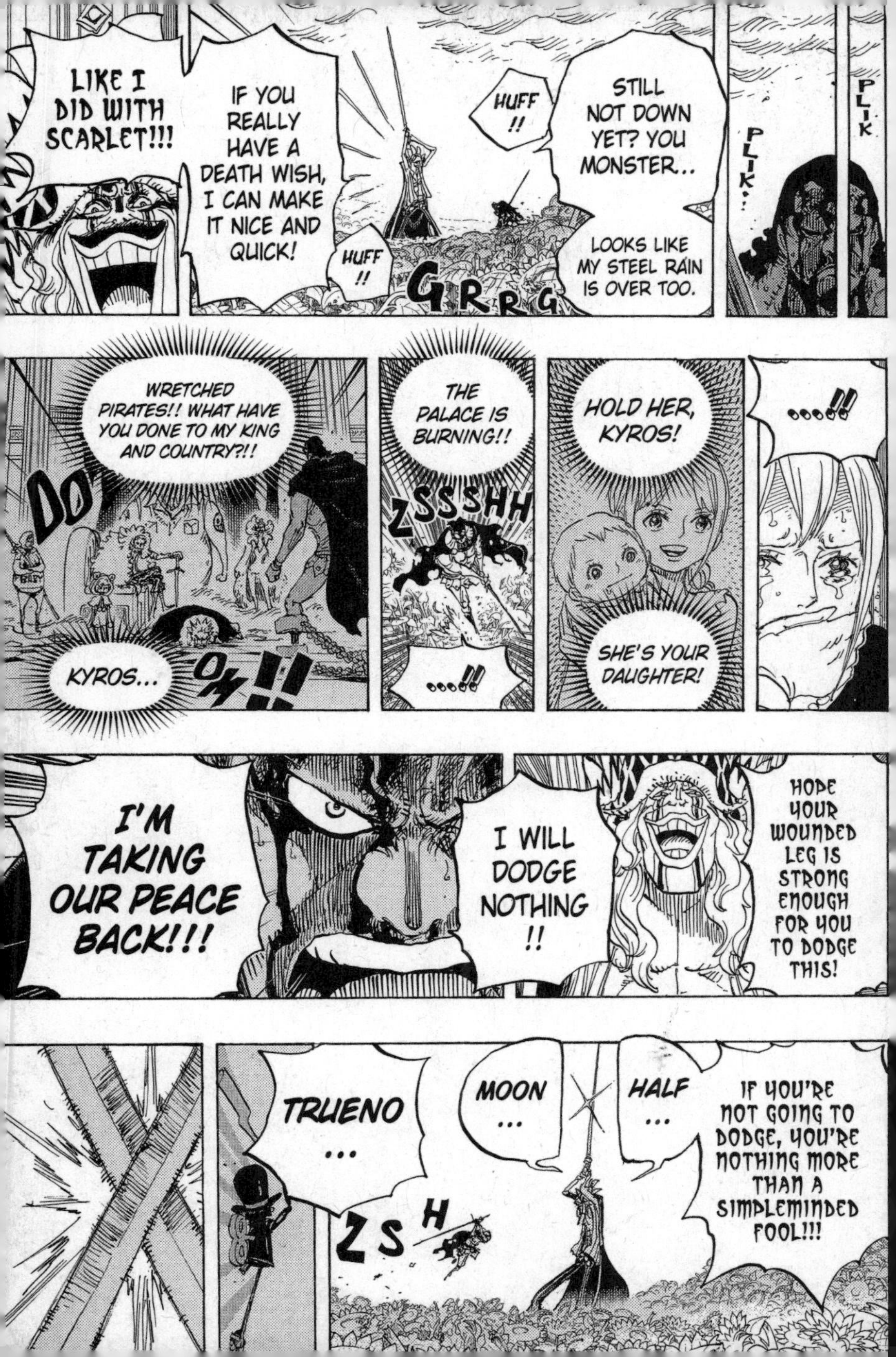

PLIK
PLIK...
STILL NOT DOWN YET? YOU MONSTER...
HUFF !!
LOOKS LIKE MY STEEL RAIN IS OVER TOO.
IF YOU REALLY HAVE A DEATH WISH, I CAN MAKE IT NICE AND QUICK!
HUFF !!
GRRG
LIKE I DID WITH SCARLET!!!
...!!
HOLD HER, KYROS!
SHE'S YOUR DAUGHTER!
THE PALACE IS BURNING!!
ZSSSHH
...!!
WRETCHED PIRATES!! WHAT HAVE YOU DONE TO MY KING AND COUNTRY?!!
DOOM!!
KYROS...
HOPE YOUR WOUNDED LEG IS STRONG ENOUGH FOR YOU TO DODGE THIS!
I WILL DODGE NOTHING !!
I'M TAKING OUR PEACE BACK!!!
IF YOU'RE NOT GOING TO DODGE, YOU'RE NOTHING MORE THAN A SIMPLEMINDED FOOL!!!
HALF ...
MOON ...
TRUENO ...
ZSH

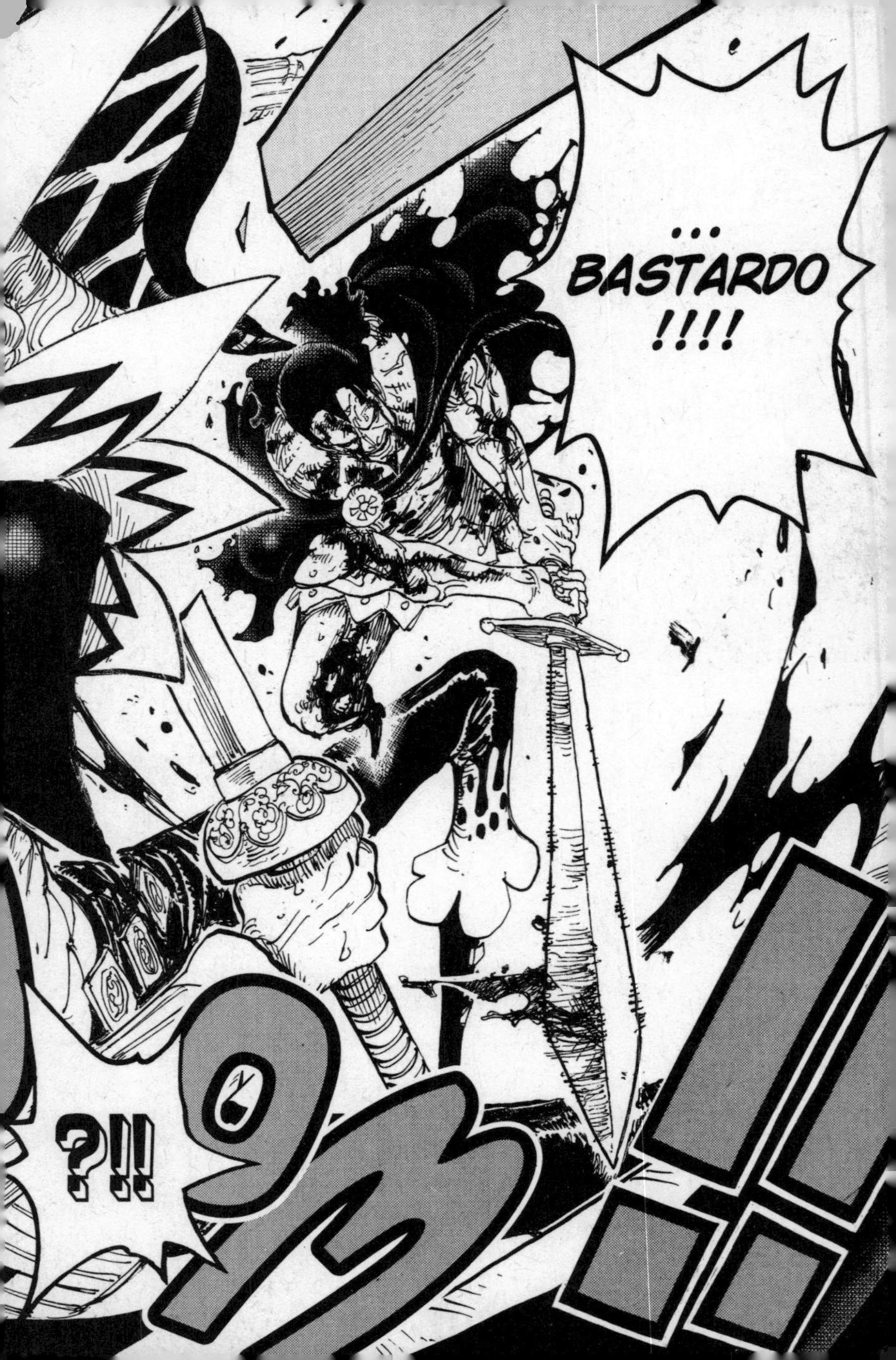
... BASTARDO !!!!
?!!

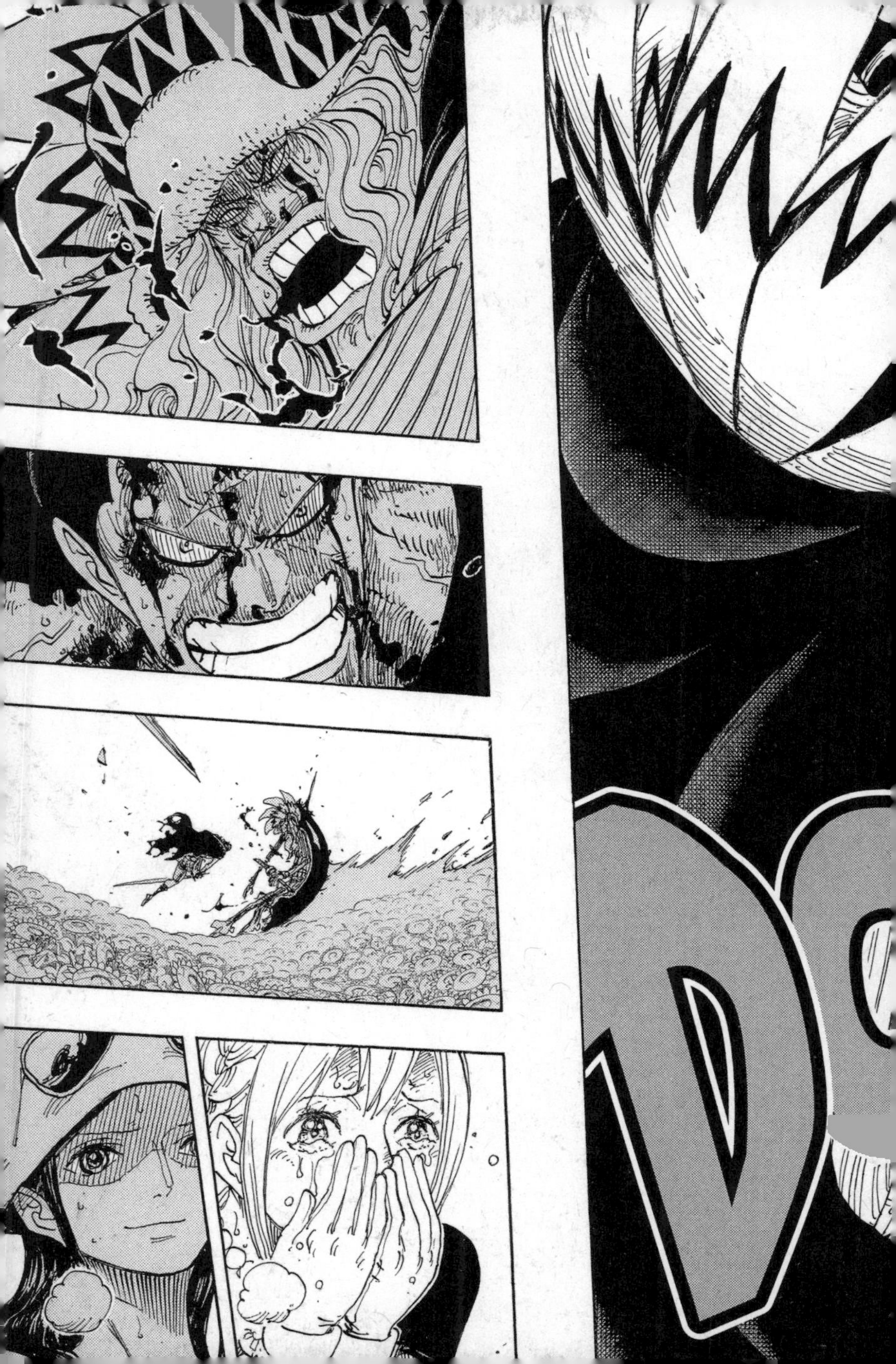

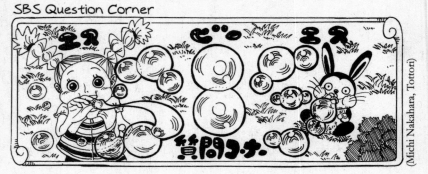

(Michi Nakahara, Tottori)

Q: Odacchi… I was cleaning up my room today and found a note that Cora left here, years ago… Just looking at it made me start thinking about him… *Sniff!* I'm sending it along, because I want you to see it.

--Mirucle

Went to go cure Law's disease

Went to go start the SBS

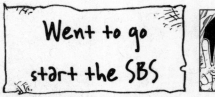

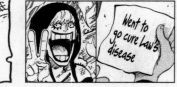

A: Waaaah! (cries) Oh, Cora!! The SBS…
Wait, the SBS already started!!

Q: When I chug a carbonated beverage, I get a tummy ache. What should I do?

--Dog Lover

A: I think you should not chug it.

Q: I want to make Pandaman's parents…so I designed them for you! Please make this official!!!

--Kanahasa

A: I'm very disturbed by the fact that his mother's body is obviously male. Thanks for the letter. (^^)
Also, rejected.

Mother
Daddy (Buff)
Bamboo Sword

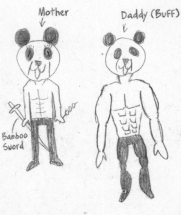

Chapter 777:
ZOLO VS. PICA

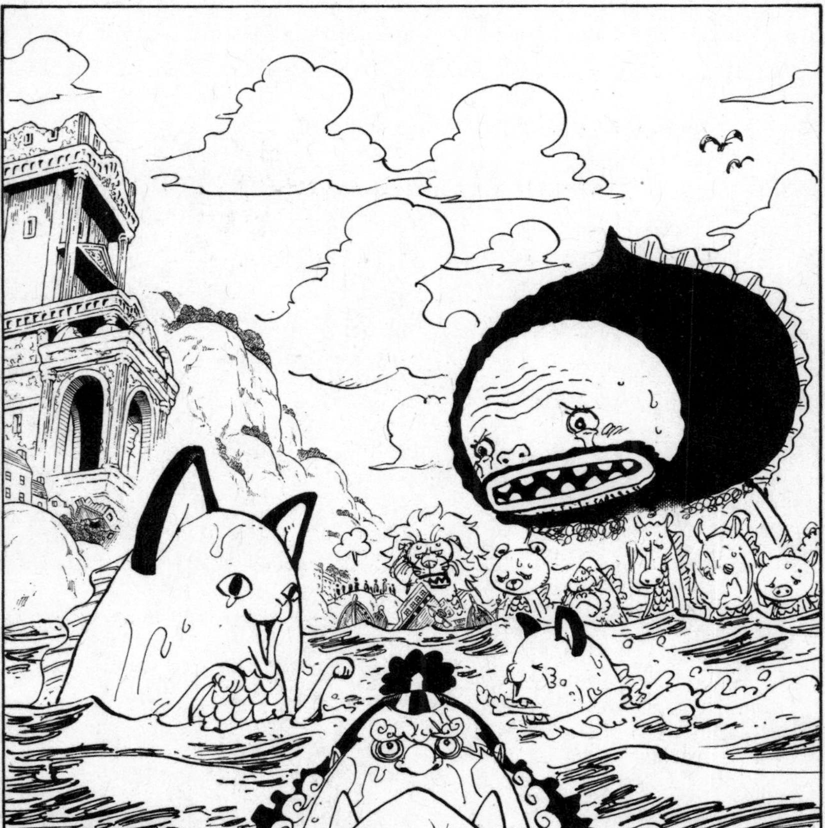

THE SOLITARY JOURNEY OF JIMBEI, FIRST SON OF THE SEA, VOL. 22: "A BIG MESS OF APOLOGIES, UNDERSTANDINGS AND REUNIONS"

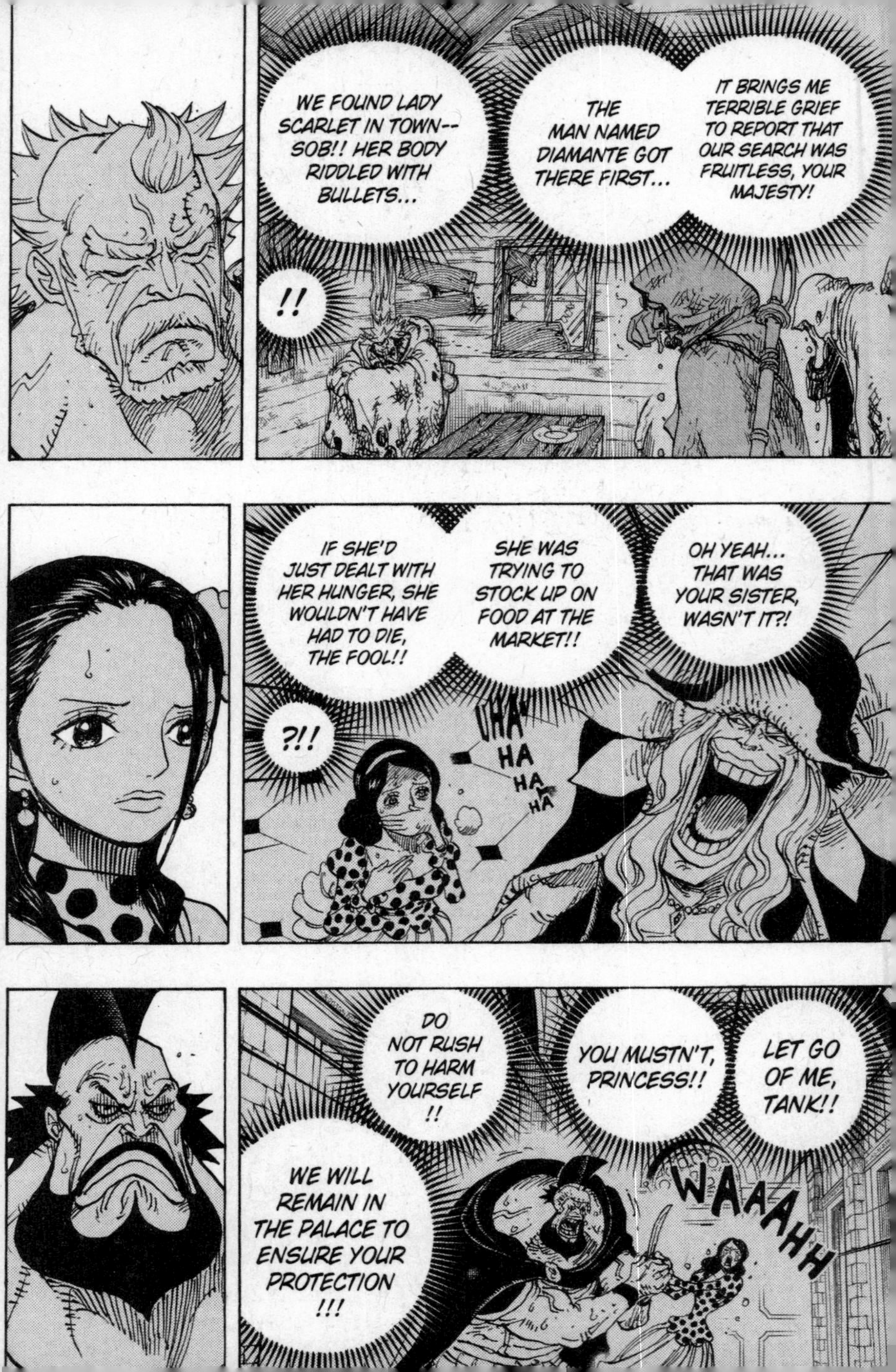
IT BRINGS ME TERRIBLE GRIEF TO REPORT THAT OUR SEARCH WAS FRUITLESS, YOUR MAJESTY!
THE MAN NAMED DIAMANTE GOT THERE FIRST...
WE FOUND LADY SCARLET IN TOWN--SOB!! HER BODY RIDDLED WITH BULLETS...
!!
OH YEAH... THAT WAS YOUR SISTER, WASN'T IT?!
SHE WAS TRYING TO STOCK UP ON FOOD AT THE MARKET!!
IF SHE'D JUST DEALT WITH HER HUNGER, SHE WOULDN'T HAVE HAD TO DIE, THE FOOL!!
UHA HA HA HA HA
?!!
LET GO OF ME, TANK!!
YOU MUSTN'T, PRINCESS!!
DO NOT RUSH TO HARM YOURSELF!!
WAAAHH
WE WILL REMAIN IN THE PALACE TO ENSURE YOUR PROTECTION!!!

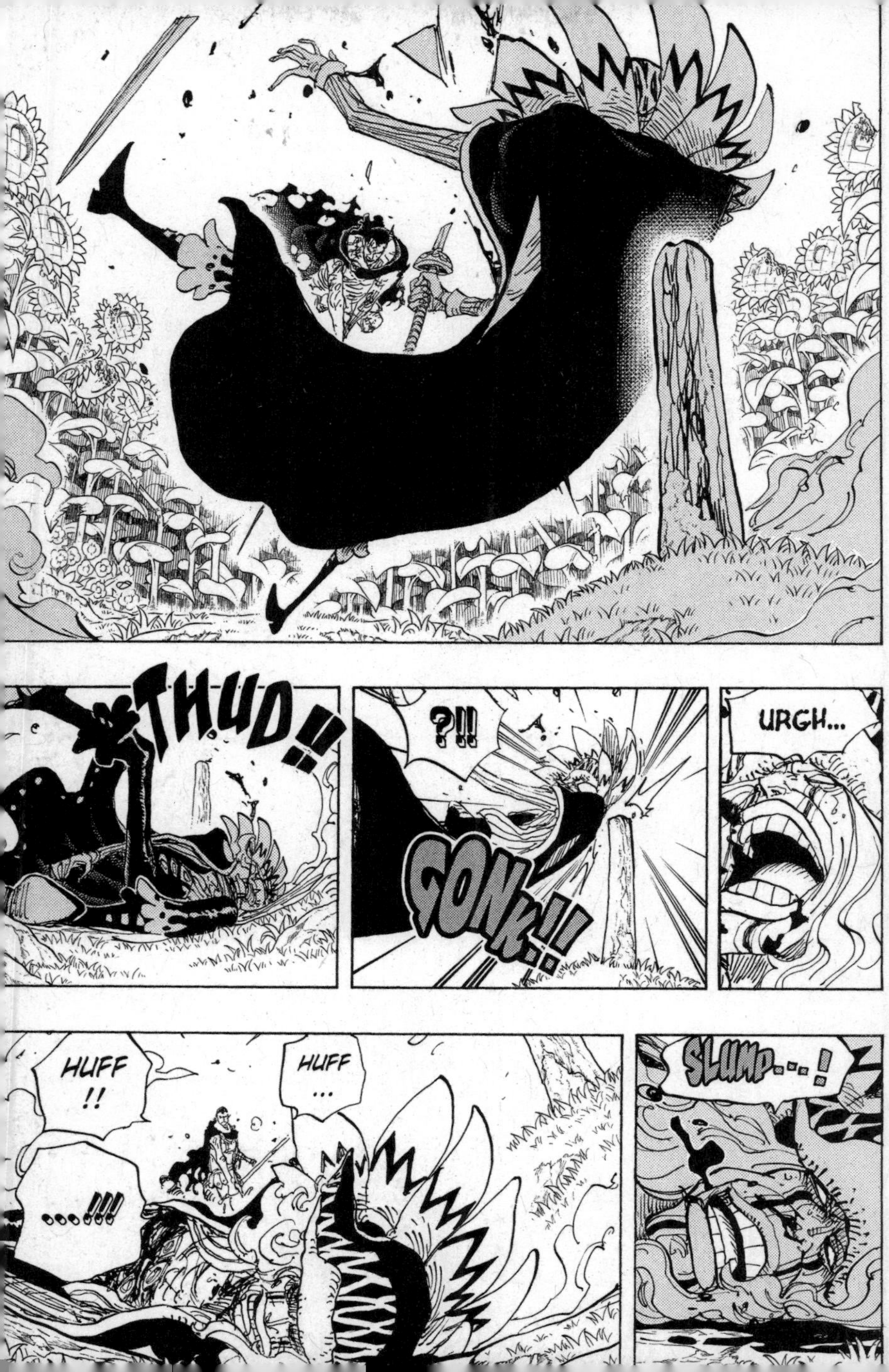
URGH...
?!!
GONK!!
THUD!!
SLUMP...!
HUFF
...
HUFF
!!
...!!!

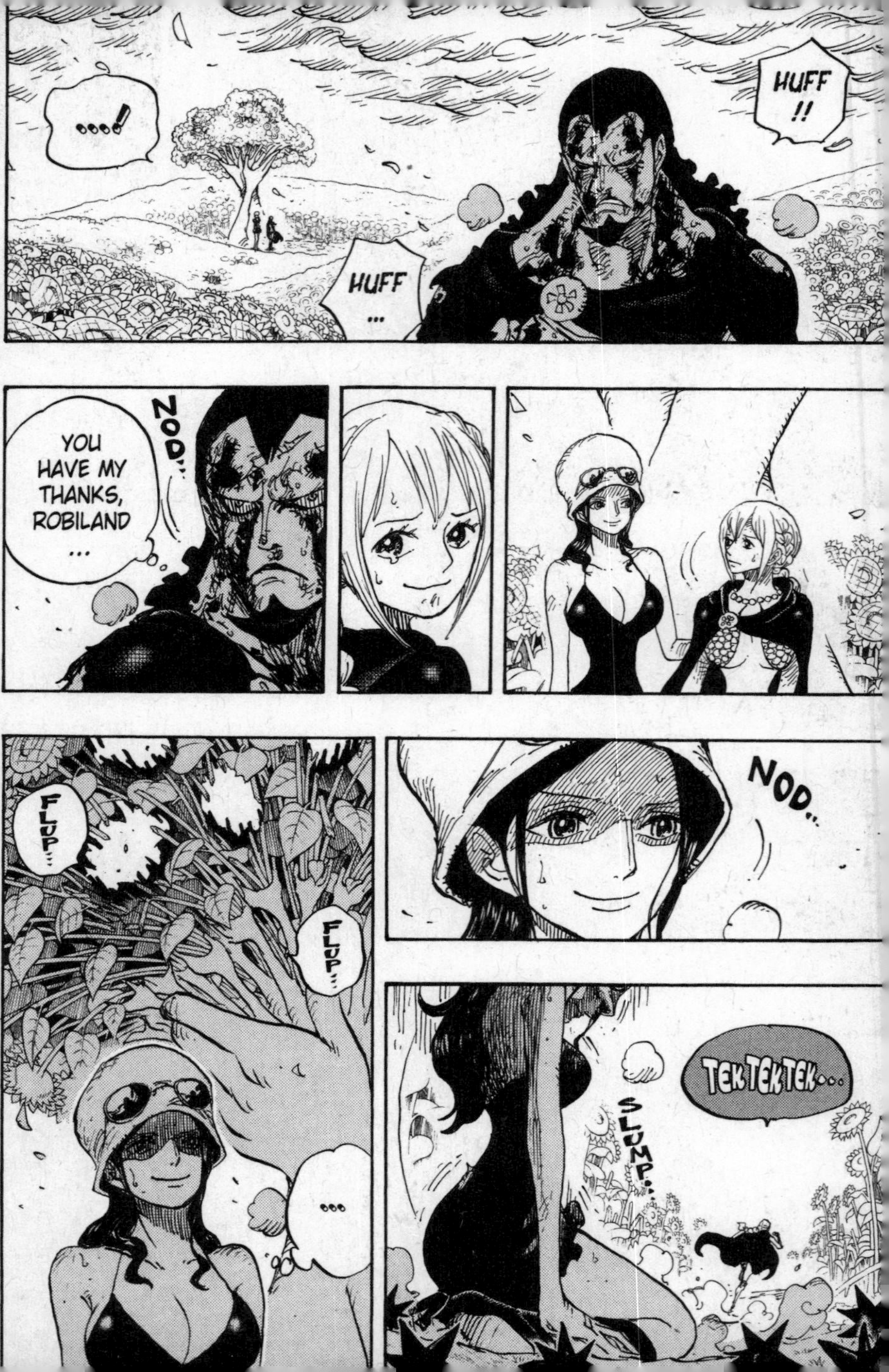
HUFF !!
HUFF ...
....!
NOD...
YOU HAVE MY THANKS, ROBILAND ...
NOD...
TEK TEK TEK...
SLUMP...
FLUP...
FLUP...
...

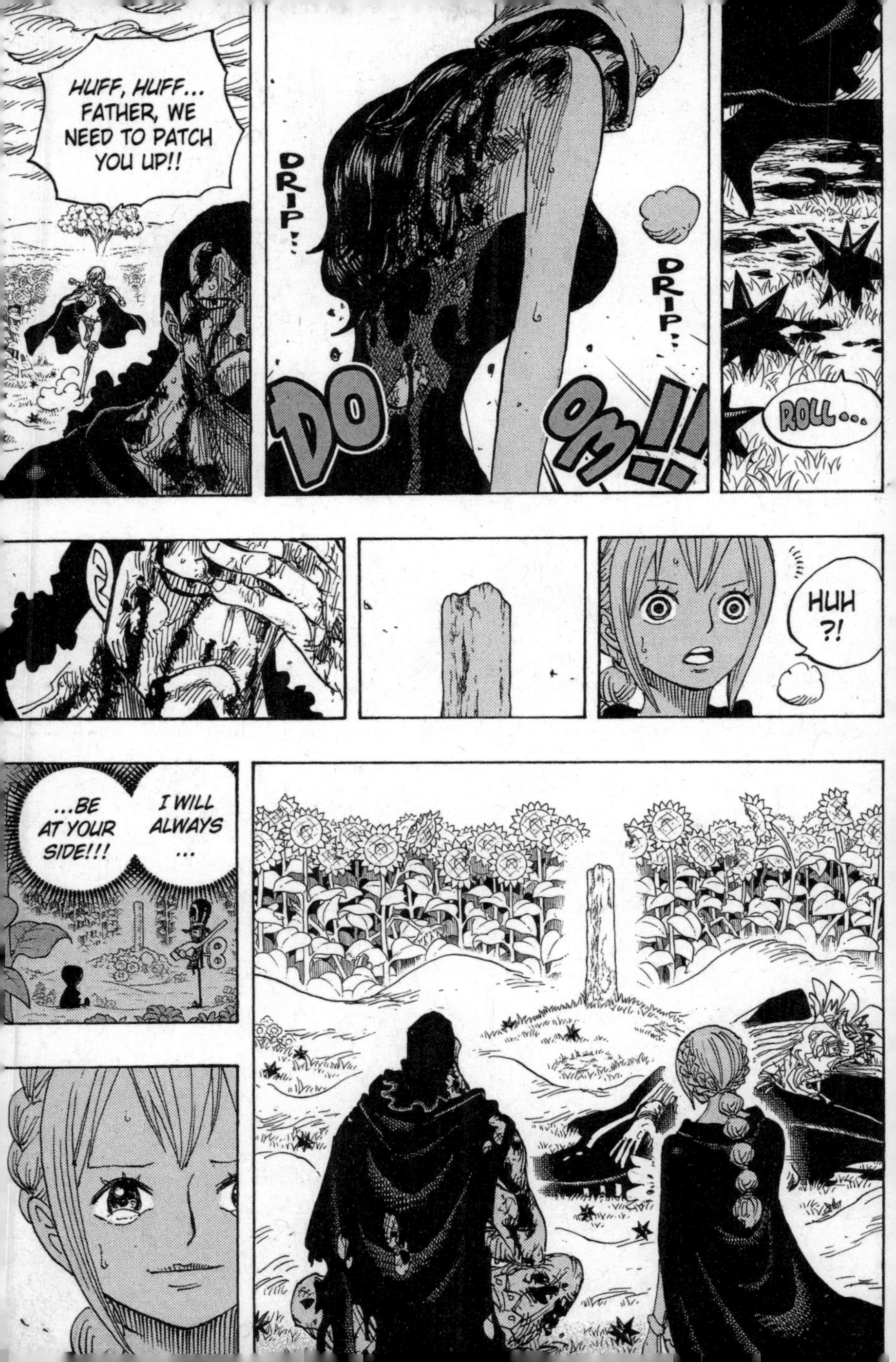
ROLL...
DRIP..
DRIP..
DOOM!!
HUFF, HUFF... FATHER, WE NEED TO PATCH YOU UP!!
HUH ?!
I WILL ALWAYS ...
...BE AT YOUR SIDE!!!

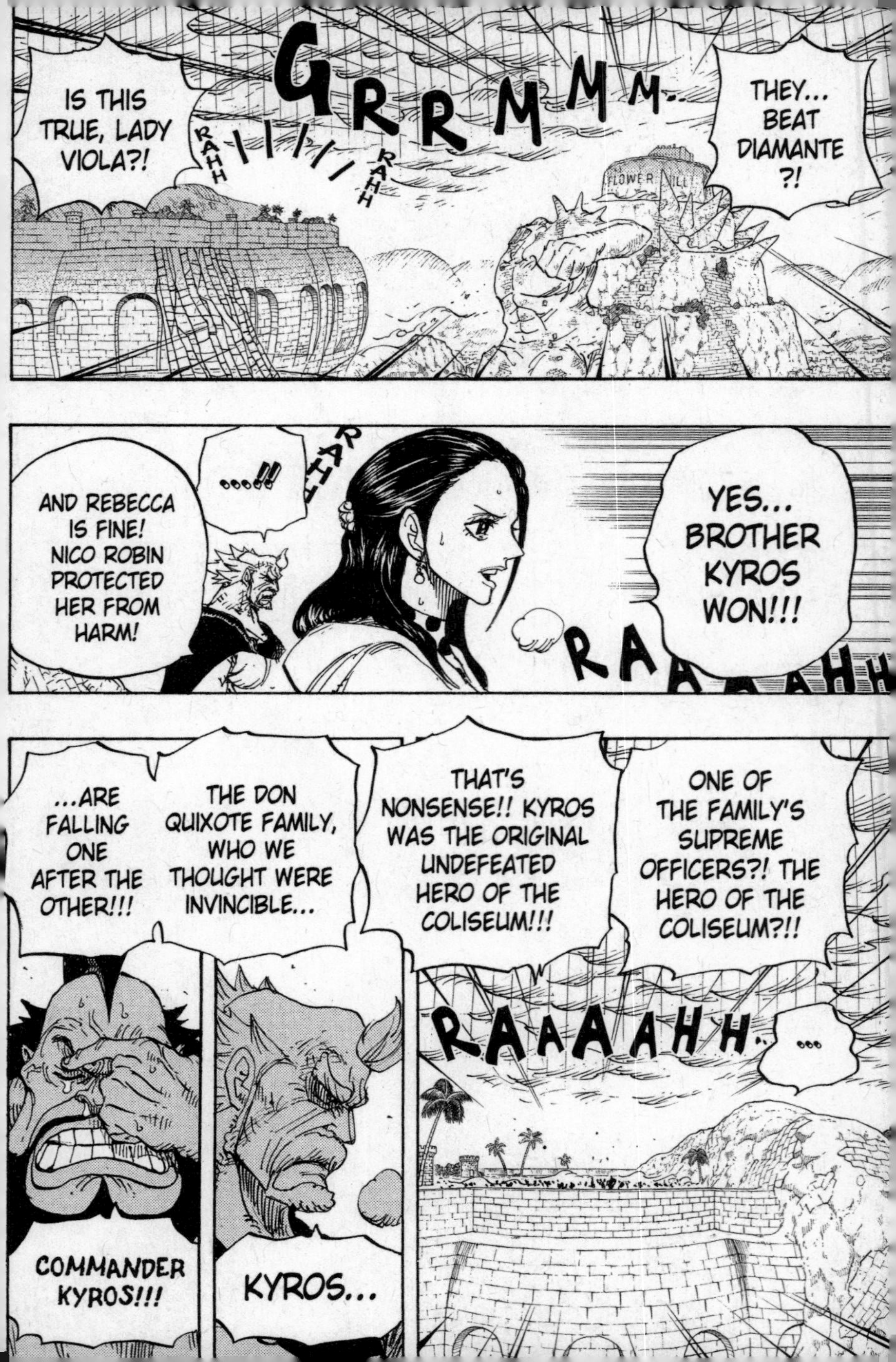
THEY... BEAT DIAMANTE ?!
GRRRMMM..
IS THIS TRUE, LADY VIOLA?!
RAHH
RAHH
YES... BROTHER KYROS WON!!!
RAAAAHH
...!!
AND REBECCA IS FINE! NICO ROBIN PROTECTED HER FROM HARM!
RAHH
ONE OF THE FAMILY'S SUPREME OFFICERS?! THE HERO OF THE COLISEUM?!!
THAT'S NONSENSE!! KYROS WAS THE ORIGINAL UNDEFEATED HERO OF THE COLISEUM!!!
RAAAAHH..
...
THE DON QUIXOTE FAMILY, WHO WE THOUGHT WERE INVINCIBLE...
KYROS...
...ARE FALLING ONE AFTER THE OTHER!!!
COMMANDER KYROS!!!

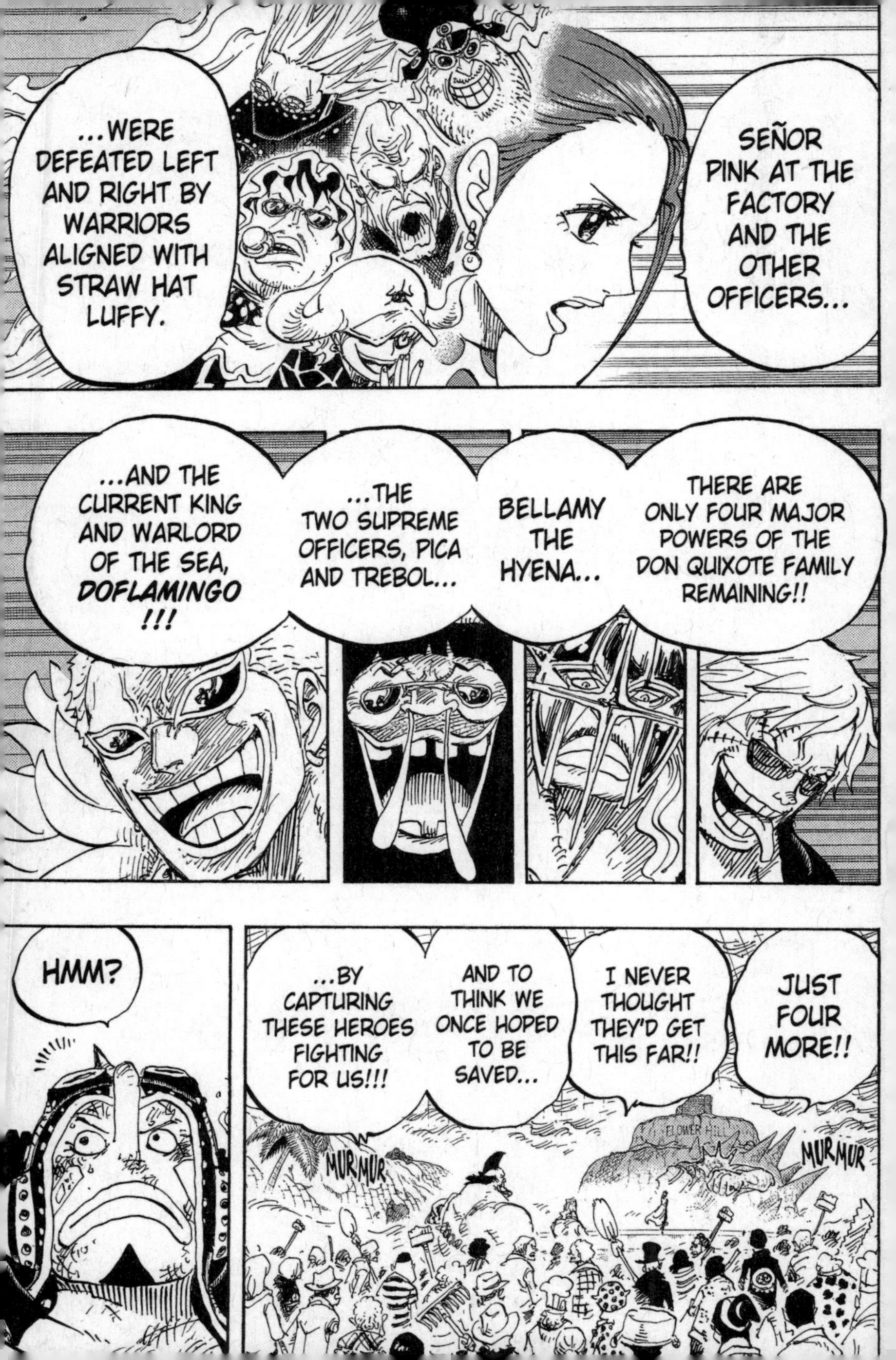
SEÑOR PINK AT THE FACTORY AND THE OTHER OFFICERS...
...WERE DEFEATED LEFT AND RIGHT BY WARRIORS ALIGNED WITH STRAW HAT LUFFY.
THERE ARE ONLY FOUR MAJOR POWERS OF THE DON QUIXOTE FAMILY REMAINING!!
BELLAMY THE HYENA...
...THE TWO SUPREME OFFICERS, PICA AND TREBOL...
...AND THE CURRENT KING AND WARLORD OF THE SEA, *DOFLAMINGO* !!!
JUST FOUR MORE!!
I NEVER THOUGHT THEY'D GET THIS FAR!!
AND TO THINK WE ONCE HOPED TO BE SAVED...
...BY CAPTURING THESE HEROES FIGHTING FOR US!!!
MURMUR
FLOWER HILL
MURMUR
HMM?

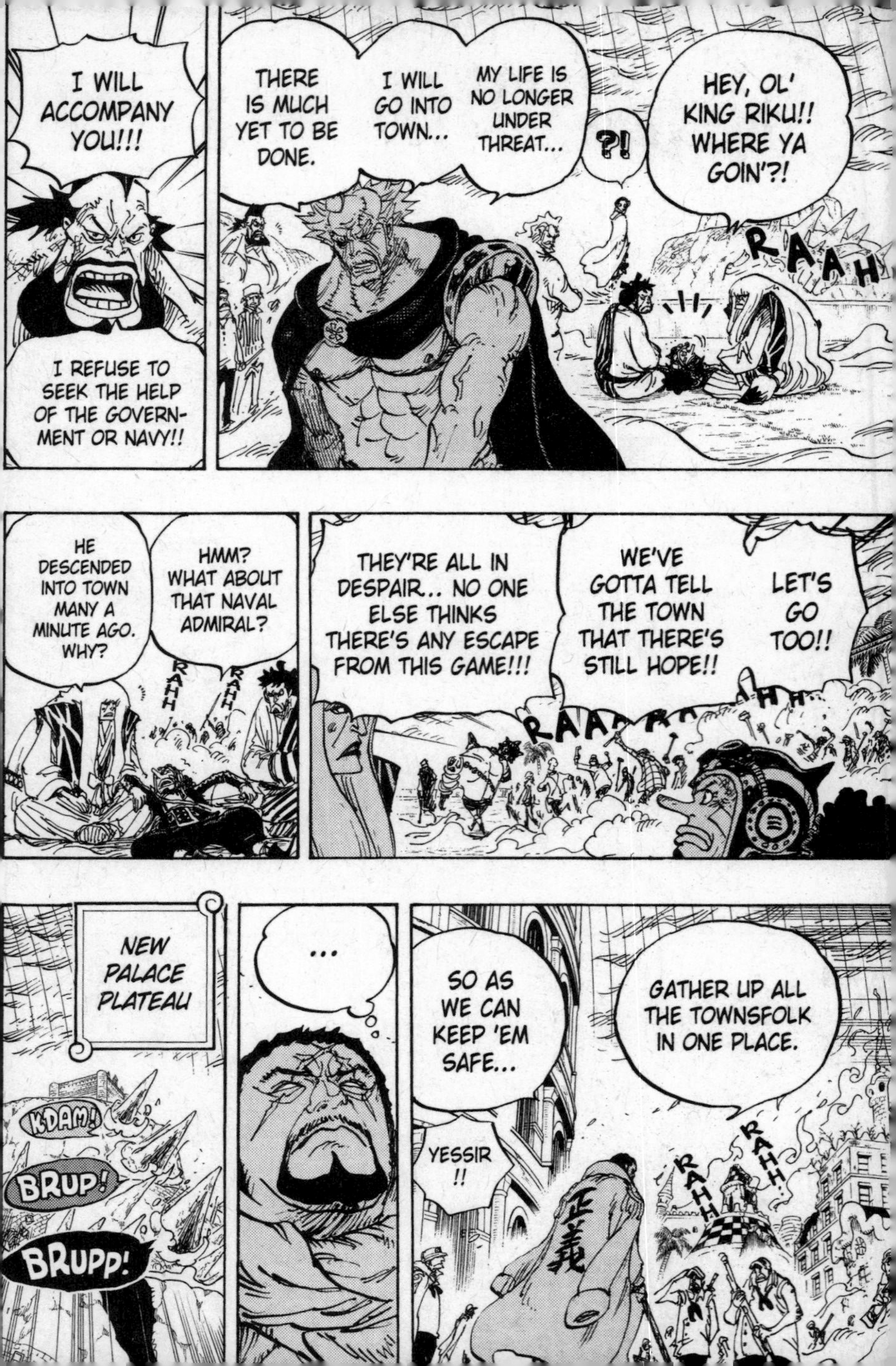
HEY, OL' KING RIKU!! WHERE YA GOIN'?!
?!
MY LIFE IS NO LONGER UNDER THREAT...
I WILL GO INTO TOWN...
THERE IS MUCH YET TO BE DONE.
RAAH
I WILL ACCOMPANY YOU!!!
I REFUSE TO SEEK THE HELP OF THE GOVERNMENT OR NAVY!!
LET'S GO TOO!!
WE'VE GOTTA TELL THE TOWN THAT THERE'S STILL HOPE!!
THEY'RE ALL IN DESPAIR... NO ONE ELSE THINKS THERE'S ANY ESCAPE FROM THIS GAME!!!
HMM? WHAT ABOUT THAT NAVAL ADMIRAL?
HE DESCENDED INTO TOWN MANY A MINUTE AGO. WHY?
RAHH
RAHH
GATHER UP ALL THE TOWNSFOLK IN ONE PLACE.
SO AS WE CAN KEEP 'EM SAFE...
YESSIR!!
RAHH
RAHH..
正義
...
NEW PALACE PLATEAU
KDAM!
BRUP!
BRUPP!

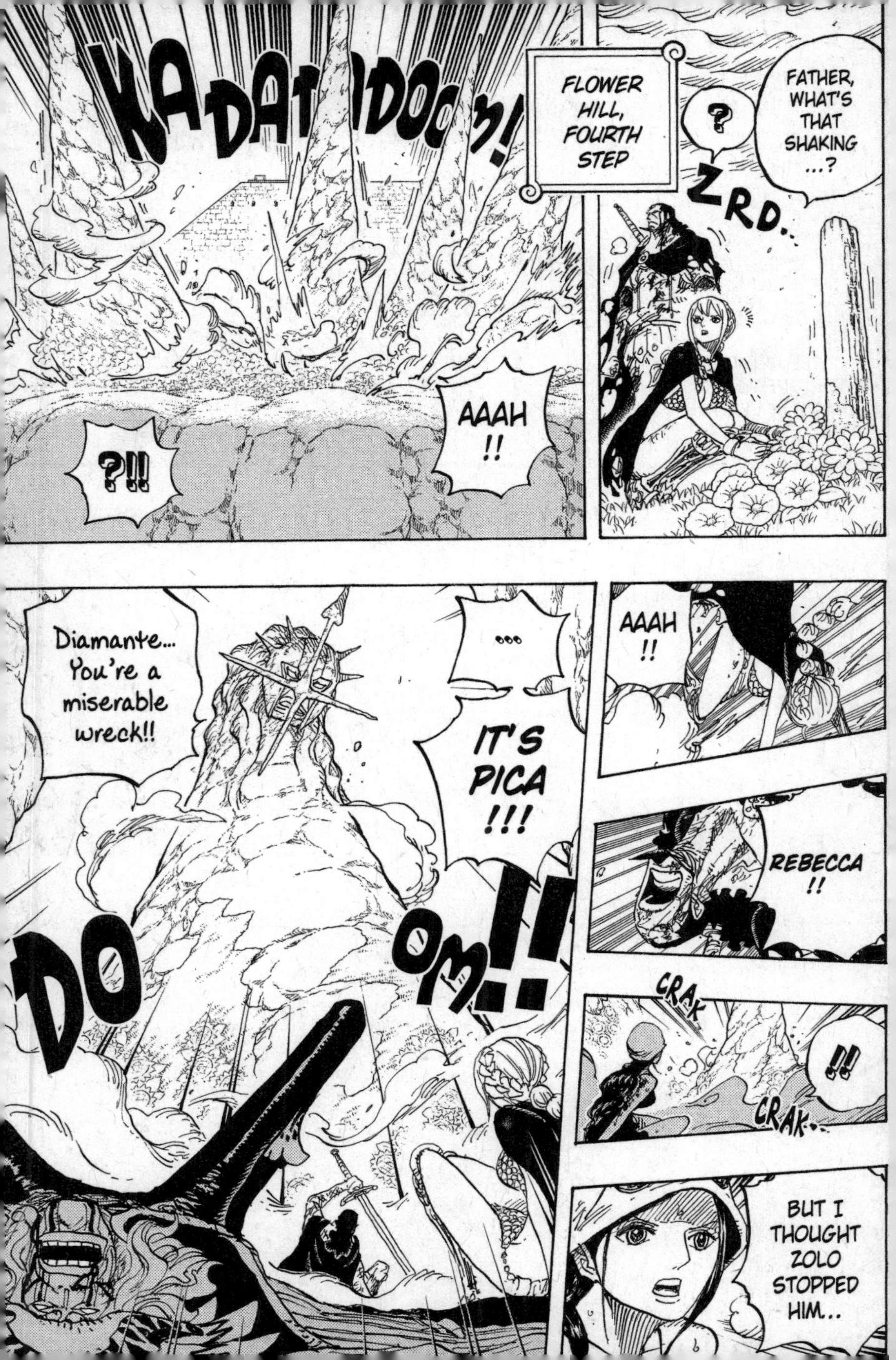
FLOWER HILL, FOURTH STEP
FATHER, WHAT'S THAT SHAKING ...?
?
ZRD..
KADATDOOM!
AAAH !!
?!!
AAAH !!
REBECCA !!
CRAK
!!
CRAK..
BUT I THOUGHT ZOLO STOPPED HIM...
...
IT'S PICA !!!
Diamante... You're a miserable wreck!!
DOOM!!

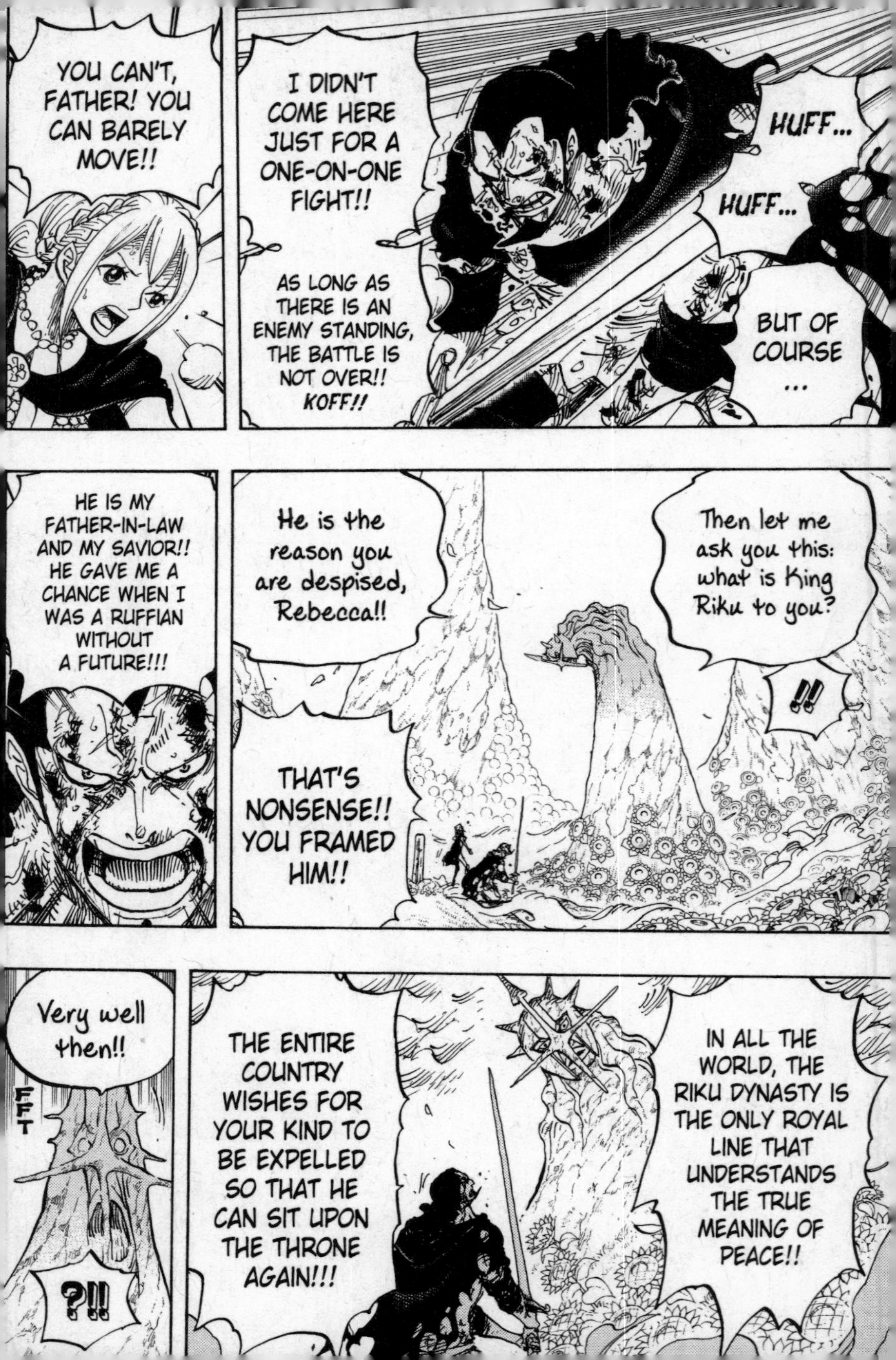
HUFF...
HUFF...
BUT OF COURSE ...
I DIDN'T COME HERE JUST FOR A ONE-ON-ONE FIGHT!!
AS LONG AS THERE IS AN ENEMY STANDING, THE BATTLE IS NOT OVER!! KOFF!!
YOU CAN'T, FATHER! YOU CAN BARELY MOVE!!
Then let me ask you this: what is King Riku to you?
!!
He is the reason you are despised, Rebecca!!
THAT'S NONSENSE!! YOU FRAMED HIM!!
HE IS MY FATHER-IN-LAW AND MY SAVIOR!! HE GAVE ME A CHANCE WHEN I WAS A RUFFIAN WITHOUT A FUTURE!!!
IN ALL THE WORLD, THE RIKU DYNASTY IS THE ONLY ROYAL LINE THAT UNDERSTANDS THE TRUE MEANING OF PEACE!!
THE ENTIRE COUNTRY WISHES FOR YOUR KIND TO BE EXPELLED SO THAT HE CAN SIT UPON THE THRONE AGAIN!!!
Very well then!!
FFT
?!!

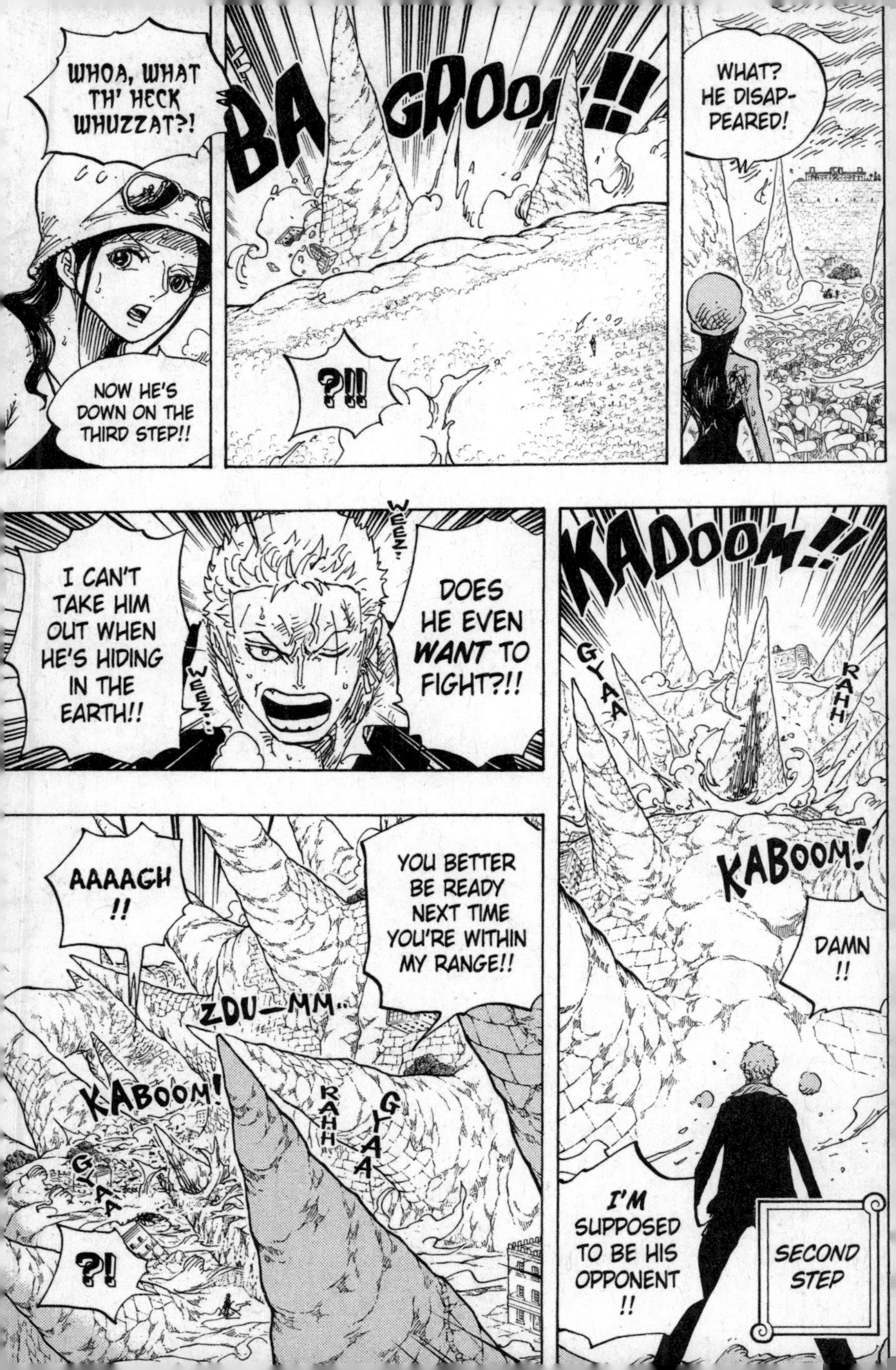
WHAT? HE DISAP-PEARED!
BAGROOM!!
?!!
WHOA, WHAT TH' HECK WHUZZAT?!
NOW HE'S DOWN ON THE THIRD STEP!!
KADOOM!!
RAHH
GYAA
KABOOM!
DAMN!!
SECOND STEP
I'M SUPPOSED TO BE HIS OPPONENT!!
WEEZ
DOES HE EVEN WANT TO FIGHT?!!
I CAN'T TAKE HIM OUT WHEN HE'S HIDING IN THE EARTH!!
WEEZ..
YOU BETTER BE READY NEXT TIME YOU'RE WITHIN MY RANGE!!
AAAAGH!!
ZDU—MM..
GYAA
RAHH
KABOOM!
GYAA
?!

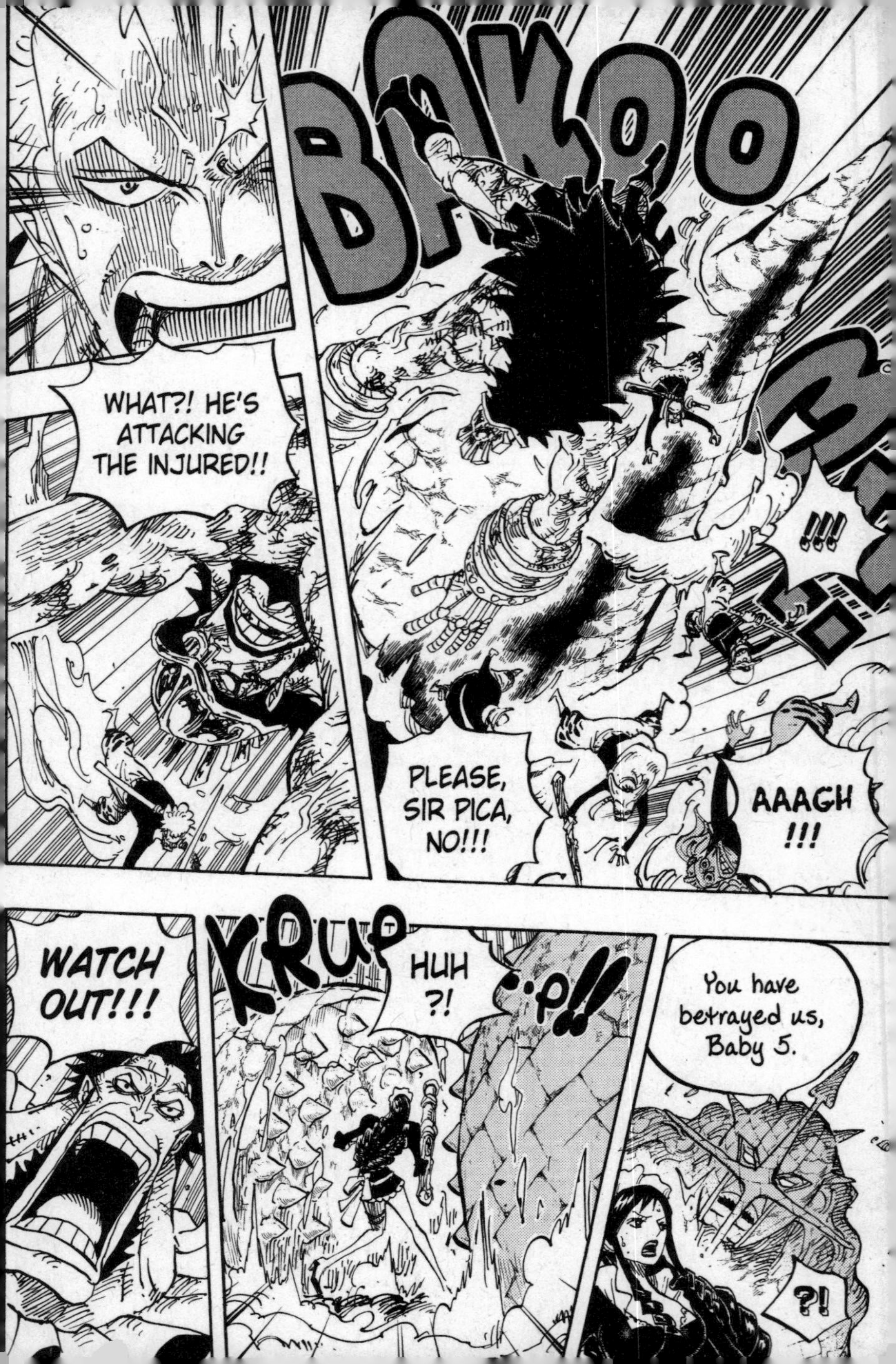
BAKOO
!!!
PLEASE, SIR PICA, NO!!!
AAAGH !!!
WHAT?! HE'S ATTACKING THE INJURED!!
You have betrayed us, Baby 5.
?!
KRUP
HUH ?!
WATCH OUT!!!

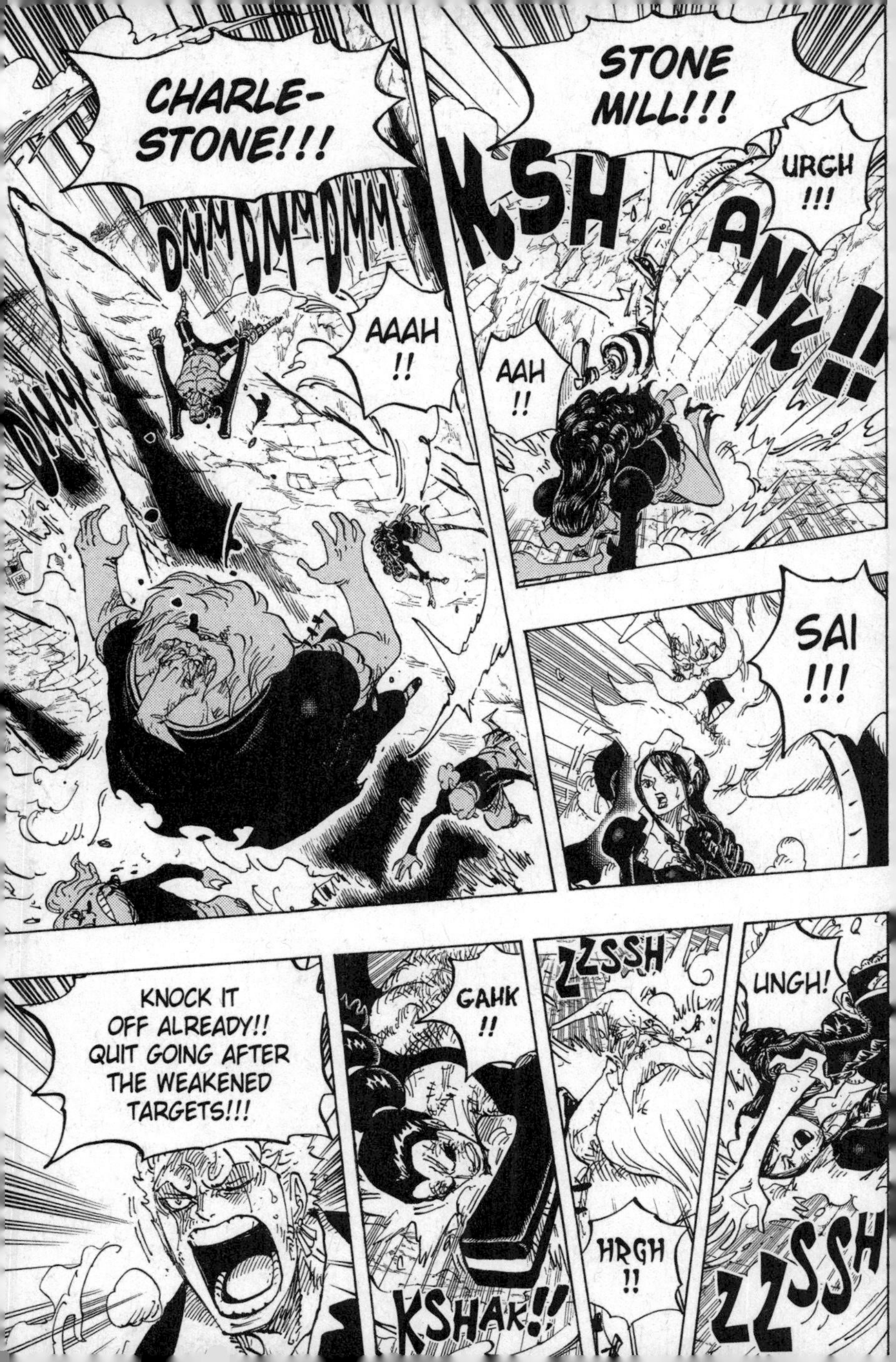

STONE MILL!!!
URGH !!!
KSH
ANK!!
AAH !!
SAI !!!
CHARLE-STONE!!!
DMMDMMDMM
AAAH !!
DMM
UNGH!
ZZSSH
ZZSSH
HRGH !!
GAHK !!
KSHAK!!
KNOCK IT OFF ALREADY!! QUIT GOING AFTER THE WEAKENED TARGETS!!!

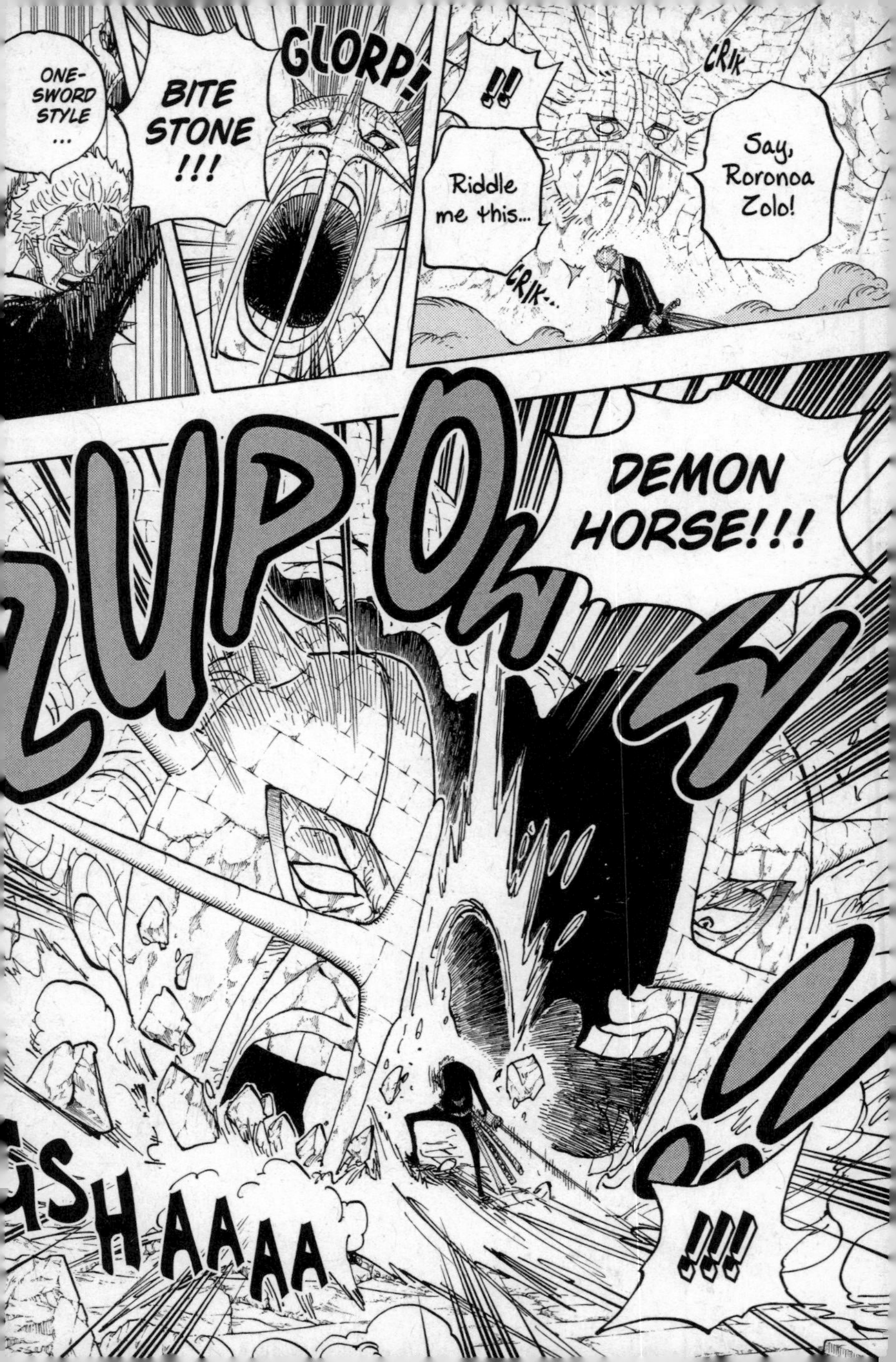

CRIK
Say, Roronoa Zolo!
Riddle me this...
CRIK...
!!
GLORP!
ONE-SWORD STYLE ...
BITE STONE!!!
DEMON HORSE!!!
ZUPOW
!!!
SHAAAA

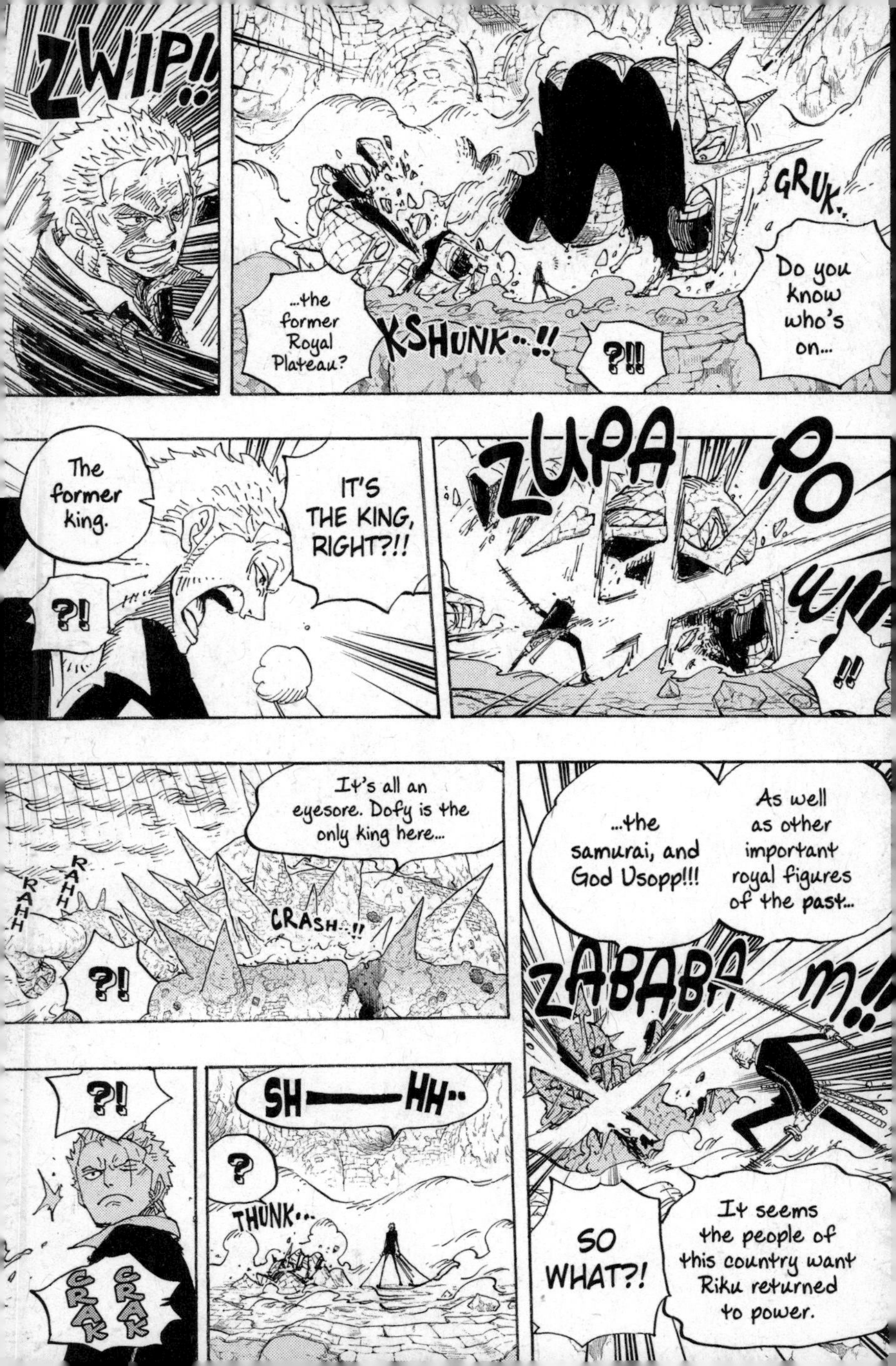
GRUK..
Do you know who's on...
?!!
KSHUNK..!!
...the former Royal Plateau?
ZWIP!!
ZUPA POW!!
IT'S THE KING, RIGHT?!!
The former king.
?!
As well as other important royal figures of the past...
...the samurai, and God Usopp!!!
ZABABAM..!!
It seems the people of this country want Riku returned to power.
SO WHAT?!
It's all an eyesore. Dofy is the only king here...
CRASH..!!
RAHH
RAHH
?!
SH——HH..
?
THUNK...
?!
CRAK
CRAK

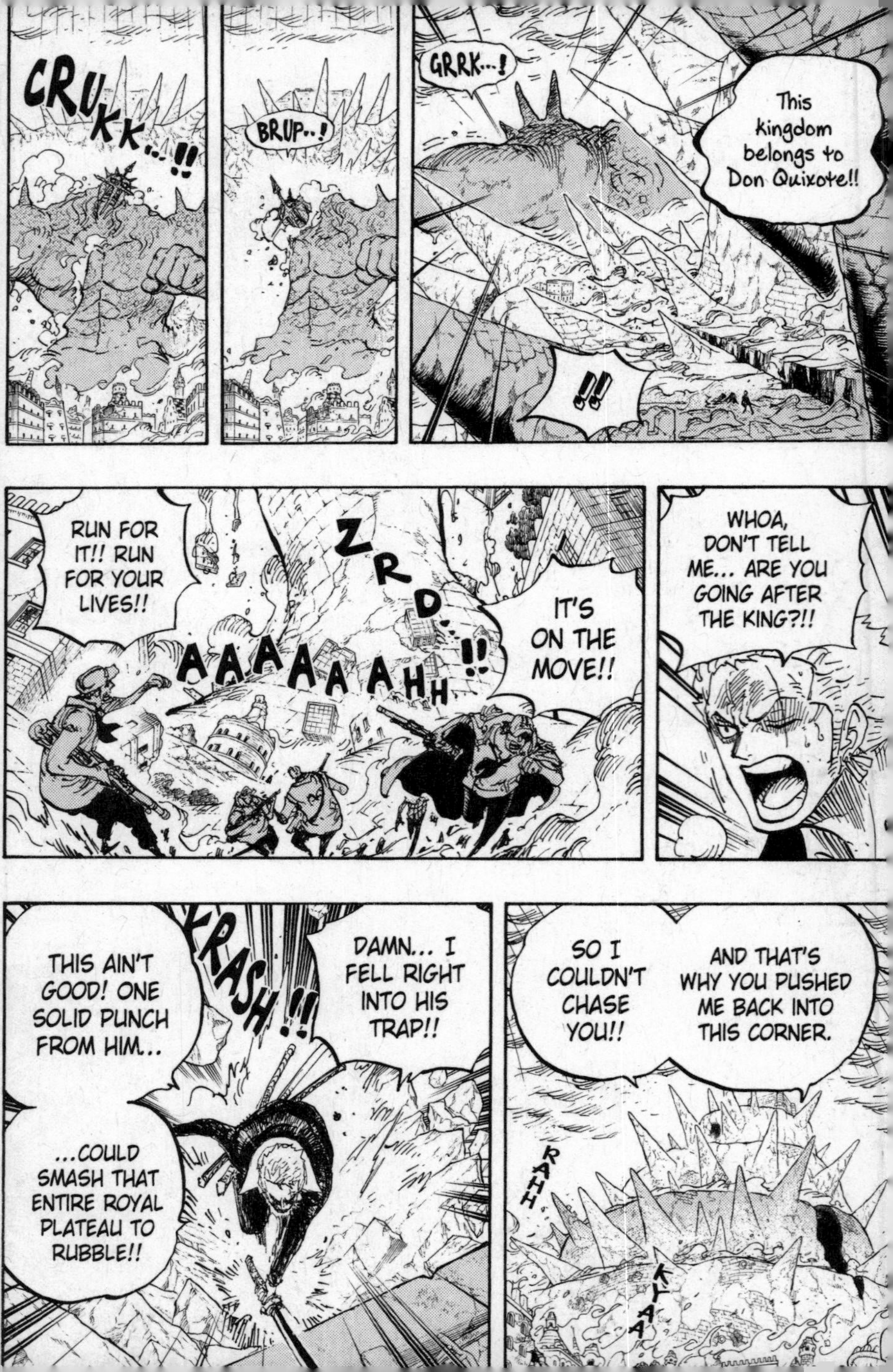
This kingdom belongs to Don Quixote!!
GRRK...!
!!
BRUP..!
CRUKK...!!
WHOA, DON'T TELL ME... ARE YOU GOING AFTER THE KING?!!
IT'S ON THE MOVE!!
ZRD...!!
RUN FOR IT!! RUN FOR YOUR LIVES!!
AAAAAAHH
AND THAT'S WHY YOU PUSHED ME BACK INTO THIS CORNER.
SO I COULDN'T CHASE YOU!!
RAHH
KYAA
DAMN... I FELL RIGHT INTO HIS TRAP!!
KRASH!!
THIS AIN'T GOOD! ONE SOLID PUNCH FROM HIM...
...COULD SMASH THAT ENTIRE ROYAL PLATEAU TO RUBBLE!!

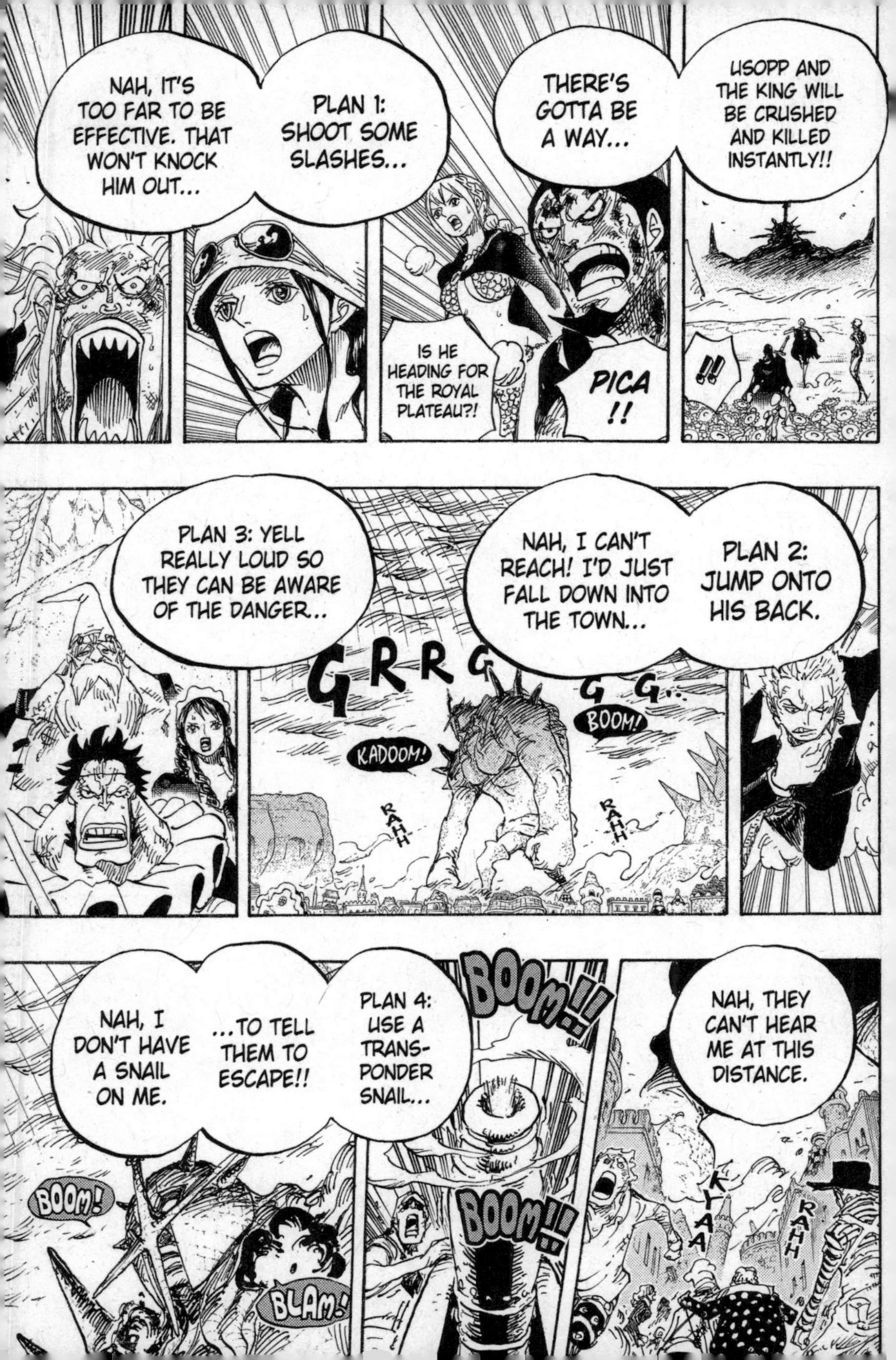
USOPP AND THE KING WILL BE CRUSHED AND KILLED INSTANTLY!!
!!
THERE'S GOTTA BE A WAY...
PICA !!
IS HE HEADING FOR THE ROYAL PLATEAU?!
PLAN 1: SHOOT SOME SLASHES...
NAH, IT'S TOO FAR TO BE EFFECTIVE. THAT WON'T KNOCK HIM OUT...
PLAN 2: JUMP ONTO HIS BACK.
NAH, I CAN'T REACH! I'D JUST FALL DOWN INTO THE TOWN...
GRRRGGG..
BOOM!
KADOOM!
RAHH
RAHH
PLAN 3: YELL REALLY LOUD SO THEY CAN BE AWARE OF THE DANGER...
NAH, THEY CAN'T HEAR ME AT THIS DISTANCE.
KYAA
RAHH
BOOM!!!
PLAN 4: USE A TRANS-PONDER SNAIL...
BOOM!!!
...TO TELL THEM TO ESCAPE!!
NAH, I DON'T HAVE A SNAIL ON ME.
BOOM!
BLAM!

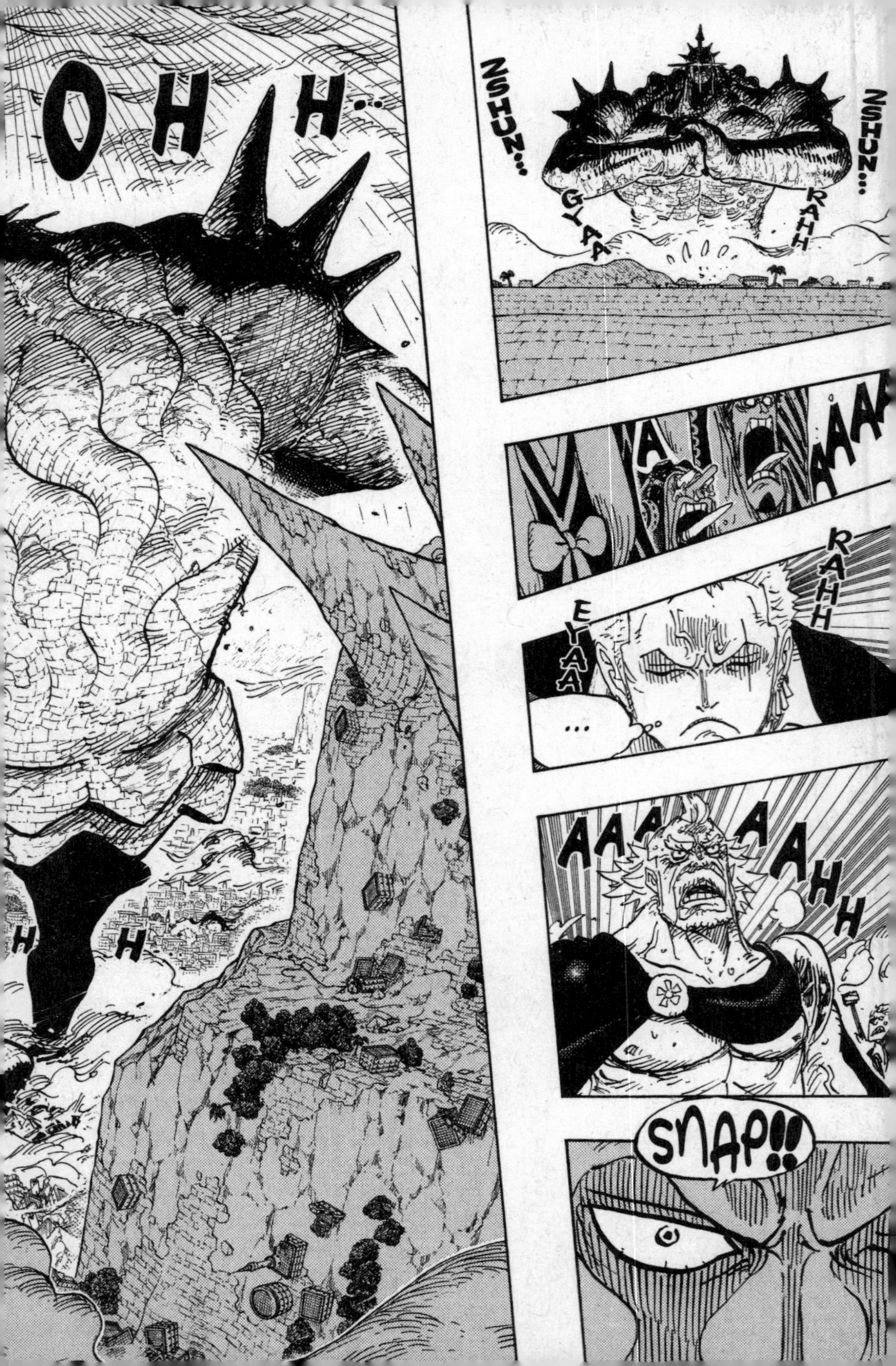
ZSHUN...
RAHH
GYAA
ZSHUN...
AAAAA
RAHH
EYAA
...
AAAAAAHH
SNAP!!
OHH...
HH

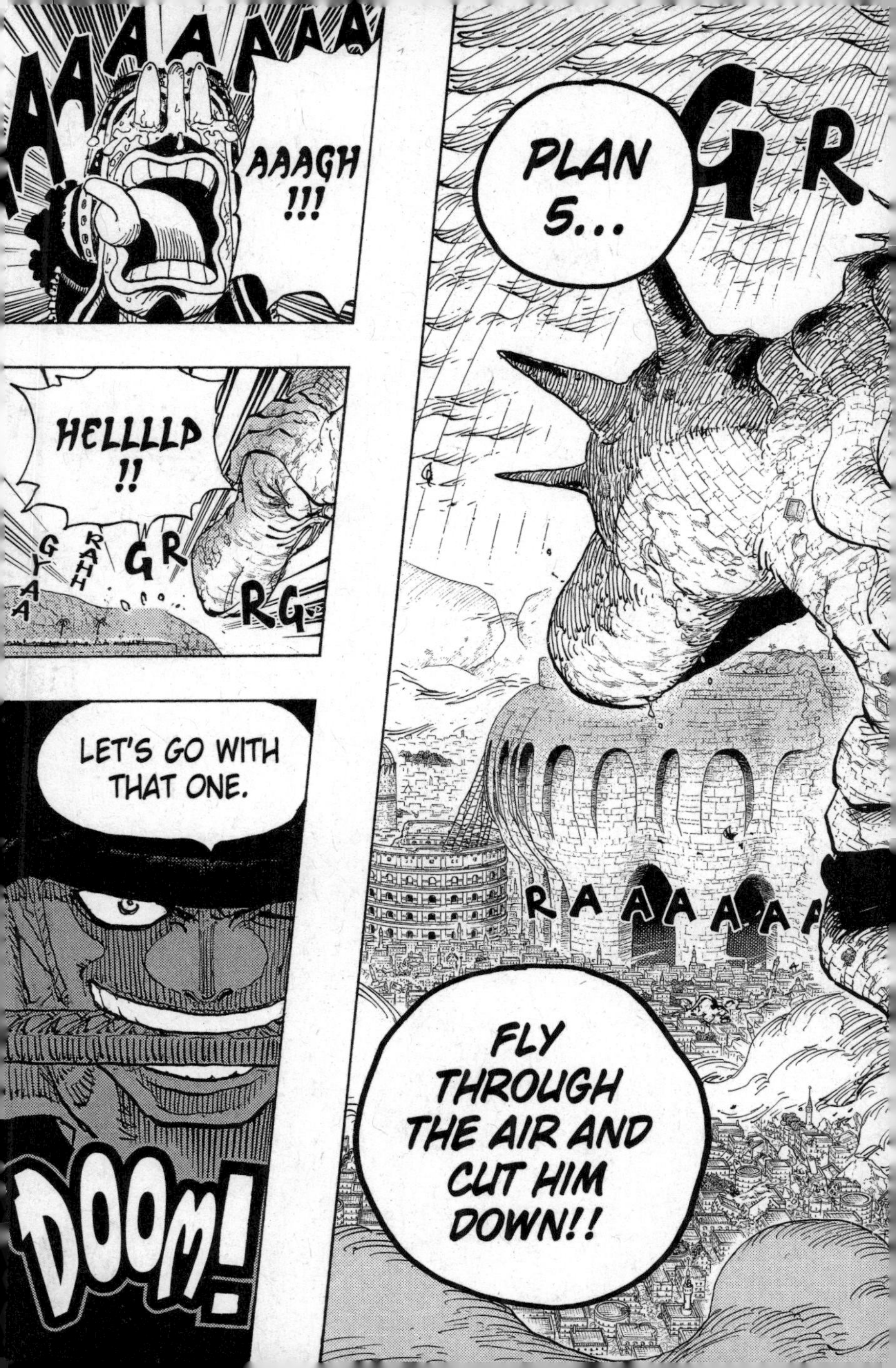
PLAN 5...
GR
RAAAAAAA
FLY THROUGH THE AIR AND CUT HIM DOWN!!
AAAAAAA
AAAGH !!!
HELLLLP !!
GYAA
RAHH
GR
RG
LET'S GO WITH THAT ONE.
DOOM!

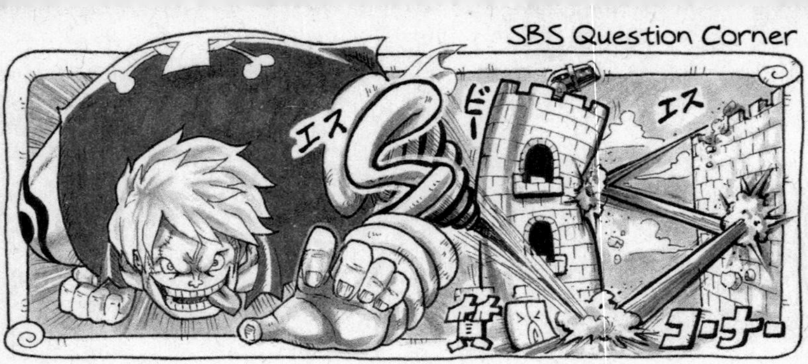
エス
ビー
エス
コーナー

(Hippo Iron, Saitama)

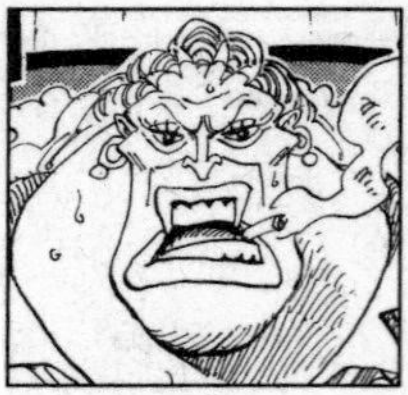

Q: Here's a question for you, Odacchi. Why is it that so many characters in *One Piece* have mothers who are unknown or deceased?

--Kon'iro

A: I see. Well, the answer is simple. The antonym of **"adventure"** is **"mother."**
*Please do not write this on a test.

Q: The Gimlet who appears in Chapter 755 has to be named after the gimlet cocktail, right?! Are you a fan of Raymond Chandler, Oda Sensei? Or do you just like alcoholic beverages? (laughs)

--Law's Second Assistant

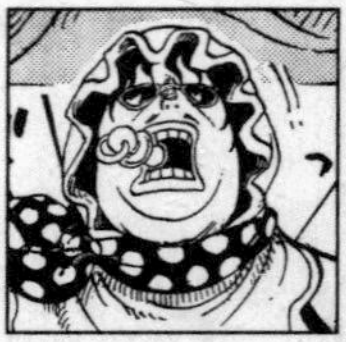

A: Yes, that's where I got the name. This is actually a tricky one to explain in full. It's a bit of wordplay on a famous line about gimlets in Chandler's classic hardboiled novel, The Long Goodbye. So I figured, if I'm going to do a hardboiled bit, I needed to get that name in there. You should look it up, if you're curious. Gimlet's mother "Russian" also came from a cocktail. Also, while I am from the alcohol-producing region of Kyushu, I draw a story about pirates, and I love hardboiled fiction...I cannot handle my liquor.

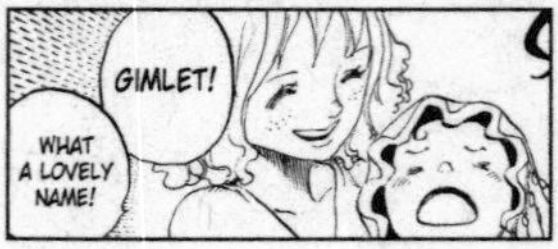
GIMLET!
WHAT A LOVELY NAME!

Q: I noticed that Robin's breasts have grown very large. Later on, I noticed that Nami's breasts are large too. Why are their breasts so large? Is that what you like, Mr. Oda? This question is from two 10-year-olds.

--Sakucchan & Yuzu

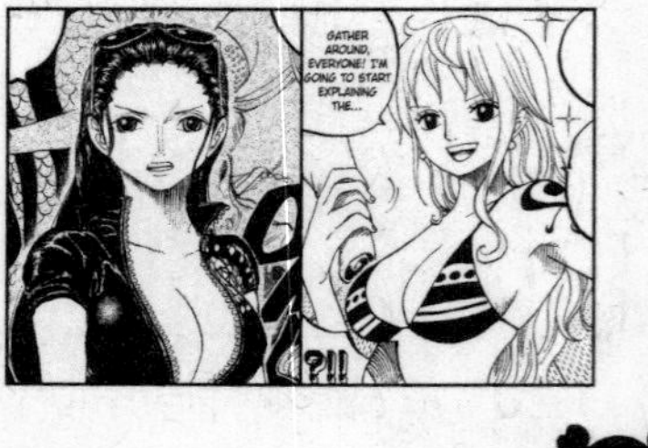
GATHER AROUND, EVERYONE! I'M GOING TO START EXPLAINING THE...
?!!

A: I'll say it a million times: I'm drawing the dreams of boys everywhere. People of the world! Grow big BOOBS!

Chapter 778:
TACTICS NO. 5

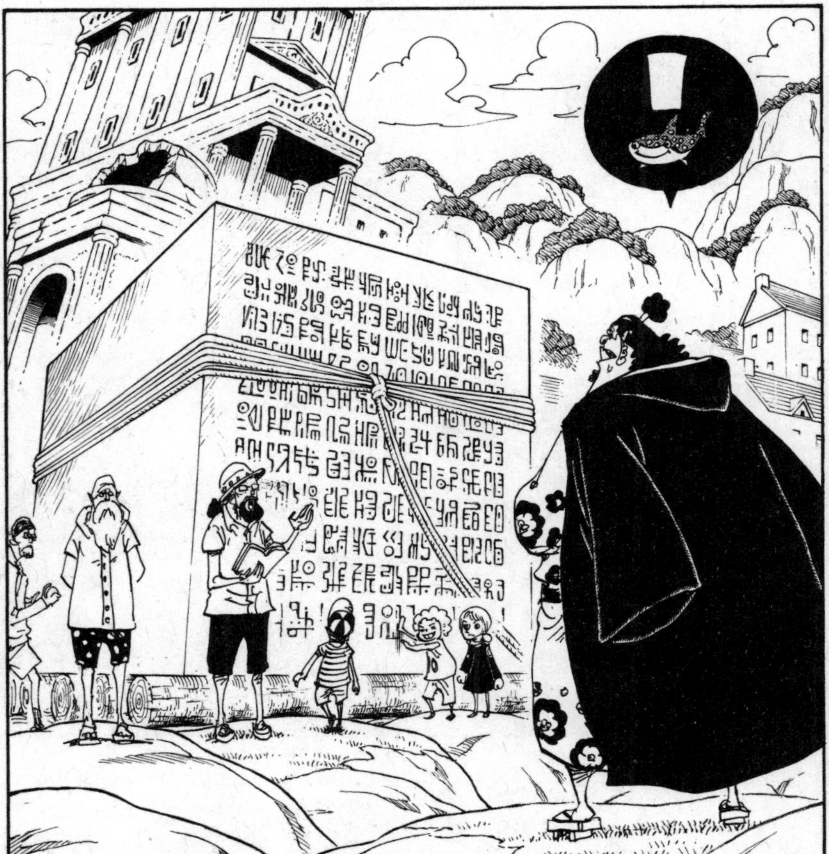

THE SOLITARY JOURNEY OF JIMBEI, FIRST SON OF THE SEA, VOL. 23: "OH YEAH, WE FOUND THIS IN THE RUINS"

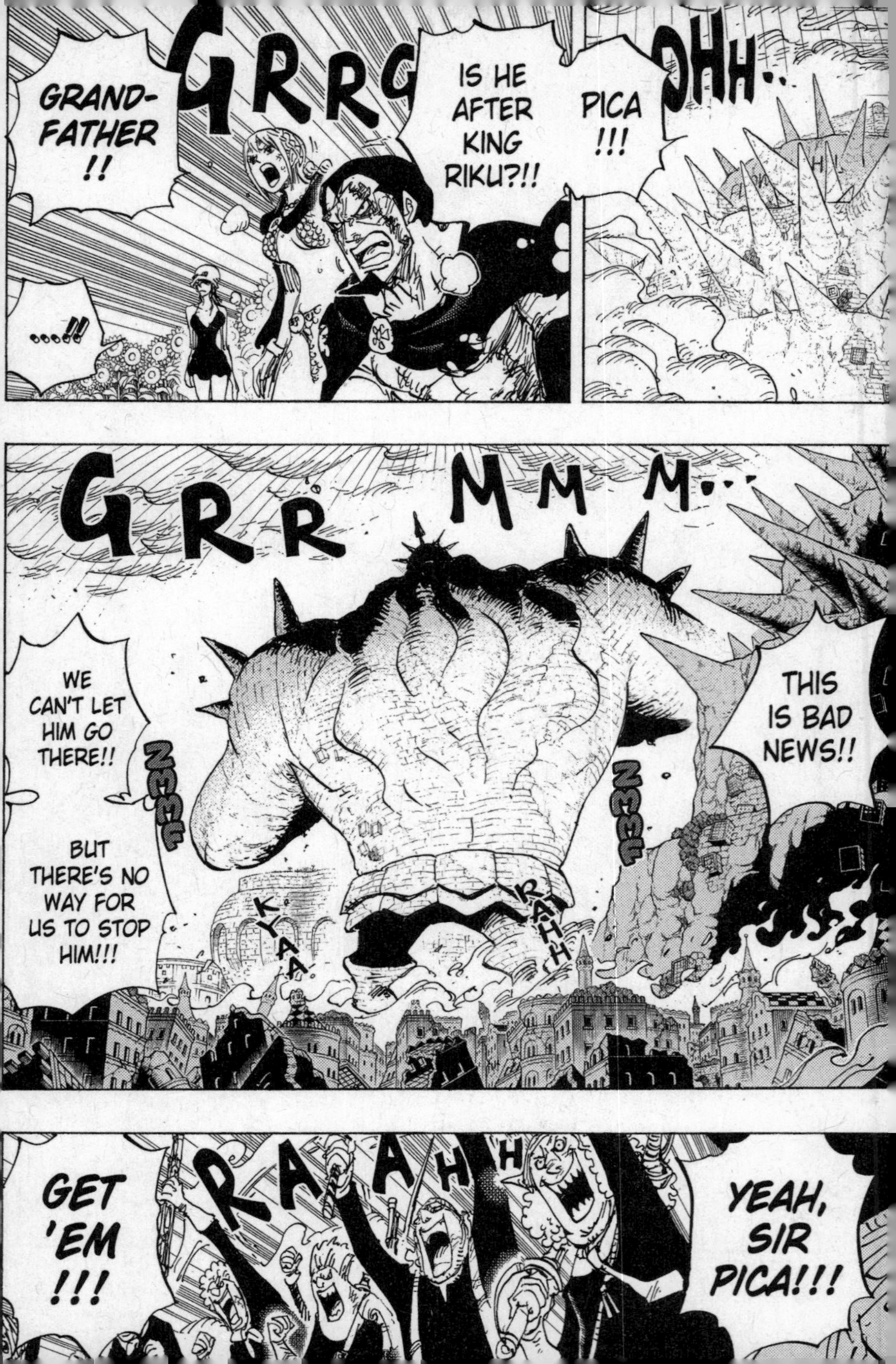
GRRRGOHH..
PICA!!!
IS HE AFTER KING RIKU?!!
GRAND-FATHER!!
....!!
GRRRMMM...
THIS IS BAD NEWS!!
WE CAN'T LET HIM GO THERE!!
BUT THERE'S NO WAY FOR US TO STOP HIM!!!
ZMMF
ZMMF
RAHHH
KYAAA
YEAH, SIR PICA!!!
RAAHHH
GET 'EM!!!

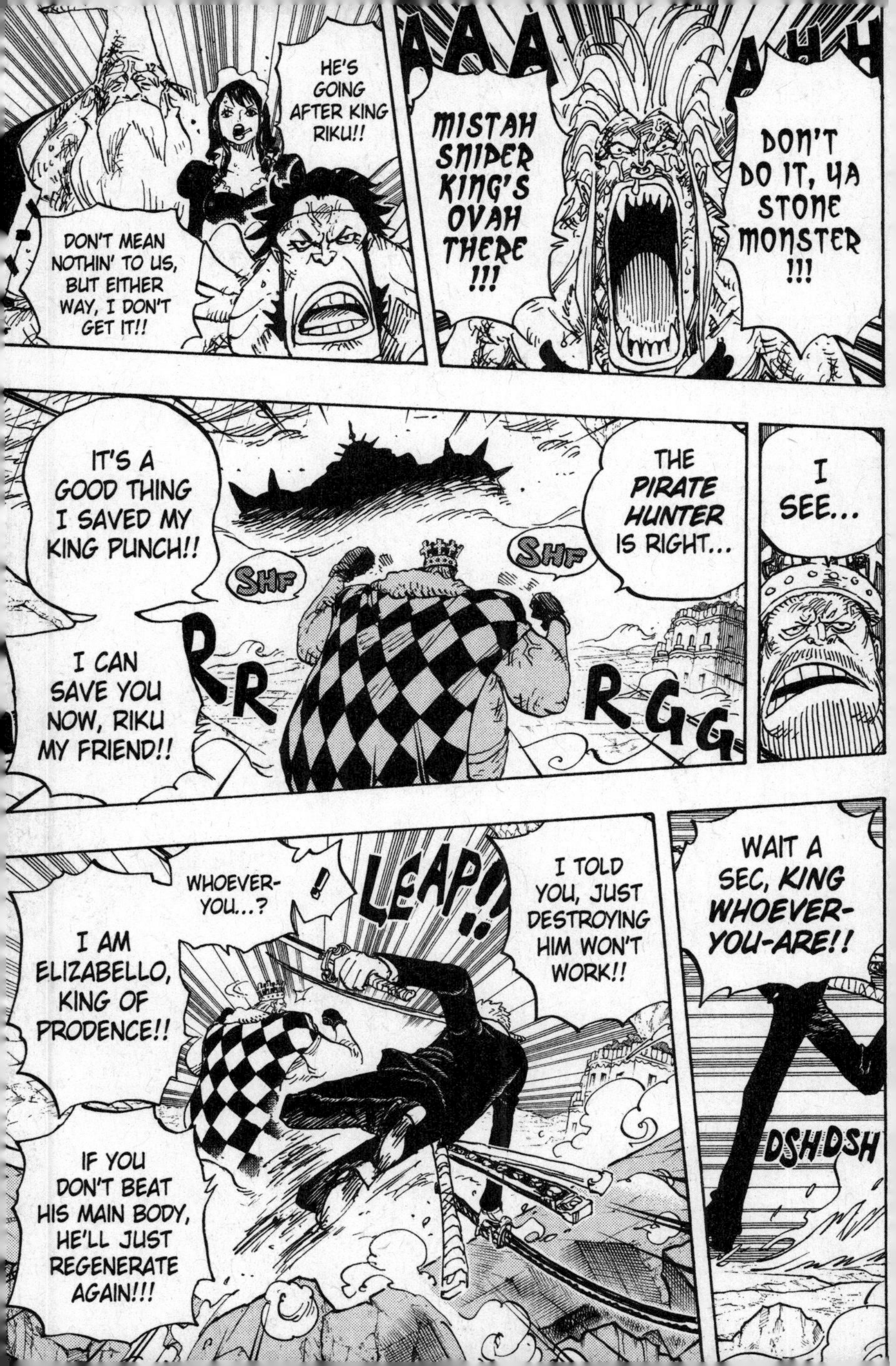
AAAAYH
DON'T DO IT, YA STONE MONSTER!!!
MISTAH SNIPER KING'S OVAH THERE!!!
HE'S GOING AFTER KING RIKU!!
DON'T MEAN NOTHIN' TO US, BUT EITHER WAY, I DON'T GET IT!!
I SEE...
THE *PIRATE HUNTER* IS RIGHT...
SHF
RGG
SHF
RR
IT'S A GOOD THING I SAVED MY KING PUNCH!!
I CAN SAVE YOU NOW, RIKU MY FRIEND!!
WAIT A SEC, *KING WHOEVER-YOU-ARE!!*
DSHDSH
I TOLD YOU, JUST DESTROYING HIM WON'T WORK!!
LEAP!!
!
WHOEVER-YOU...?
I AM ELIZABELLO, KING OF PRODENCE!!
IF YOU DON'T BEAT HIS MAIN BODY, HE'LL JUST REGENERATE AGAIN!!!

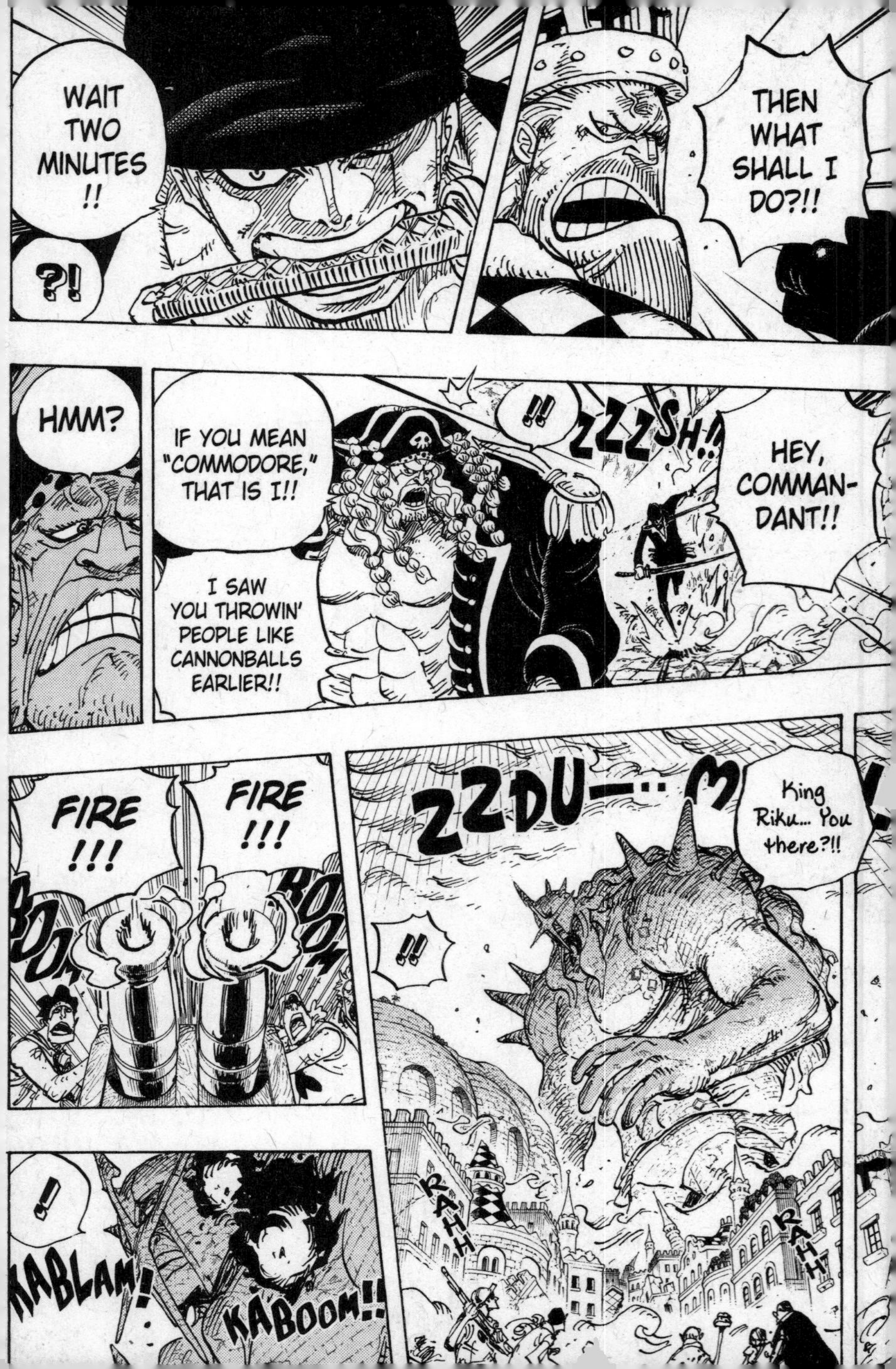
THEN WHAT SHALL I DO?!!
WAIT TWO MINUTES!!
?!
HEY, COMMANDANT!!
ZZZSH!!
!!
IF YOU MEAN "COMMODORE," THAT IS I!!
I SAW YOU THROWIN' PEOPLE LIKE CANNONBALLS EARLIER!!
HMM?
King Riku... You there?!!
ZZDU—..M
!!
RAHH
RAHH
FIRE!!!
FIRE!!!
BOOM
BOOM
!
KABOOM!!
KABLAM!

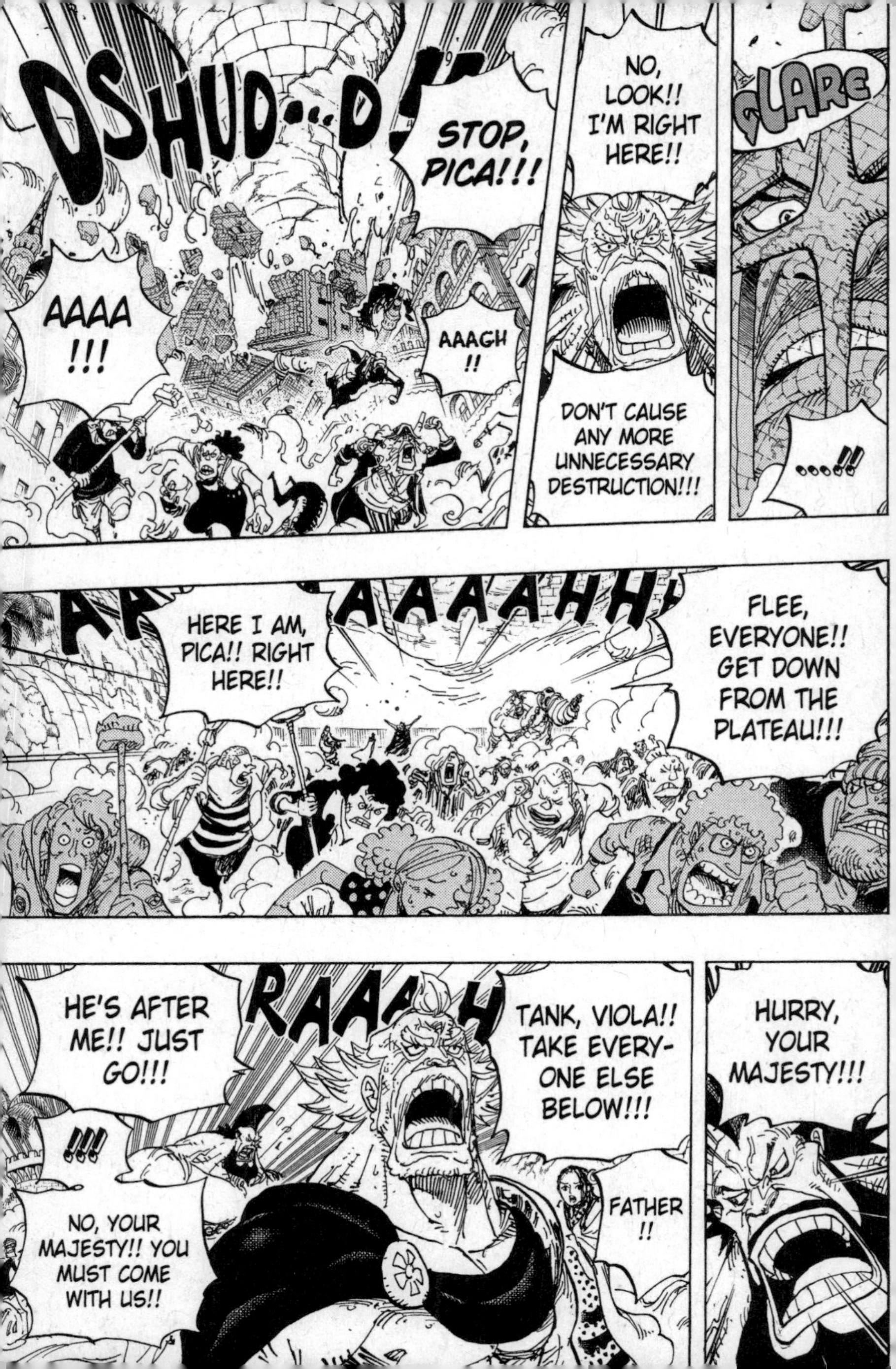
GLARE
....!!
NO, LOOK!! I'M RIGHT HERE!!
DON'T CAUSE ANY MORE UNNECESSARY DESTRUCTION!!!
DSHUD...D
STOP, PICA!!!
AAAGH!!
AAAA!!!
AAAAAAHH
FLEE, EVERYONE!! GET DOWN FROM THE PLATEAU!!!
HERE I AM, PICA!! RIGHT HERE!!
HURRY, YOUR MAJESTY!!!
TANK, VIOLA!! TAKE EVERY-ONE ELSE BELOW!!!
RAAAH
HE'S AFTER ME!! JUST GO!!!
FATHER!!
!!!
NO, YOUR MAJESTY!! YOU MUST COME WITH US!!

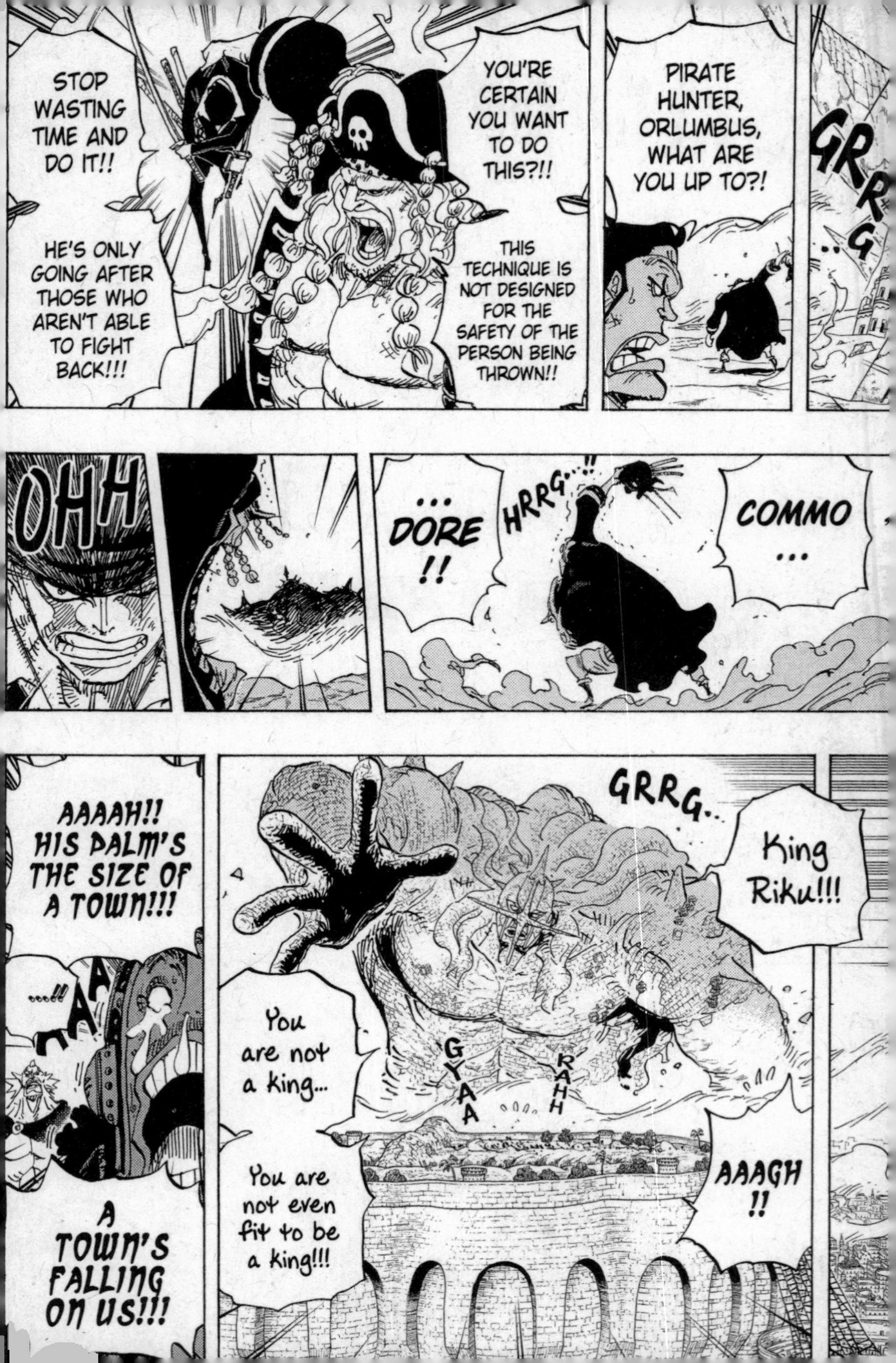
GRRRG
...
PIRATE HUNTER, ORLUMBUS, WHAT ARE YOU UP TO?!
YOU'RE CERTAIN YOU WANT TO DO THIS?!!
THIS TECHNIQUE IS NOT DESIGNED FOR THE SAFETY OF THE PERSON BEING THROWN!!
STOP WASTING TIME AND DO IT!!
HE'S ONLY GOING AFTER THOSE WHO AREN'T ABLE TO FIGHT BACK!!!
COMMO ...
HRRG...!!
... DORE !!
OHH
GRRG..
King Riku!!!
You are not a king...
You are not even fit to be a king!!!
GYAA
RAHH
AAAGH !!
AAAAH!! HIS PALM'S THE SIZE OF A TOWN!!!
...!!
AA
A TOWN'S FALLING ON US!!!

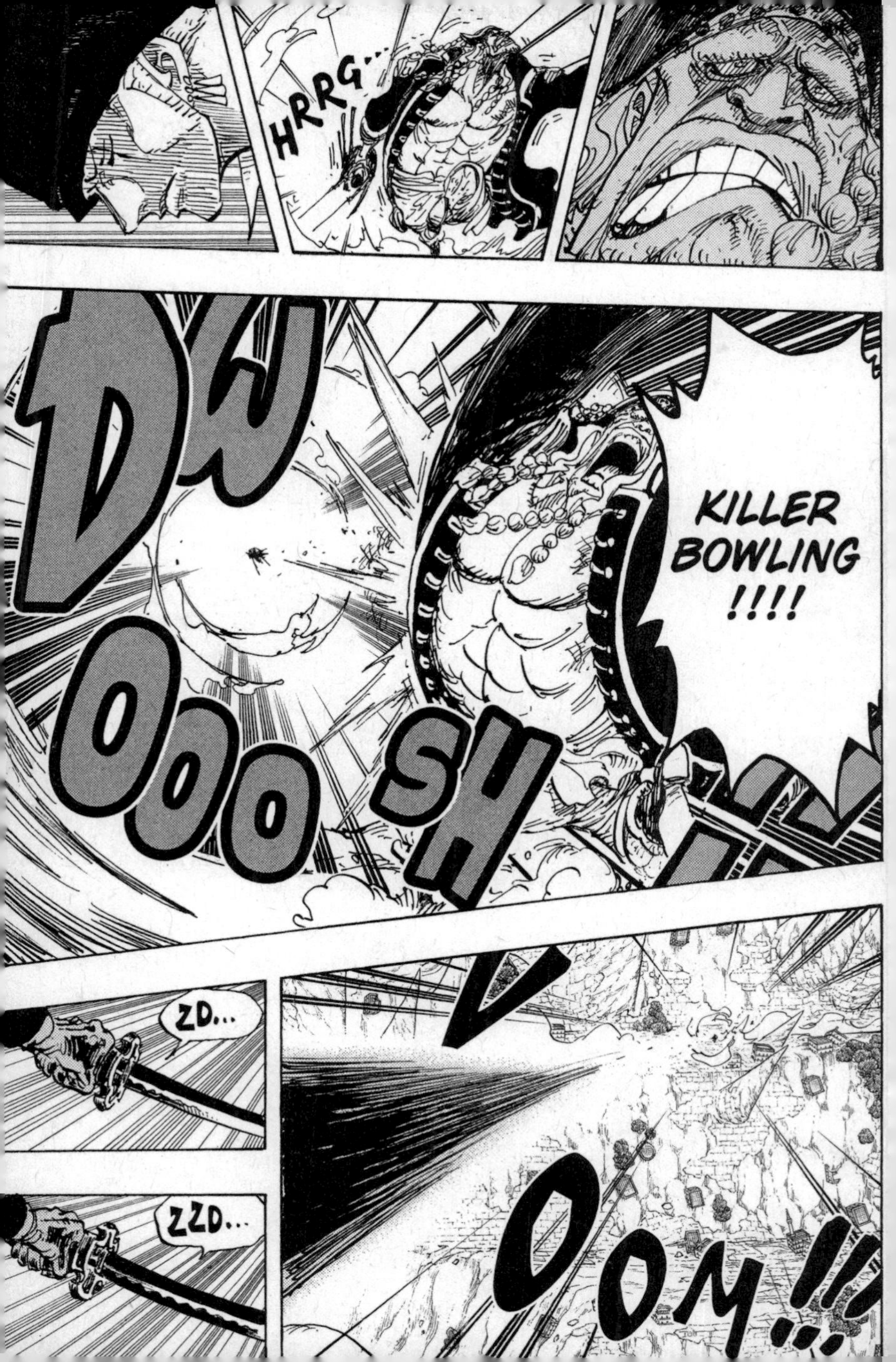
HRRG...
KILLER BOWLING !!!!
DWOOOSH
VOOM!!!
ZD...
ZZD...

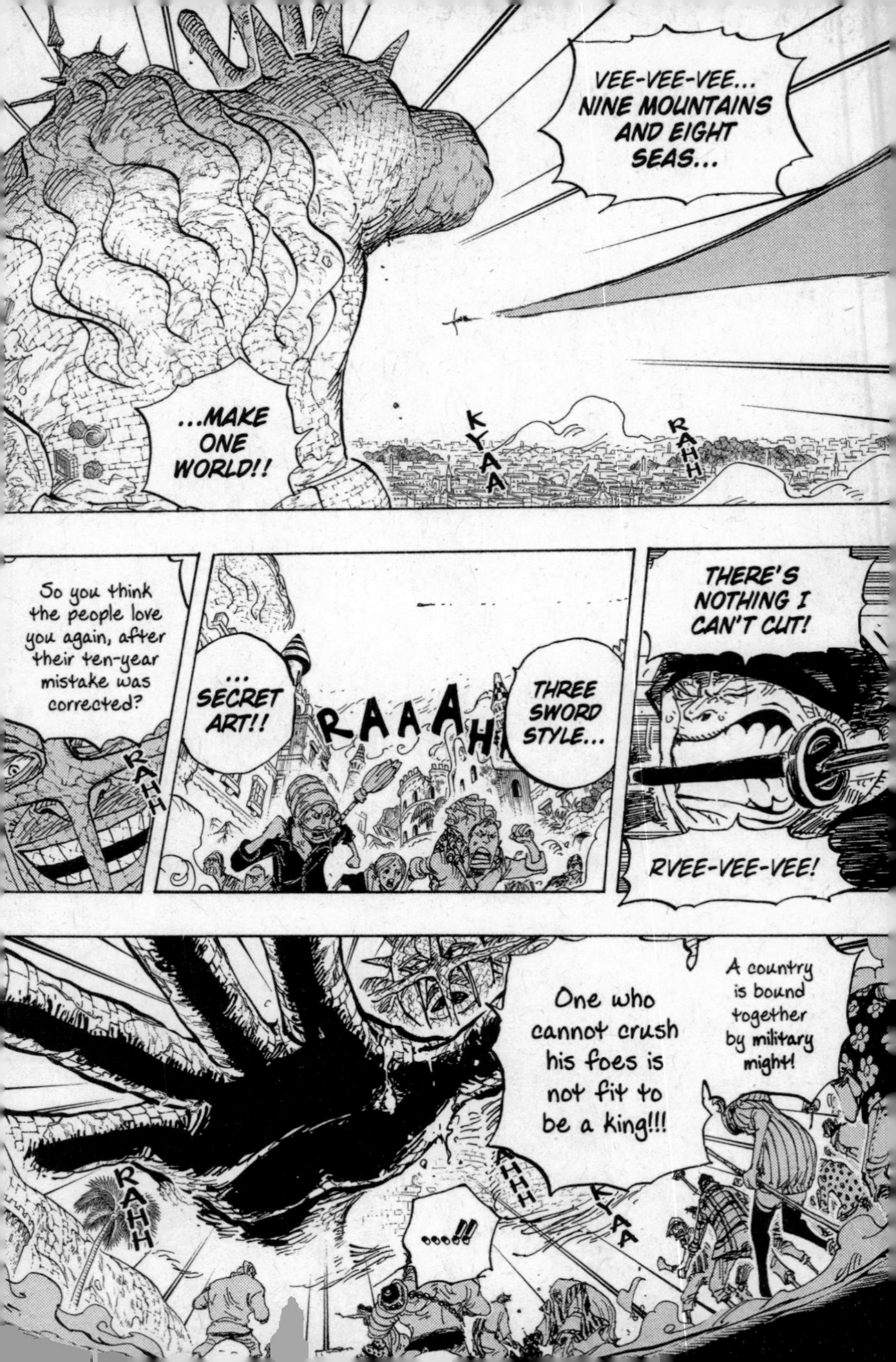
VEE-VEE-VEE... NINE MOUNTAINS AND EIGHT SEAS...
...MAKE ONE WORLD!!
RAHH
KYAA
THERE'S NOTHING I CAN'T CUT!
RVEE-VEE-VEE!
THREE SWORD STYLE...
RAAAH
...SECRET ART!!
So you think the people love you again, after their ten-year mistake was corrected?
RAHH
A country is bound together by military might!
One who cannot crush his foes is not fit to be a king!!!
KYAA
AHHH
...!!
RAHH

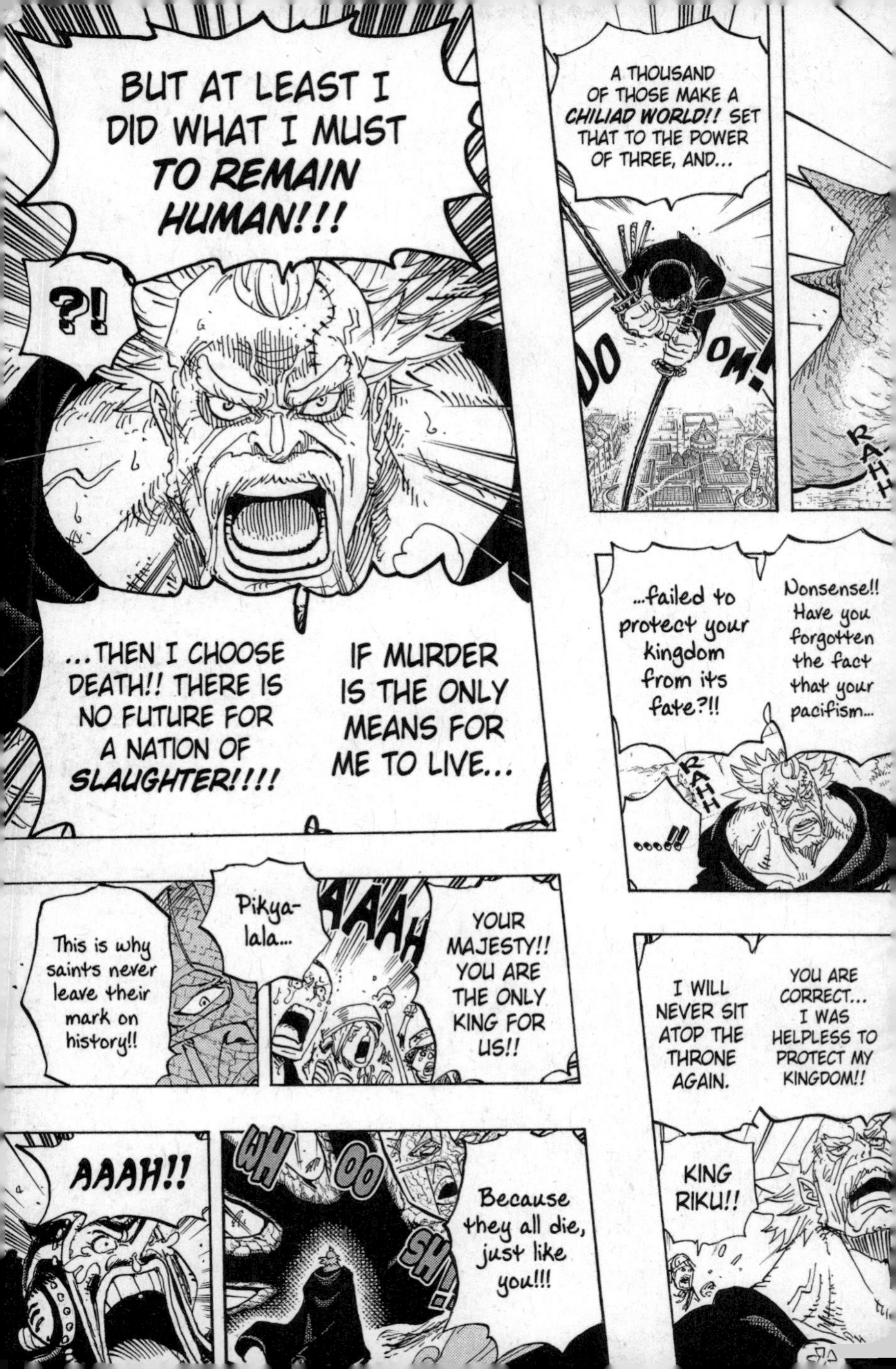
RAHH
A THOUSAND OF THOSE MAKE A *CHILIAD WORLD!!* SET THAT TO THE POWER OF THREE, AND...
DOOM!
Nonsense!! Have you forgotten the fact that your pacifism...
...failed to protect your kingdom from its fate?!!
RAHH
...!!
BUT AT LEAST I DID WHAT I MUST *TO REMAIN HUMAN!!!*
?!
IF MURDER IS THE ONLY MEANS FOR ME TO LIVE...
...THEN I CHOOSE DEATH!! THERE IS NO FUTURE FOR A NATION OF *SLAUGHTER!!!!*
YOU ARE CORRECT... I WAS HELPLESS TO PROTECT MY KINGDOM!!
I WILL NEVER SIT ATOP THE THRONE AGAIN.
KING RIKU!!
YOUR MAJESTY!! YOU ARE THE ONLY KING FOR US!!
AAAH
Pikya-lala...
This is why saints never leave their mark on history!!
Because they all die, just like you!!!
WHOOSH
AAAH!!

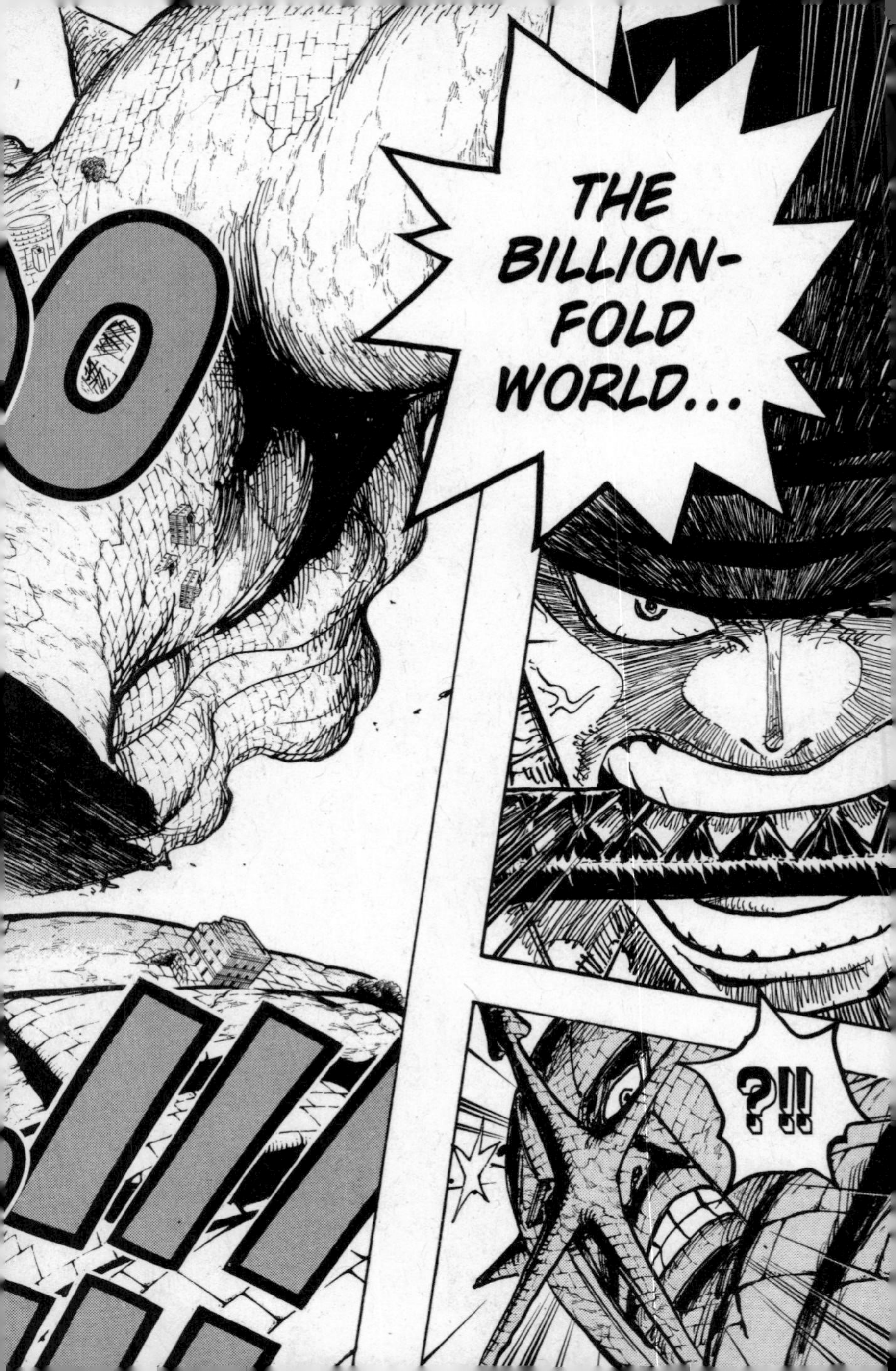
THE BILLION-FOLD WORLD...
?!!

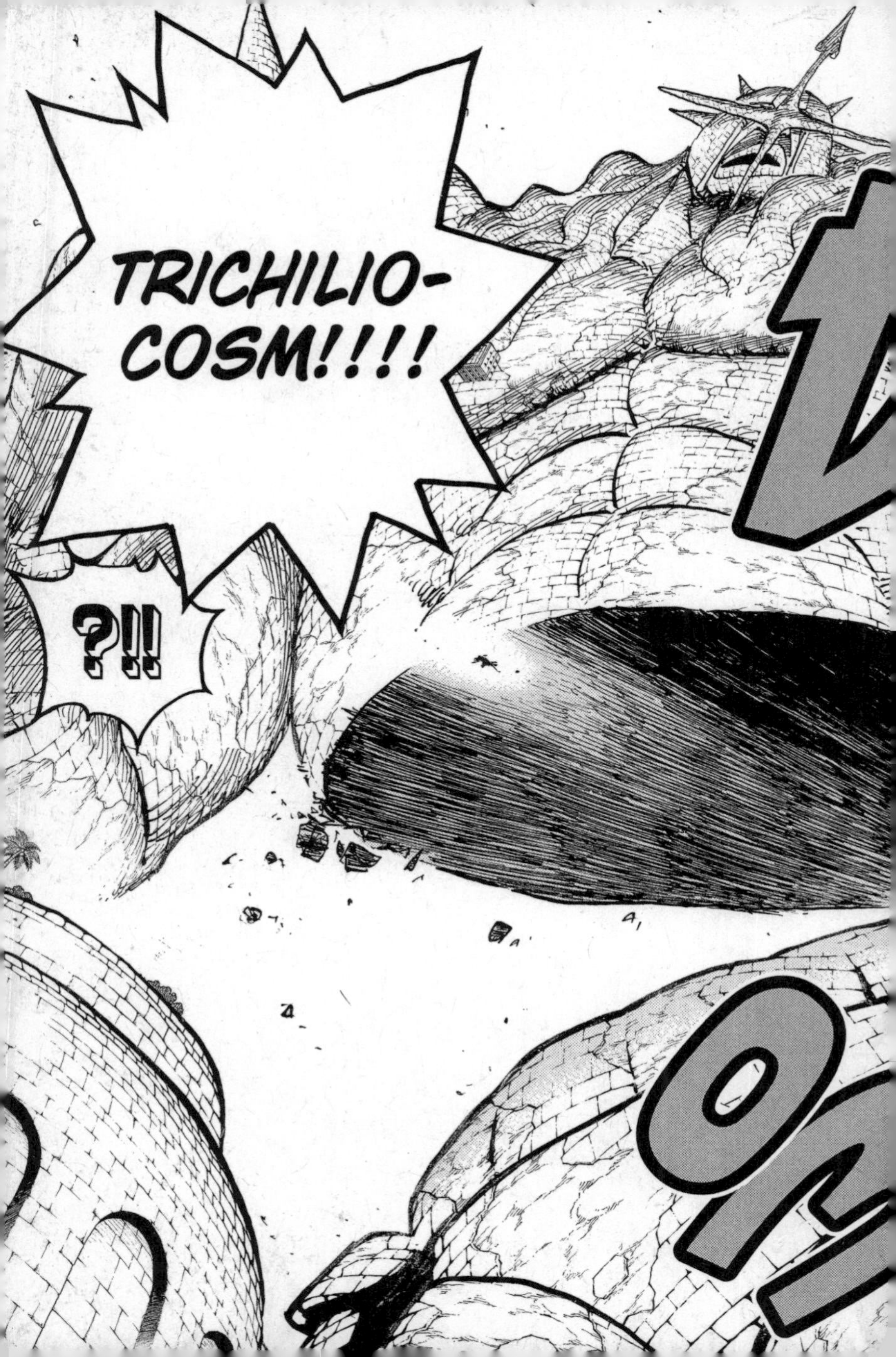
TRICHILIO-COSM!!!!
?!!

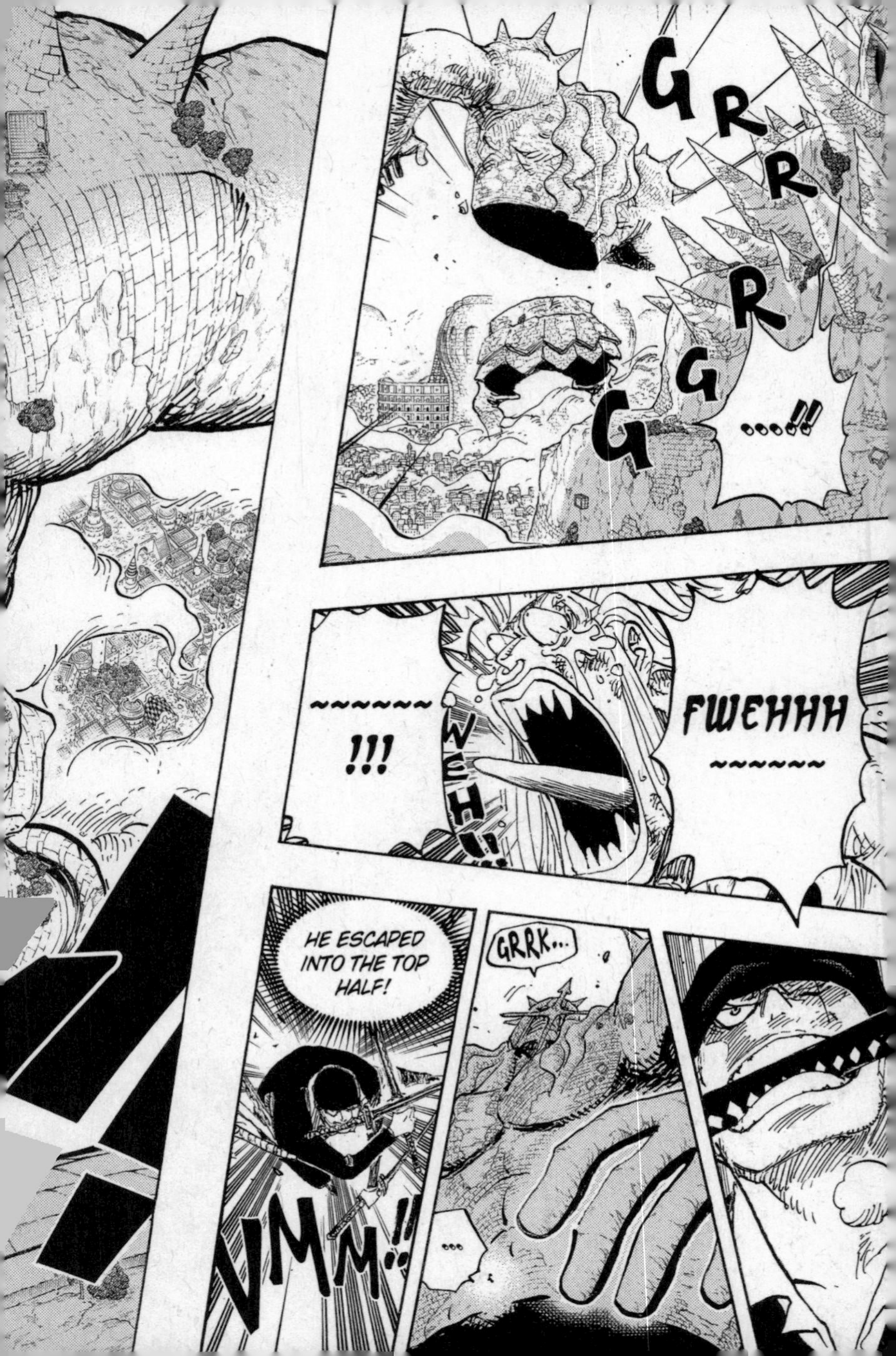
GRRRGGG...!!
FWEHHH ~~~~~~~
~~~~~~~ !!!
WEH!!
GRRK...
...
HE ESCAPED INTO THE TOP HALF!
VMM!!
~~~~~~~

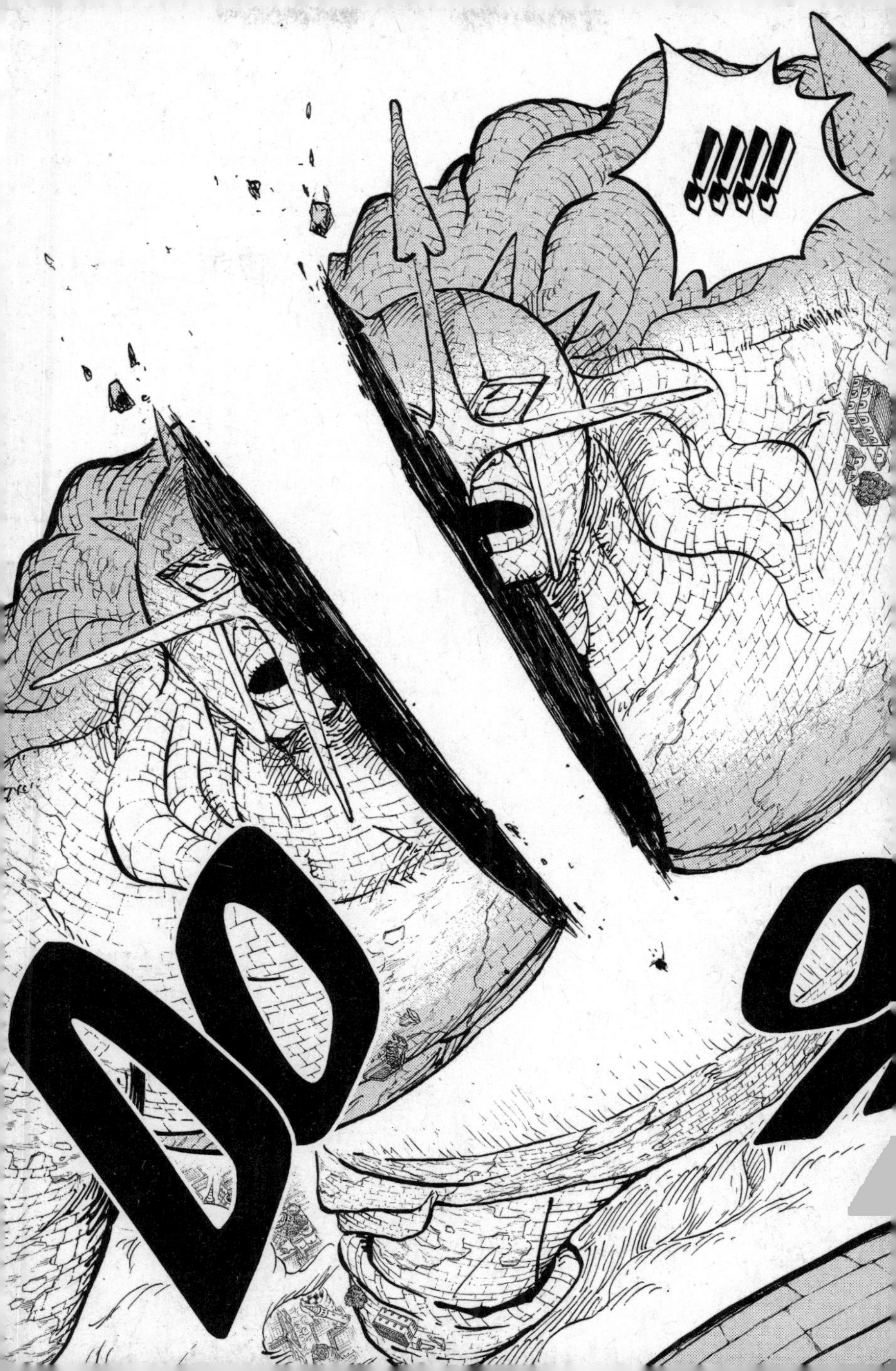
!!!!
DO

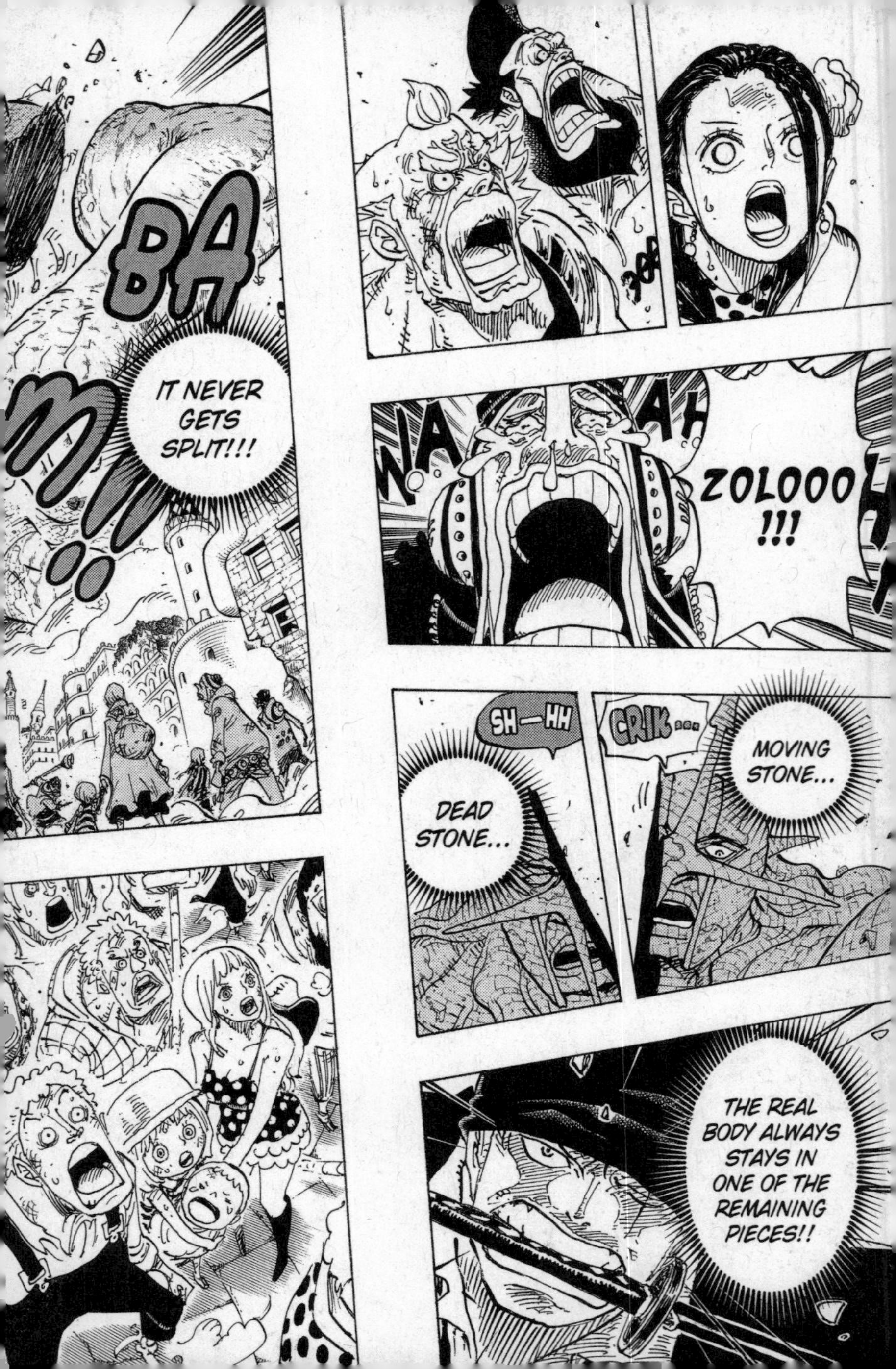
WA
AH
ZOLOOO!!!
CRIK...
MOVING STONE...
SH-HH
DEAD STONE...
THE REAL BODY ALWAYS STAYS IN ONE OF THE REMAINING PIECES!!
BAM!!
IT NEVER GETS SPLIT!!!

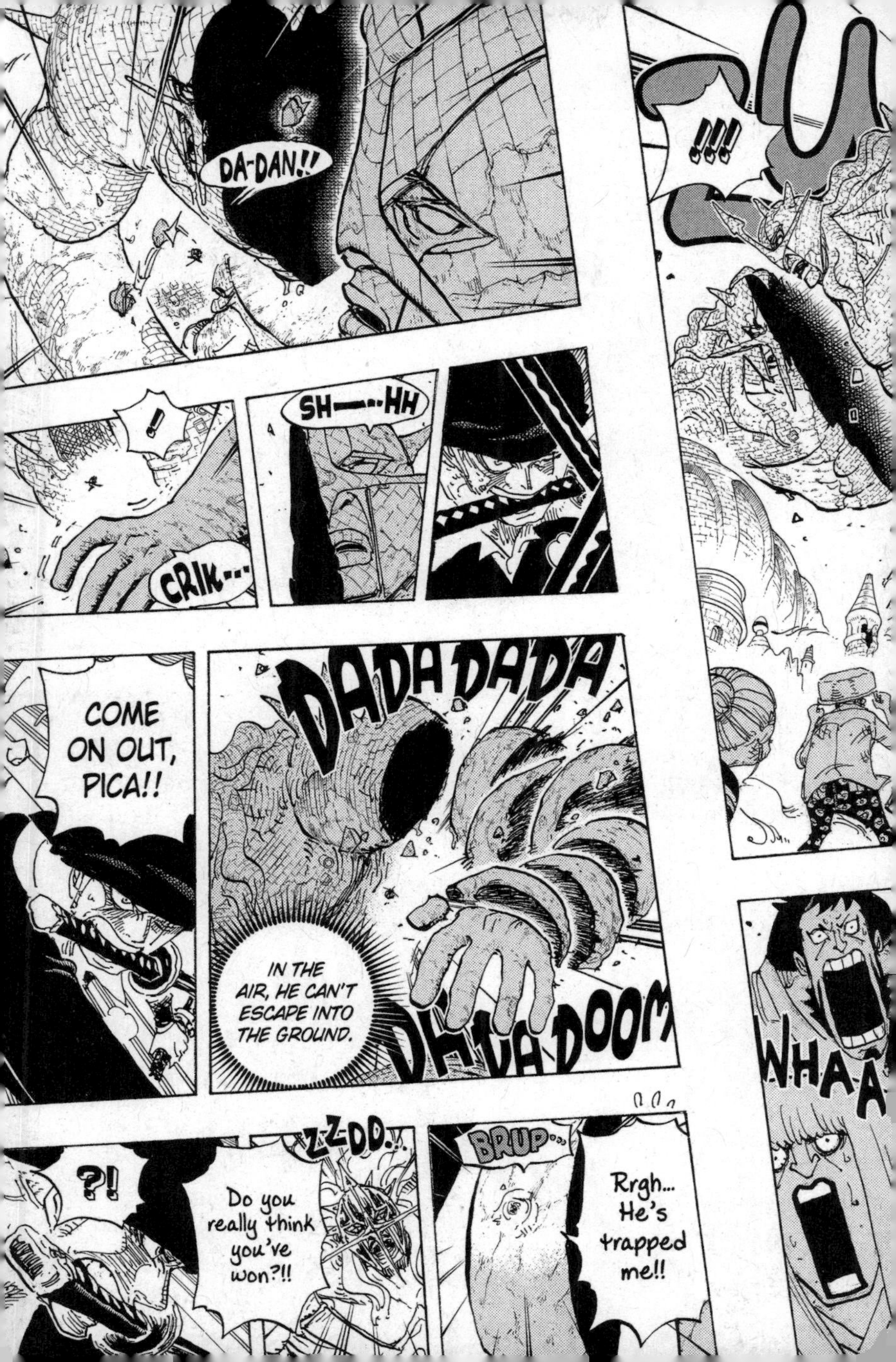
!!!
DA-DAN!!
SH——HH
!
CRIK...
DADADADA
IN THE AIR, HE CAN'T ESCAPE INTO THE GROUND.
DHA-DOOM
COME ON OUT, PICA!!
WHAA
BRUP...
Rrgh... He's trapped me!!
Z-Z-DD...
Do you really think you've won?!!
?!

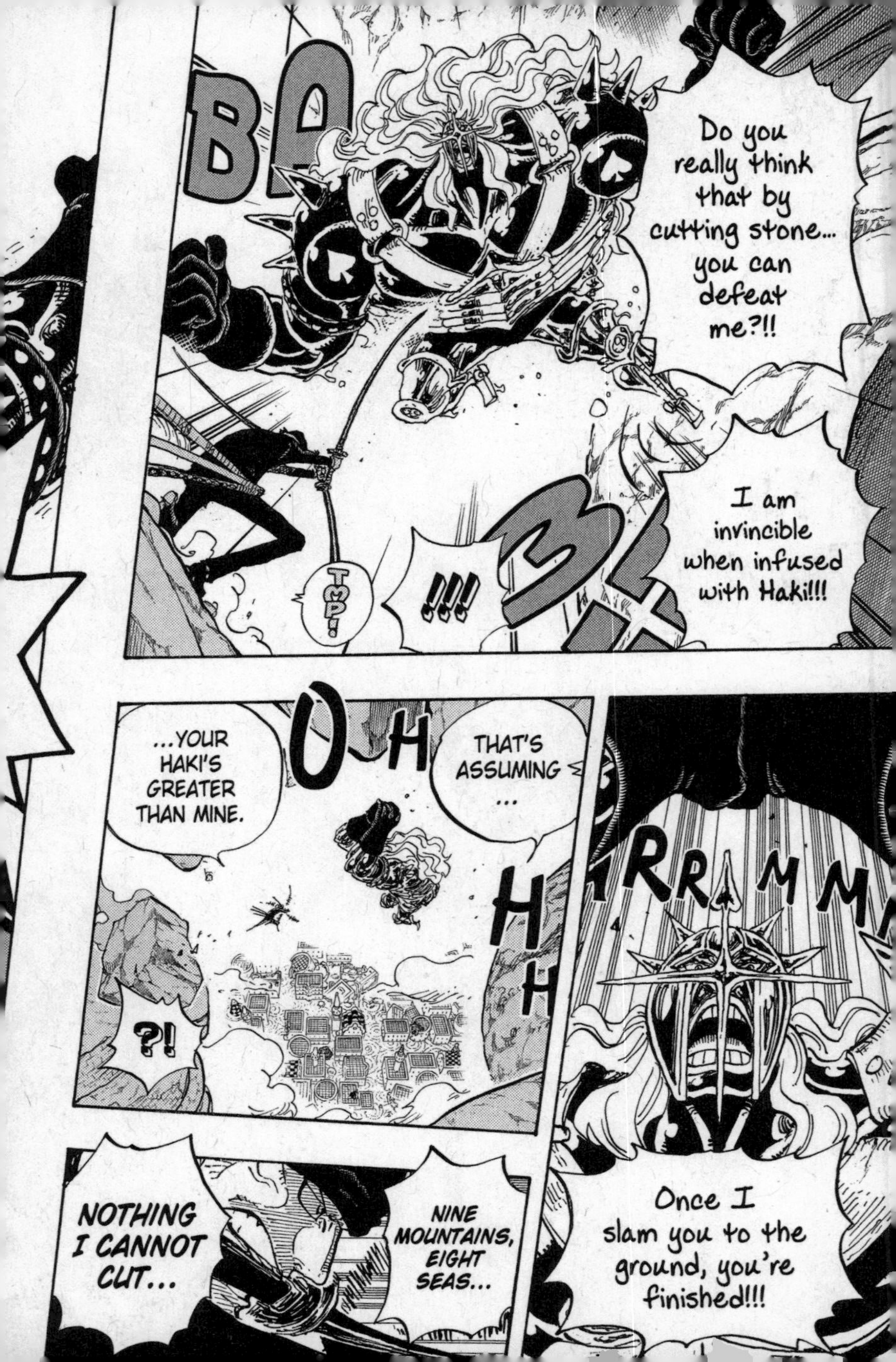

Do you really think that by cutting stone... you can defeat me?!!
I am invincible when infused with Haki!!!
!!!
TMP!
Once I slam you to the ground, you're finished!!!
THAT'S ASSUMING ...
...YOUR HAKI'S GREATER THAN MINE.
?!
NINE MOUNTAINS, EIGHT SEAS...
NOTHING I CANNOT CUT...

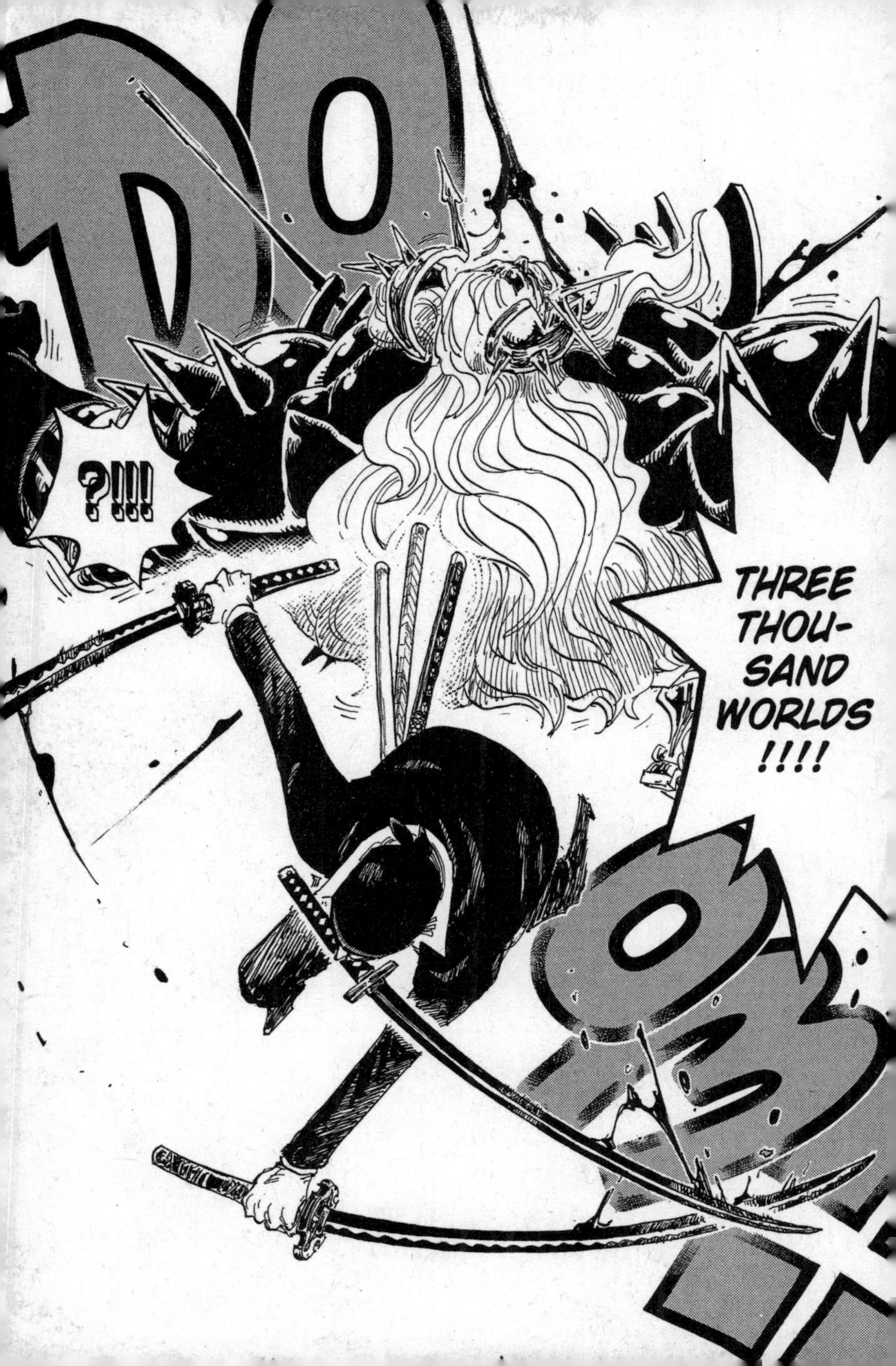
THREE THOUSAND WORLDS !!!!
?!!!

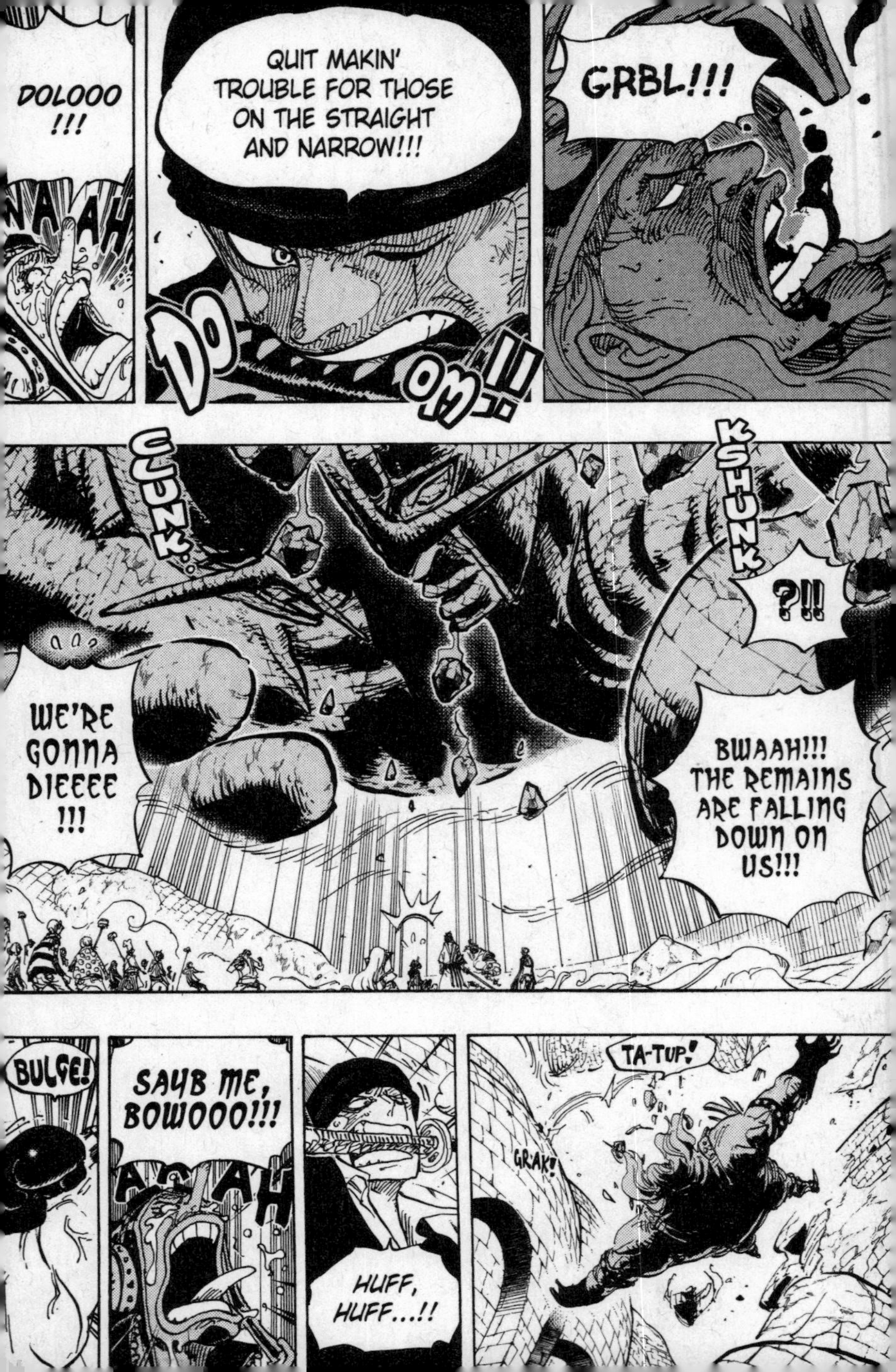
GRBL!!!
QUIT MAKIN' TROUBLE FOR THOSE ON THE STRAIGHT AND NARROW!!!
DOOM!!
DOLOOO !!!
KSHUNK
?!!
BWAAH!!! THE REMAINS ARE FALLING DOWN ON US!!!
CLUNK
WE'RE GONNA DIEEEE !!!
TA-TUP!
GRAK!
HUFF, HUFF...!!
SAYB ME, BOWOOO!!!
BULGE!

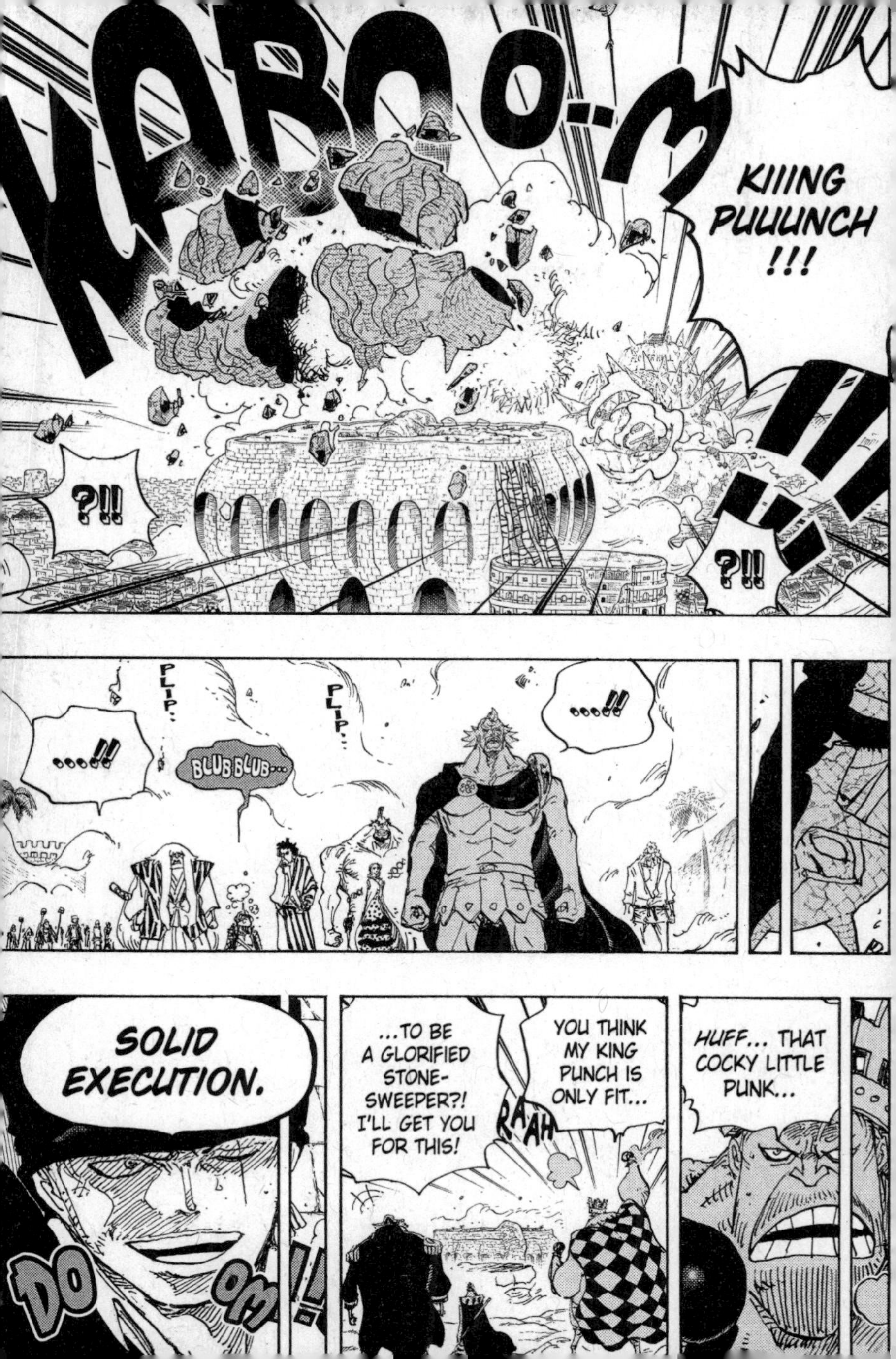
KIIING PUUUNCH !!!
KABOO..M
?!!
?!!
...!!
PLIP..
PLIP..
BLUB BLUB...
...!!
HUFF... THAT COCKY LITTLE PUNK...
YOU THINK MY KING PUNCH IS ONLY FIT...
RAAH
...TO BE A GLORIFIED STONE-SWEEPER?! I'LL GET YOU FOR THIS!
SOLID EXECUTION.
DOOM!!

HIS FINAL BATTLE

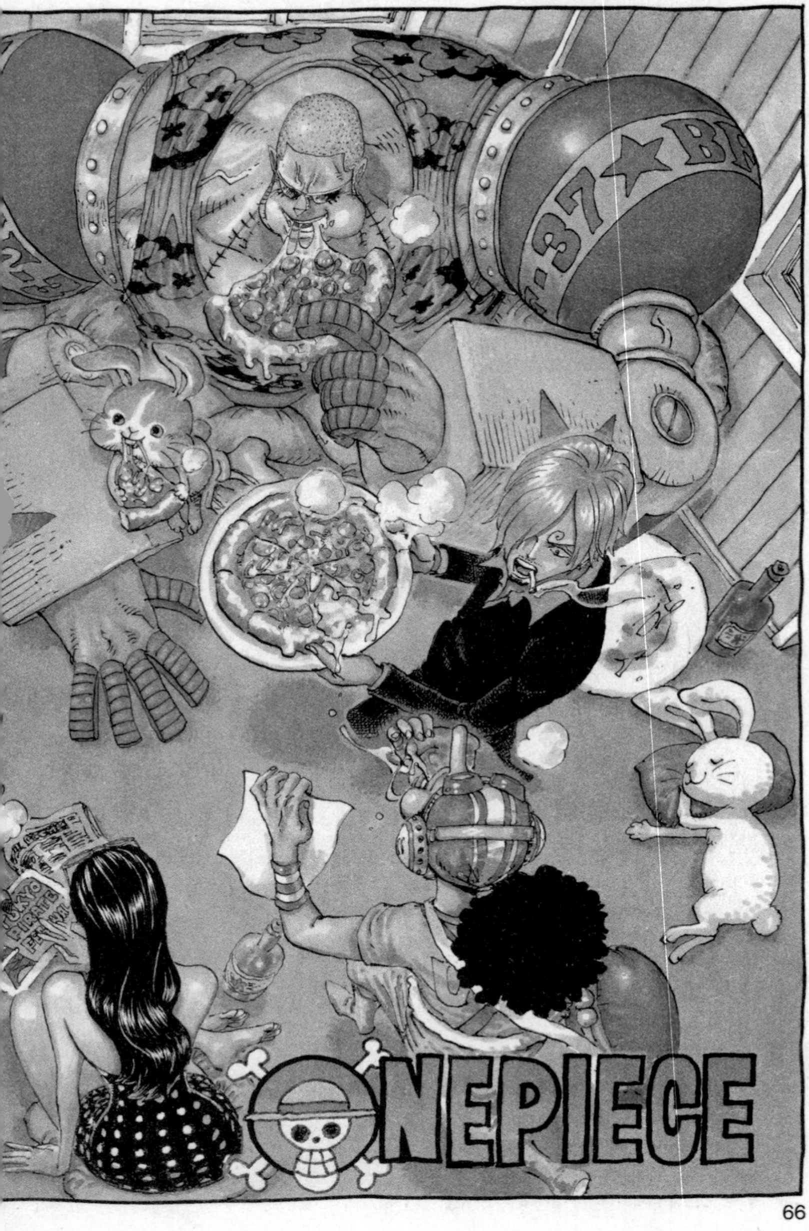
ONE PIECE

Chapter 779:

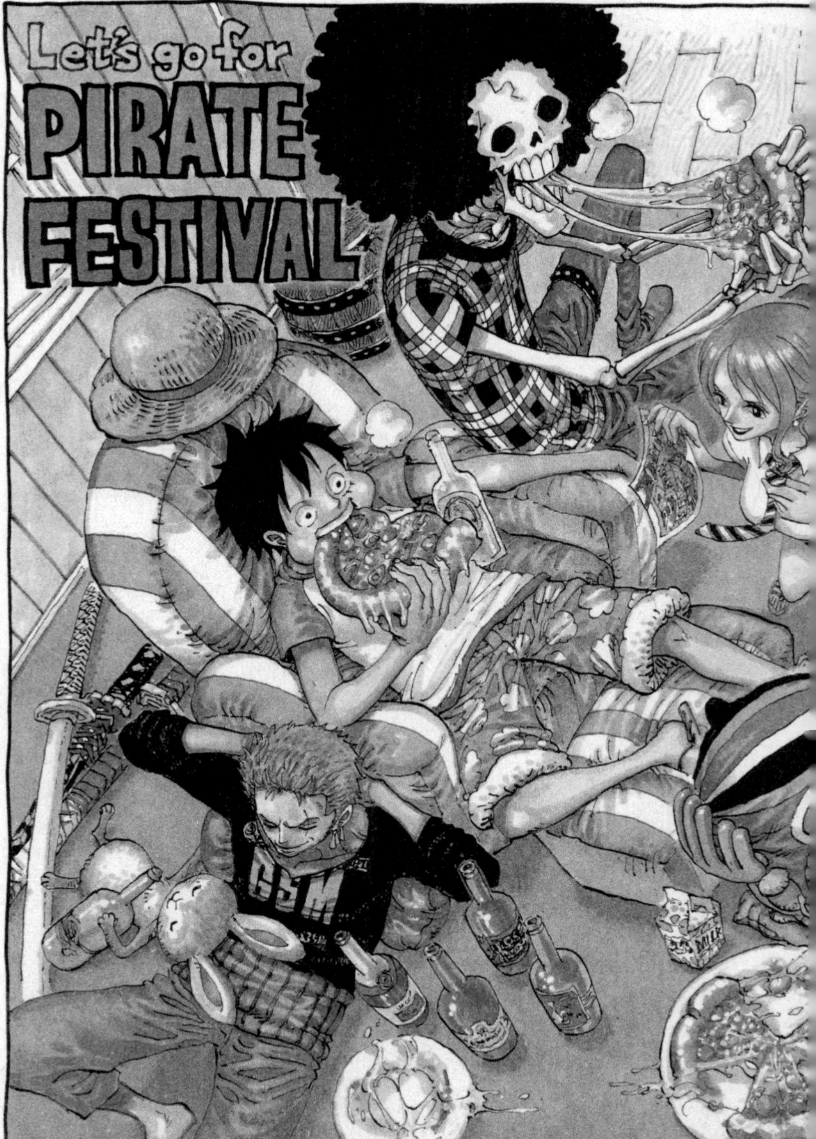
Let's go for
PIRATE
FESTIVAL
GSM
MILK

vol.78

ONE PIECE

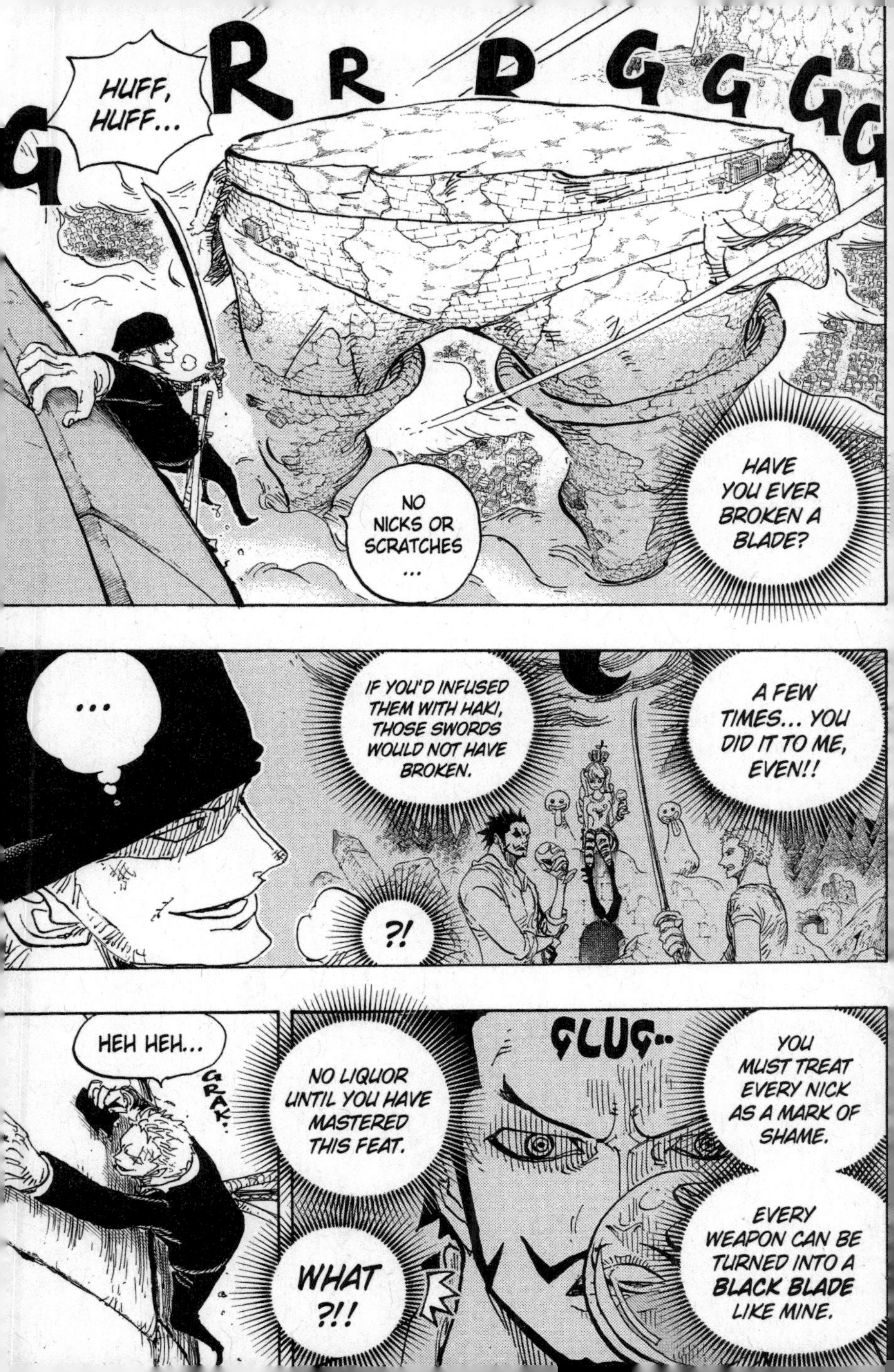
GRRRGGGG
HUFF, HUFF...
HAVE YOU EVER BROKEN A BLADE?
NO NICKS OR SCRATCHES ...
A FEW TIMES... YOU DID IT TO ME, EVEN!!
IF YOU'D INFUSED THEM WITH HAKI, THOSE SWORDS WOULD NOT HAVE BROKEN.
?!
...
GLUG..
YOU MUST TREAT EVERY NICK AS A MARK OF SHAME.
EVERY WEAPON CAN BE TURNED INTO A BLACK BLADE LIKE MINE.
NO LIQUOR UNTIL YOU HAVE MASTERED THIS FEAT.
WHAT ?!!
HEH HEH...
GRAK.

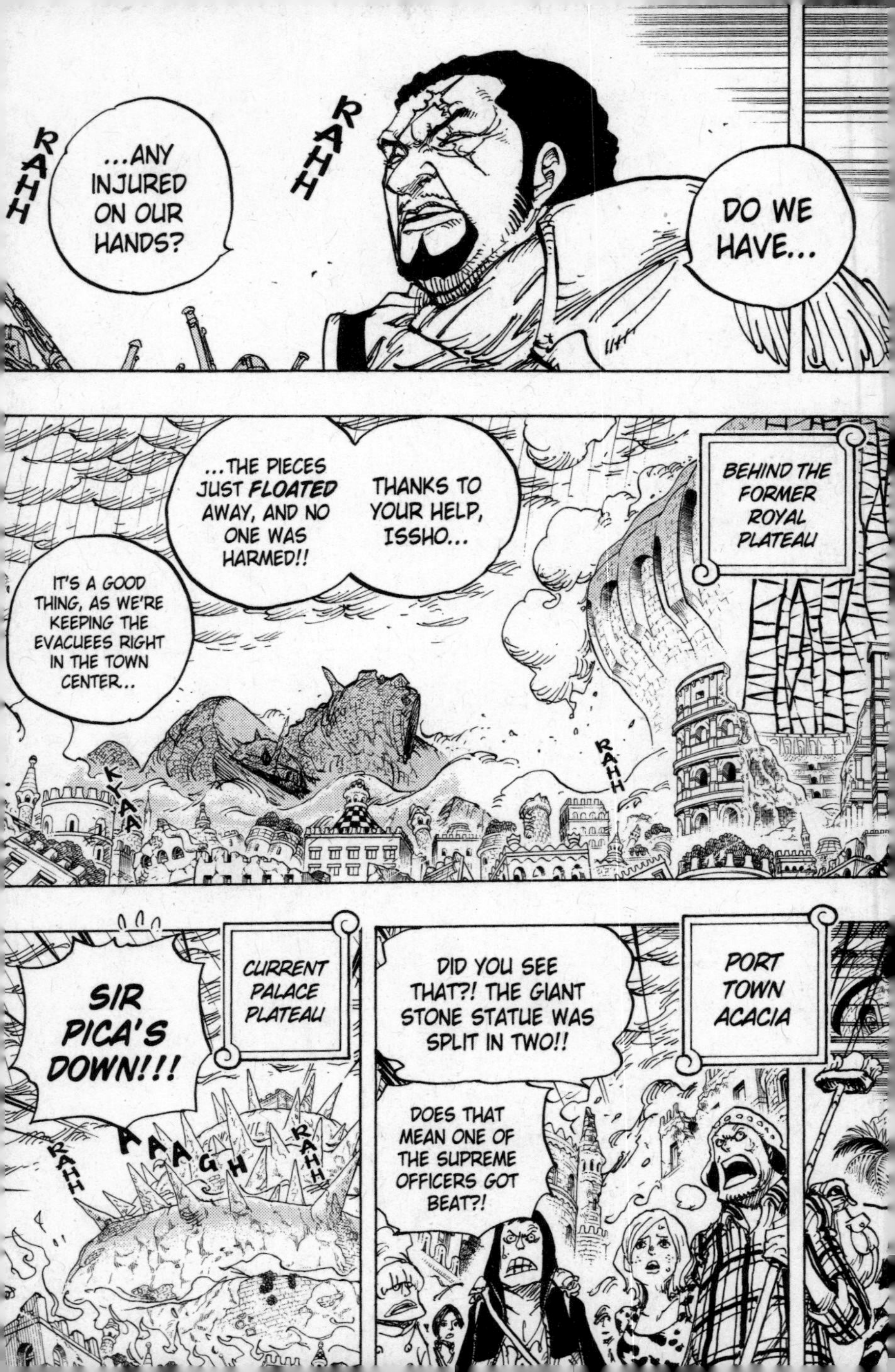
DO WE HAVE...
...ANY INJURED ON OUR HANDS?
RAHH
RAHH
BEHIND THE FORMER ROYAL PLATEAU
THANKS TO YOUR HELP, ISSHO...
...THE PIECES JUST FLOATED AWAY, AND NO ONE WAS HARMED!!
IT'S A GOOD THING, AS WE'RE KEEPING THE EVACUEES RIGHT IN THE TOWN CENTER...
RAHH
KYAA
PORT TOWN ACACIA
DID YOU SEE THAT?! THE GIANT STONE STATUE WAS SPLIT IN TWO!!
DOES THAT MEAN ONE OF THE SUPREME OFFICERS GOT BEAT?!
CURRENT PALACE PLATEAU
SIR PICA'S DOWN!!!
RAHH
AAAGH
RAHH

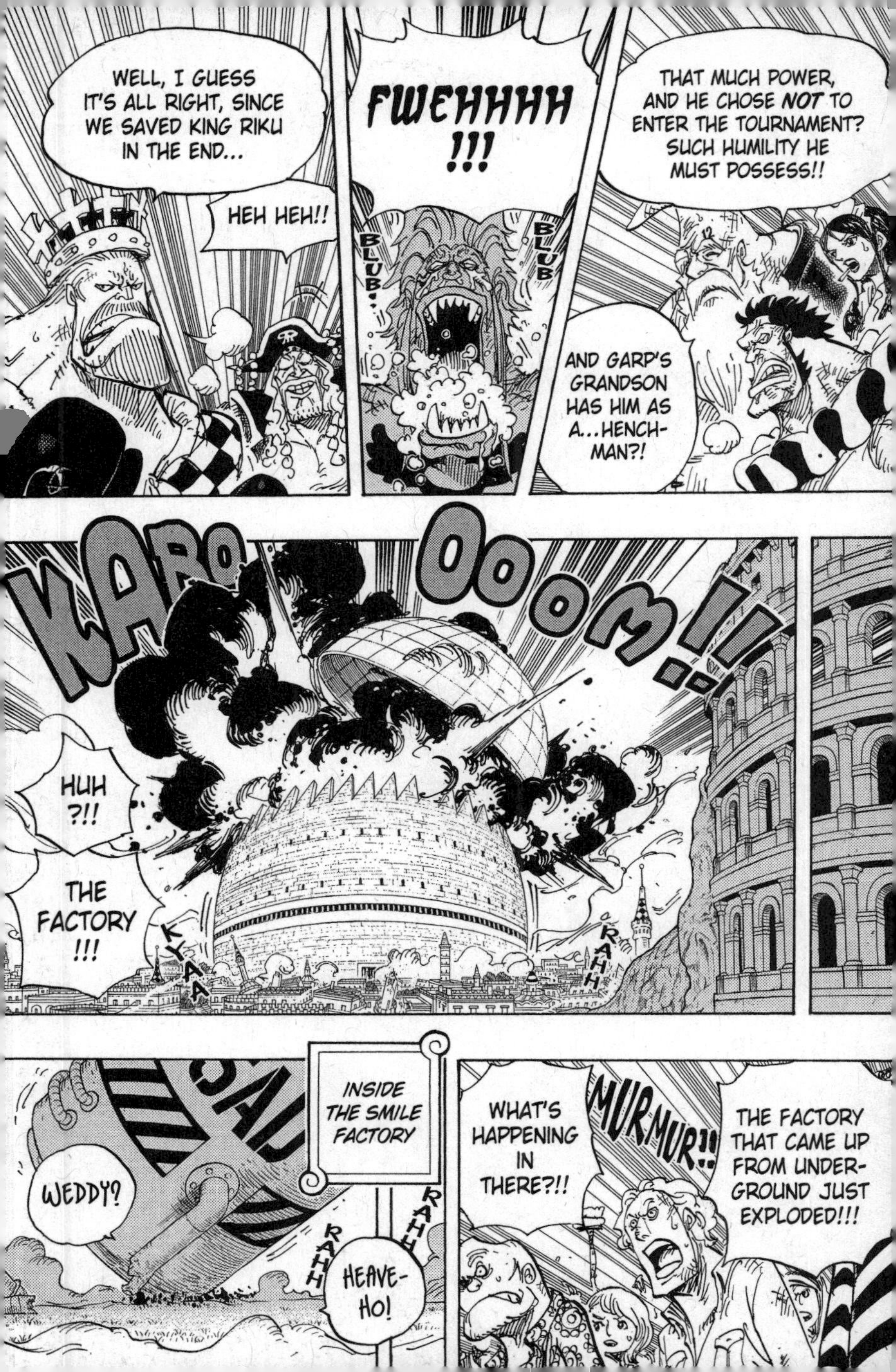
THAT MUCH POWER, AND HE CHOSE NOT TO ENTER THE TOURNAMENT? SUCH HUMILITY HE MUST POSSESS!!
AND GARP'S GRANDSON HAS HIM AS A...HENCH-MAN?!
FWEHHHH !!!
BLUB
BLUB
WELL, I GUESS IT'S ALL RIGHT, SINCE WE SAVED KING RIKU IN THE END...
HEH HEH!!
KAROOOOM!!
HUH ?!!
THE FACTORY !!!
KYAA
RAHH
THE FACTORY THAT CAME UP FROM UNDER-GROUND JUST EXPLODED!!!
MURMUR!!
WHAT'S HAPPENING IN THERE?!!
INSIDE THE SMILE FACTORY
RAHH
RAHH
HEAVE-HO!
WEDDY?

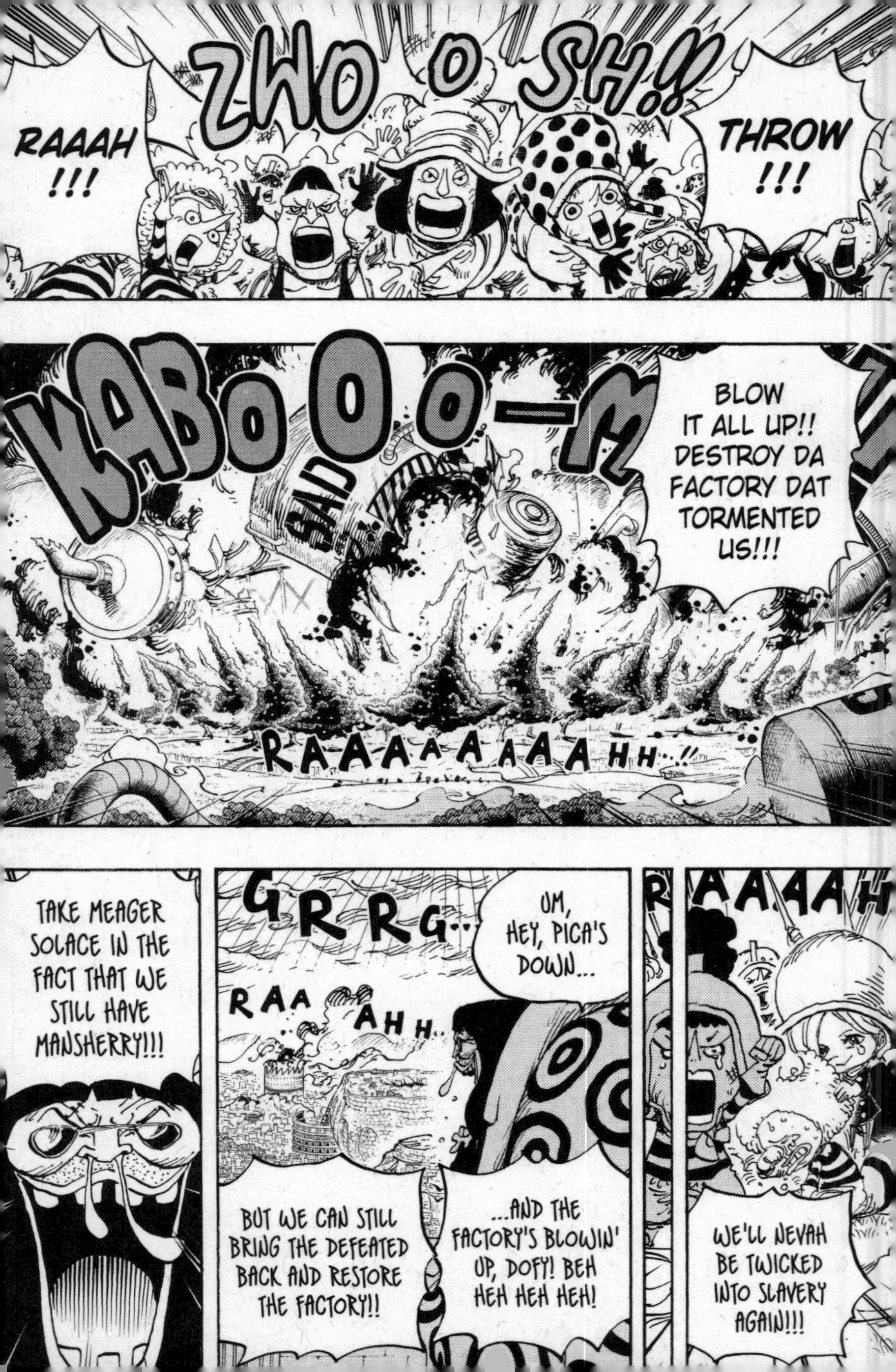
THROW !!!
ZWOOSH!!
RAAAH !!!
BLOW IT ALL UP!! DESTROY DA FACTORY DAT TORMENTED US!!!
KABOOO-M
RAAAAAAAAAHH...!!
RAAAAAH
WE'LL NEVAH BE TWICKED INTO SLAVERY AGAIN!!!
UM, HEY, PICA'S DOWN...
GRRRG...
RAAAHH...
...AND THE FACTORY'S BLOWIN' UP, DOFY! BEH HEH HEH HEH!
BUT WE CAN STILL BRING THE DEFEATED BACK AND RESTORE THE FACTORY!!
TAKE MEAGER SOLACE IN THE FACT THAT WE STILL HAVE MANSHERRY!!!

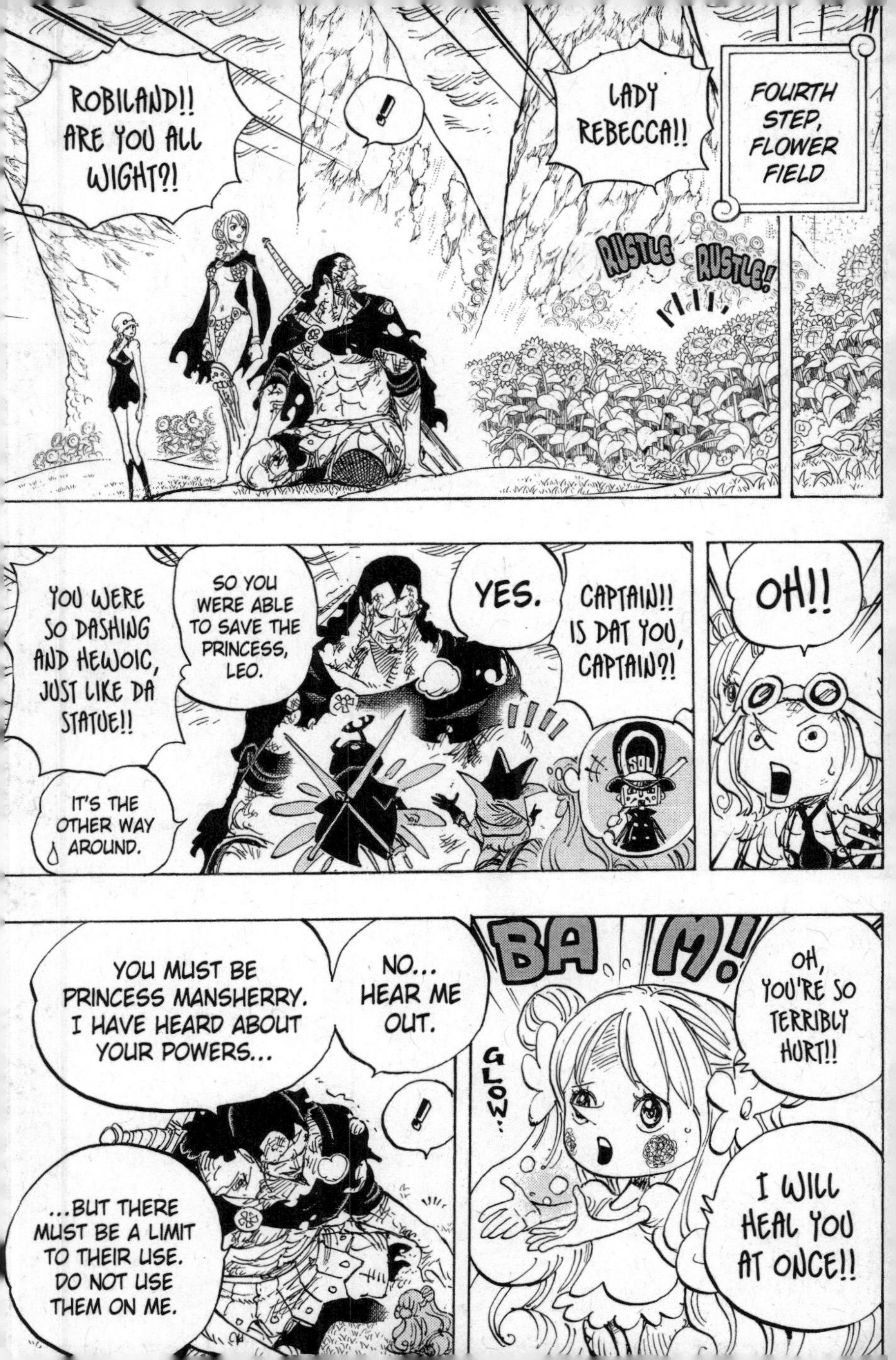
FOURTH STEP, FLOWER FIELD
RUSTLE RUSTLE!
LADY REBECCA!!
!
ROBILAND!! ARE YOU ALL WIGHT?!
OH!!
CAPTAIN!! IS DAT YOU, CAPTAIN?!
YES.
SO YOU WERE ABLE TO SAVE THE PRINCESS, LEO.
YOU WERE SO DASHING AND HEWOIC, JUST LIKE DA STATUE!!
IT'S THE OTHER WAY AROUND.
BAM!
OH, YOU'RE SO TERRIBLY HURT!!
GLOW
I WILL HEAL YOU AT ONCE!!
NO... HEAR ME OUT.
YOU MUST BE PRINCESS MANSHERRY. I HAVE HEARD ABOUT YOUR POWERS...
!
...BUT THERE MUST BE A LIMIT TO THEIR USE. DO NOT USE THEM ON ME.

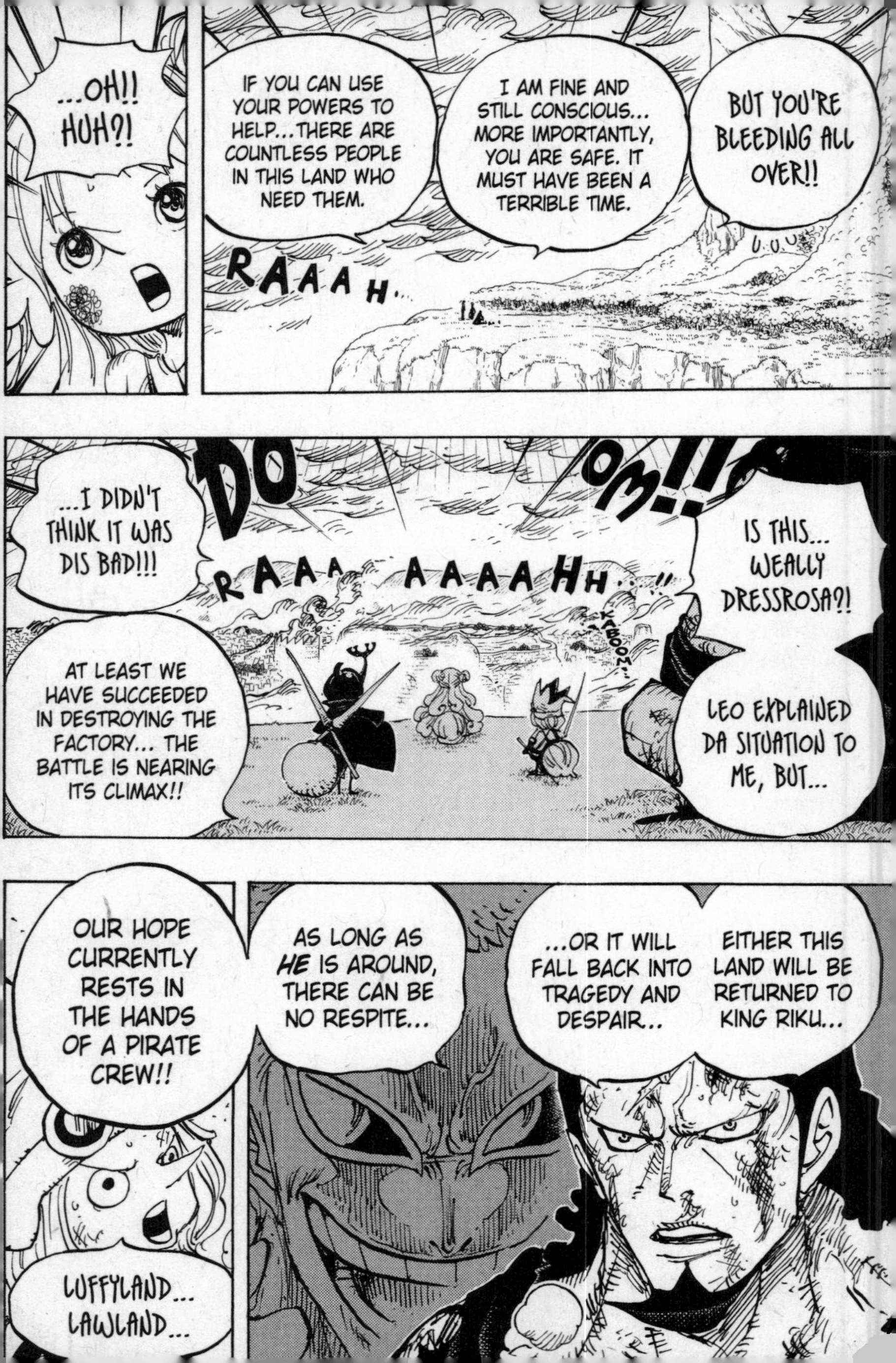

BUT YOU'RE BLEEDING ALL OVER!!
I AM FINE AND STILL CONSCIOUS... MORE IMPORTANTLY, YOU ARE SAFE. IT MUST HAVE BEEN A TERRIBLE TIME.
IF YOU CAN USE YOUR POWERS TO HELP...THERE ARE COUNTLESS PEOPLE IN THIS LAND WHO NEED THEM.
RAAAH...
...OH!! HUH?!
IS THIS... WEALLY DRESSROSA?!
DOOM!!
...I DIDN'T THINK IT WAS DIS BAD!!!
RAAAAAAAAHH...!!
KABOOM
LEO EXPLAINED DA SITUATION TO ME, BUT...
AT LEAST WE HAVE SUCCEEDED IN DESTROYING THE FACTORY... THE BATTLE IS NEARING ITS CLIMAX!!
EITHER THIS LAND WILL BE RETURNED TO KING RIKU...
...OR IT WILL FALL BACK INTO TRAGEDY AND DESPAIR...
AS LONG AS *HE* IS AROUND, THERE CAN BE NO RESPITE...
OUR HOPE CURRENTLY RESTS IN THE HANDS OF A PIRATE CREW!!
LUFFYLAND... LAWLAND...

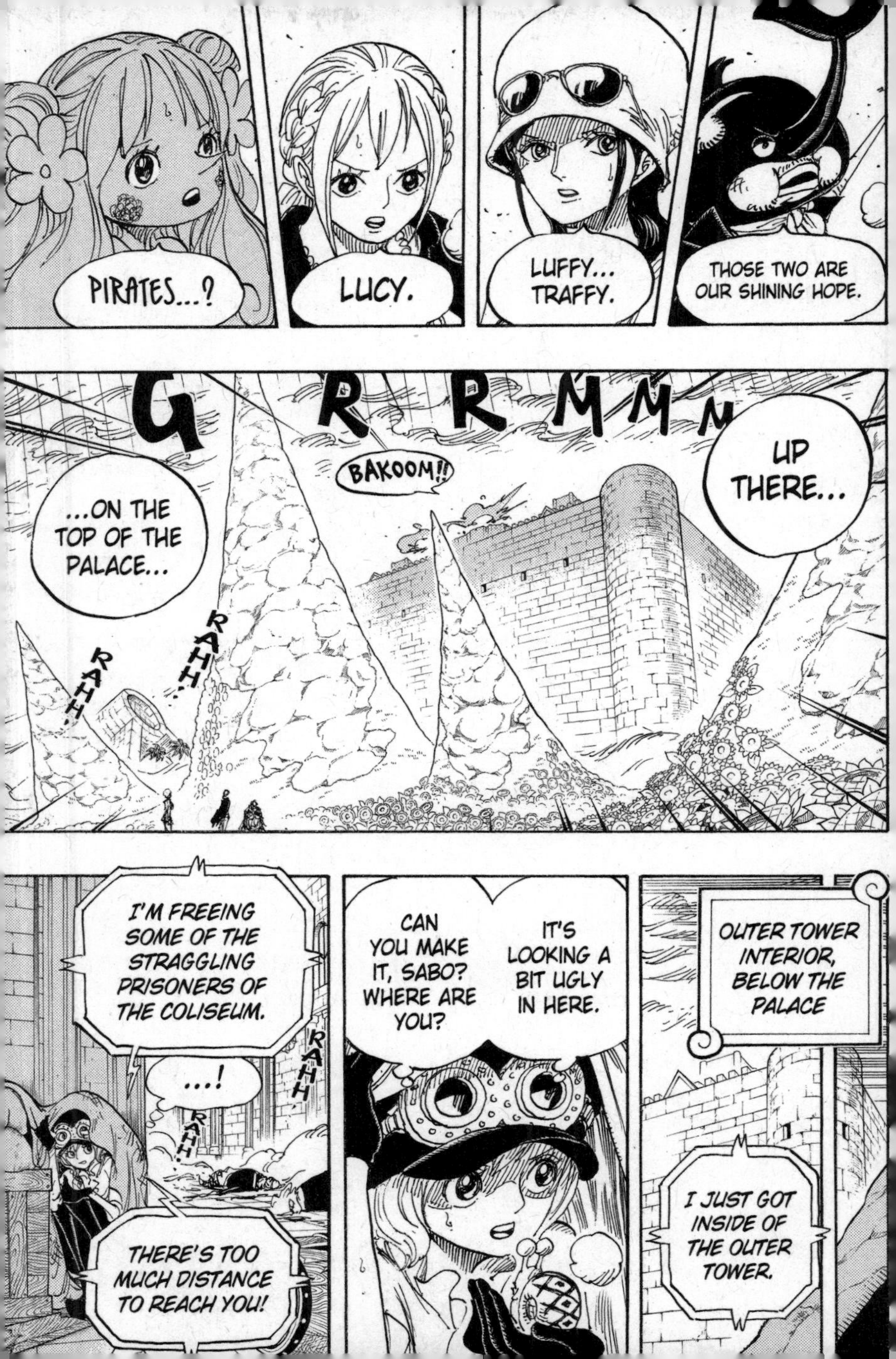
THOSE TWO ARE OUR SHINING HOPE.
LUFFY... TRAFFY.
LUCY.
PIRATES...?
GRRMMN
UP THERE...
BAKOOM!!
...ON THE TOP OF THE PALACE...
RAHH
RAHH
OUTER TOWER INTERIOR, BELOW THE PALACE
I JUST GOT INSIDE OF THE OUTER TOWER.
IT'S LOOKING A BIT UGLY IN HERE.
CAN YOU MAKE IT, SABO? WHERE ARE YOU?
I'M FREEING SOME OF THE STRAGGLING PRISONERS OF THE COLISEUM.
RAHH
...!
RAHH
THERE'S TOO MUCH DISTANCE TO REACH YOU!

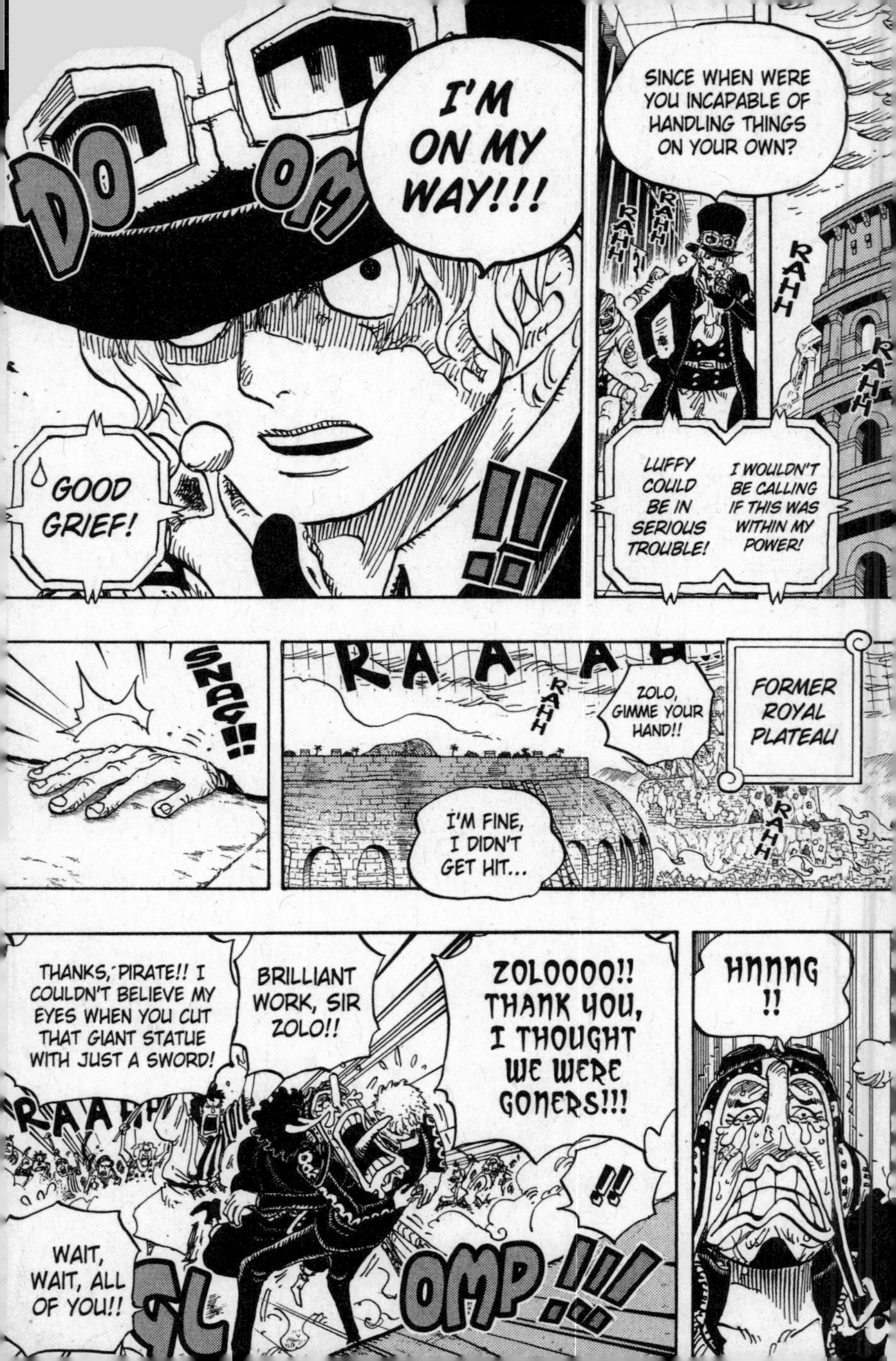
SINCE WHEN WERE YOU INCAPABLE OF HANDLING THINGS ON YOUR OWN?
RAHH
RAHH
RAHH
RAHH
I WOULDN'T BE CALLING IF THIS WAS WITHIN MY POWER!
LUFFY COULD BE IN SERIOUS TROUBLE!
DOOM
I'M ON MY WAY!!!
!!
GOOD GRIEF!
FORMER ROYAL PLATEAU
RAAAAH
RAHH
ZOLO, GIMME YOUR HAND!!
RAHH
I'M FINE, I DIDN'T GET HIT...
SNAG!!
HNNNG !!
ZOLOOOO!! THANK YOU, I THOUGHT WE WERE GONERS!!!
BRILLIANT WORK, SIR ZOLO!!
THANKS, PIRATE!! I COULDN'T BELIEVE MY EYES WHEN YOU CUT THAT GIANT STATUE WITH JUST A SWORD!
RAAAH
!!
WAIT, WAIT, ALL OF YOU!!
GLOMP!!!

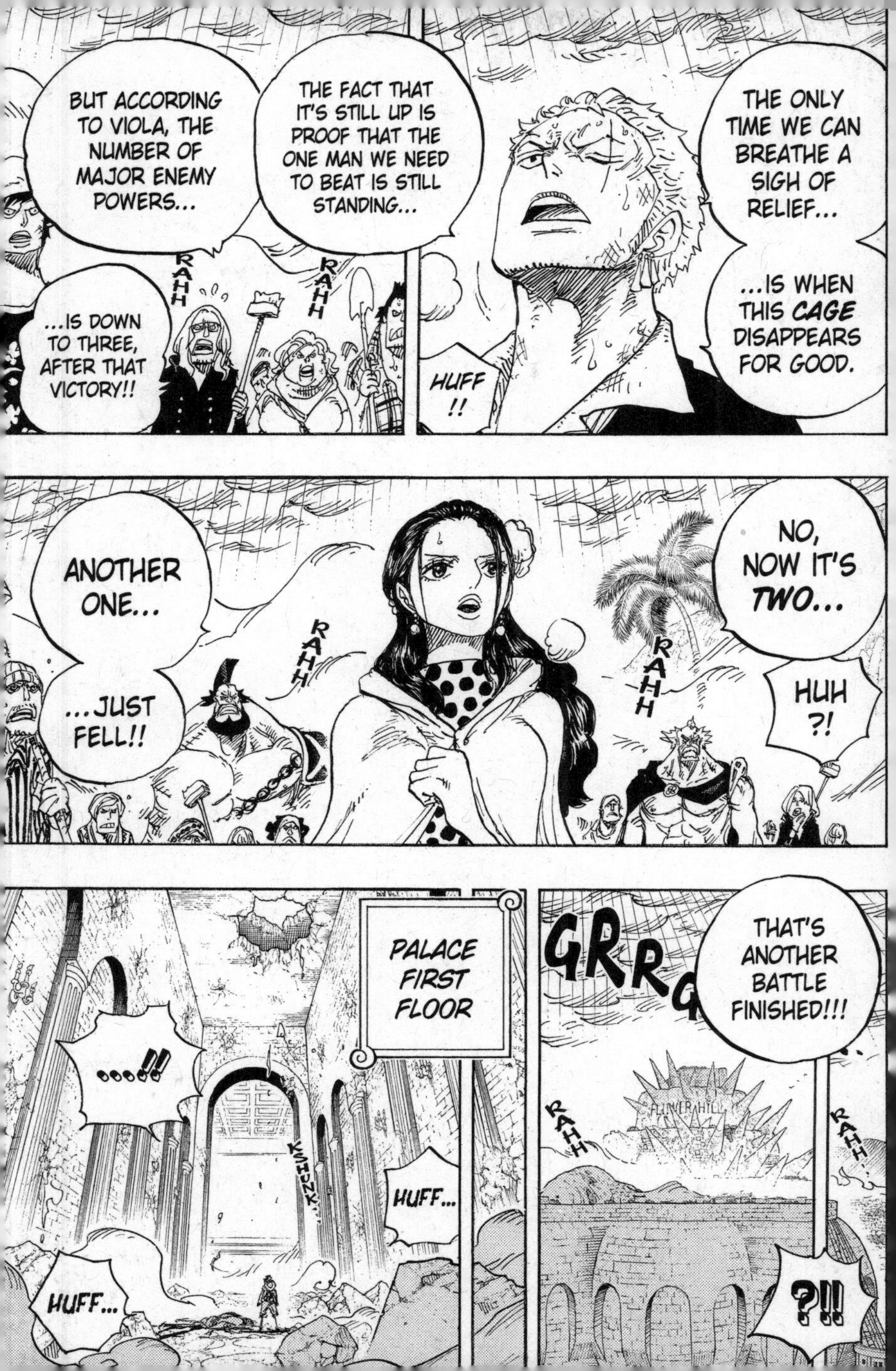
THE ONLY TIME WE CAN BREATHE A SIGH OF RELIEF...
...IS WHEN THIS CAGE DISAPPEARS FOR GOOD.
HUFF!!
THE FACT THAT IT'S STILL UP IS PROOF THAT THE ONE MAN WE NEED TO BEAT IS STILL STANDING...
RAHH
RAHH
BUT ACCORDING TO VIOLA, THE NUMBER OF MAJOR ENEMY POWERS...
...IS DOWN TO THREE, AFTER THAT VICTORY!!
NO, NOW IT'S TWO...
HUH?!
RAHH
RAHH
ANOTHER ONE...
...JUST FELL!!
GRRR
THAT'S ANOTHER BATTLE FINISHED!!!
RAHH
RAHH
?!!
PALACE FIRST FLOOR
....!!
KSHUNK...
HUFF...
HUFF...

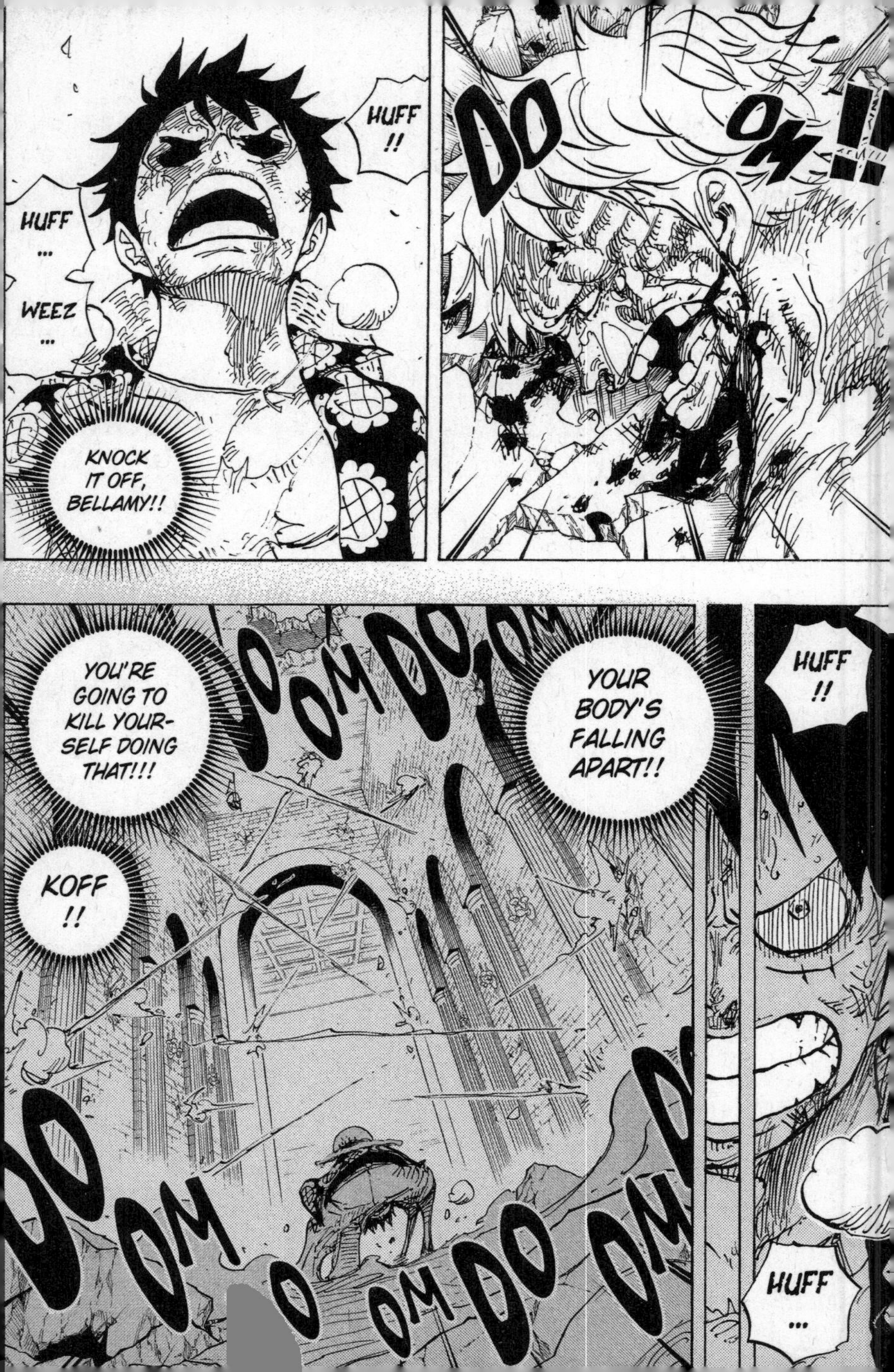
DO-OM!!
HUFF !!
HUFF ... WEEZ ...
KNOCK IT OFF, BELLAMY!!
HUFF !!
HUFF ...
DOOM DOOM
YOUR BODY'S FALLING APART!!
YOU'RE GOING TO KILL YOUR-SELF DOING THAT!!!
KOFF !!
DOOM DOOM DOOM DOOM

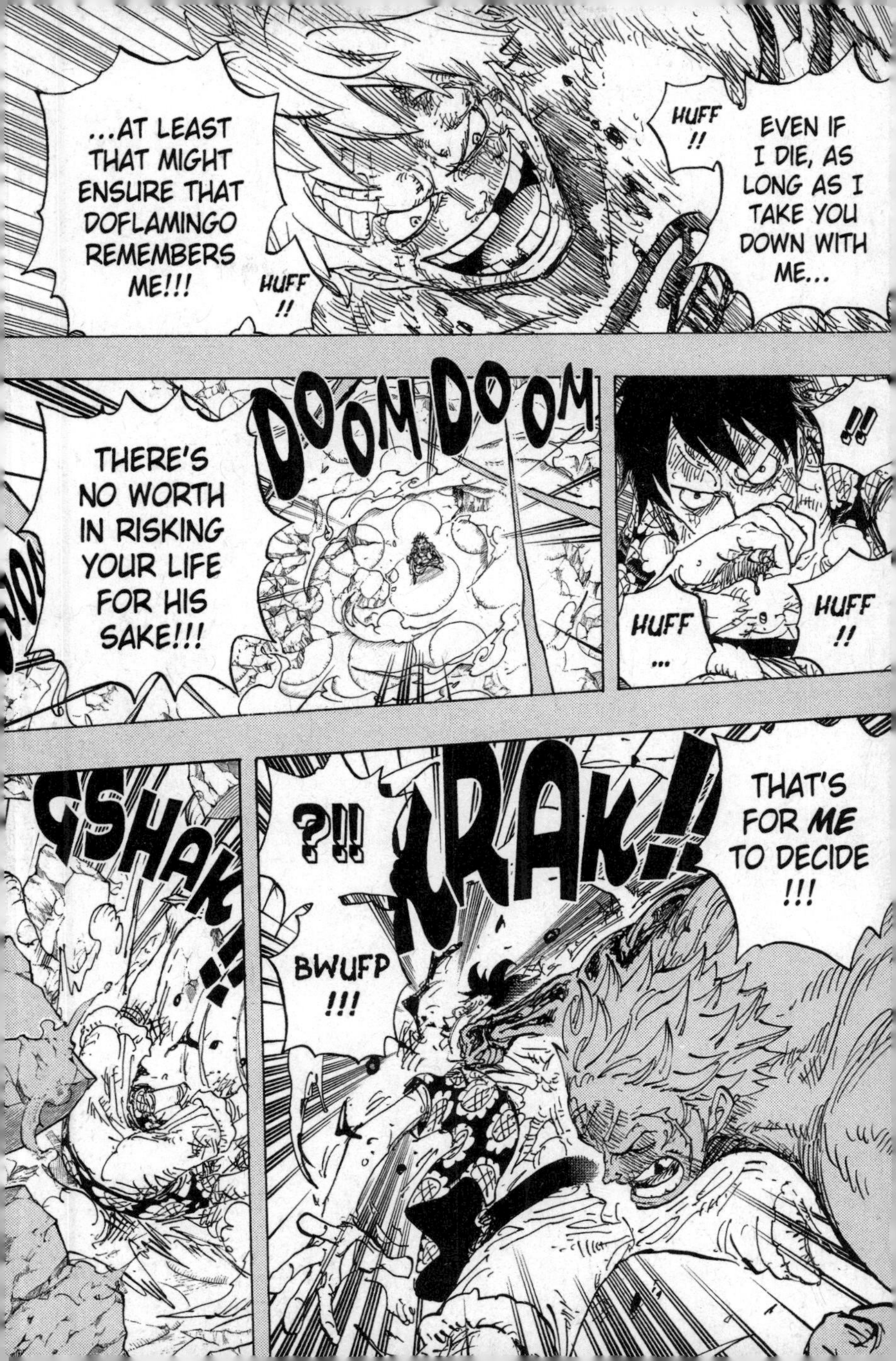
EVEN IF I DIE, AS LONG AS I TAKE YOU DOWN WITH ME...
HUFF !!
...AT LEAST THAT MIGHT ENSURE THAT DOFLAMINGO REMEMBERS ME!!!
HUFF !!
!!
HUFF !!
HUFF ...
DOOM DOOM
THERE'S NO WORTH IN RISKING YOUR LIFE FOR HIS SAKE!!!
THAT'S FOR ME TO DECIDE !!!
KRAK!!
?!!
BWUFP !!!
GSHAK!!

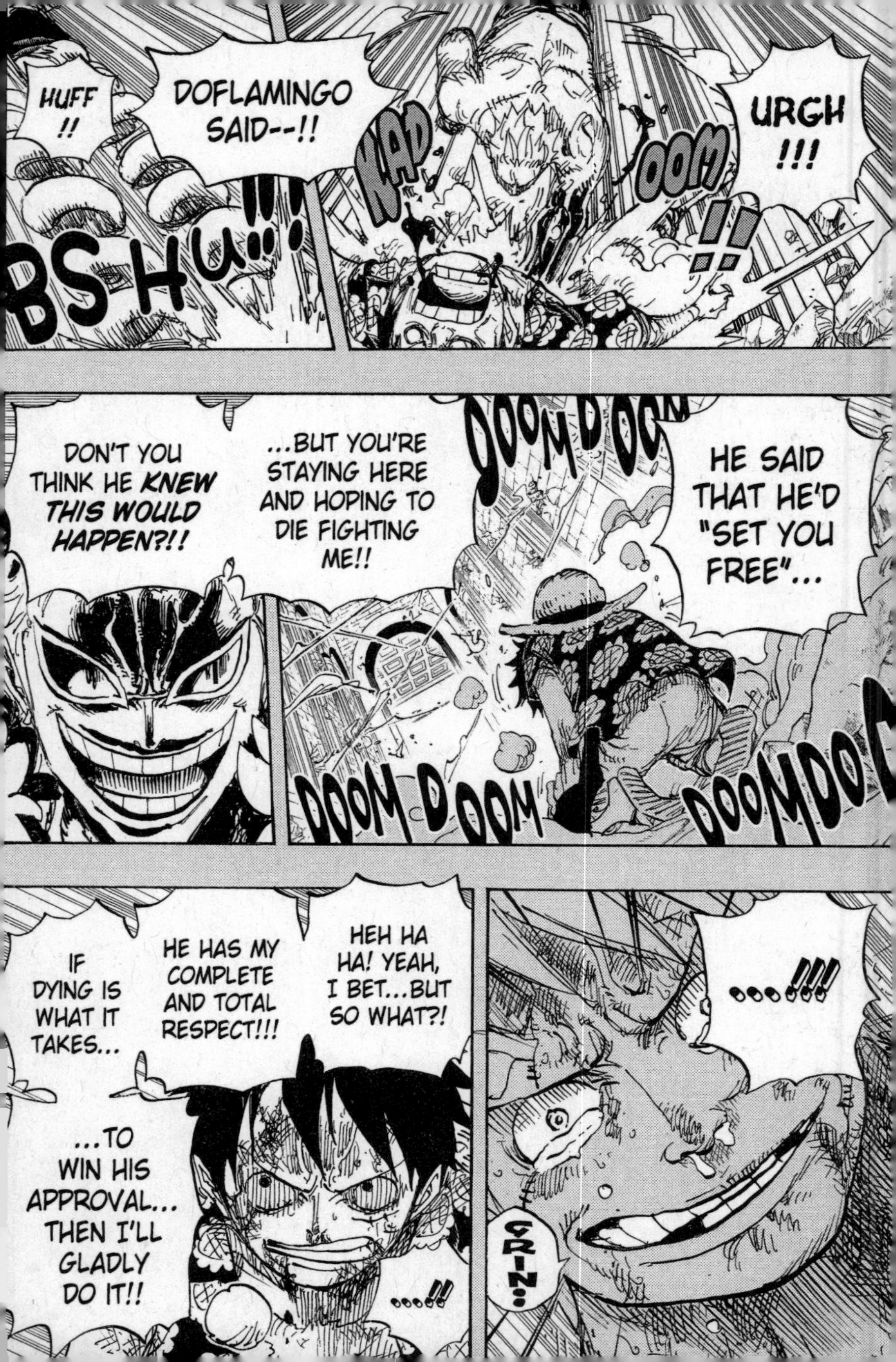

URGH !!!
OOM!!
KAP
DOFLAMINGO SAID--!!
HUFF !!
BS-HU!!!
HE SAID THAT HE'D "SET YOU FREE"...
DOOM DOOM
...BUT YOU'RE STAYING HERE AND HOPING TO DIE FIGHTING ME!!
DOOM DOOM
DON'T YOU THINK HE *KNEW THIS WOULD HAPPEN?!!*
...!!!
GRIN...
HEH HA HA! YEAH, I BET...BUT SO WHAT?!
HE HAS MY COMPLETE AND TOTAL RESPECT!!!
IF DYING IS WHAT IT TAKES...
...TO WIN HIS APPROVAL... THEN I'LL GLADLY DO IT!!
...!!

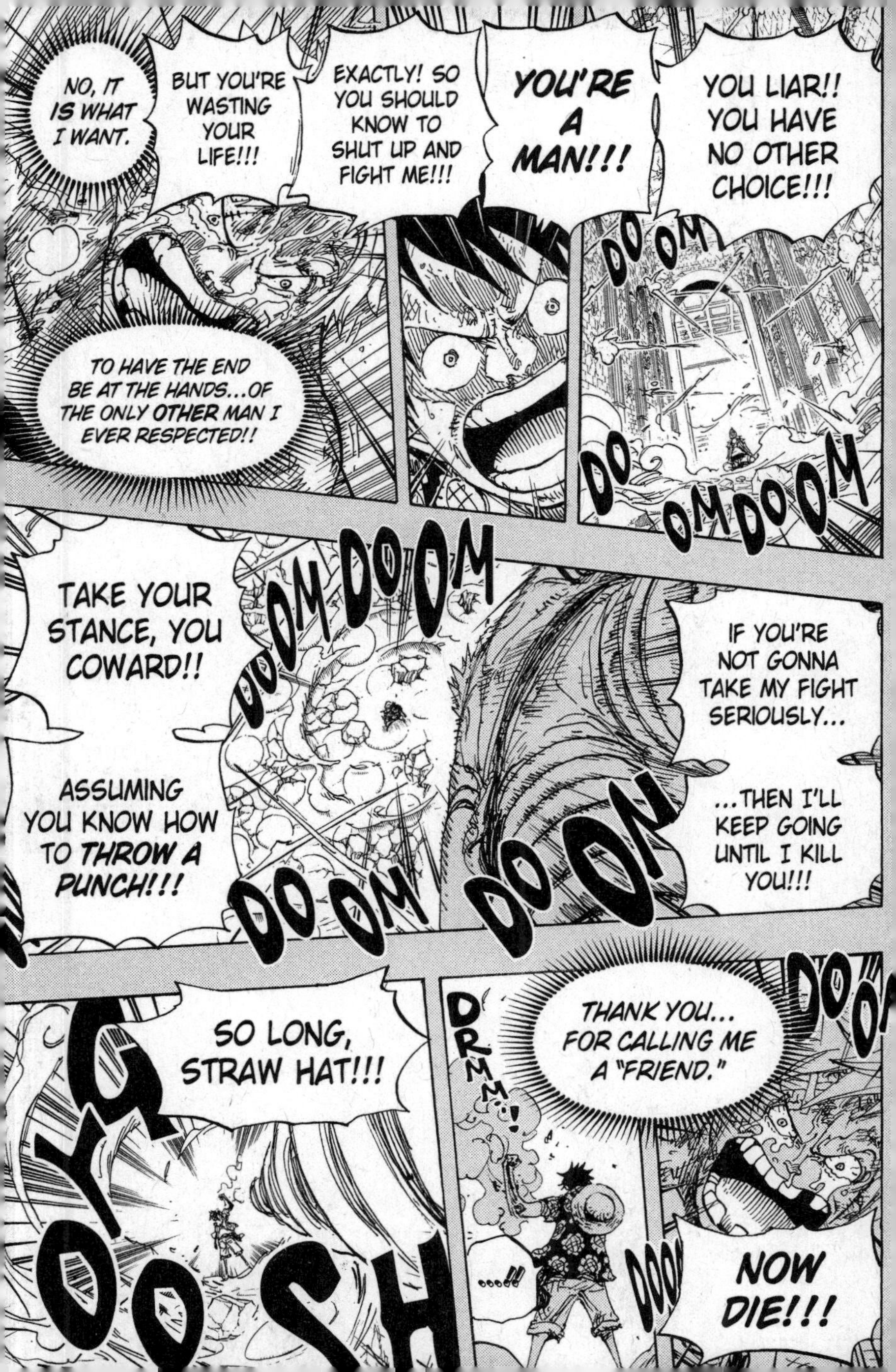

YOU LIAR!! YOU HAVE NO OTHER CHOICE!!!
DOOM
DOOMDOOM
YOU'RE A MAN!!!
EXACTLY! SO YOU SHOULD KNOW TO SHUT UP AND FIGHT ME!!!
BUT YOU'RE WASTING YOUR LIFE!!!
NO, IT IS WHAT I WANT.
TO HAVE THE END BE AT THE HANDS...OF THE ONLY OTHER MAN I EVER RESPECTED!!
IF YOU'RE NOT GONNA TAKE MY FIGHT SERIOUSLY...
...THEN I'LL KEEP GOING UNTIL I KILL YOU!!!
DOOM
DOOMDOOM
DOOM
TAKE YOUR STANCE, YOU COWARD!!
ASSUMING YOU KNOW HOW TO THROW A PUNCH!!!
DOOM
NOW DIE!!!
THANK YOU... FOR CALLING ME A "FRIEND."
DRMMM!
....!!
SO LONG, STRAW HAT!!!

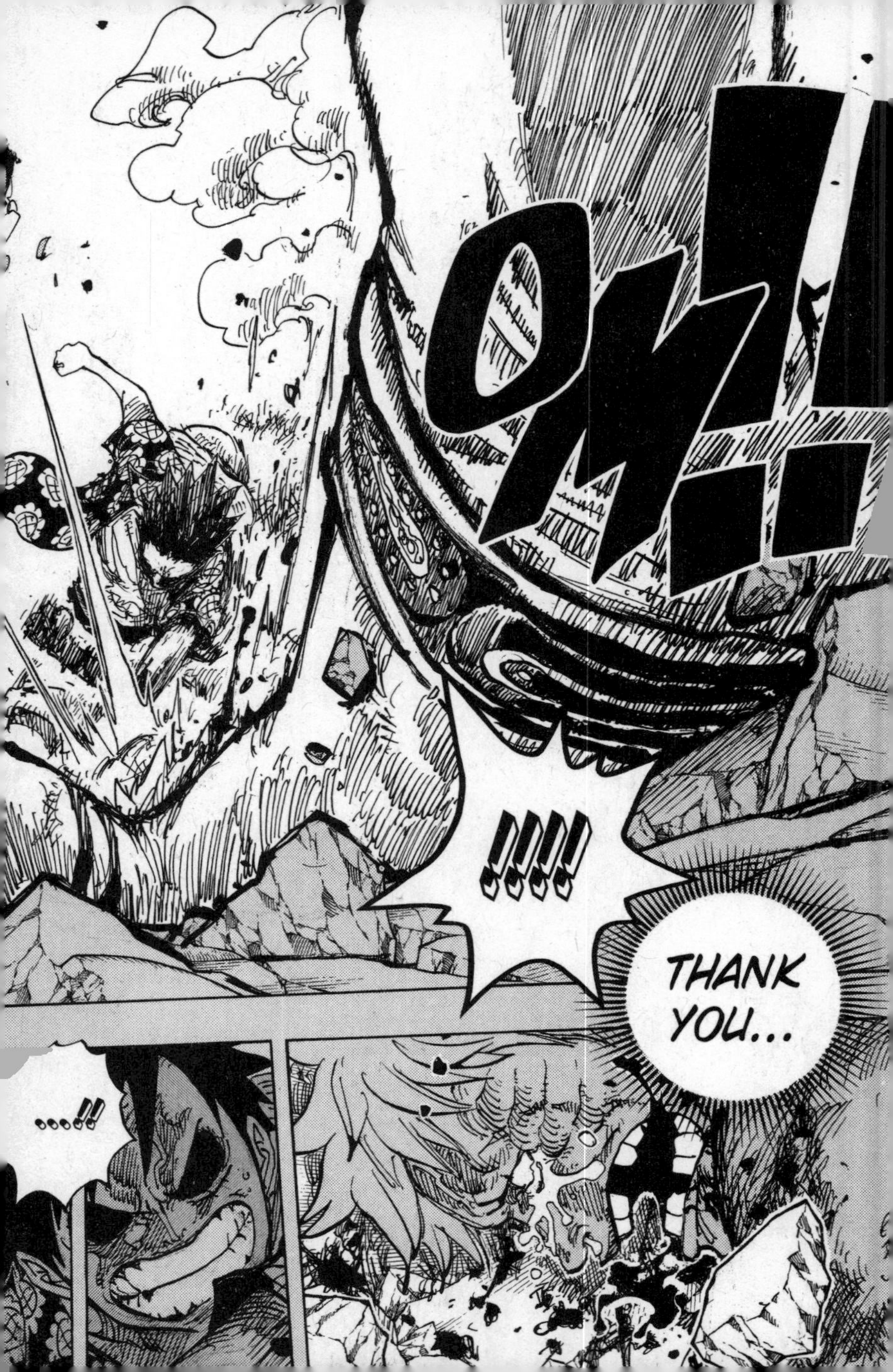
OW!!
!!!!
THANK YOU...
...!!

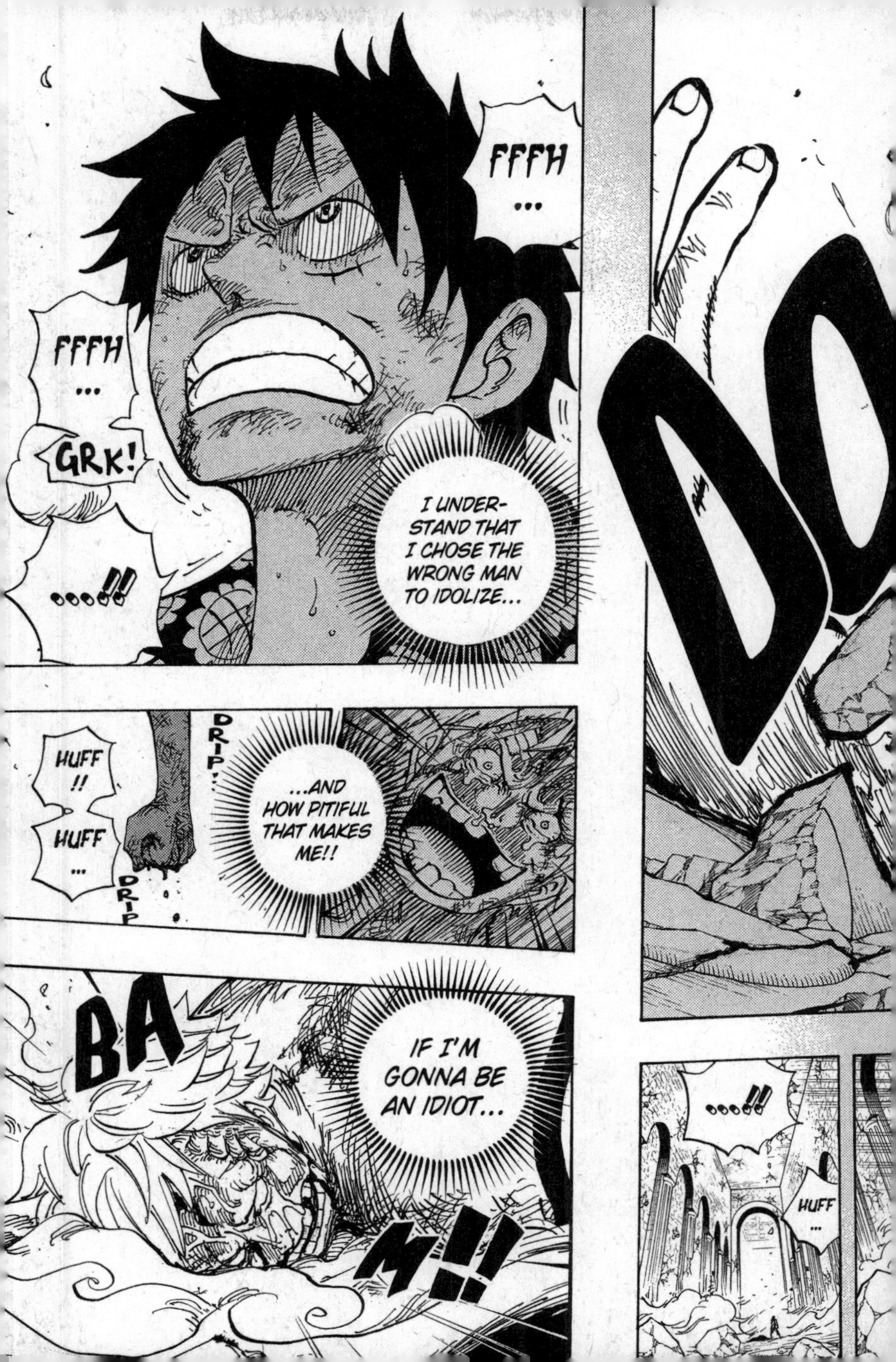
DO
FFFH...
FFFH...
GRK!
I UNDER-STAND THAT I CHOSE THE WRONG MAN TO IDOLIZE...
....!!
...AND HOW PITIFUL THAT MAKES ME!!
DRIP
HUFF!!
HUFF...
DRIP
....!!
HUFF...
IF I'M GONNA BE AN IDIOT...
BA
M!!

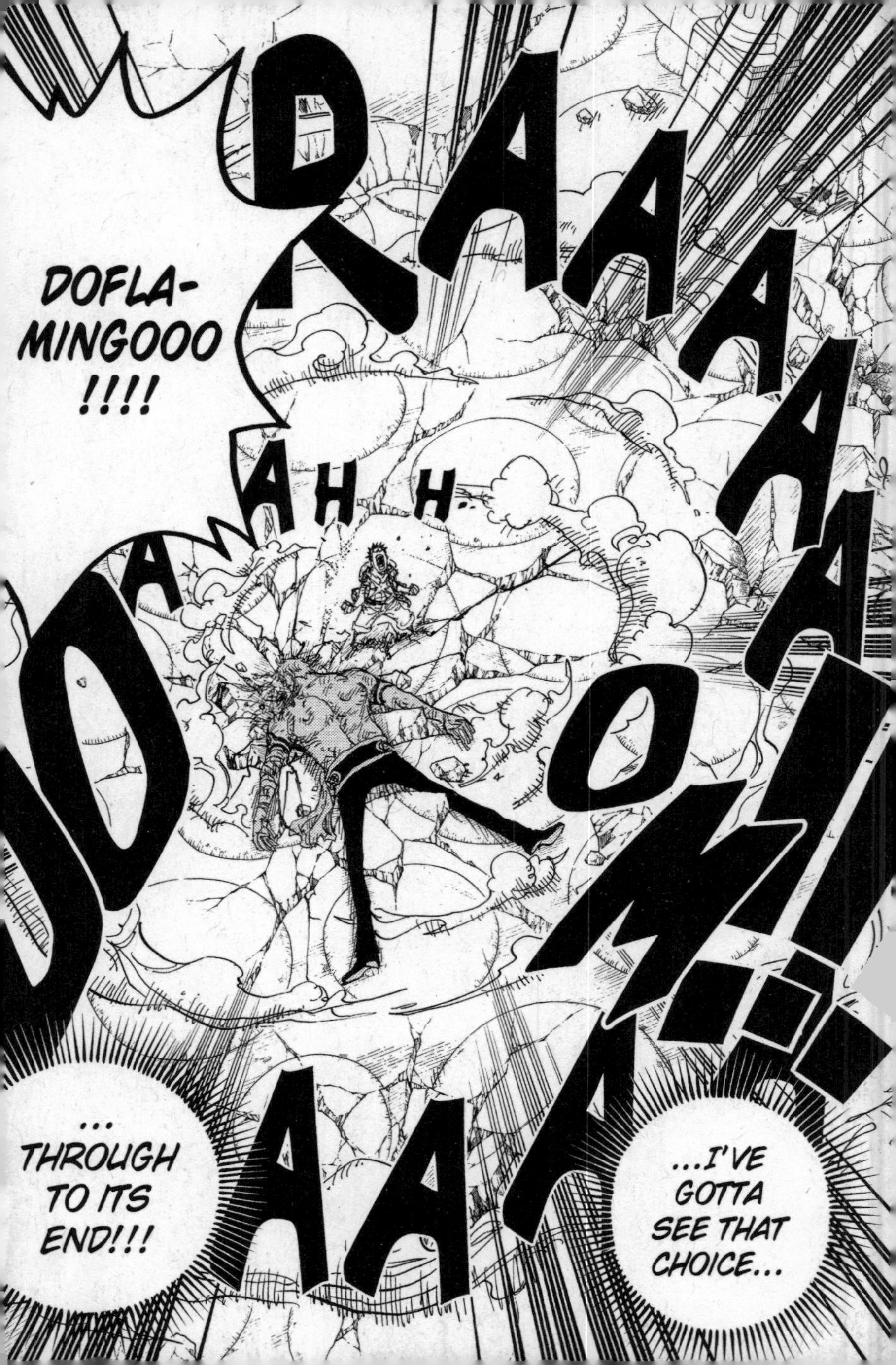
DOFLA-MINGOOO!!!!
...I'VE GOTTA SEE THAT CHOICE...
... THROUGH TO ITS END!!!

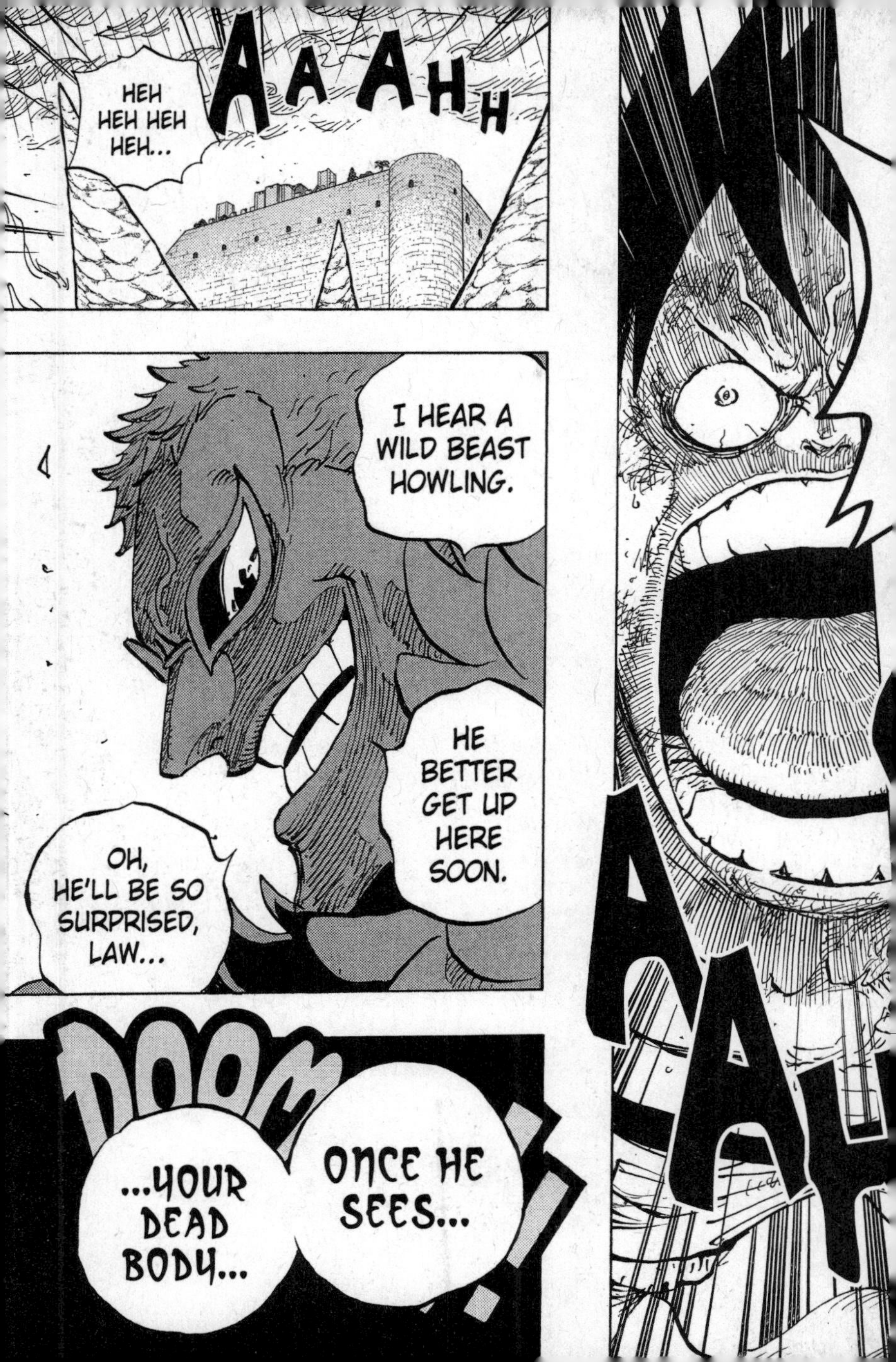
AAAHH
HEH HEH HEH HEH...
I HEAR A WILD BEAST HOWLING.
HE BETTER GET UP HERE SOON.
OH, HE'LL BE SO SURPRISED, LAW...
DOOM
ONCE HE SEES...
...YOUR DEAD BODY...

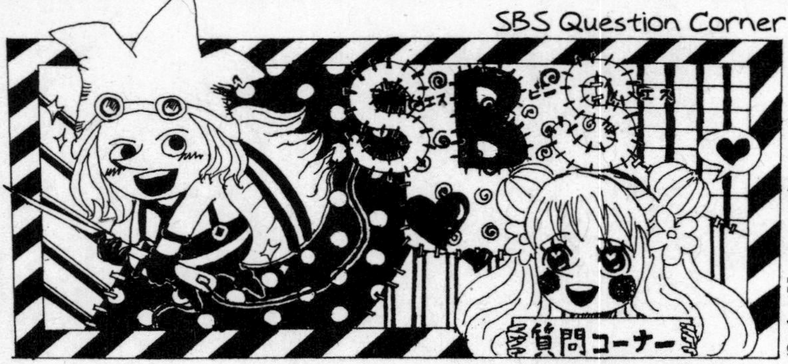
SBS!!!!
質問コーナー

(Saeka, Kumamoto)

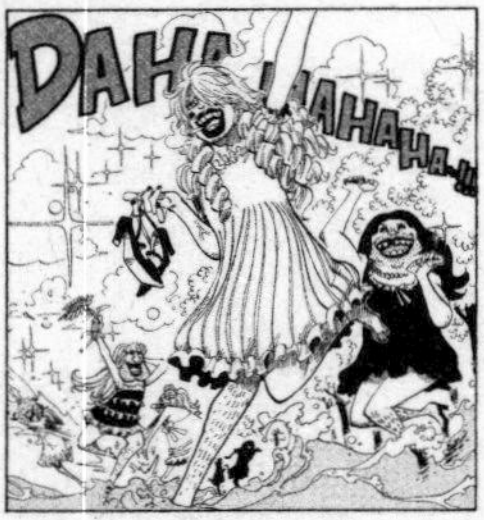
DAHA

Q: Hello. How are you? I am fine. I have a question about my beloved one-piece. I can't decide between flower print or plain. I mean, flowers are nice, but I'm wondering if going with plain will make me look more like a grown-up lady. What do you think is better, Mr. Oda?

--The Invincible Haru-Haru

A: Good question. In my case, I prefer to go out on trips in a nice frilly one-piece with a flower design. Seems like I often wind up down at the police station answering questions for some nice policemen, but other than that, I'm fine, thanks for asking! I just love a good one-piece dress!

Q: Here's a question, Odacchi. In Chapter 762 of Volume 76, when Law stabs Cora, I spotted Crocodile's face on his copy of the newspaper. What kind of article was it?

--Yamamoto/Sugiyama/Hori

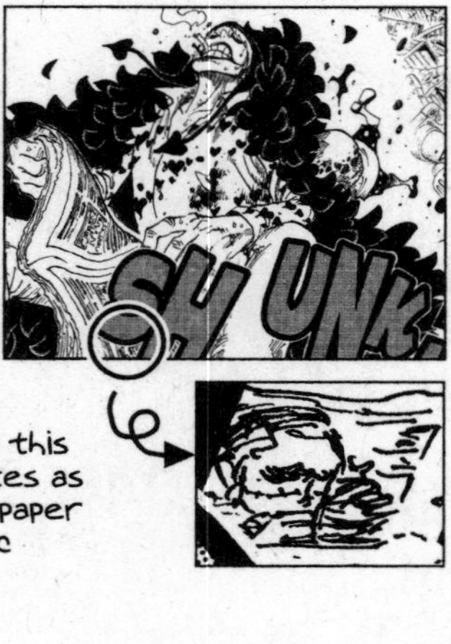
SHUNK

A: Nice job spotting that. Indeed, it is Crocodile. This happened 16 years ago, when Law was 10 and Doflamingo was 25. Crocodile was 30 at this time. When he was younger, he blew up quick, just like Luffy, but he joined the Seven Warlords fairly early on, in his early twenties. After that, he challenged Whitebeard and lost. While he stayed quiet after that, his ambitions were turning on Alabasta instead, and this is when he started hunting pirates as a Warlord. So the article in the paper is actually a story about his heroic exploits saving the country!

Chapter 780:
THE HEART CURSE

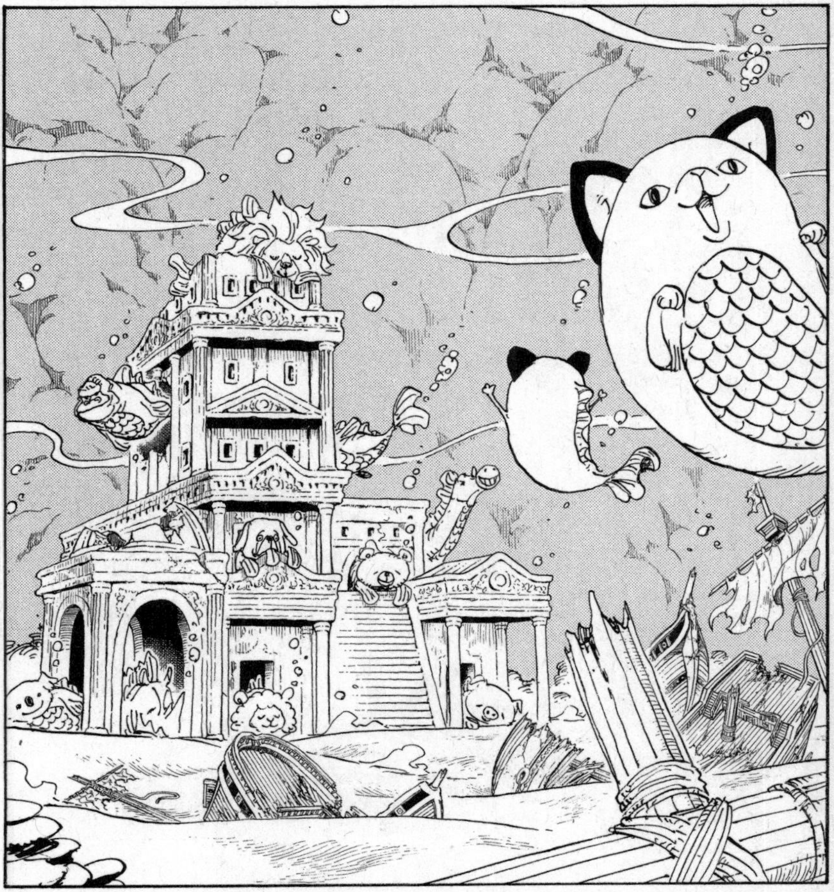

THE SOLITARY JOURNEY OF JIMBEI, FIRST SON OF THE SEA, VOL. 24: "SANK THE RUINS DOWN NEXT TO THE PORT"

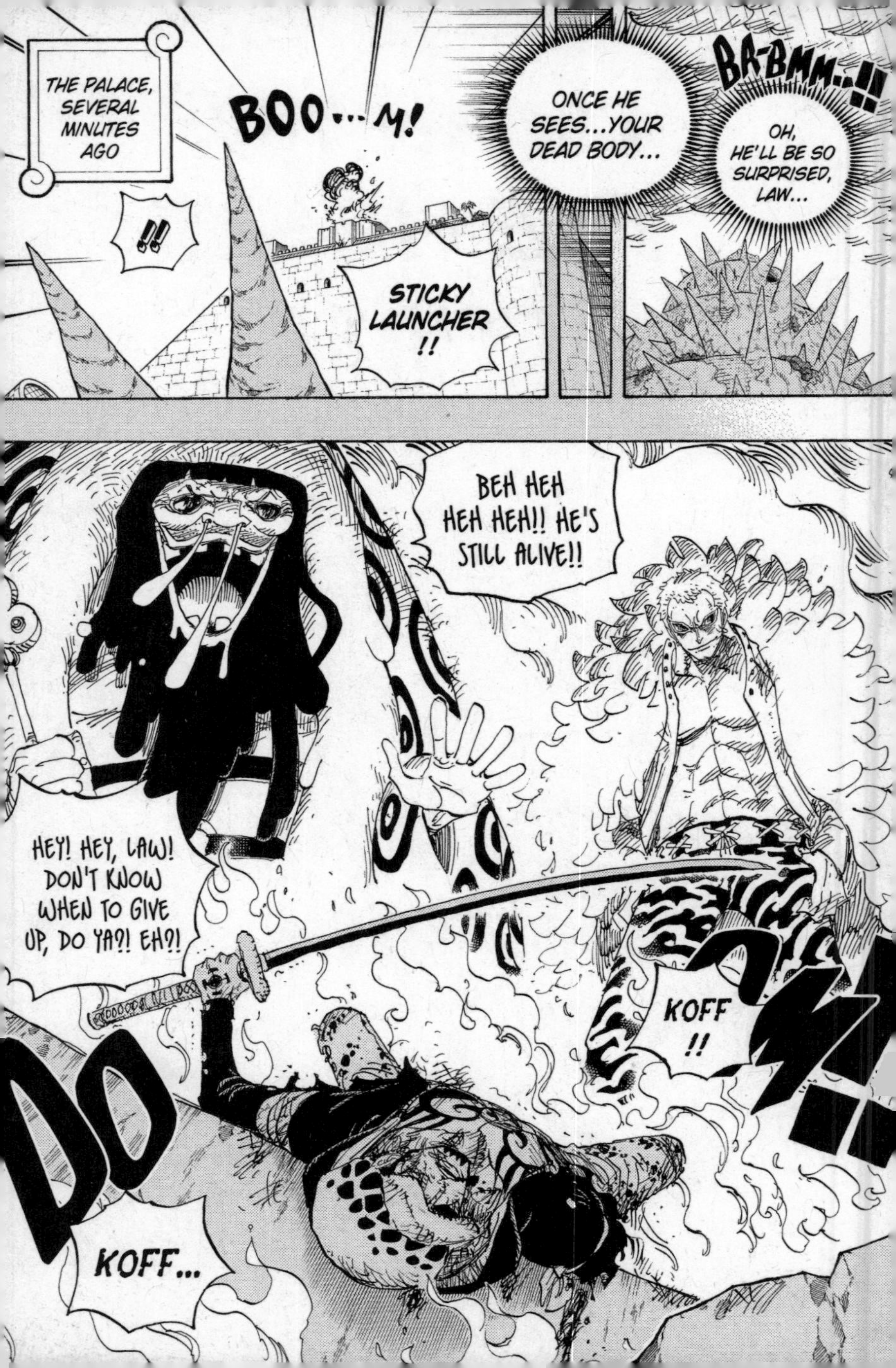
BA-BMM..!!
ONCE HE SEES...YOUR DEAD BODY...
OH, HE'LL BE SO SURPRISED, LAW...
THE PALACE, SEVERAL MINUTES AGO
BOO...M!
!!
STICKY LAUNCHER !!
BEH HEH HEH HEH!! HE'S STILL ALIVE!!
KOFF !!
DOM!!
HEY! HEY, LAW! DON'T KNOW WHEN TO GIVE UP, DO YA?! EH?!
KOFF...

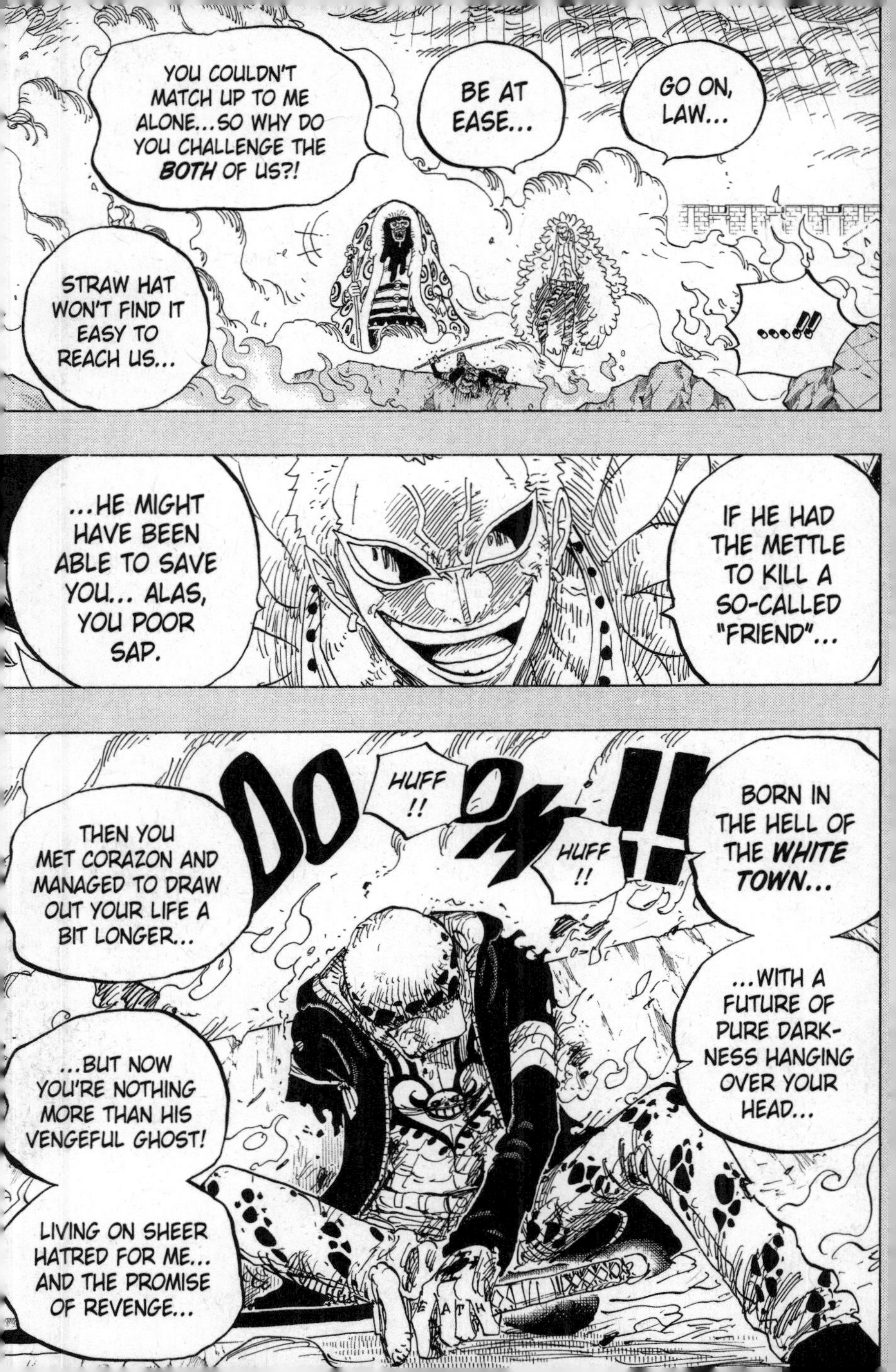
GO ON, LAW...
BE AT EASE...
YOU COULDN'T MATCH UP TO ME ALONE...SO WHY DO YOU CHALLENGE THE *BOTH* OF US?!
....!!
STRAW HAT WON'T FIND IT EASY TO REACH US...
IF HE HAD THE METTLE TO KILL A SO-CALLED "FRIEND"...
...HE MIGHT HAVE BEEN ABLE TO SAVE YOU... ALAS, YOU POOR SAP.
BORN IN THE HELL OF THE *WHITE TOWN*...
DOON!!
HUFF !!
HUFF !!
THEN YOU MET CORAZON AND MANAGED TO DRAW OUT YOUR LIFE A BIT LONGER...
...WITH A FUTURE OF PURE DARKNESS HANGING OVER YOUR HEAD...
...BUT NOW YOU'RE NOTHING MORE THAN HIS VENGEFUL GHOST!
LIVING ON SHEER HATRED FOR ME... AND THE PROMISE OF REVENGE...

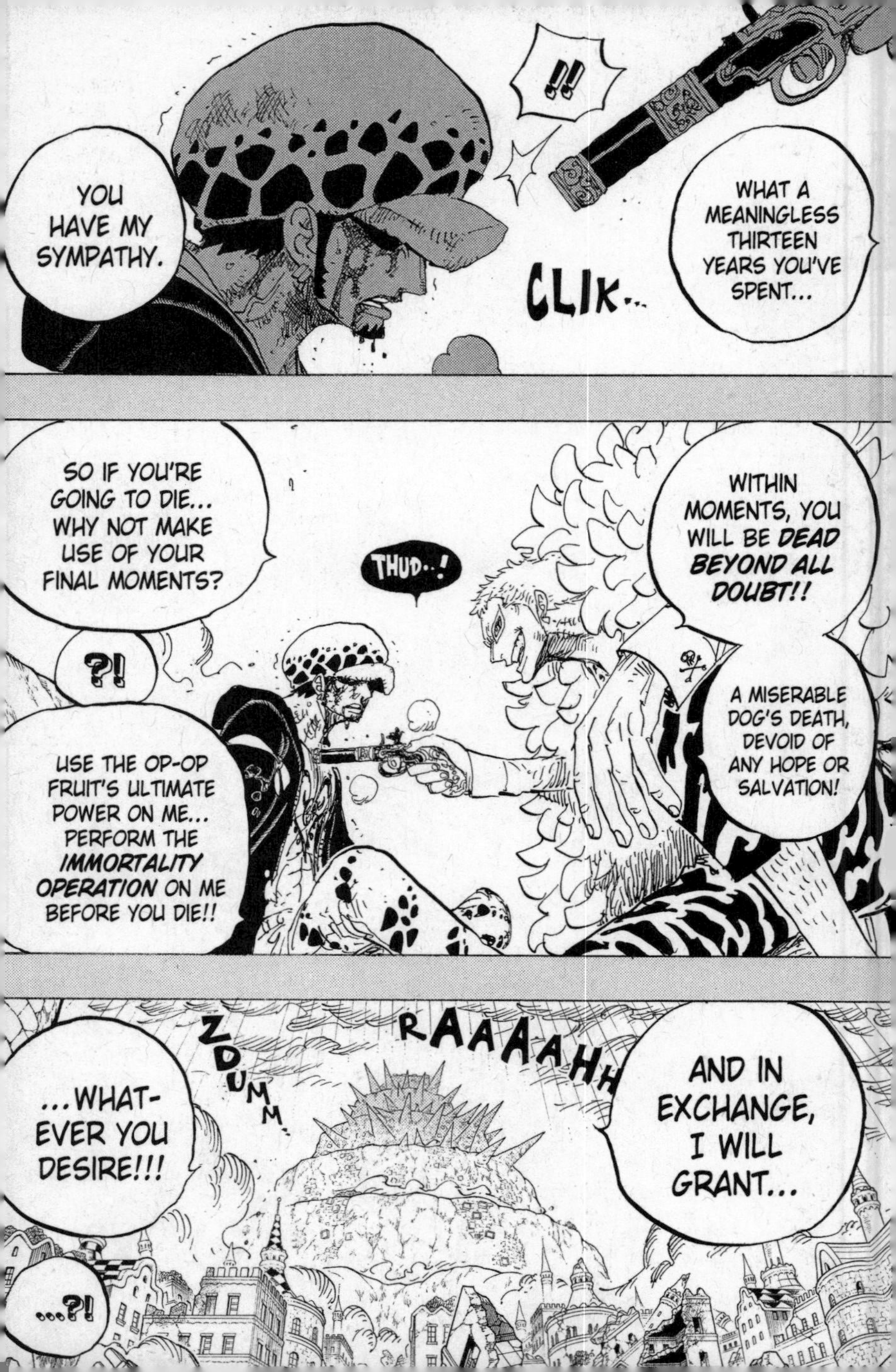
!!
WHAT A MEANINGLESS THIRTEEN YEARS YOU'VE SPENT...
CLIK...
YOU HAVE MY SYMPATHY.
WITHIN MOMENTS, YOU WILL BE DEAD BEYOND ALL DOUBT!!
A MISERABLE DOG'S DEATH, DEVOID OF ANY HOPE OR SALVATION!
THUD..!
SO IF YOU'RE GOING TO DIE... WHY NOT MAKE USE OF YOUR FINAL MOMENTS?
?!
USE THE OP-OP FRUIT'S ULTIMATE POWER ON ME... PERFORM THE IMMORTALITY OPERATION ON ME BEFORE YOU DIE!!
RAAAAHH
AND IN EXCHANGE, I WILL GRANT...
ZDUMM
...WHAT-EVER YOU DESIRE!!!
...?!

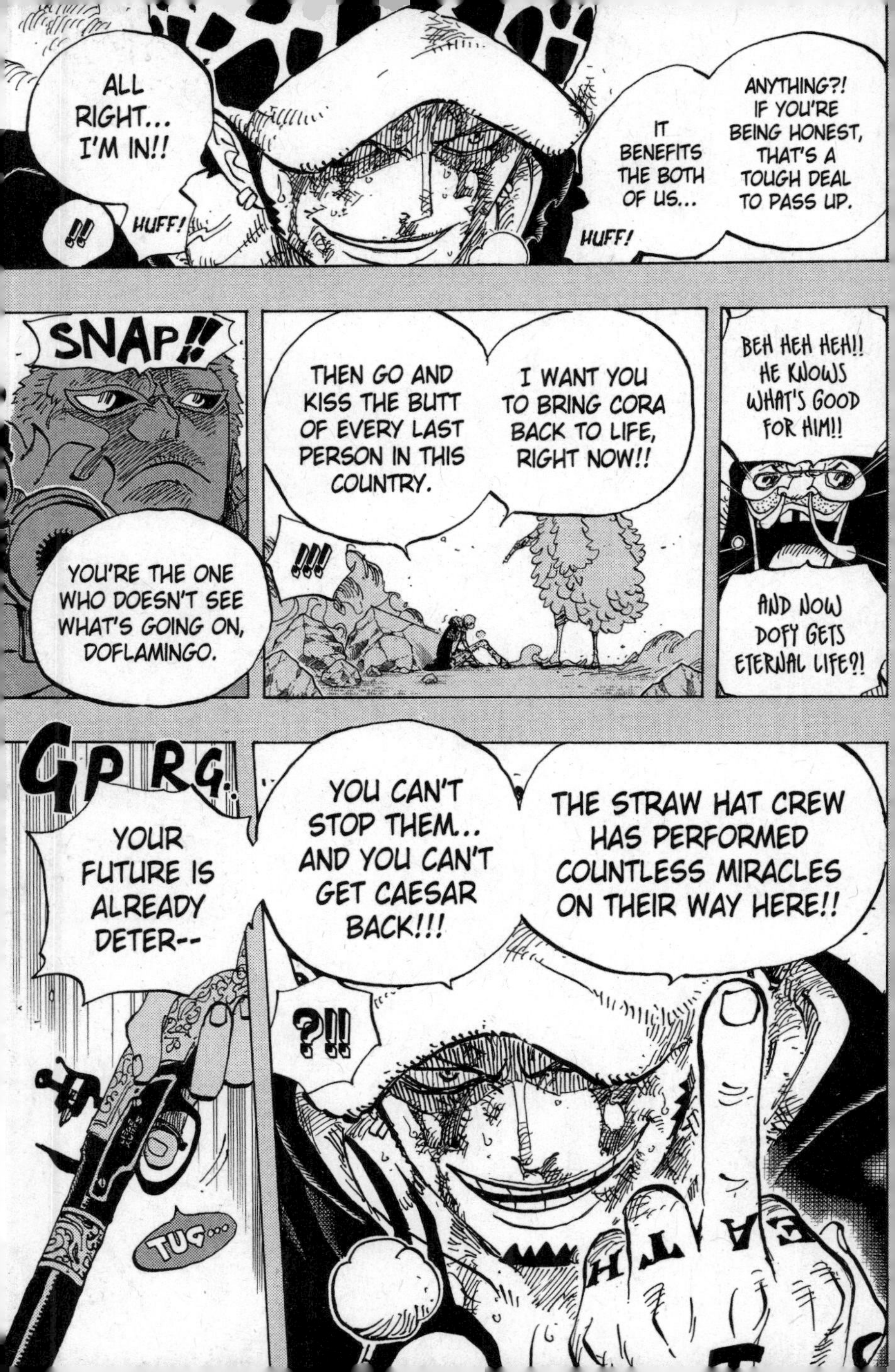
ANYTHING?! IF YOU'RE BEING HONEST, THAT'S A TOUGH DEAL TO PASS UP.
IT BENEFITS THE BOTH OF US...
HUFF!
ALL RIGHT... I'M IN!!
HUFF!
!!
BEH HEH HEH!! HE KNOWS WHAT'S GOOD FOR HIM!!
AND NOW DOFY GETS ETERNAL LIFE?!
I WANT YOU TO BRING CORA BACK TO LIFE, RIGHT NOW!!
THEN GO AND KISS THE BUTT OF EVERY LAST PERSON IN THIS COUNTRY.
!!!
SNAP!!
YOU'RE THE ONE WHO DOESN'T SEE WHAT'S GOING ON, DOFLAMINGO.
THE STRAW HAT CREW HAS PERFORMED COUNTLESS MIRACLES ON THEIR WAY HERE!!
YOU CAN'T STOP THEM... AND YOU CAN'T GET CAESAR BACK!!!
?!!
TUG...
GPRG
YOUR FUTURE IS ALREADY DETER--

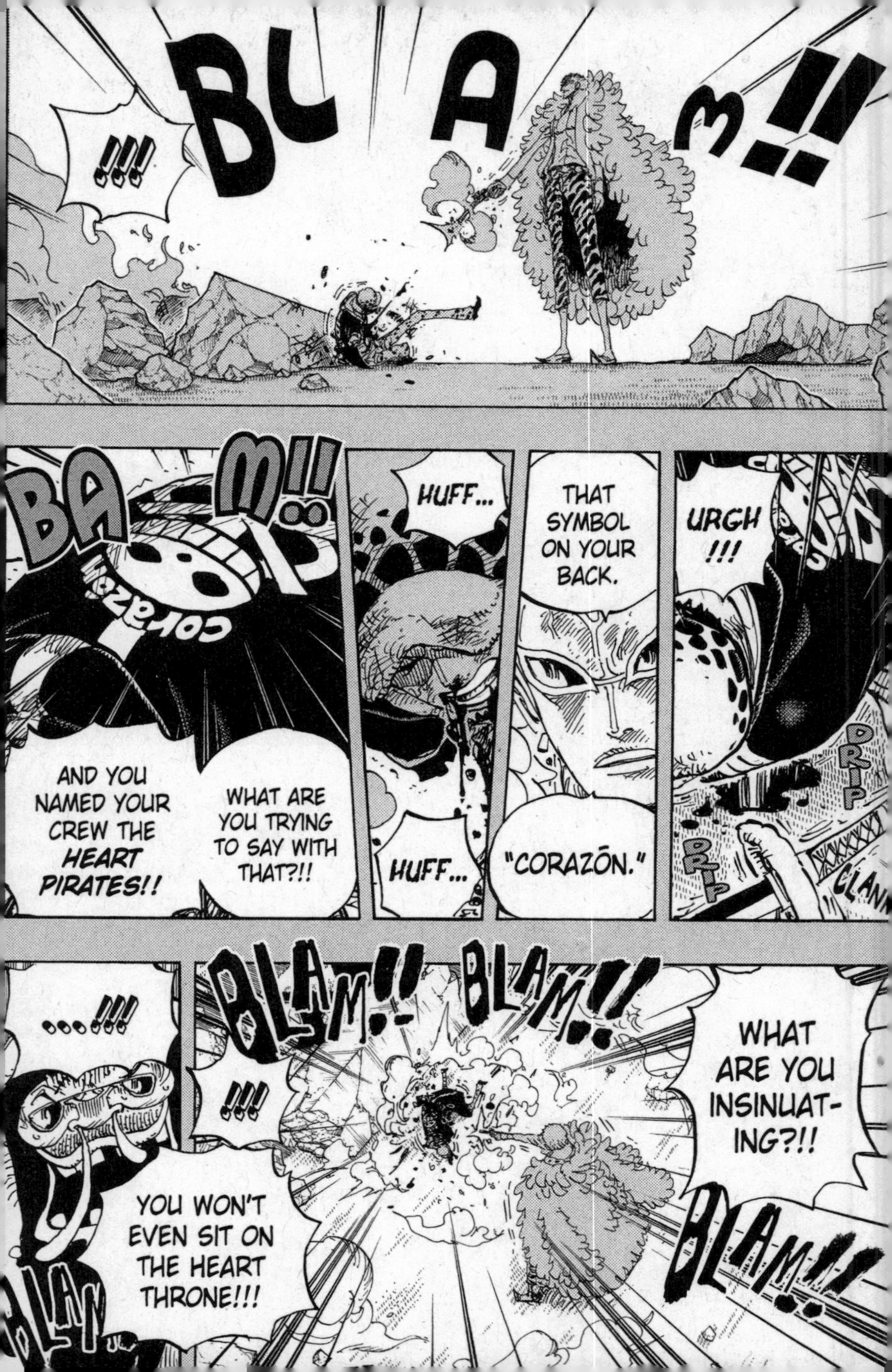
BLAM!!
!!!
URGH !!!
DRIP
DRIP
CLANK
THAT SYMBOL ON YOUR BACK.
"CORAZÓN."
HUFF...
HUFF...
BAM!!
WHAT ARE YOU TRYING TO SAY WITH THAT?!!
AND YOU NAMED YOUR CREW THE HEART PIRATES!!
WHAT ARE YOU INSINUATING?!!
BLAM!!
BLAM!! BLAM!!
!!!
...!!!
YOU WON'T EVEN SIT ON THE HEART THRONE!!!

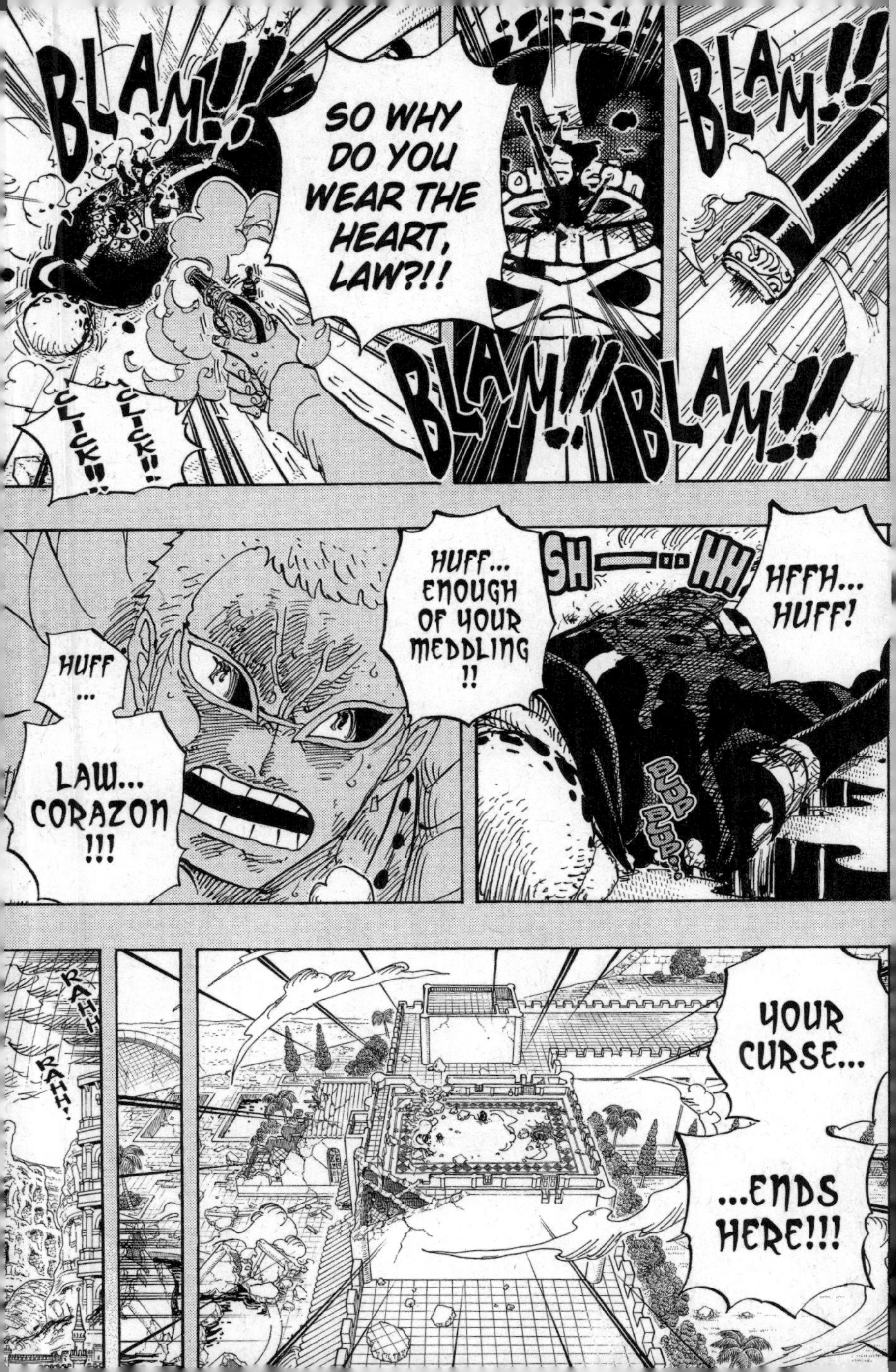
BLAM!!
SO WHY DO YOU WEAR THE HEART, LAW?!!
BLAM!! BLAM!!
BLAM!!
CLICK!!
CLICK!!
SH—...HH
HFFH... HUFF!
BUP BUP
HUFF... ENOUGH OF YOUR MEDDLING!!
HUFF...
LAW... CORAZON!!!
YOUR CURSE...
...ENDS HERE!!!
RAHH
RAHH!

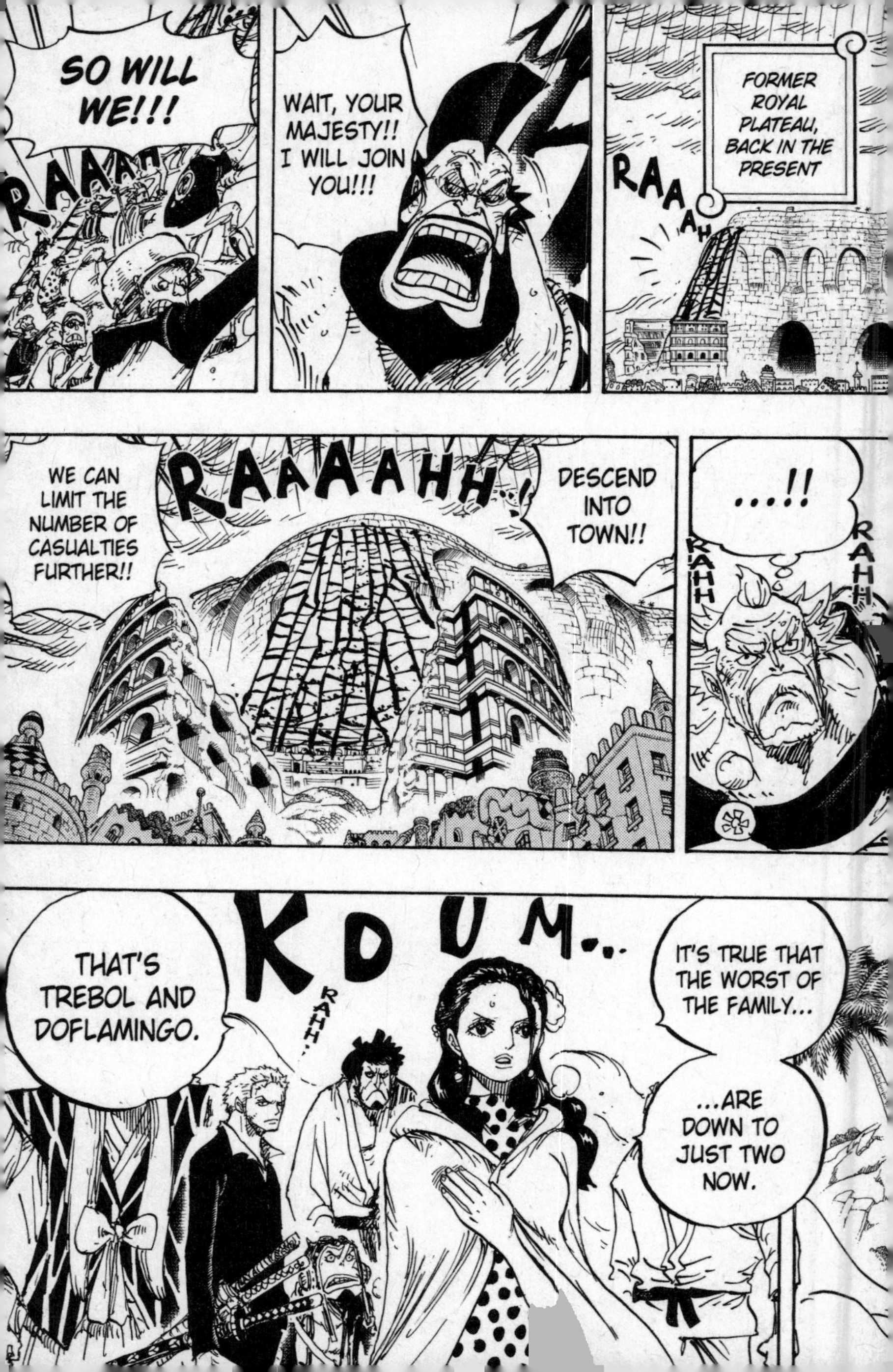
FORMER ROYAL PLATEAU, BACK IN THE PRESENT
RAAAAH
WAIT, YOUR MAJESTY!! I WILL JOIN YOU!!!
SO WILL WE!!!
RAAAAH
....!!
RAHH
RAHH
DESCEND INTO TOWN!!
RAAAAHH..
WE CAN LIMIT THE NUMBER OF CASUALTIES FURTHER!!
IT'S TRUE THAT THE WORST OF THE FAMILY...
...ARE DOWN TO JUST TWO NOW.
KDUM..
RAHH..
THAT'S TREBOL AND DOFLAMINGO.

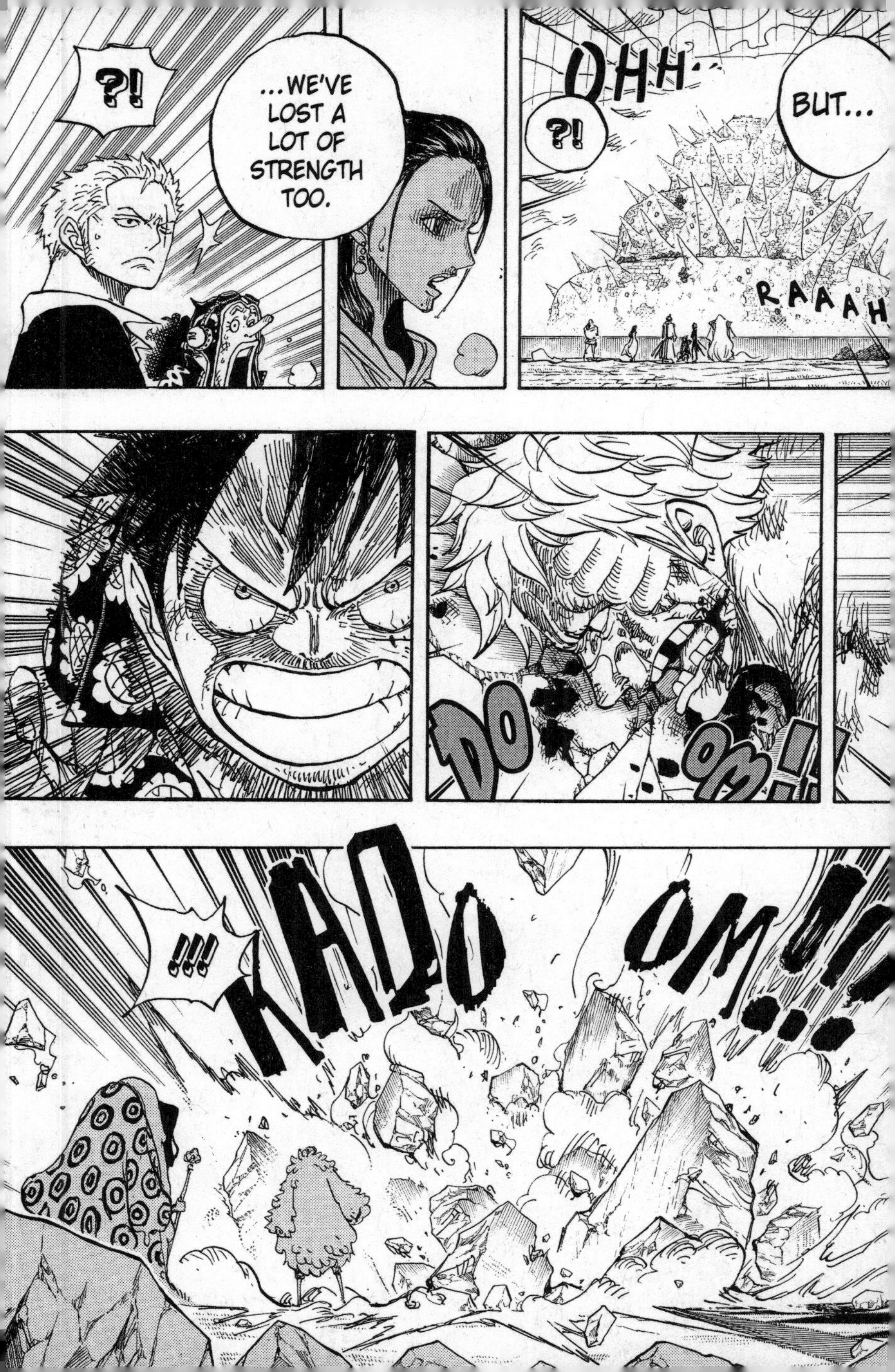
BUT...
OHH
?!
RAAAH
...WE'VE LOST A LOT OF STRENGTH TOO.
?!
DO OM!!
KADO OM!!
!!!

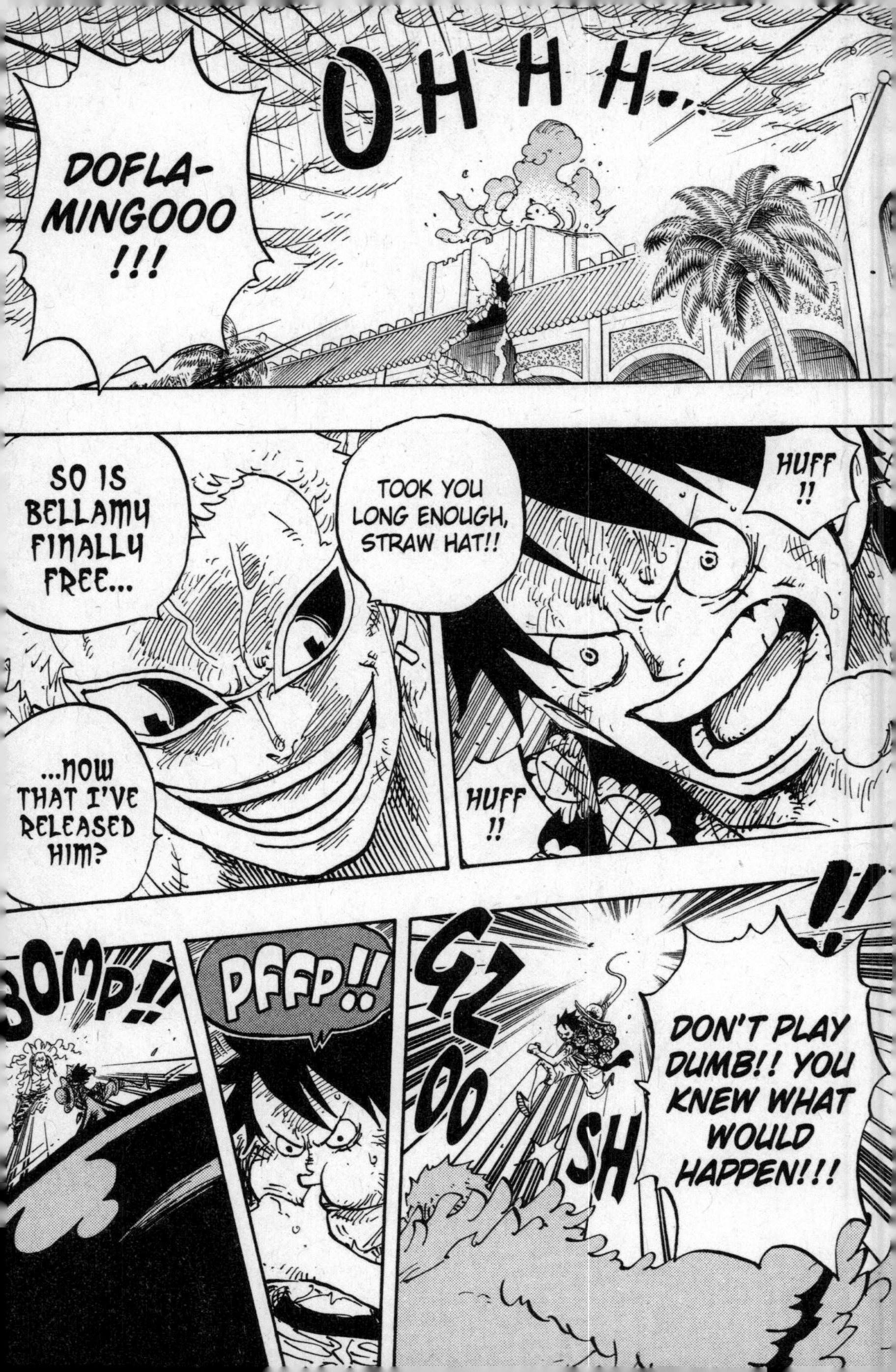

OHHH..
DOFLA-MINGOOO!!!
HUFF!!
HUFF!!
TOOK YOU LONG ENOUGH, STRAW HAT!!
SO IS BELLAMY FINALLY FREE...
...NOW THAT I'VE RELEASED HIM?
!!
GZOOSH
DON'T PLAY DUMB!! YOU KNEW WHAT WOULD HAPPEN!!!
PFFP!!
BOMP!!

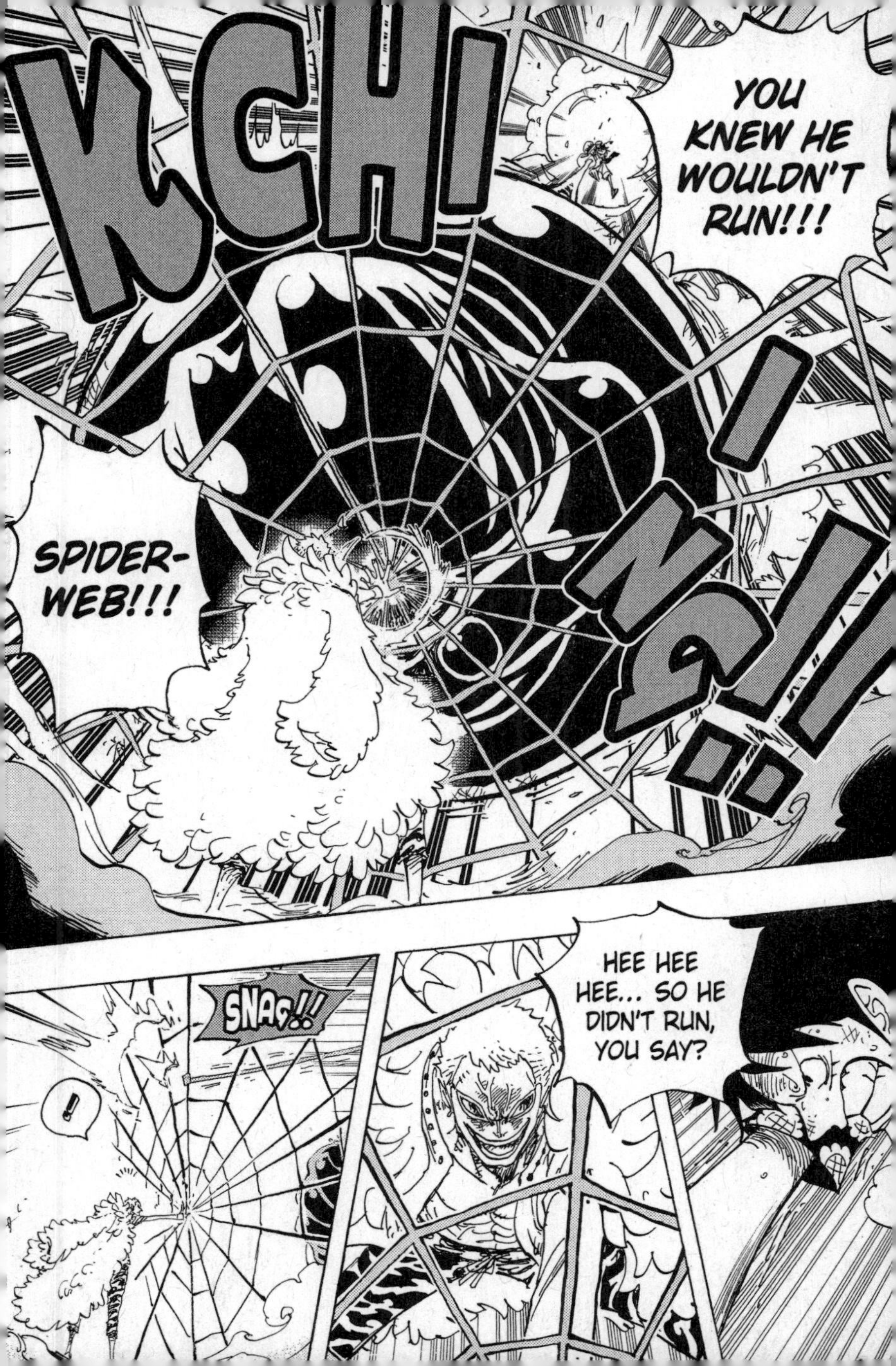
YOU KNEW HE WOULDN'T RUN!!!
KCHI
ING!!
SPIDER-WEB!!!
HEE HEE HEE... SO HE DIDN'T RUN, YOU SAY?
SNAG!!
!

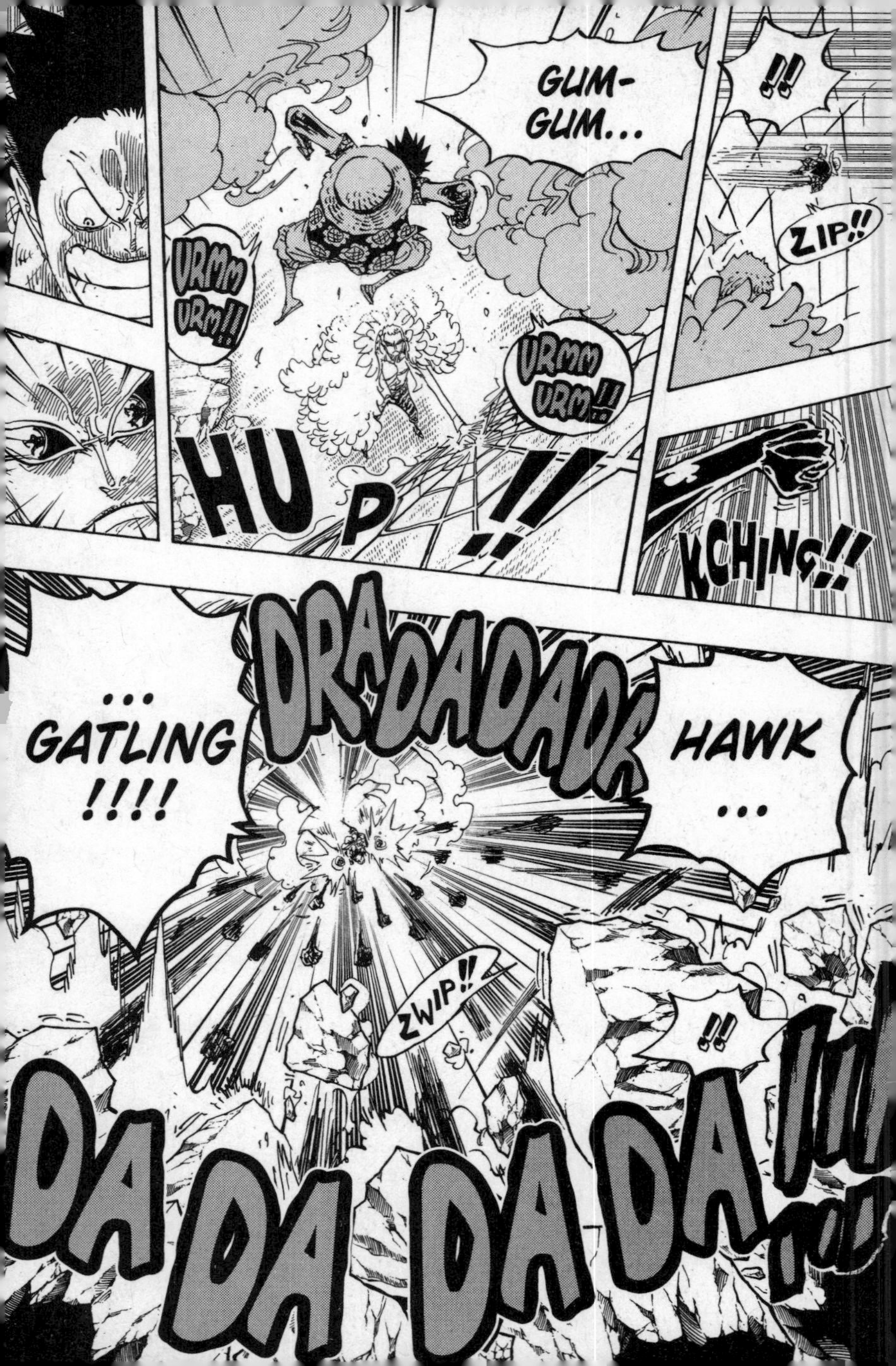
!!
ZIP!!
KCHING!!
GUM-GUM...
URMM URM!!
URMM URM!!
HUP!!
HAWK...
DRADADADA
...GATLING!!!!
!!
ZWIP!!
DA DA DA DA!!!...

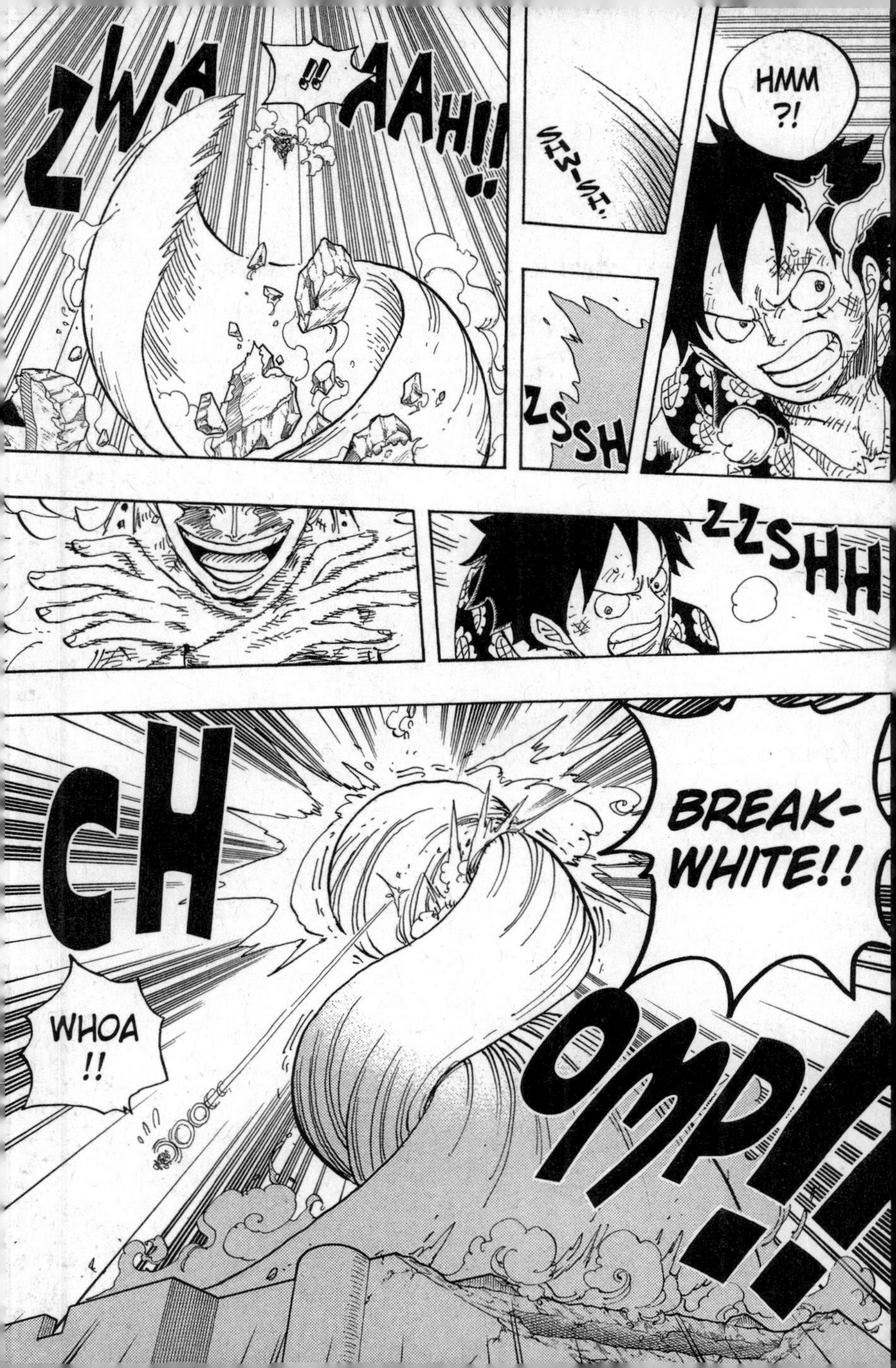
HMM ?!
SHWISH
ZSSH
!!
ZWA
AAH!!
ZZSHH
BREAK-WHITE!!
CH
OMP!!
WHOA !!

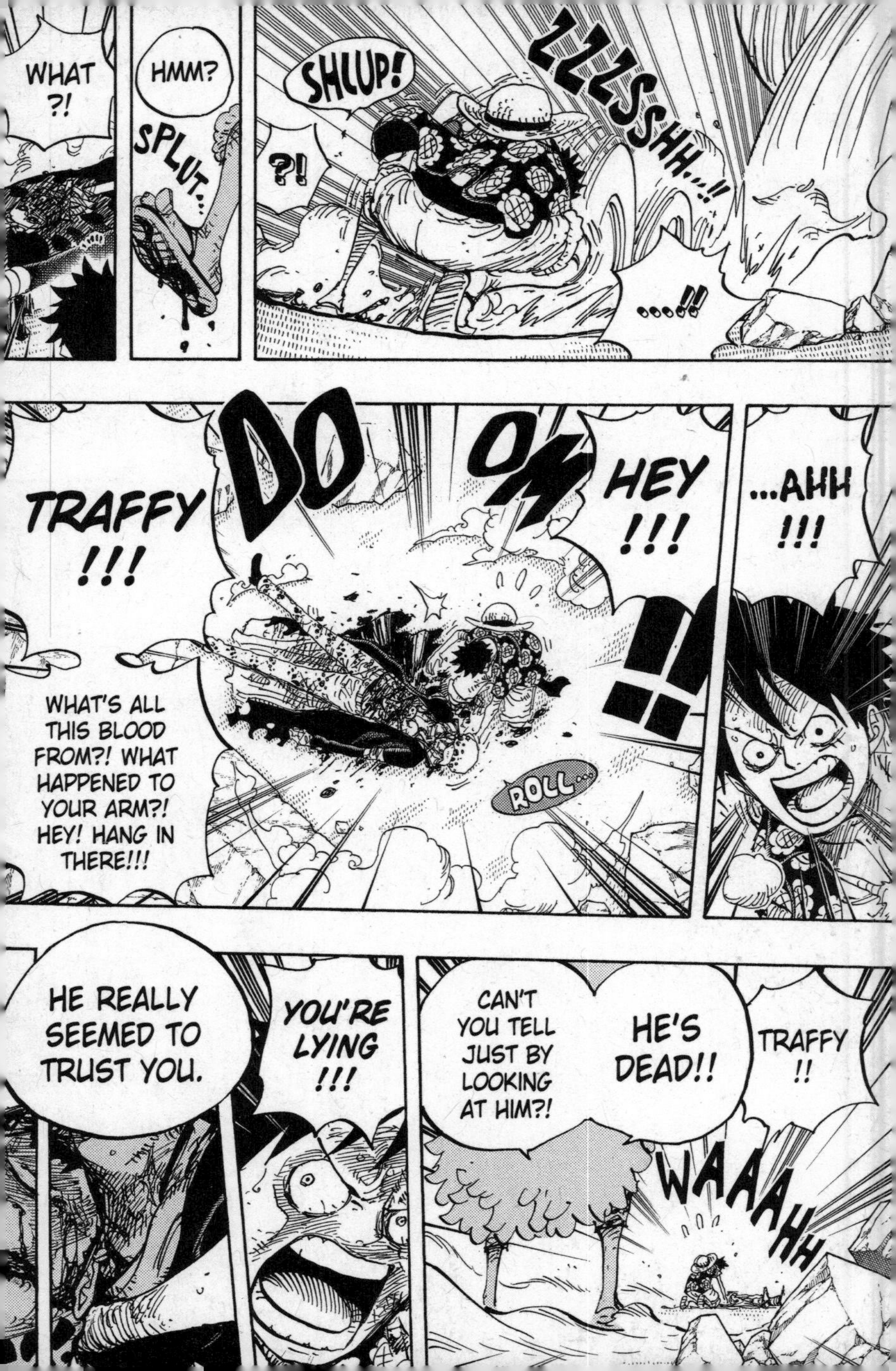
ZZZSSHH...!!
SHLUP!
?!
....!!
HMM?
SPLUT..
WHAT ?!
...AHH !!!
HEY !!!
DOOM
!!
TRAFFY !!!
ROLL...
WHAT'S ALL THIS BLOOD FROM?! WHAT HAPPENED TO YOUR ARM?! HEY! HANG IN THERE!!!
TRAFFY !!
HE'S DEAD!!
CAN'T YOU TELL JUST BY LOOKING AT HIM?!
WAAAHH
YOU'RE LYING !!!
HE REALLY SEEMED TO TRUST YOU.

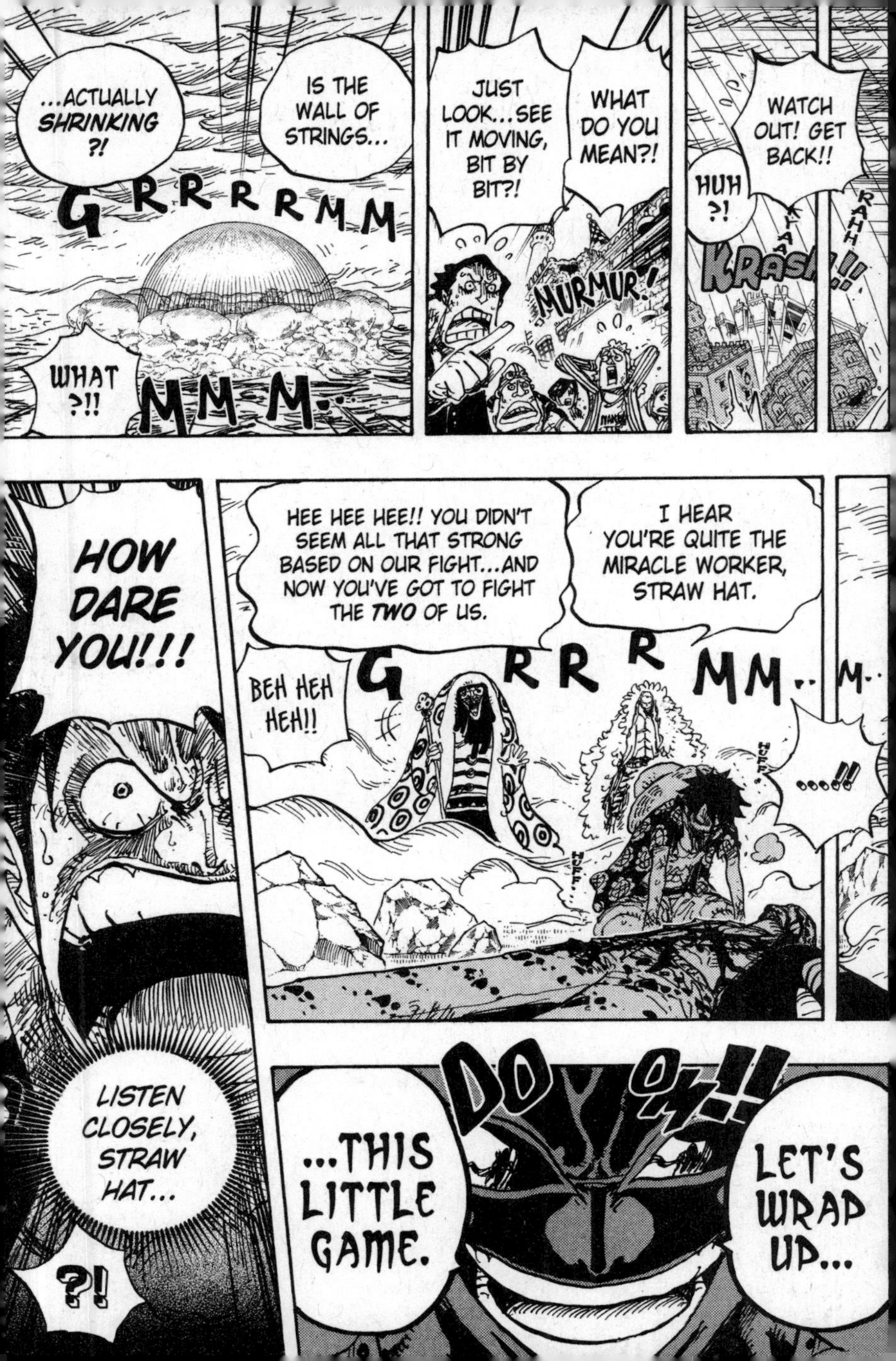
WATCH OUT! GET BACK!!
HUH?!
KYAA
RAHH
KRASH!!
WHAT DO YOU MEAN?!
JUST LOOK...SEE IT MOVING, BIT BY BIT?!
MURMUR!
IS THE WALL OF STRINGS...
...ACTUALLY SHRINKING?!
GRRRRRMM
WHAT?!!
MMM...
I HEAR YOU'RE QUITE THE MIRACLE WORKER, STRAW HAT.
HEE HEE HEE!! YOU DIDN'T SEEM ALL THAT STRONG BASED ON OUR FIGHT...AND NOW YOU'VE GOT TO FIGHT THE *TWO* OF US.
GRRRMM...M...
BEH HEH HEH!!
HUFF
HUFF
....!!
LET'S WRAP UP...
...THIS LITTLE GAME.
DOOM!!
HOW DARE YOU!!!
LISTEN CLOSELY, STRAW HAT...
?!

SBS Question Corner

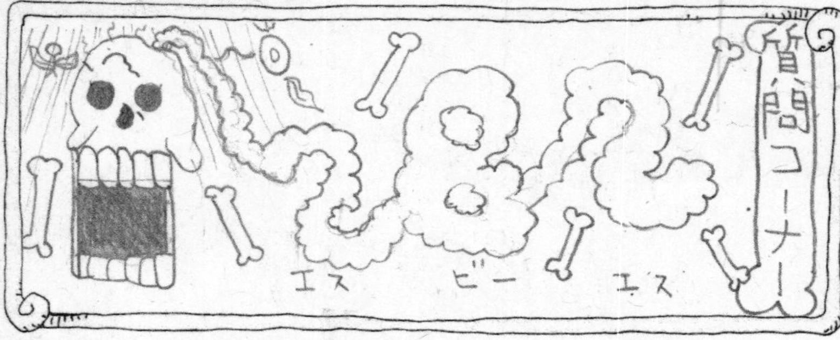

質問コーナー!
エス ビー エス

(Waka Kanda, Nagasaki)

Q: What are those spike-like things on Pica's shoulders?
--No. 73

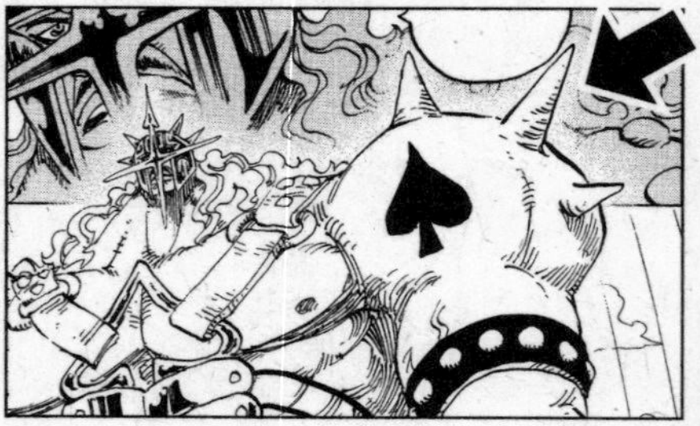

A: If you place a growing watermelon into a square container, it will eventually fill the space and result in a square watermelon. Pica wore shoulder protectors in that shape all throughout his growth spurt, so his shoulders just grew that way!!

Q: Oda Sensei!! Buggy could pass right through the Birdcage, couldn't he?!
--Pick Me Man

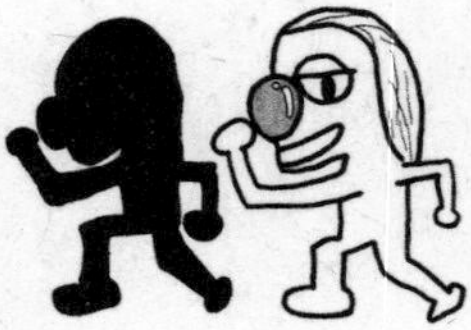

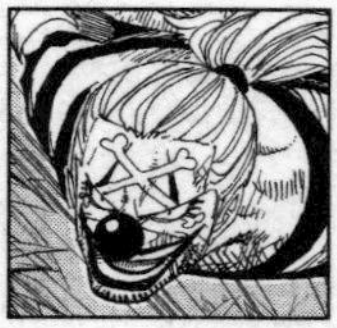

A: True, that's a good point. Buggy's entire crew could be stuck in there, and he'd split and take off on his own! I like this drawing. ➚

Q: I want Luffy and Doflamingo to fight and I want Luffy to win.

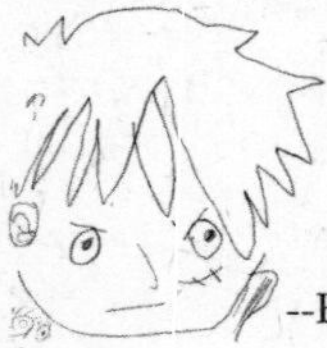

--From Taiichi in Iwate

A: I agree!! Let's root him on together!

Q: Show me a simple way to draw Zolo!
--Kanahasa

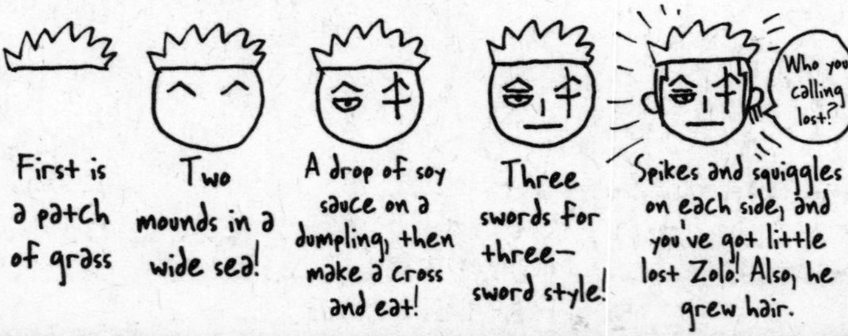

First is a patch of grass
Two mounds in a wide sea!
A drop of soy sauce on a dumpling, then make a cross and eat!
Three swords for three-sword style!
Who you calling lost?
Spikes and squiggles on each side, and you've got little lost Zolo! Also, he grew hair.

Chapter 781:
DESIRE

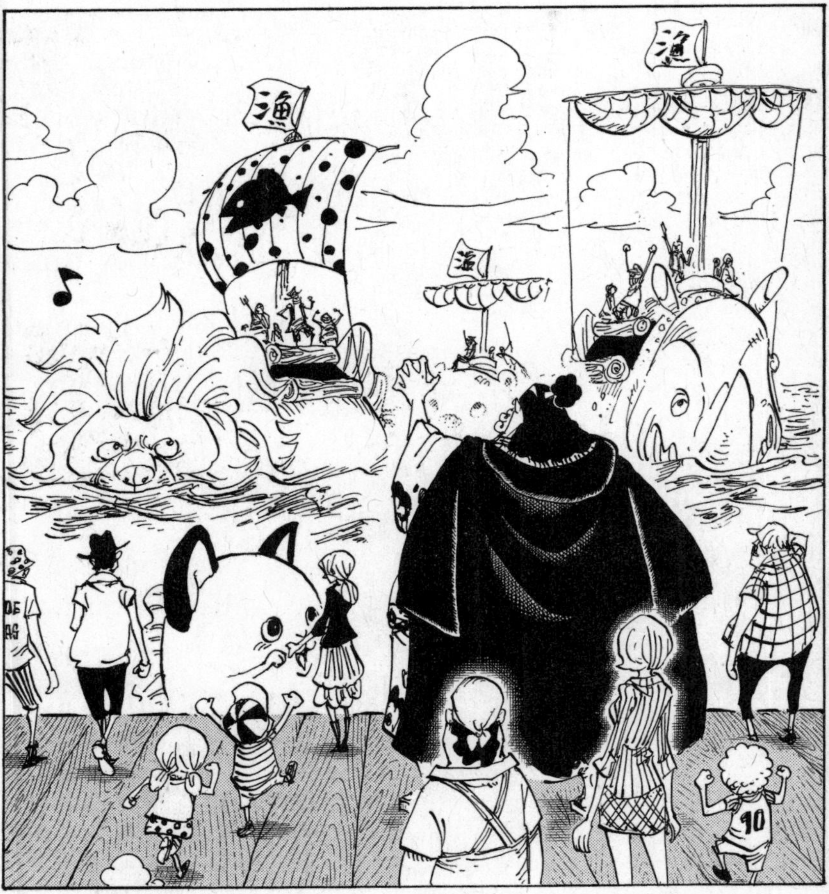
漁
漁
漁
10

THE SOLITARY JOURNEY OF JIMBEI, FIRST SON OF THE SEA, VOL. 25: "NEW FISHING BOATS TO MAKE UP FOR THE BUSTED ONES"

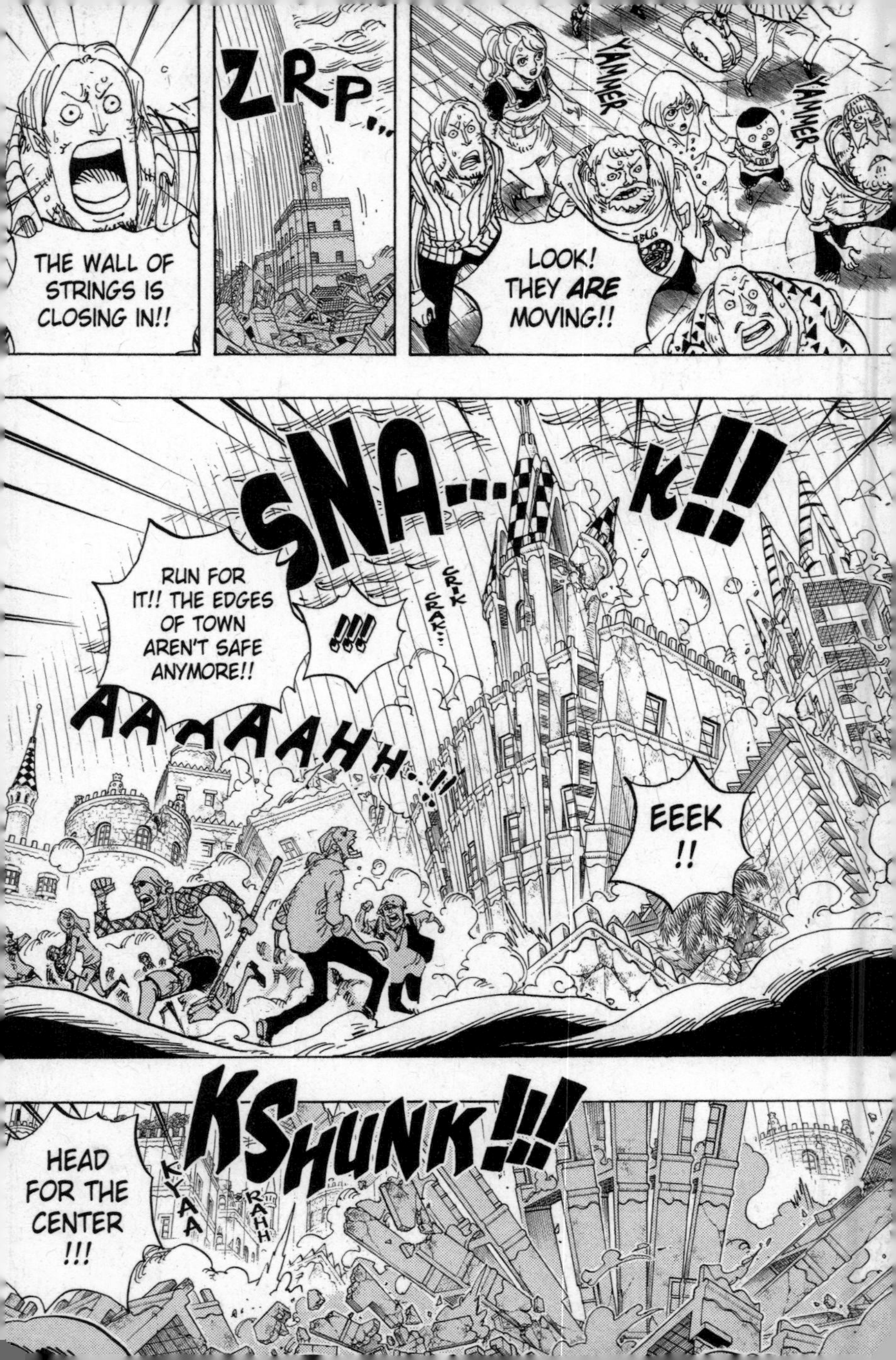
YAMMER
YAMMER
LOOK! THEY ARE MOVING!!
ZRP...
THE WALL OF STRINGS IS CLOSING IN!!
SNA...K!!
EEEK!!
CRIK CRAK...
!!!
RUN FOR IT!! THE EDGES OF TOWN AREN'T SAFE ANYMORE!!
AAAAAHH...!!
KSHUNK!!!
RAHH
KYAA
HEAD FOR THE CENTER!!!

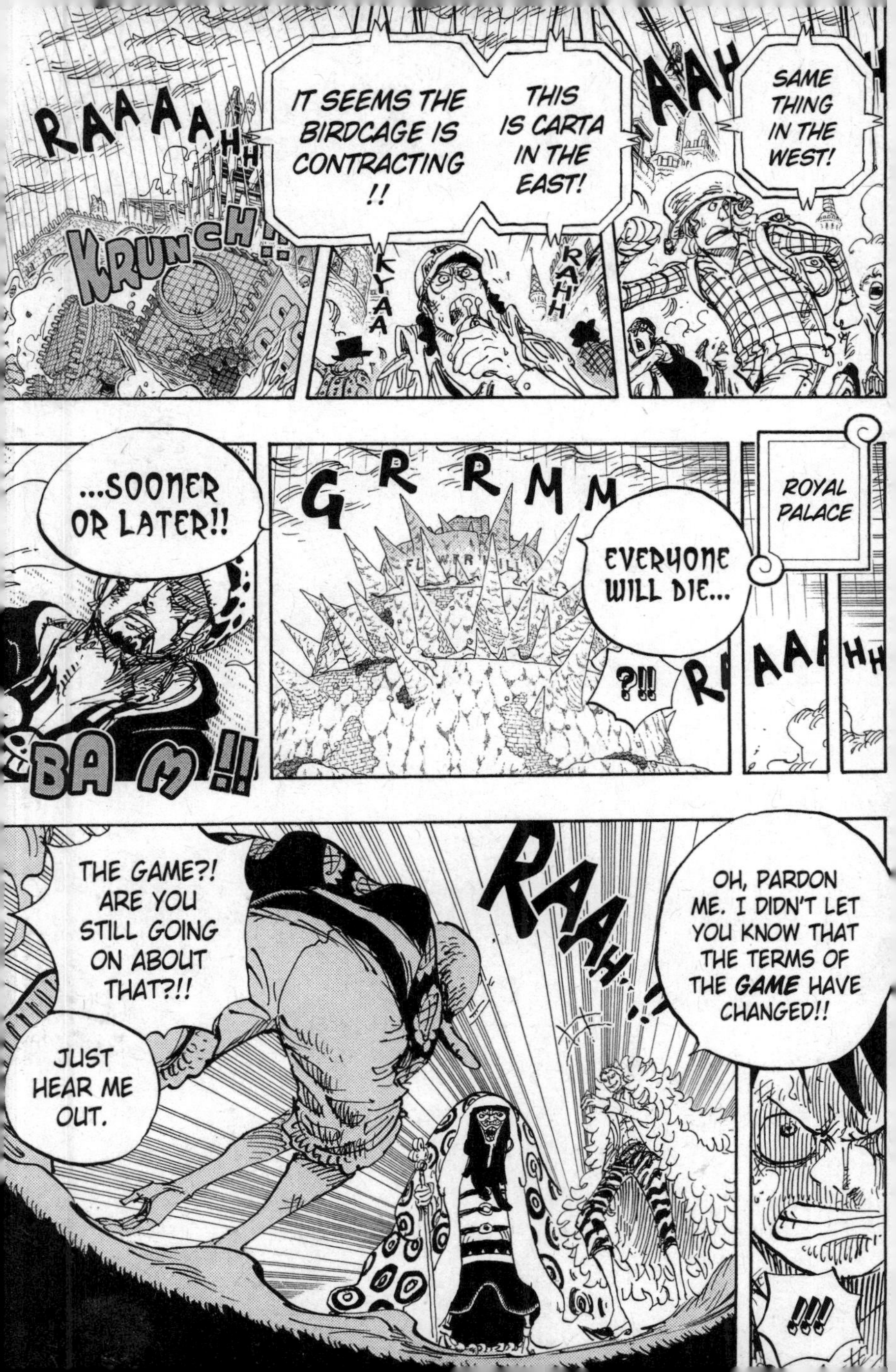

SAME THING IN THE WEST!
AAAH
THIS IS CARTA IN THE EAST!
RAHH
KYAA
IT SEEMS THE BIRDCAGE IS CONTRACTING!!
RAAAAHHH
KRUNCH!!
ROYAL PALACE
RAAAHH
GRRRMM
EVERYONE WILL DIE...
?!!
...SOONER OR LATER!!
BAM!!
!!!
OH, PARDON ME. I DIDN'T LET YOU KNOW THAT THE TERMS OF THE **GAME** HAVE CHANGED!!
RAAH!!
THE GAME?! ARE YOU STILL GOING ON ABOUT THAT?!!
JUST HEAR ME OUT.

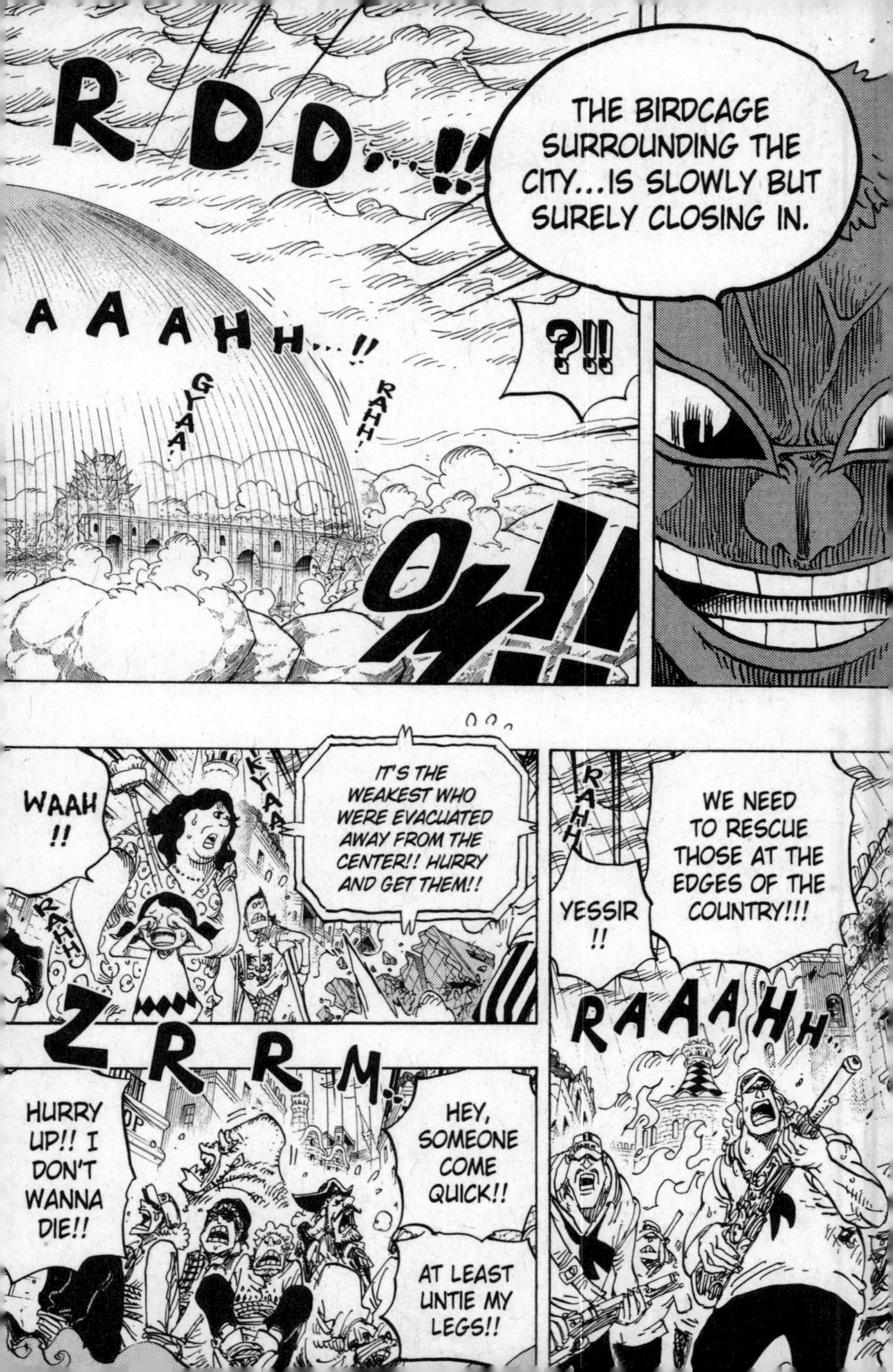
THE BIRDCAGE SURROUNDING THE CITY...IS SLOWLY BUT SURELY CLOSING IN.
?!!
RDD...!!
AAAHH...!!
GYAA
RAHH!
WE NEED TO RESCUE THOSE AT THE EDGES OF THE COUNTRY!!!
YESSIR!!
RAHH
RAAAHH...
IT'S THE WEAKEST WHO WERE EVACUATED AWAY FROM THE CENTER!! HURRY AND GET THEM!!
KYAA
WAAH!!
RAHH
ZRRRM!
HEY, SOMEONE COME QUICK!!
AT LEAST UNTIE MY LEGS!!
HURRY UP!! I DON'T WANNA DIE!!

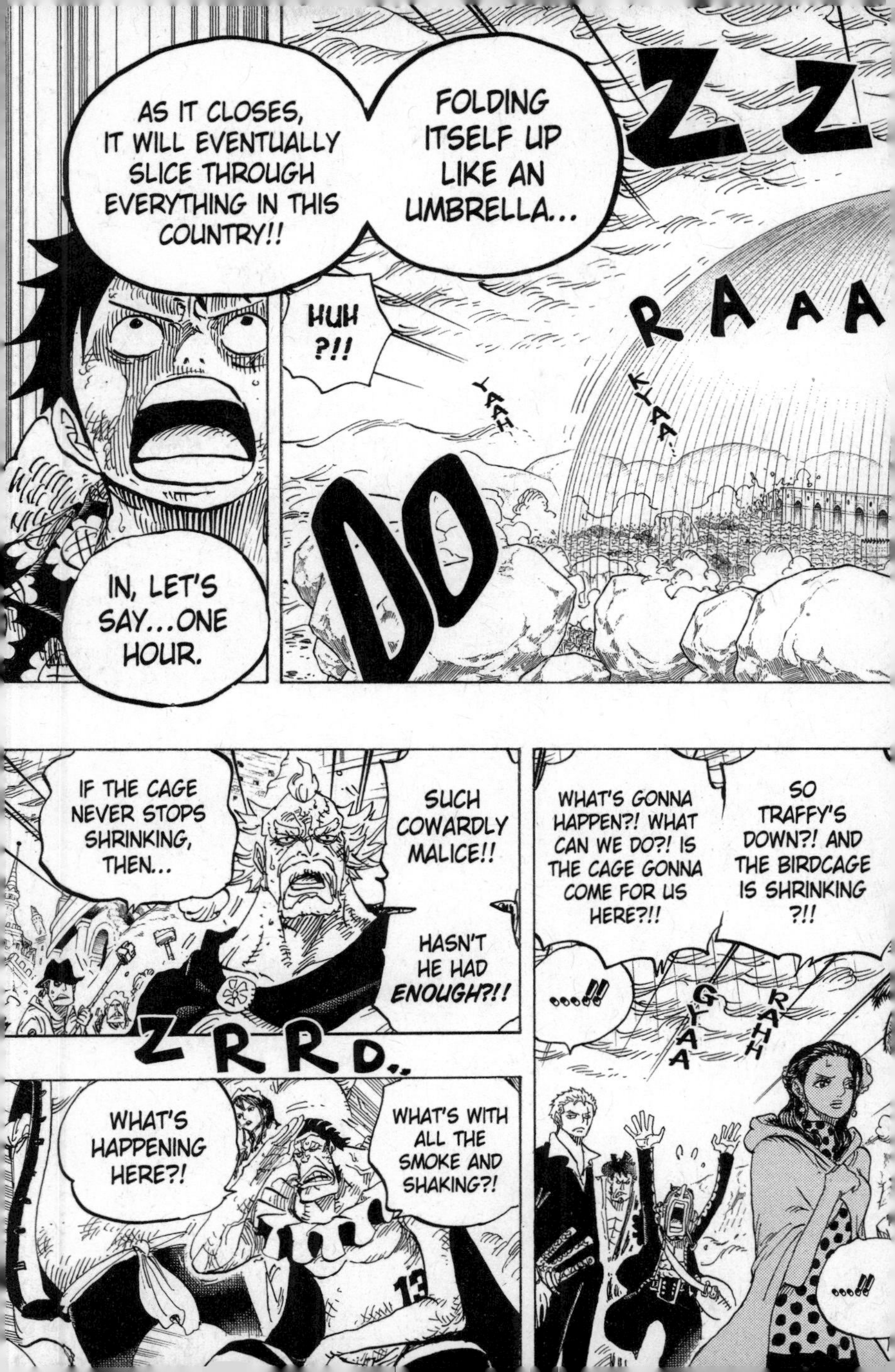
FOLDING ITSELF UP LIKE AN UMBRELLA...
AS IT CLOSES, IT WILL EVENTUALLY SLICE THROUGH EVERYTHING IN THIS COUNTRY!!
ZZRAAA
HUH ?!!
KYAA
YAAH
DO
IN, LET'S SAY...ONE HOUR.
SO TRAFFY'S DOWN?! AND THE BIRDCAGE IS SHRINKING ?!!
WHAT'S GONNA HAPPEN?! WHAT CAN WE DO?! IS THE CAGE GONNA COME FOR US HERE?!!
...!!
RAHH
GYAA
...!!
SUCH COWARDLY MALICE!!
HASN'T HE HAD ENOUGH?!!
IF THE CAGE NEVER STOPS SHRINKING, THEN...
ZRRD..
WHAT'S WITH ALL THE SMOKE AND SHAKING?!
WHAT'S HAPPENING HERE?!

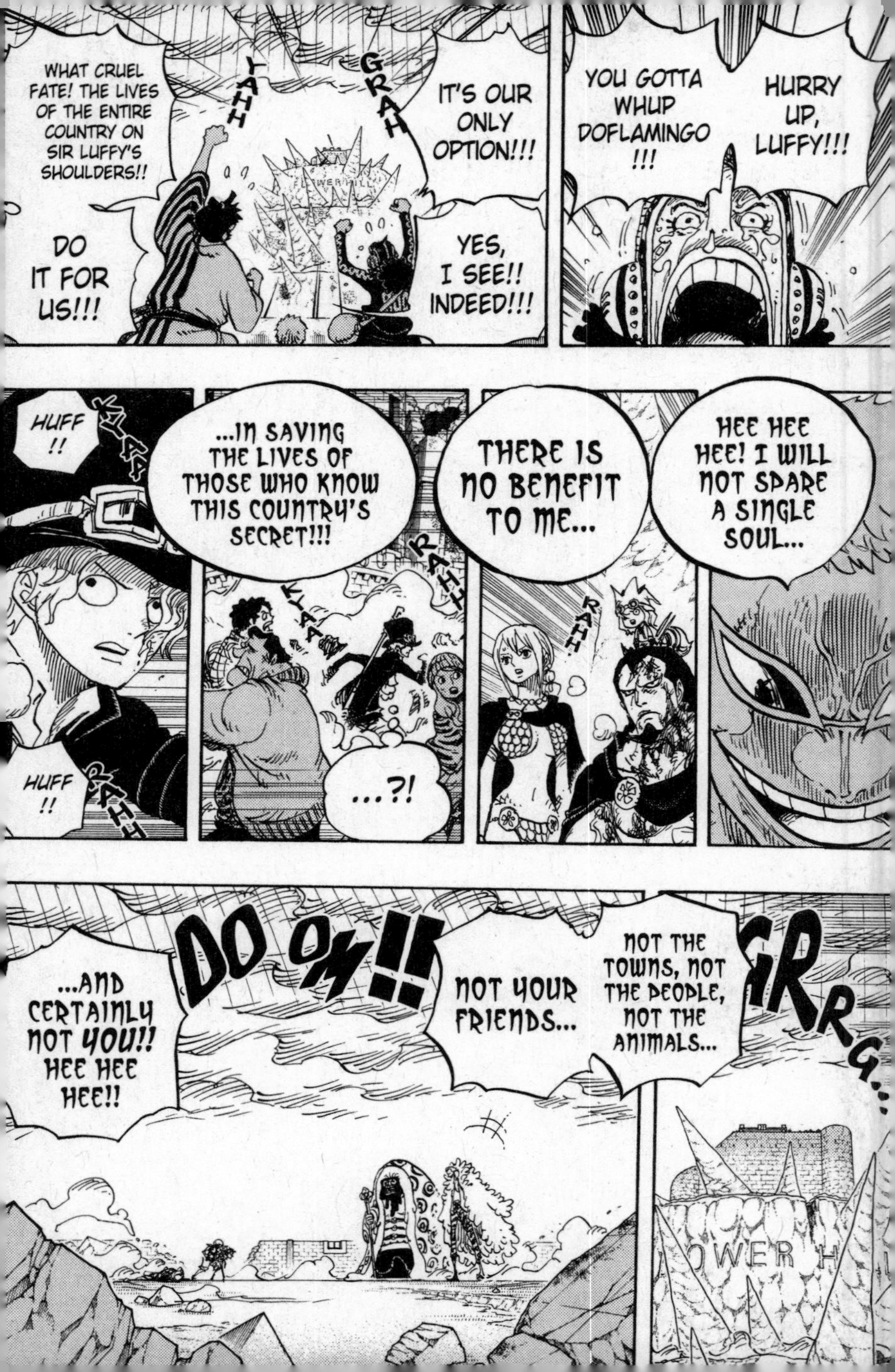
HURRY UP, LUFFY!!!
YOU GOTTA WHUP DOFLAMINGO!!!
IT'S OUR ONLY OPTION!!!
GRAH
YAHH
WHAT CRUEL FATE! THE LIVES OF THE ENTIRE COUNTRY ON SIR LUFFY'S SHOULDERS!!
YES, I SEE!! INDEED!!!
DO IT FOR US!!!
HEE HEE HEE! I WILL NOT SPARE A SINGLE SOUL...
THERE IS NO BENEFIT TO ME...
RAHH
...IN SAVING THE LIVES OF THOSE WHO KNOW THIS COUNTRY'S SECRET!!!
RAHH
KYAA
...?!
HUFF!!
KYAA
HUFF!!
RAHH
GRRRG...
NOT THE TOWNS, NOT THE PEOPLE, NOT THE ANIMALS...
NOT YOUR FRIENDS...
DOOM!!
...AND CERTAINLY NOT YOU!! HEE HEE HEE!!

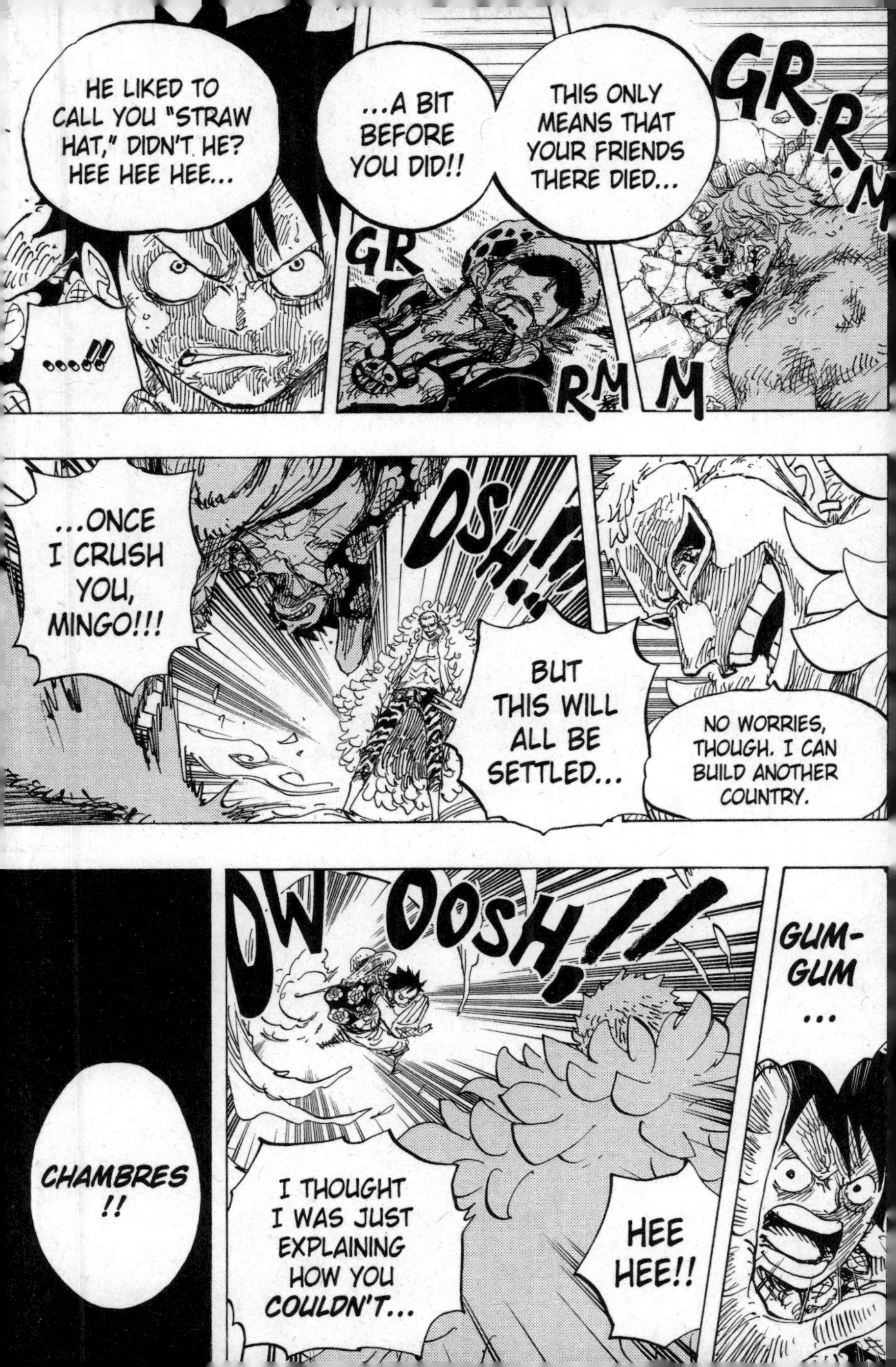
GRRRM
THIS ONLY MEANS THAT YOUR FRIENDS THERE DIED...
GR
RM
M
...A BIT BEFORE YOU DID!!
HE LIKED TO CALL YOU "STRAW HAT," DIDN'T HE? HEE HEE HEE...
....!!
NO WORRIES, THOUGH. I CAN BUILD ANOTHER COUNTRY.
BUT THIS WILL ALL BE SETTLED...
DOSH!!
...ONCE I CRUSH YOU, MINGO!!!
GUM-GUM ...
HEE HEE!!
I THOUGHT I WAS JUST EXPLAINING HOW YOU COULDN'T...
DWOOSH!!
CHAMBRES !!

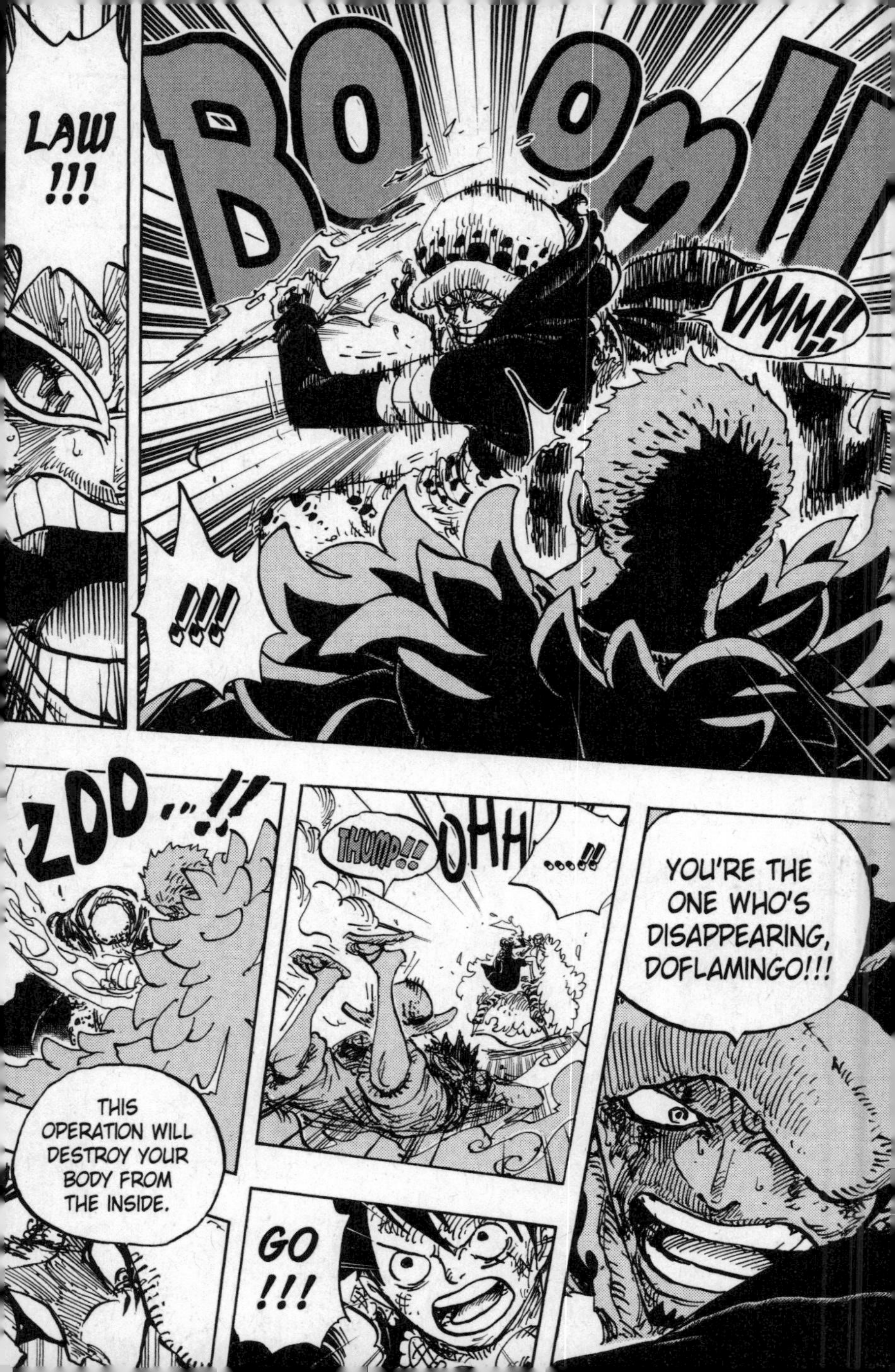

BOOM!
VMM!!
!!!
LAW !!!
YOU'RE THE ONE WHO'S DISAPPEARING, DOFLAMINGO!!!
THUMP!!
OHH...!!
ZDD...!!
THIS OPERATION WILL DESTROY YOUR BODY FROM THE INSIDE.
GO !!!

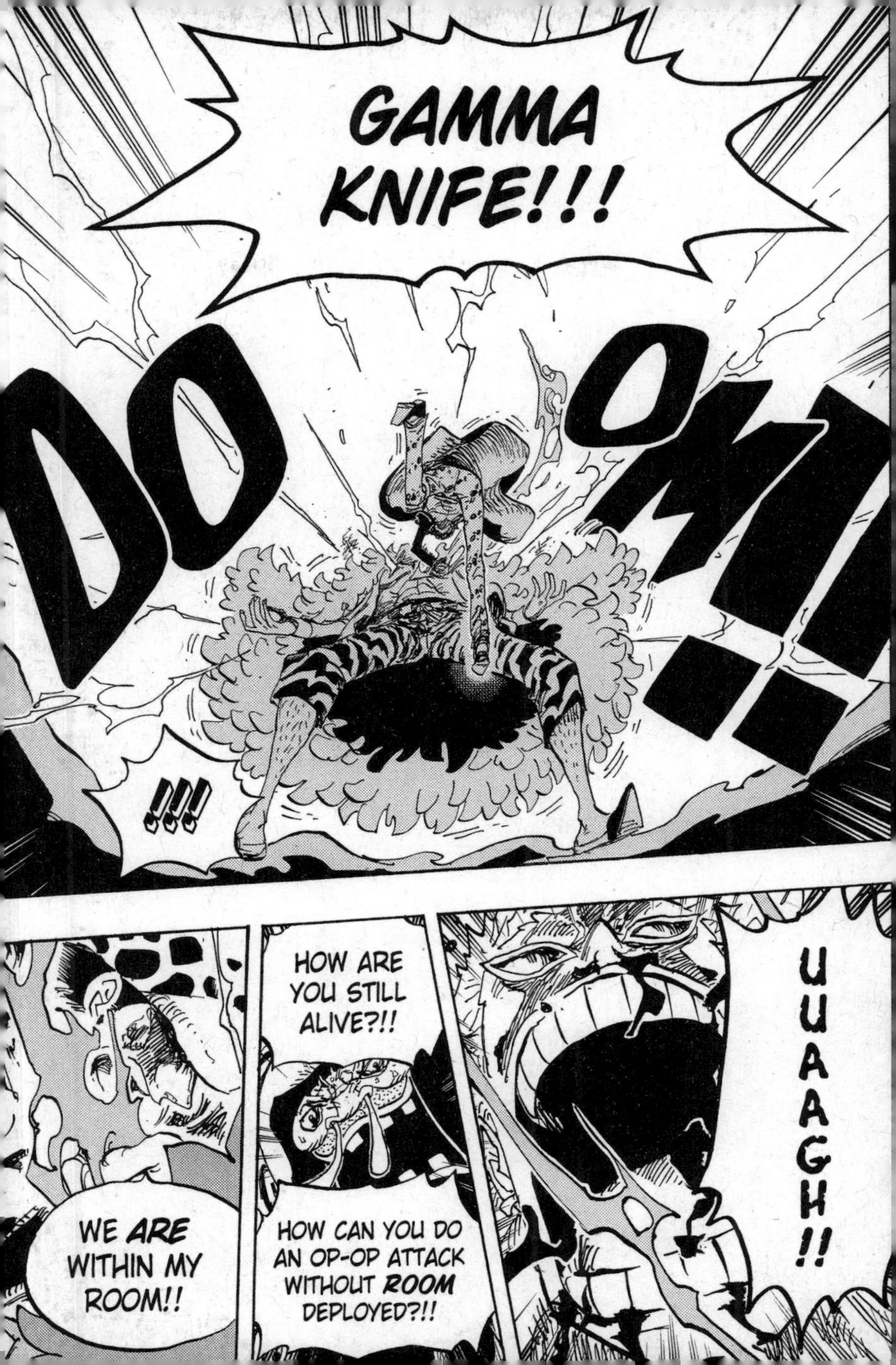
GAMMA KNIFE!!!
DOON!!
!!!
UUAAGH!!
HOW ARE YOU STILL ALIVE?!!
HOW CAN YOU DO AN OP-OP ATTACK WITHOUT *ROOM* DEPLOYED?!!
WE *ARE* WITHIN MY *ROOM*!!

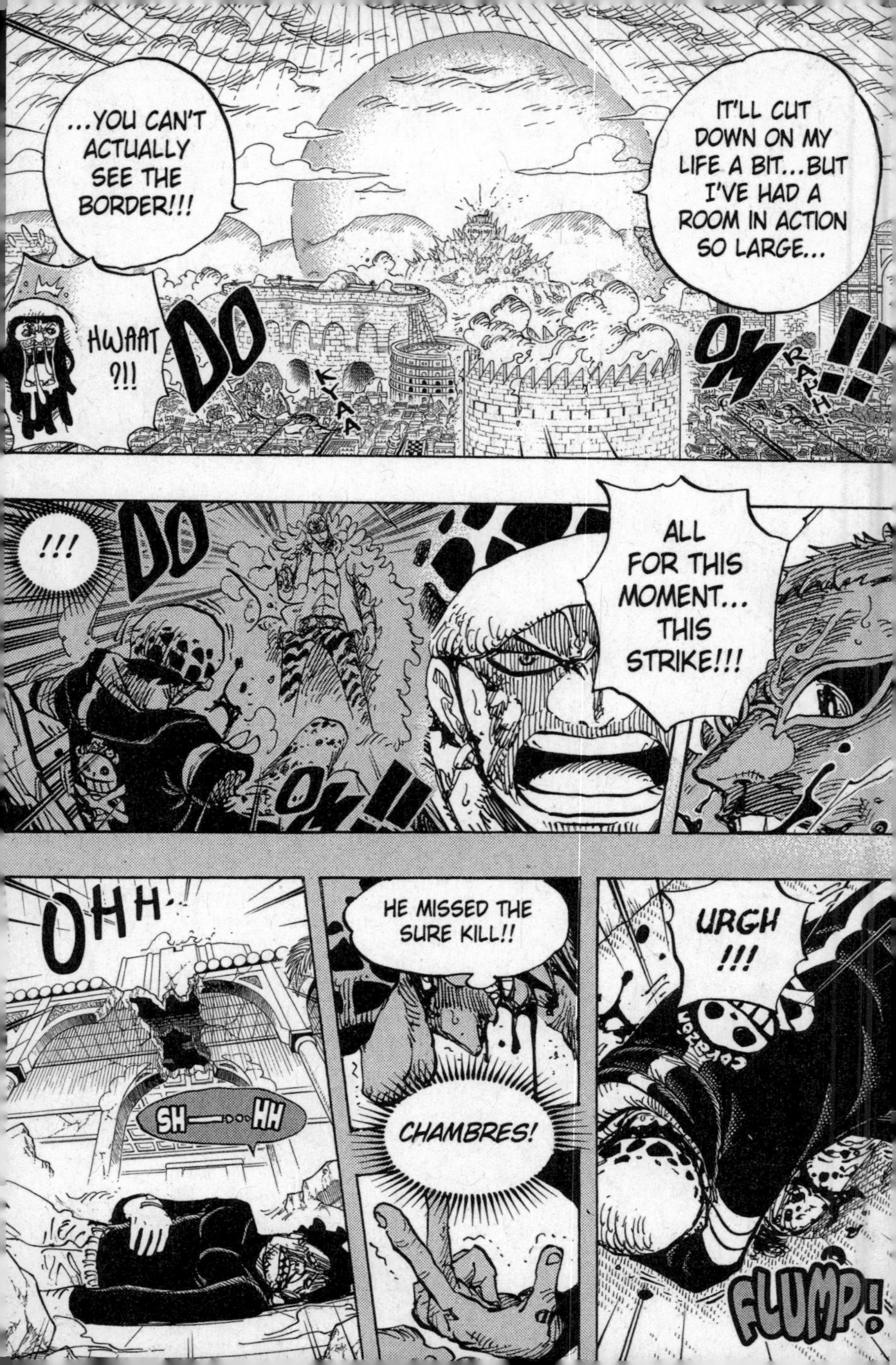
IT'LL CUT DOWN ON MY LIFE A BIT...BUT I'VE HAD A ROOM IN ACTION SO LARGE...
...YOU CAN'T ACTUALLY SEE THE BORDER!!!
RAAH
OM!!
KYAA
DO
HWAAT ?!!
ALL FOR THIS MOMENT... THIS STRIKE!!!
OM!!
DO
!!!
URGH !!!
FLUMP!
HE MISSED THE SURE KILL!!
CHAMBRES!
OHH
SH—HH

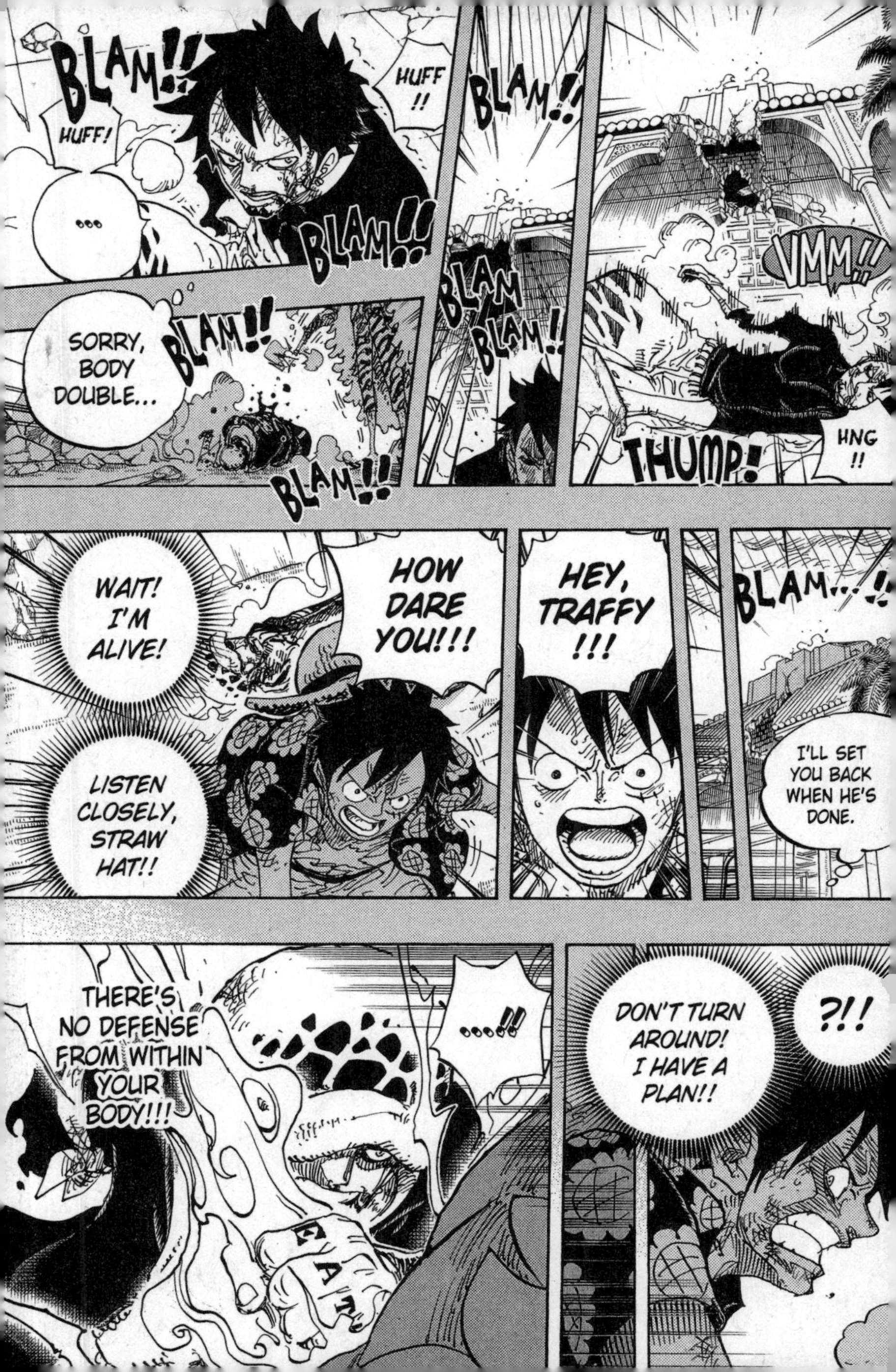
VMM!!
HNG!!
THUMP!
BLAM!!
BLAM BLAM BLAM!!
BLAM!!
HUFF!!
BLAM!!
HUFF!
...
BLAM!!
SORRY, BODY DOUBLE...
BLAM!!
BLAM...!!
I'LL SET YOU BACK WHEN HE'S DONE.
HEY, TRAFFY!!!
HOW DARE YOU!!!
WAIT! I'M ALIVE!
LISTEN CLOSELY, STRAW HAT!!
?!!
DON'T TURN AROUND! I HAVE A PLAN!!
...!!
THERE'S NO DEFENSE FROM WITHIN YOUR BODY!!!

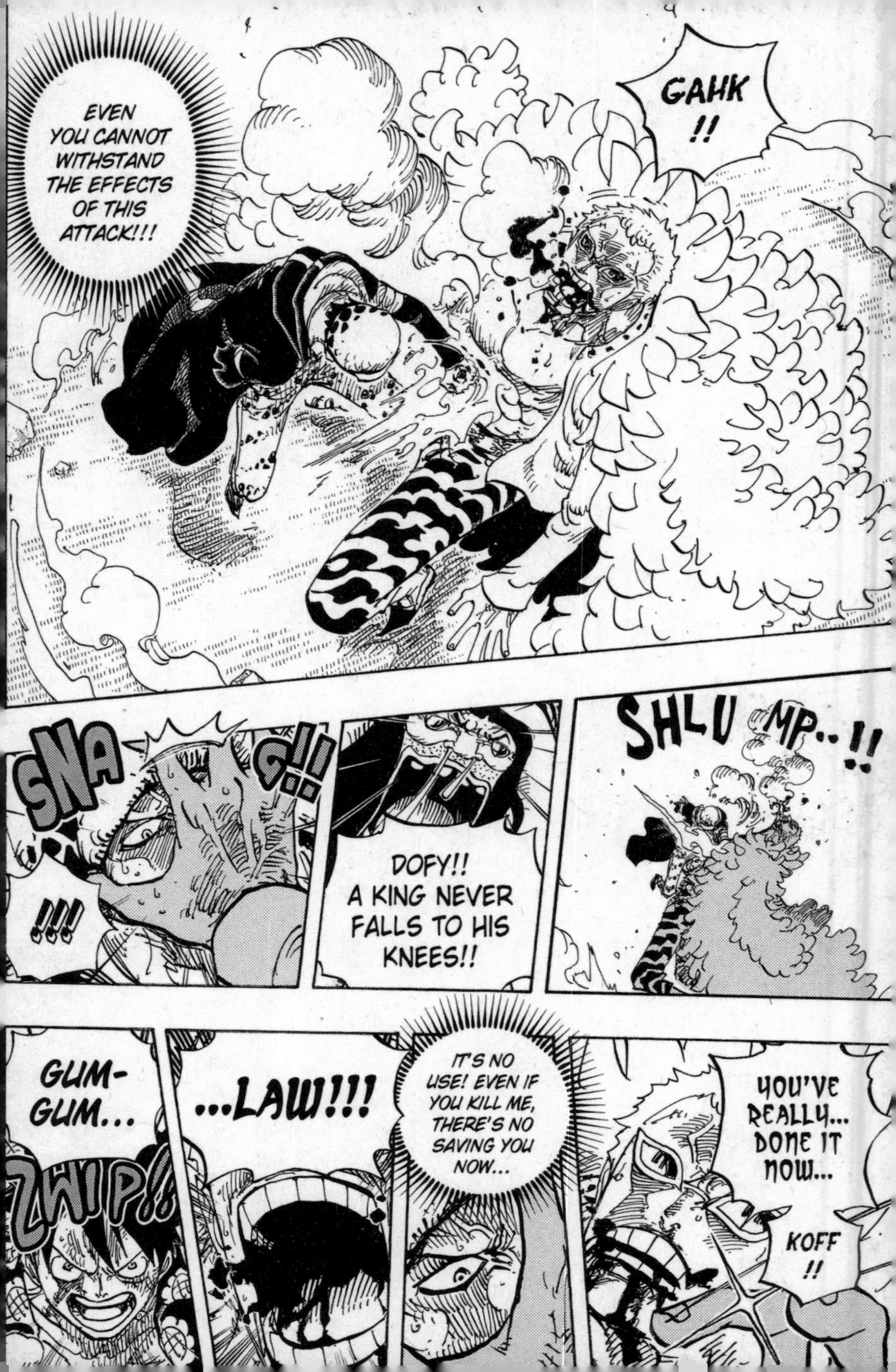
GAHK !!
EVEN YOU CANNOT WITHSTAND THE EFFECTS OF THIS ATTACK!!!
SHLUMP..!!
DOFY!! A KING NEVER FALLS TO HIS KNEES!!
SNAG!!
!!!
YOU'VE REALLY... DONE IT NOW...
KOFF !!
IT'S NO USE! EVEN IF YOU KILL ME, THERE'S NO SAVING YOU NOW...
...LAW!!!
GUM-GUM...
ZWIP!!

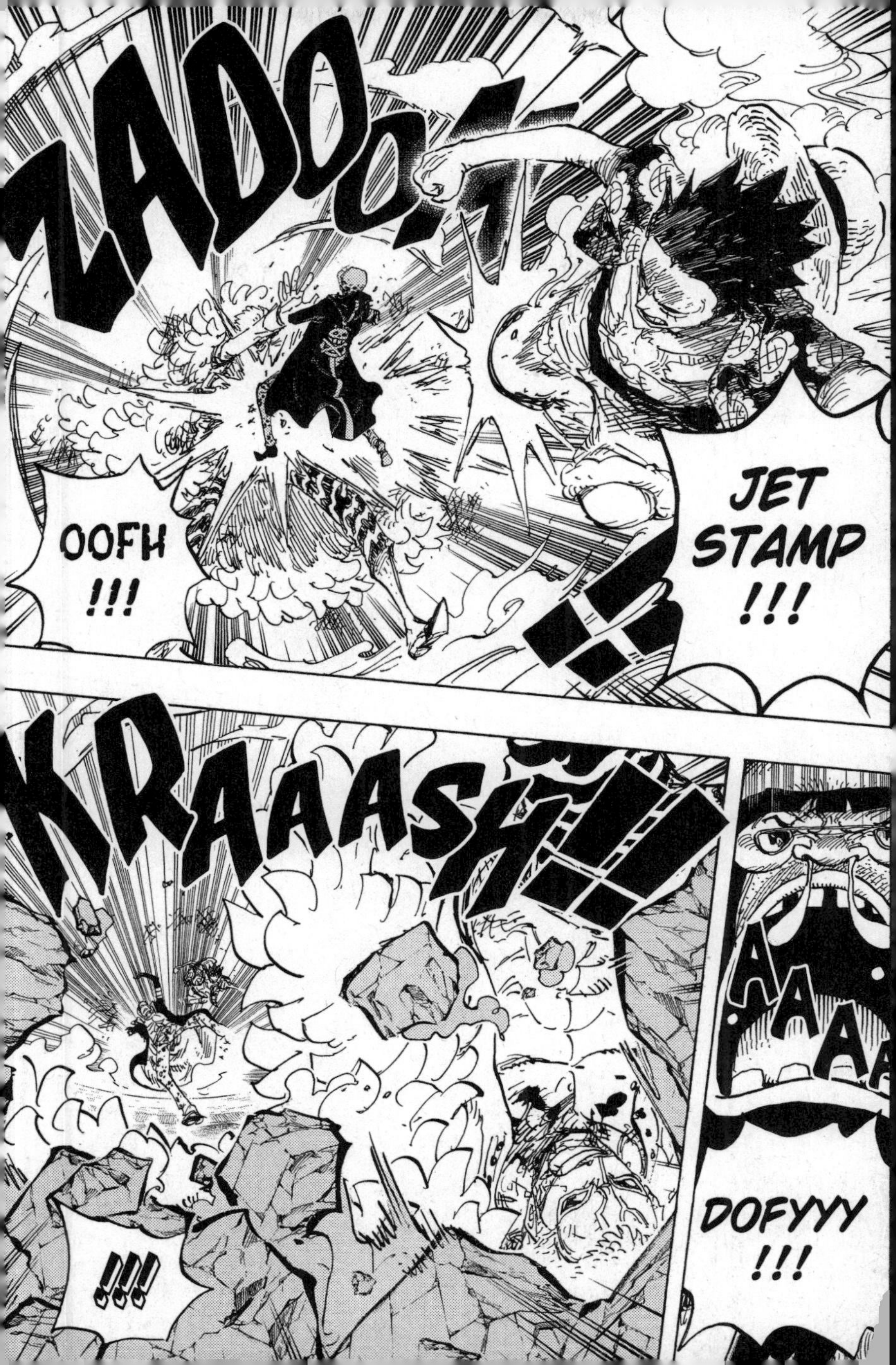
JET STAMP !!!
ZADOO
OOFH !!!
AAAA
DOFYYY !!!
KRAAASH!!
!!!

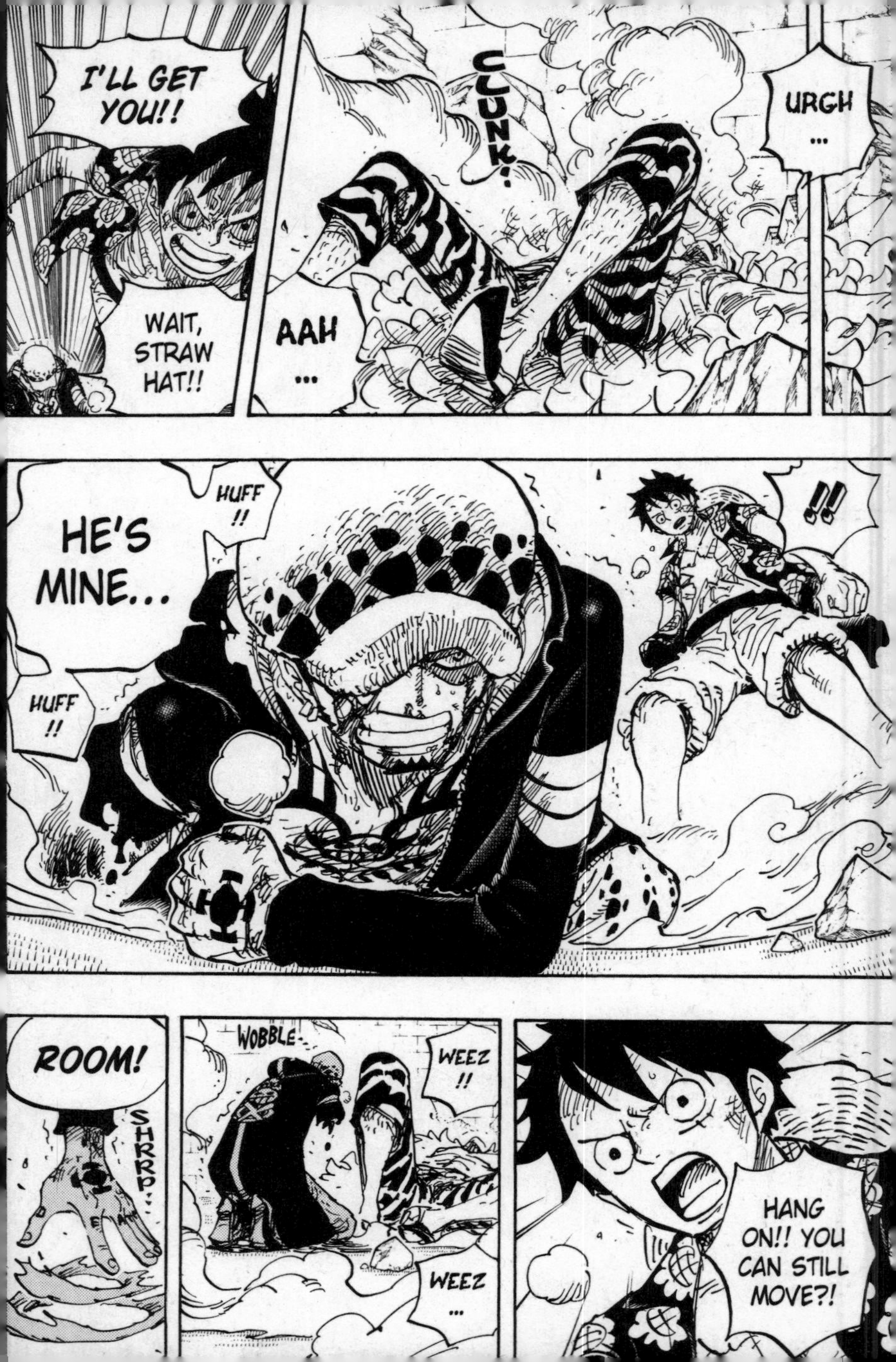
URGH ...
CLUNK!
AAH ...
I'LL GET YOU!!
WAIT, STRAW HAT!!
!!
HUFF !!
HE'S MINE...
HUFF !!
HANG ON!! YOU CAN STILL MOVE?!
WEEZ !!
WOBBLE
WEEZ ...
ROOM!
SHRRP

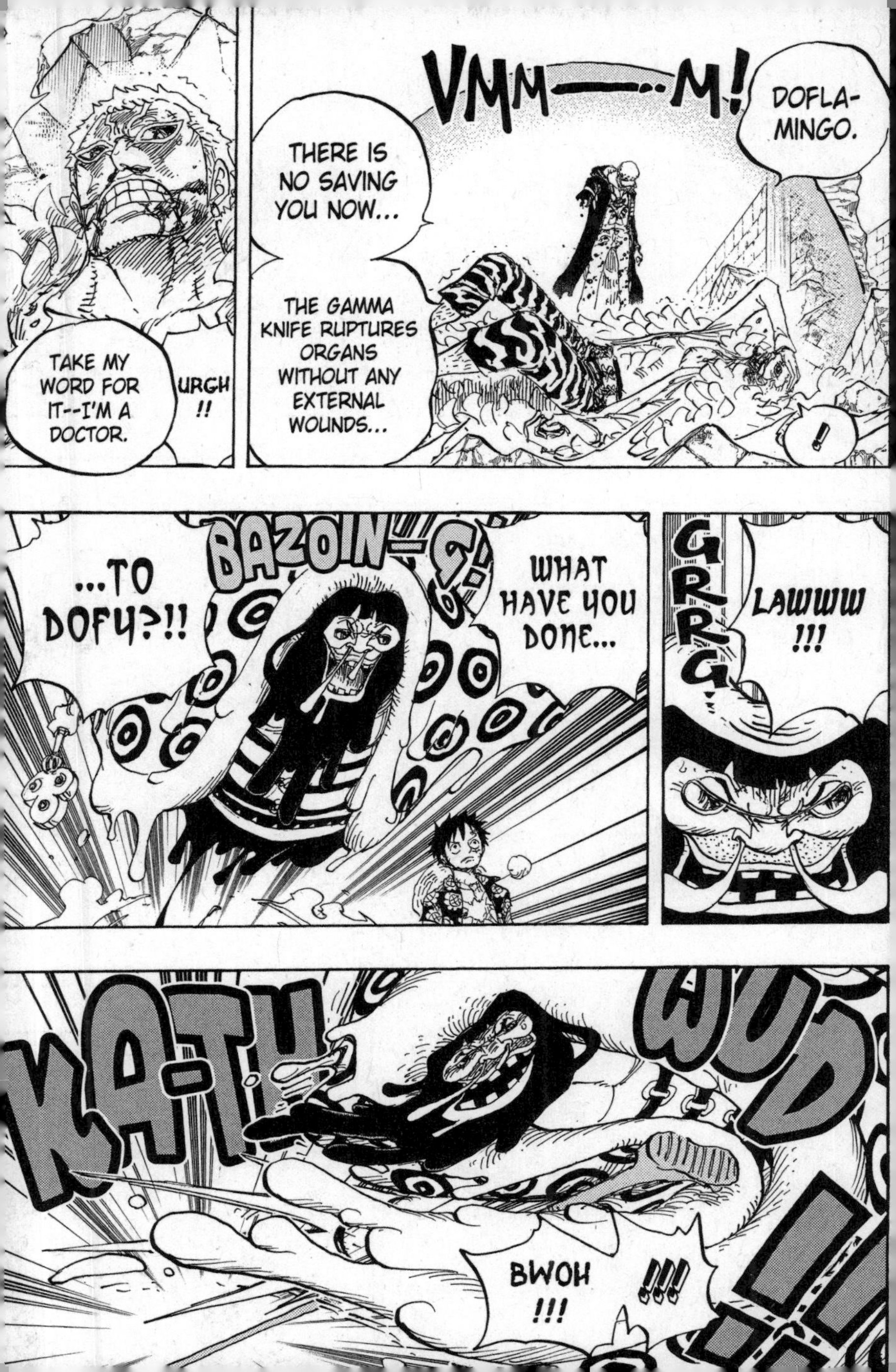
DOFLA-MINGO.
VMM———M!
THERE IS NO SAVING YOU NOW...
THE GAMMA KNIFE RUPTURES ORGANS WITHOUT ANY EXTERNAL WOUNDS...
!
URGH !!
TAKE MY WORD FOR IT--I'M A DOCTOR.
GRRRG
LAWWW !!!
WHAT HAVE YOU DONE...
BAZOIN--G!!
...TO DOFY?!!
WUD
!!
!!!
BWOH !!!
KA-TH

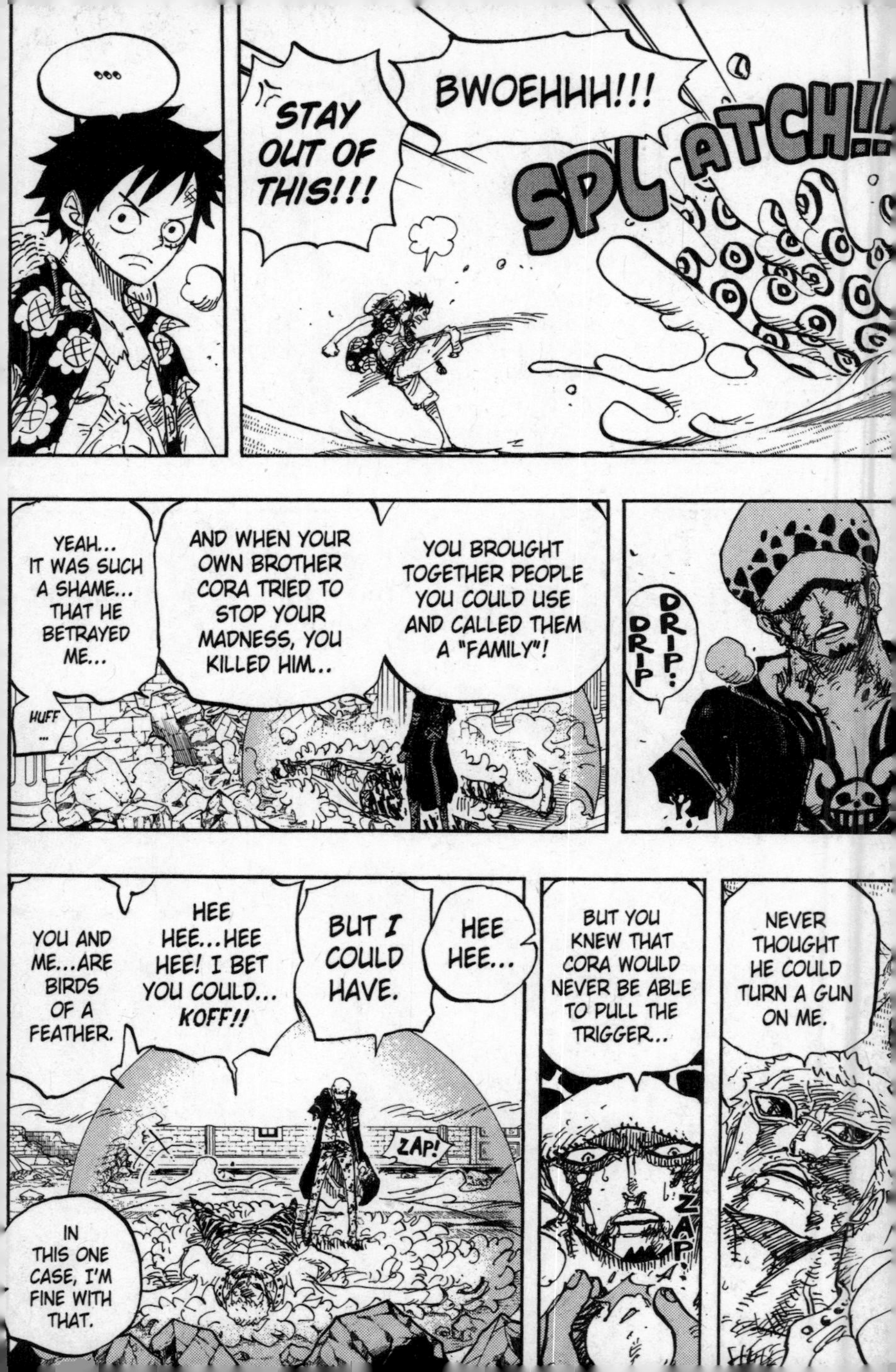
BWOEHHH!!!
STAY OUT OF THIS!!!
SPLATCH!!
...
DRIP DRIP
YOU BROUGHT TOGETHER PEOPLE YOU COULD USE AND CALLED THEM A "FAMILY"!
AND WHEN YOUR OWN BROTHER CORA TRIED TO STOP YOUR MADNESS, YOU KILLED HIM...
YEAH... IT WAS SUCH A SHAME... THAT HE BETRAYED ME...
HUFF ...
NEVER THOUGHT HE COULD TURN A GUN ON ME.
BUT YOU KNEW THAT CORA WOULD NEVER BE ABLE TO PULL THE TRIGGER...
ZAP!
HEE HEE...
BUT *I* COULD HAVE.
HEE HEE...HEE HEE! I BET YOU COULD... *KOFF!!*
YOU AND ME...ARE BIRDS OF A FEATHER.
ZAP!
IN THIS ONE CASE, I'M FINE WITH THAT.

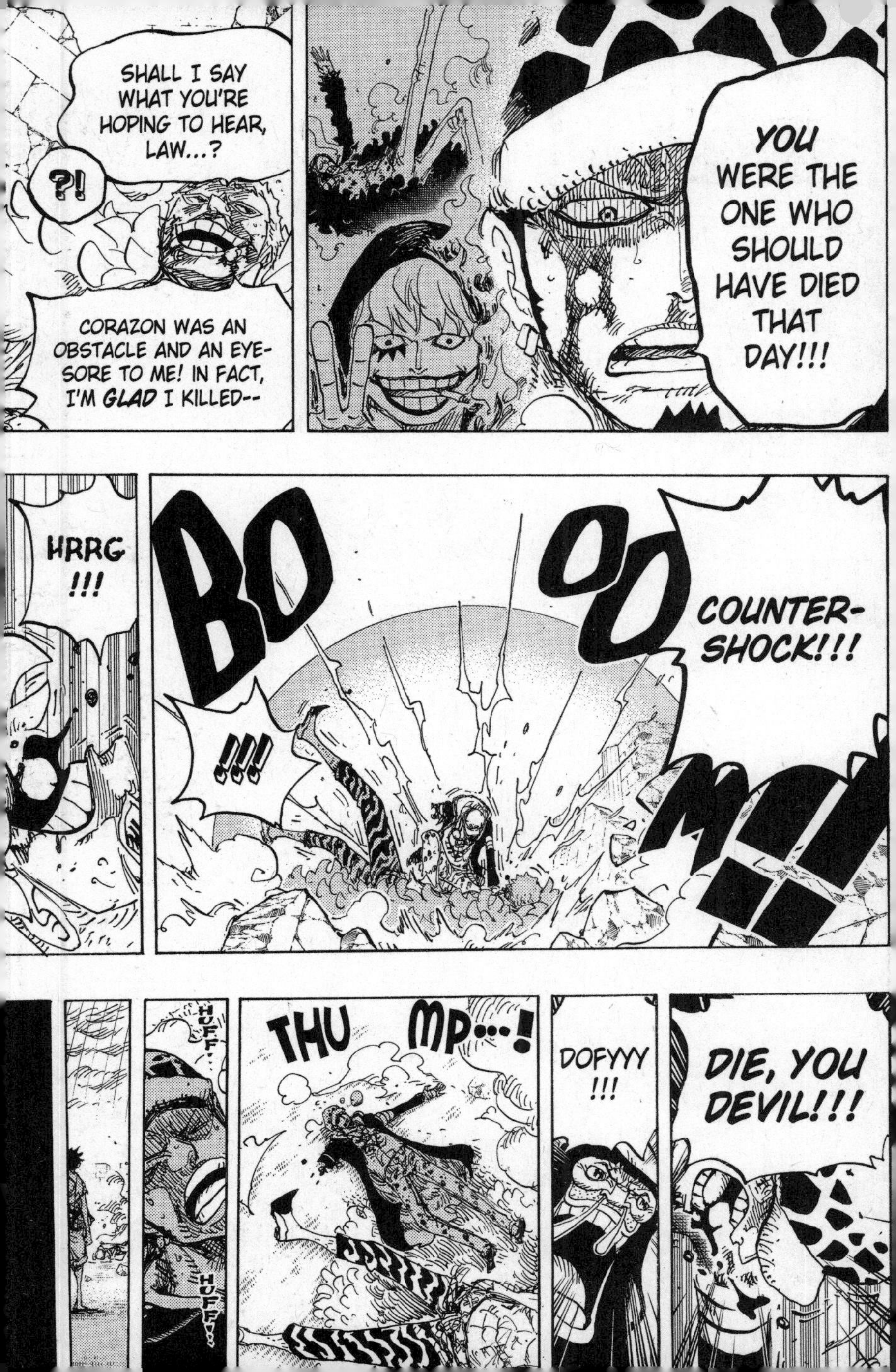
YOU WERE THE ONE WHO SHOULD HAVE DIED THAT DAY!!!
SHALL I SAY WHAT YOU'RE HOPING TO HEAR, LAW...?
?!
CORAZON WAS AN OBSTACLE AND AN EYE-SORE TO ME! IN FACT, I'M GLAD I KILLED--
BOOOM
COUNTER-SHOCK!!!
!!!
HRRG !!!
DIE, YOU DEVIL!!!
DOFYYY !!!
THUMP...!
HUFF
HUFF!!

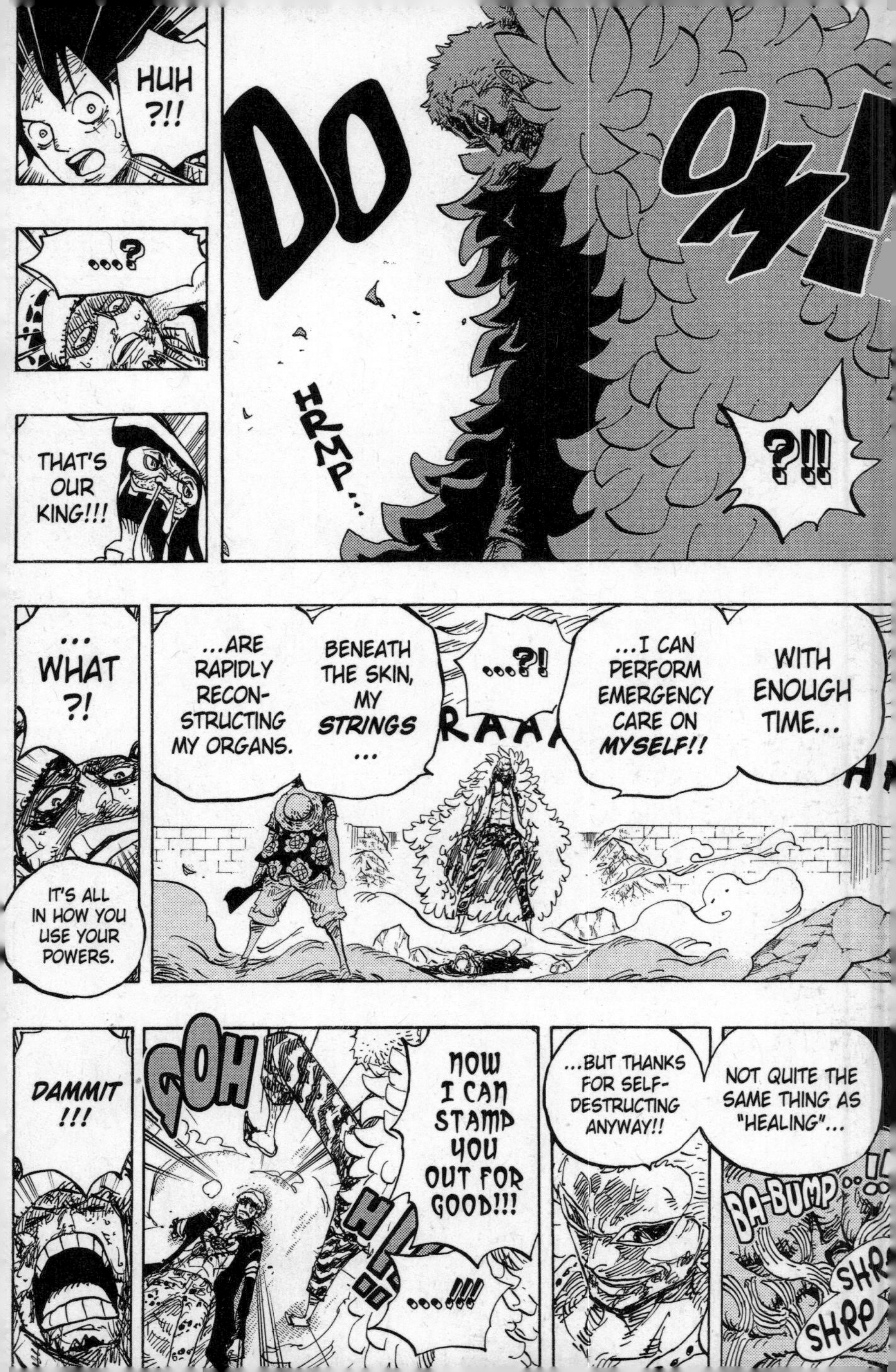
DO
OM!
?!!
HRMP...
HUH ?!!
...?
THAT'S OUR KING!!!
WITH ENOUGH TIME...
...I CAN PERFORM EMERGENCY CARE ON MYSELF!!
...?!
BENEATH THE SKIN, MY STRINGS ...
...ARE RAPIDLY RECONSTRUCTING MY ORGANS.
... WHAT ?!
IT'S ALL IN HOW YOU USE YOUR POWERS.
NOT QUITE THE SAME THING AS "HEALING"...
BA-BUMP
...BUT THANKS FOR SELF-DESTRUCTING ANYWAY!!
NOW I CAN STAMP YOU OUT FOR GOOD!!!
GOH
...!!!
DAMMIT !!!

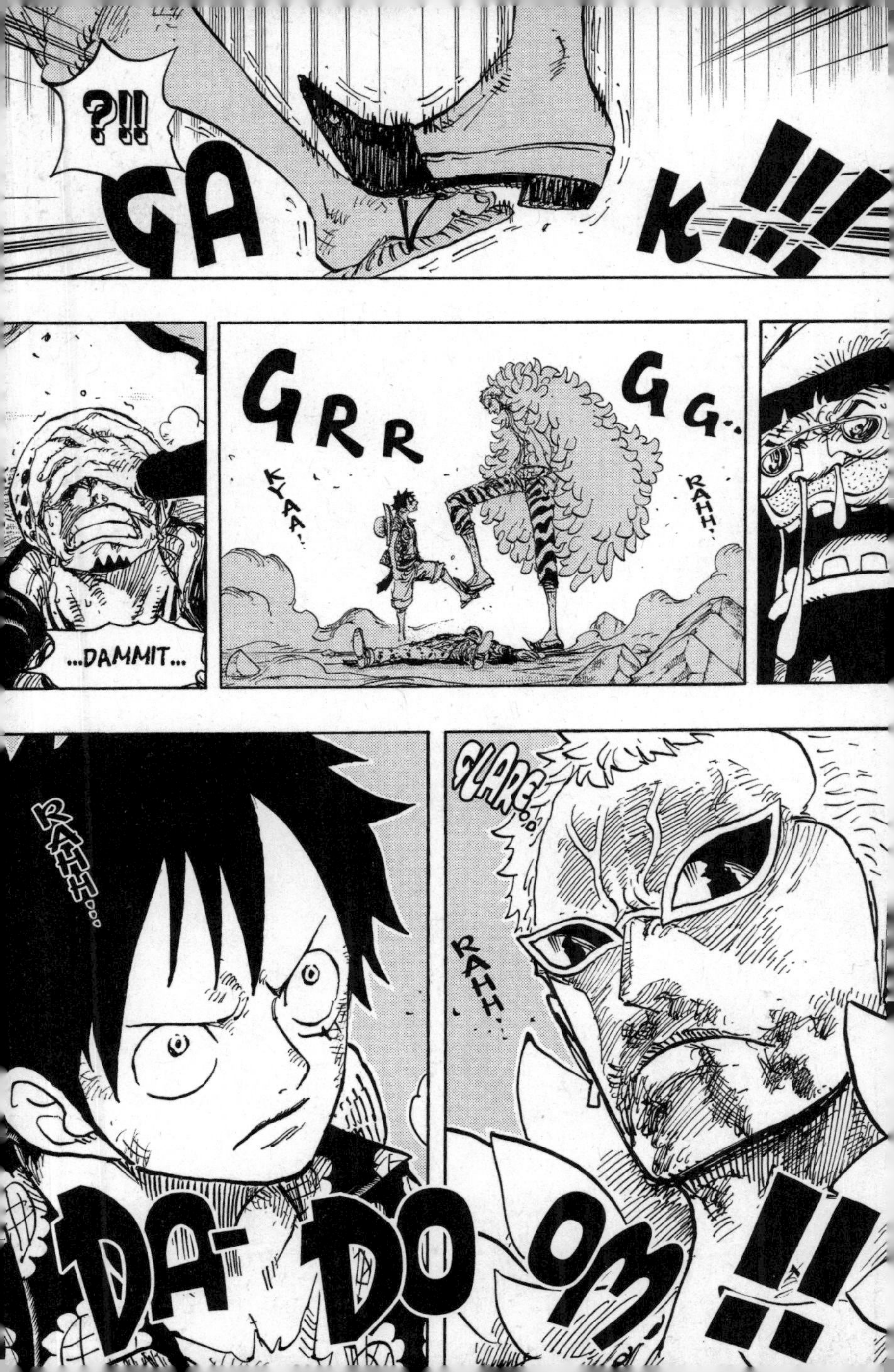
?!!
GA K!!!
GRRR GG..
RAHH!
KYAA!
...DAMMIT...
GLARE..
RAHH..
RAHH...
DA-DO-OM!!

COLORING CORNER

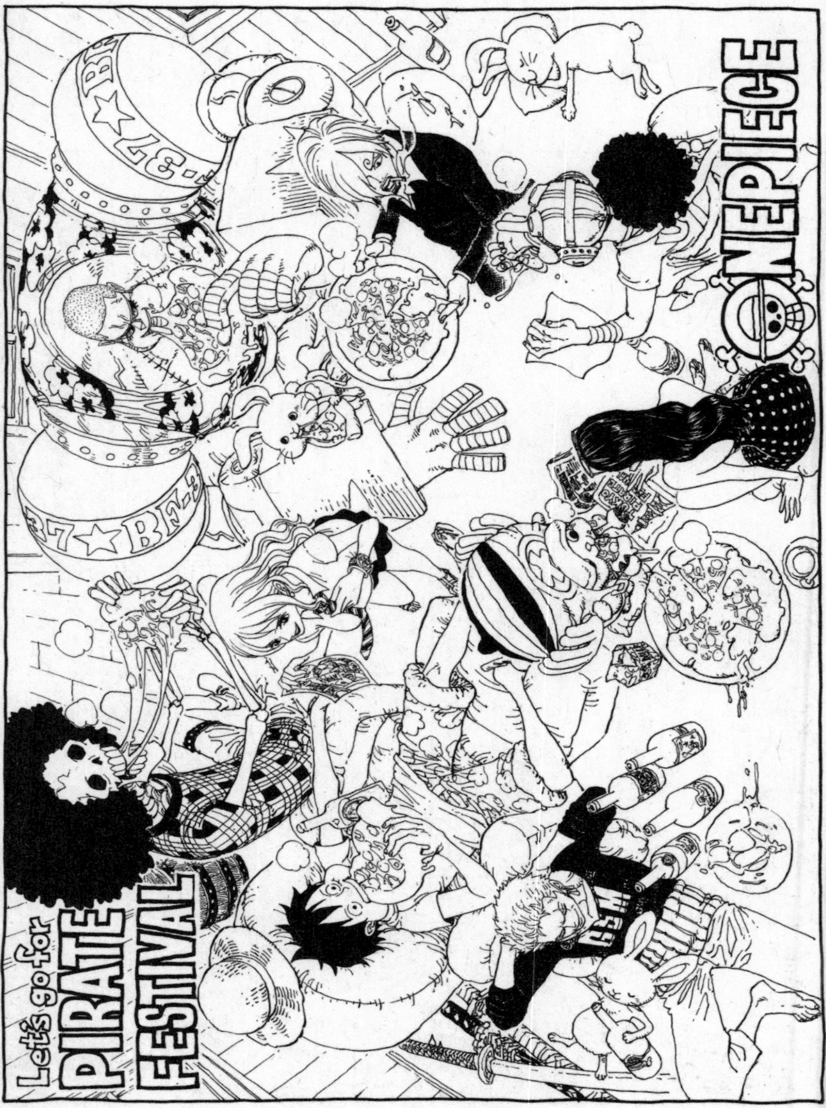

Let's go for
PIRATE
FESTIVAL
ONE PIECE

Chapter 782:
CHAMPION OF EVIL

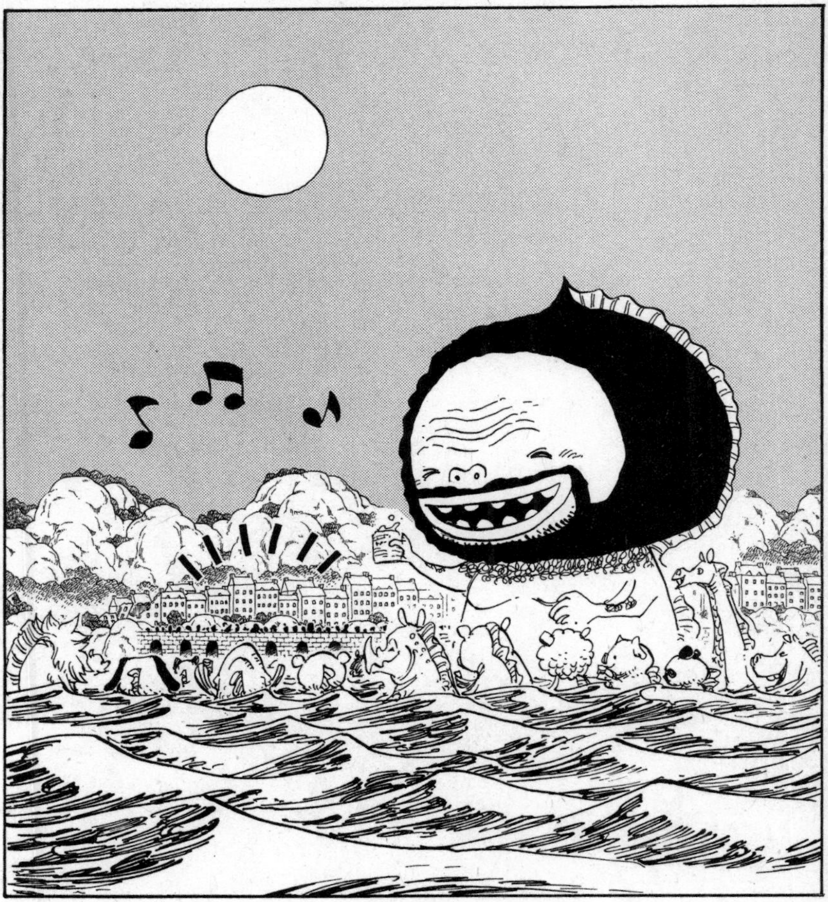

THE SOLITARY JOURNEY OF JIMBEI, FIRST SON OF THE SEA, VOL. 26: "TIME FOR A PARTY"

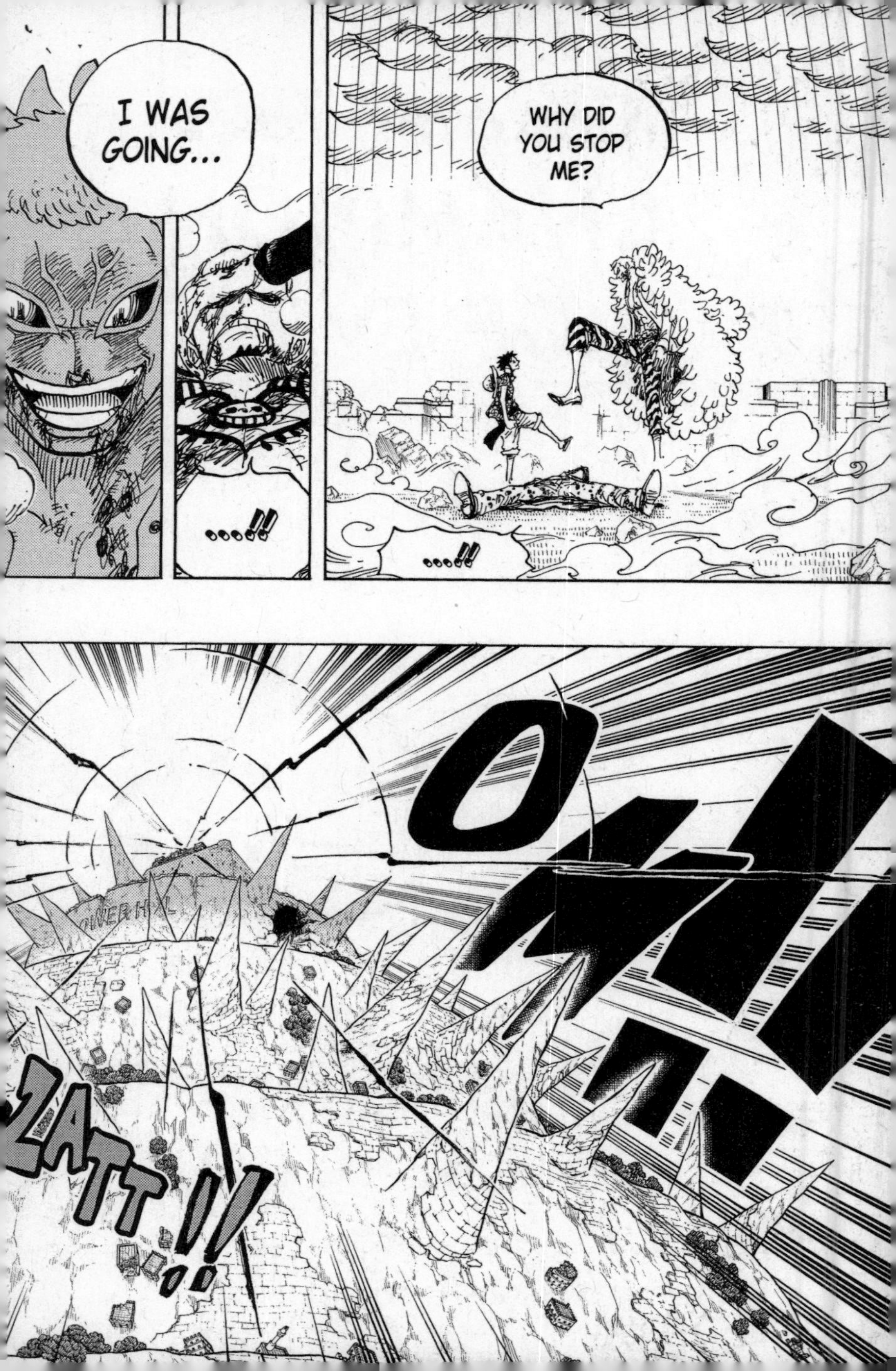
WHY DID YOU STOP ME?
....!!
....!!
I WAS GOING...
ZATT!!

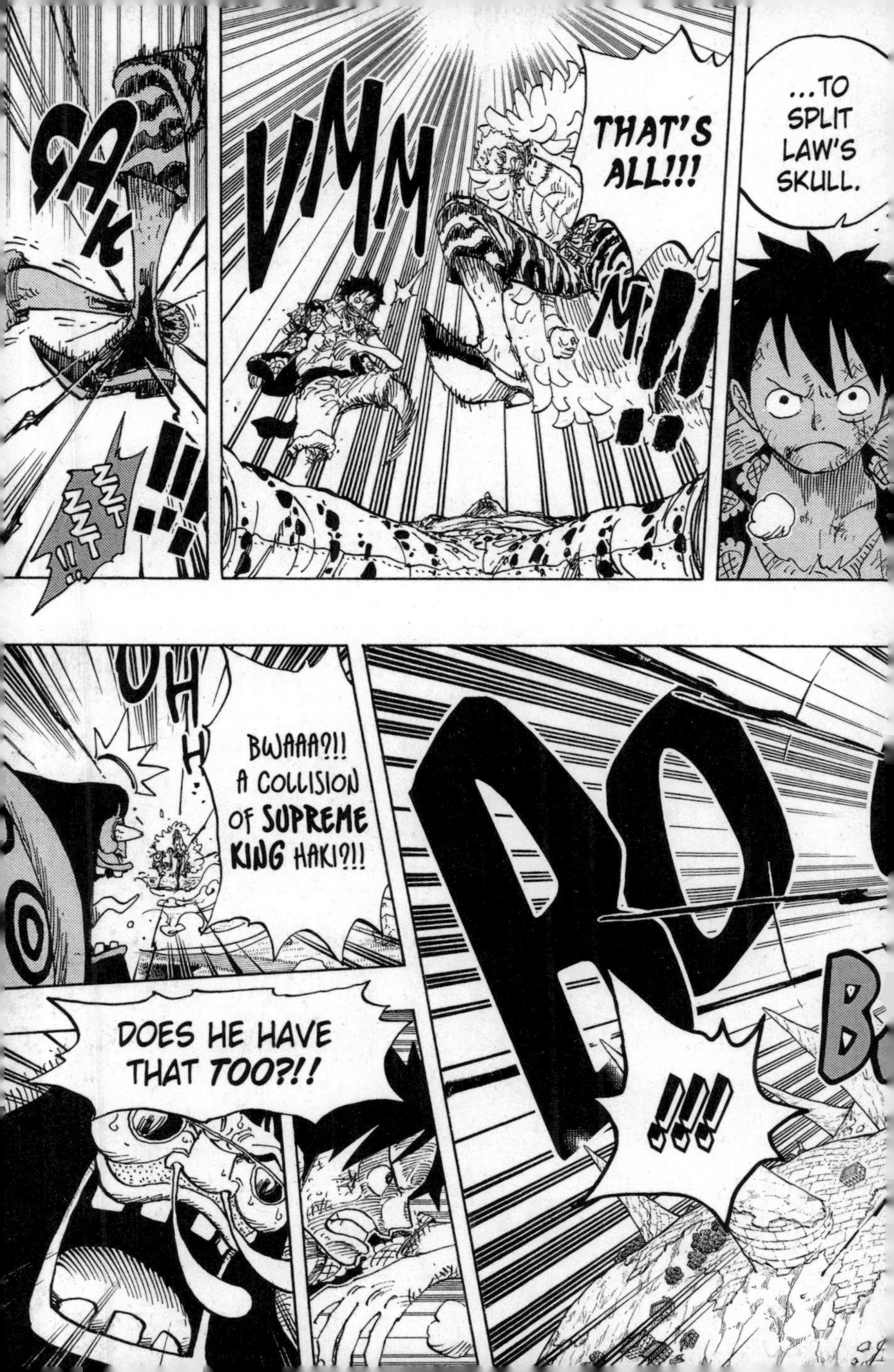
...TO SPLIT LAW'S SKULL.
THAT'S ALL!!!
VMMM!!
GAK!!!
ZZT ZZT!!
OHH
BWAAA?!! A COLLISION OF SUPREME KING HAKI?!!
DOES HE HAVE THAT TOO?!!

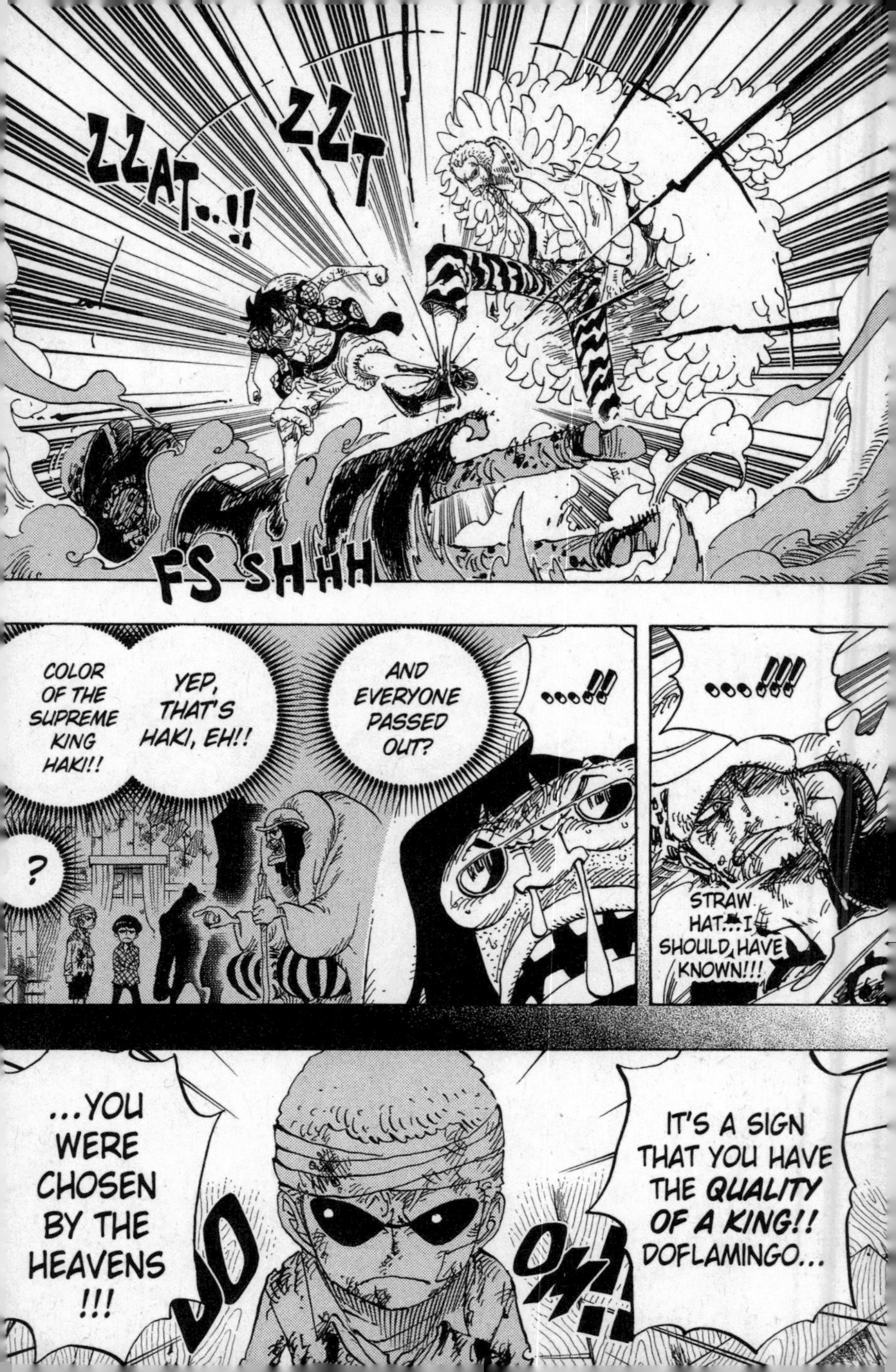
ZZT
ZZAT..!!
FS SHHH
...!!!
STRAW HAT... I SHOULD HAVE KNOWN!!!
....!!
AND EVERYONE PASSED OUT?
YEP, THAT'S HAKI, EH!!
COLOR OF THE SUPREME KING HAKI!!
?
IT'S A SIGN THAT YOU HAVE THE *QUALITY OF A KING!!* DOFLAMINGO...
DOOM!!
...YOU WERE CHOSEN BY THE HEAVENS!!!

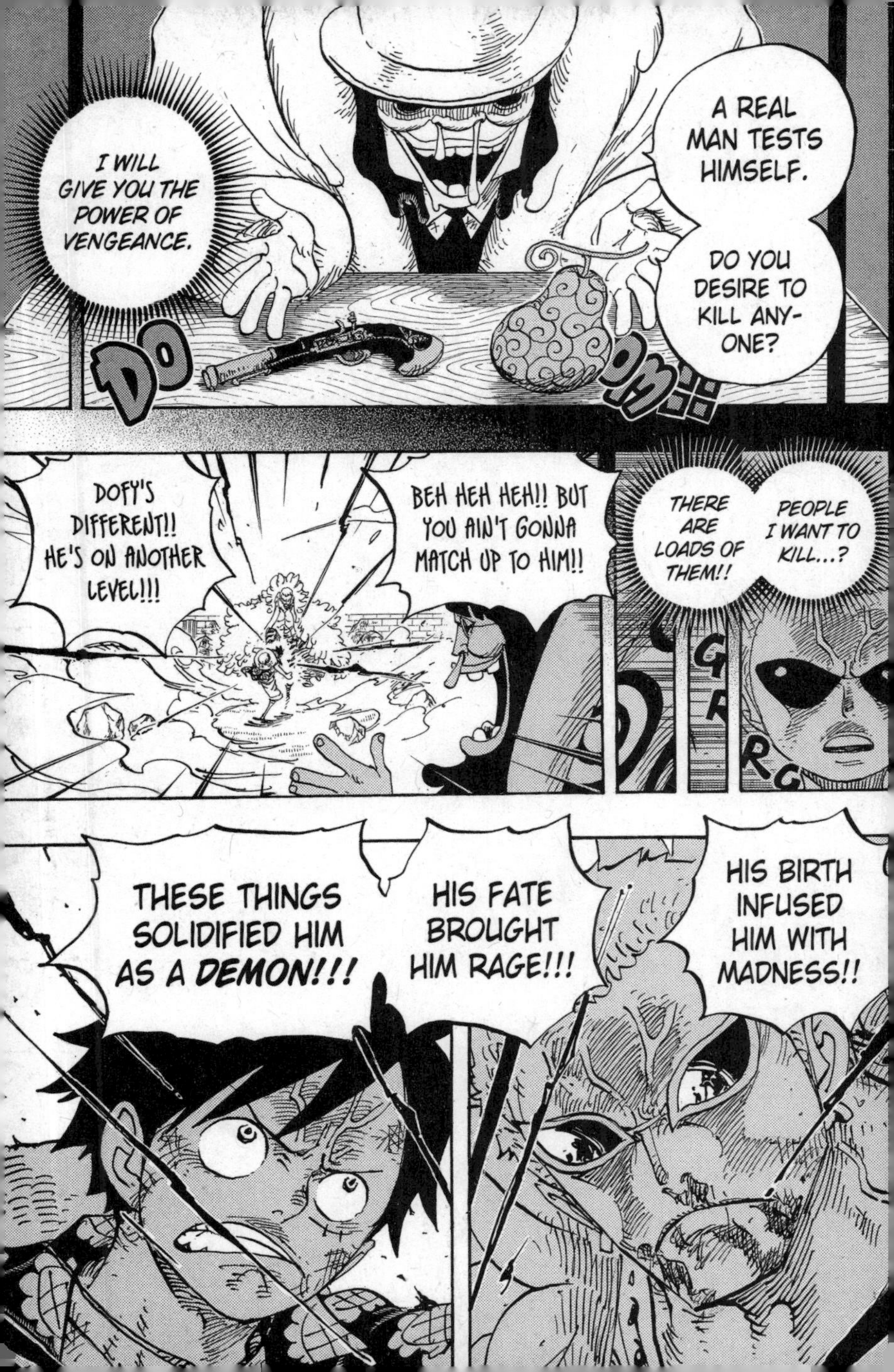
A REAL MAN TESTS HIMSELF.
DO YOU DESIRE TO KILL ANY-ONE?
I WILL GIVE YOU THE POWER OF VENGEANCE.
DOOM
PEOPLE I WANT TO KILL...?
THERE ARE LOADS OF THEM!!
GRRRG
BEH HEH HEH!! BUT YOU AIN'T GONNA MATCH UP TO HIM!!
DOFY'S DIFFERENT!! HE'S ON ANOTHER LEVEL!!!
HIS BIRTH INFUSED HIM WITH MADNESS!!
HIS FATE BROUGHT HIM RAGE!!!
THESE THINGS SOLIDIFIED HIM AS A *DEMON!!!*

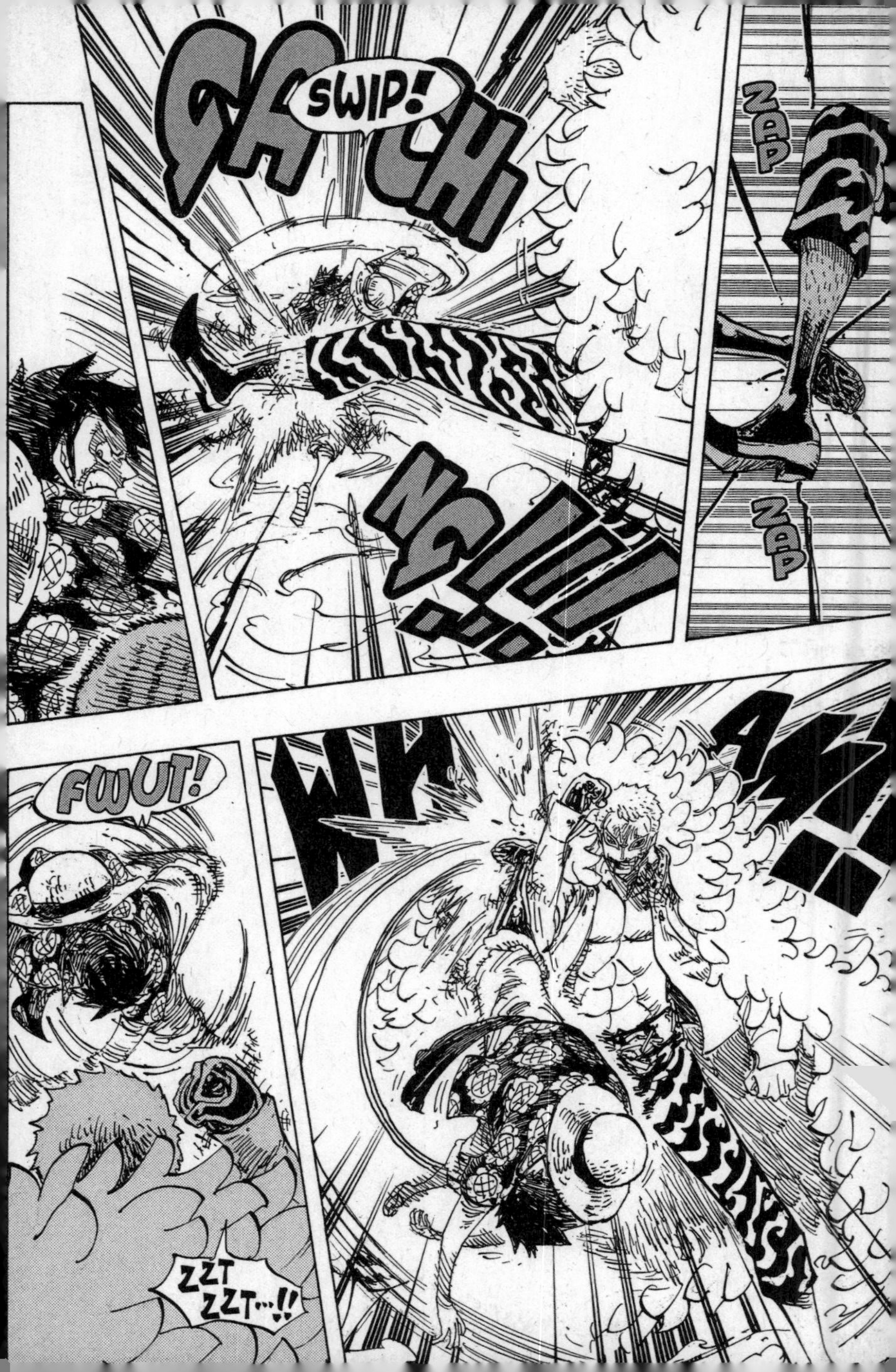
ZAP
ZAP
GACHI
SWIP!
NGUU
WHAM!!
FWUT!
ZZT ZZT…!!

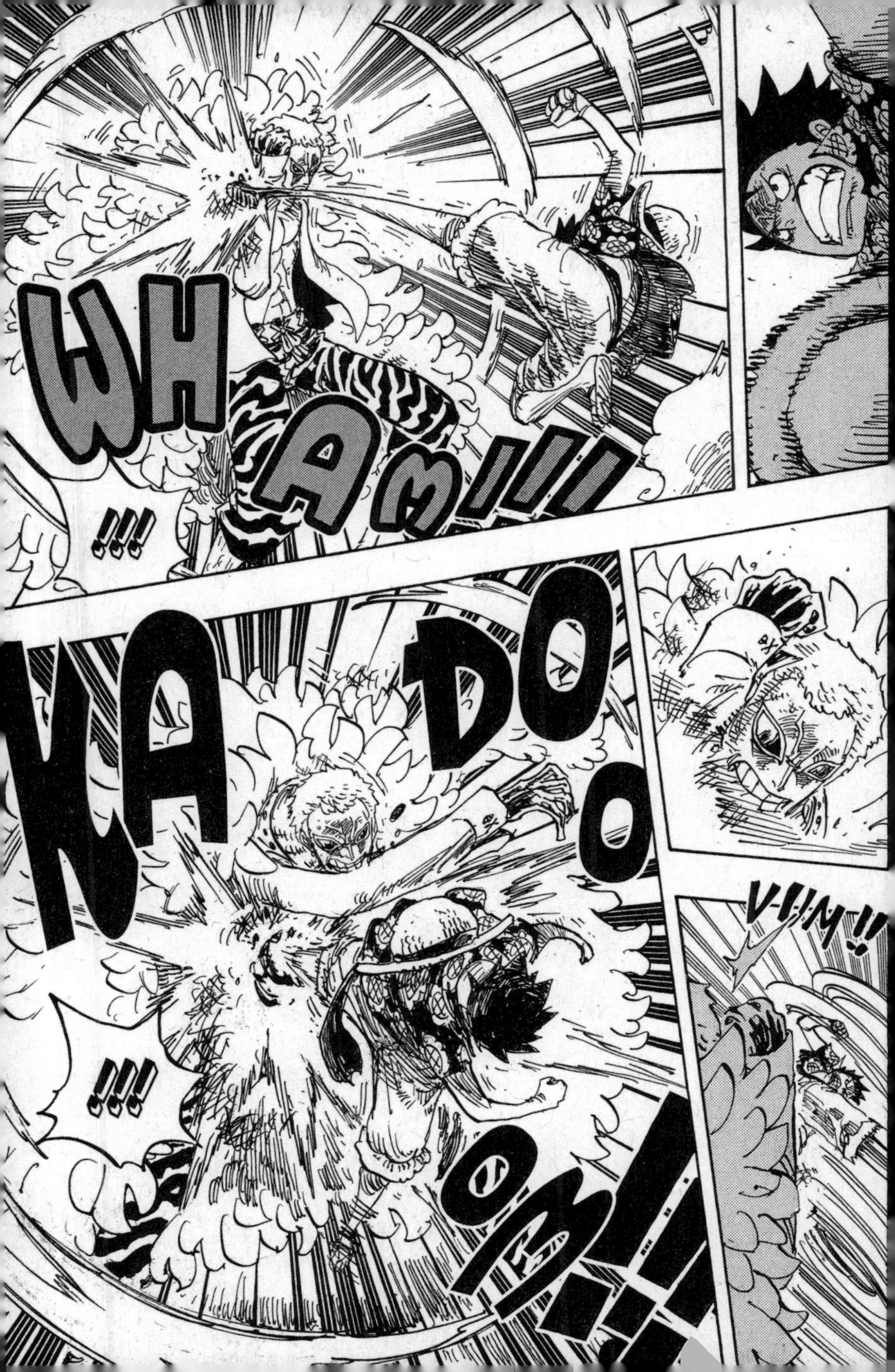

WHAM!!!
!!!
KA DOOOSH!!
V-I-M!!
!!!

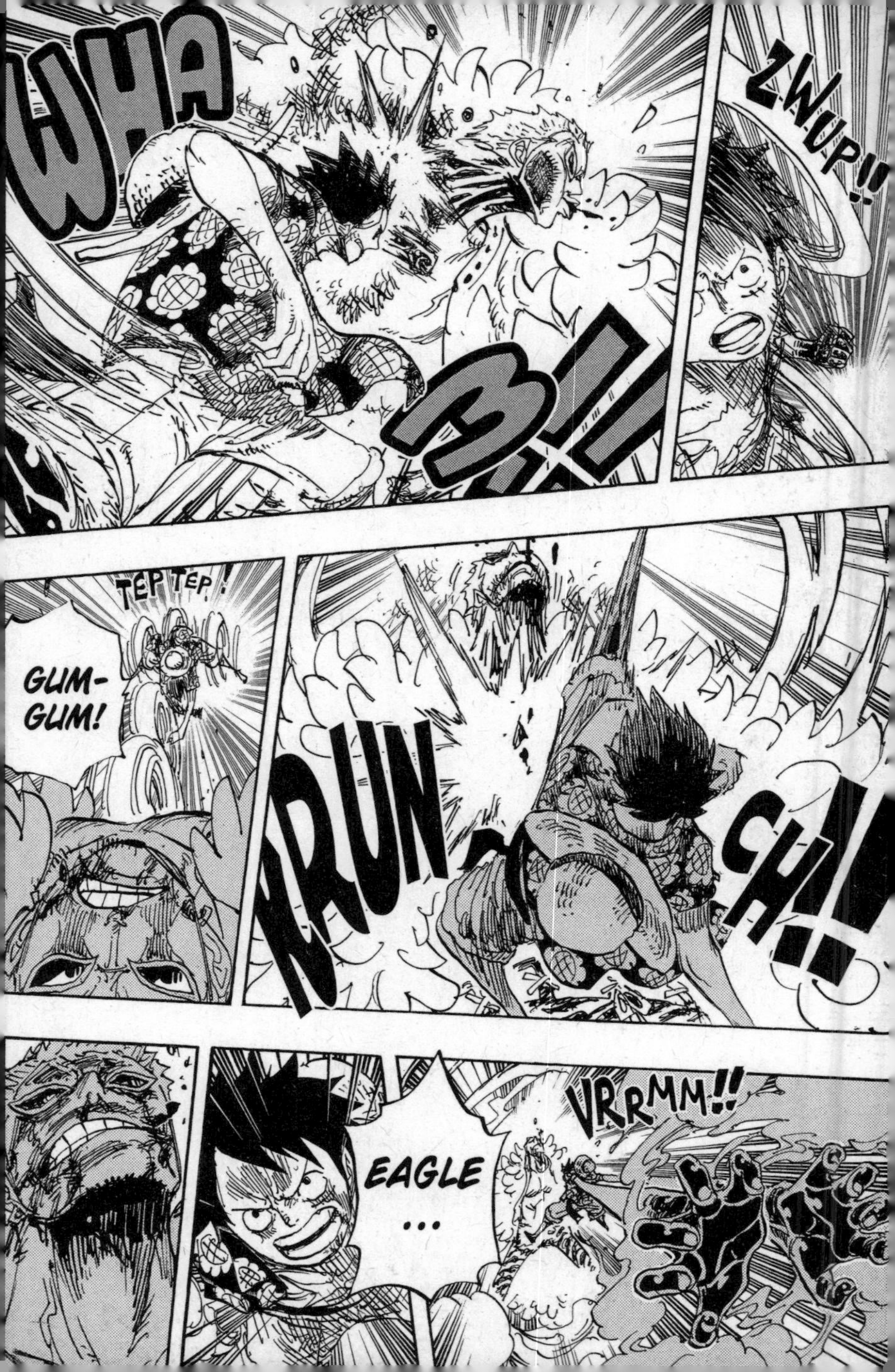
ZWUP!!
WHA
BU
KRUN
CH!!
TEP TEP!
GUM-GUM!
VRRMM!!
EAGLE
...

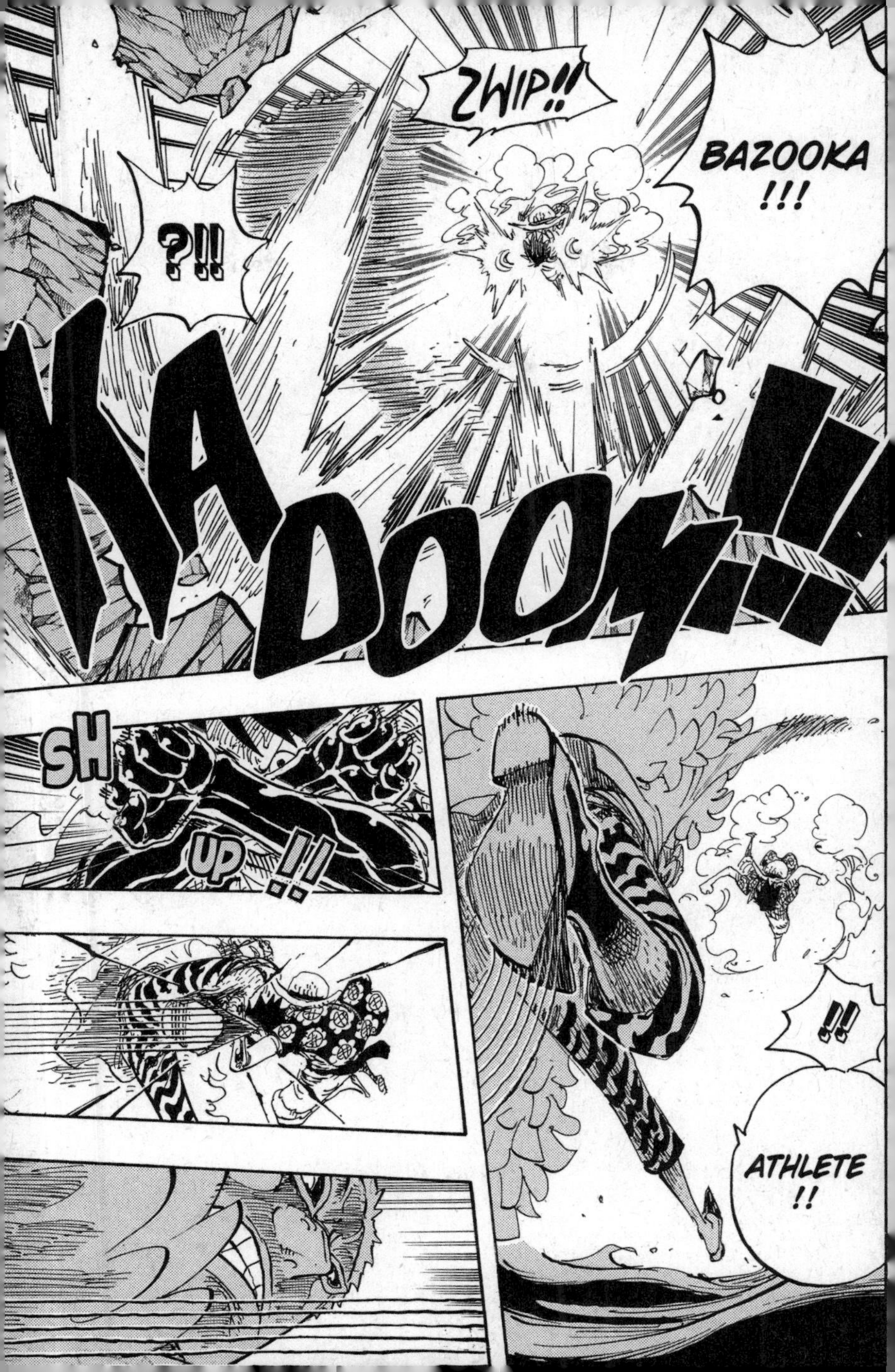

BAZOOKA !!!
ZWIP!!
?!!
KADOOM!!!
!!
ATHLETE !!
SH UP!!

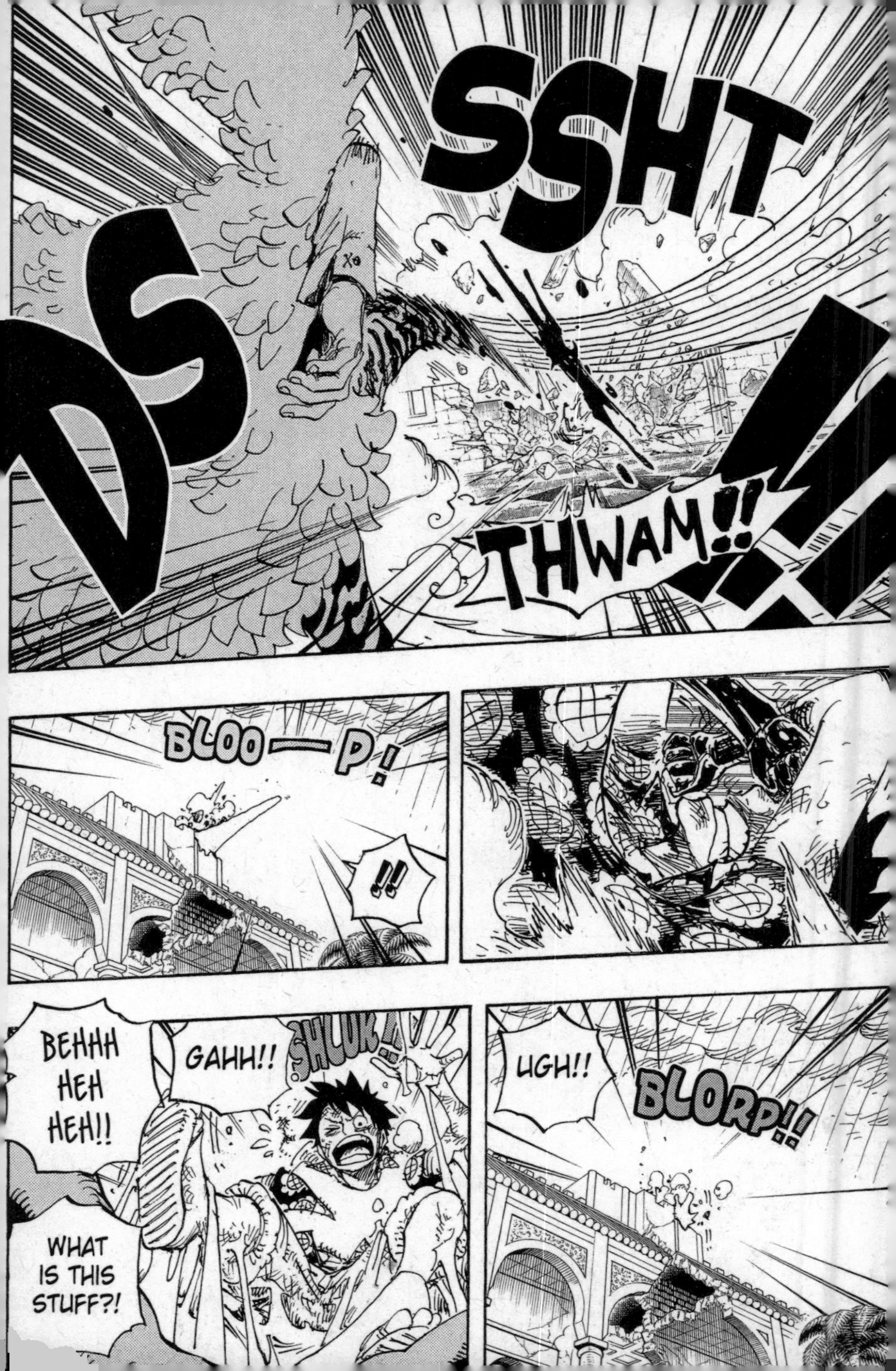
SSHT
THWAM!!
DS
BLOO—P!
!!
UGH!!
BLORP!!
SHLUK!!
GAHH!!
BEHHH HEH HEH!!
WHAT IS THIS STUFF?!

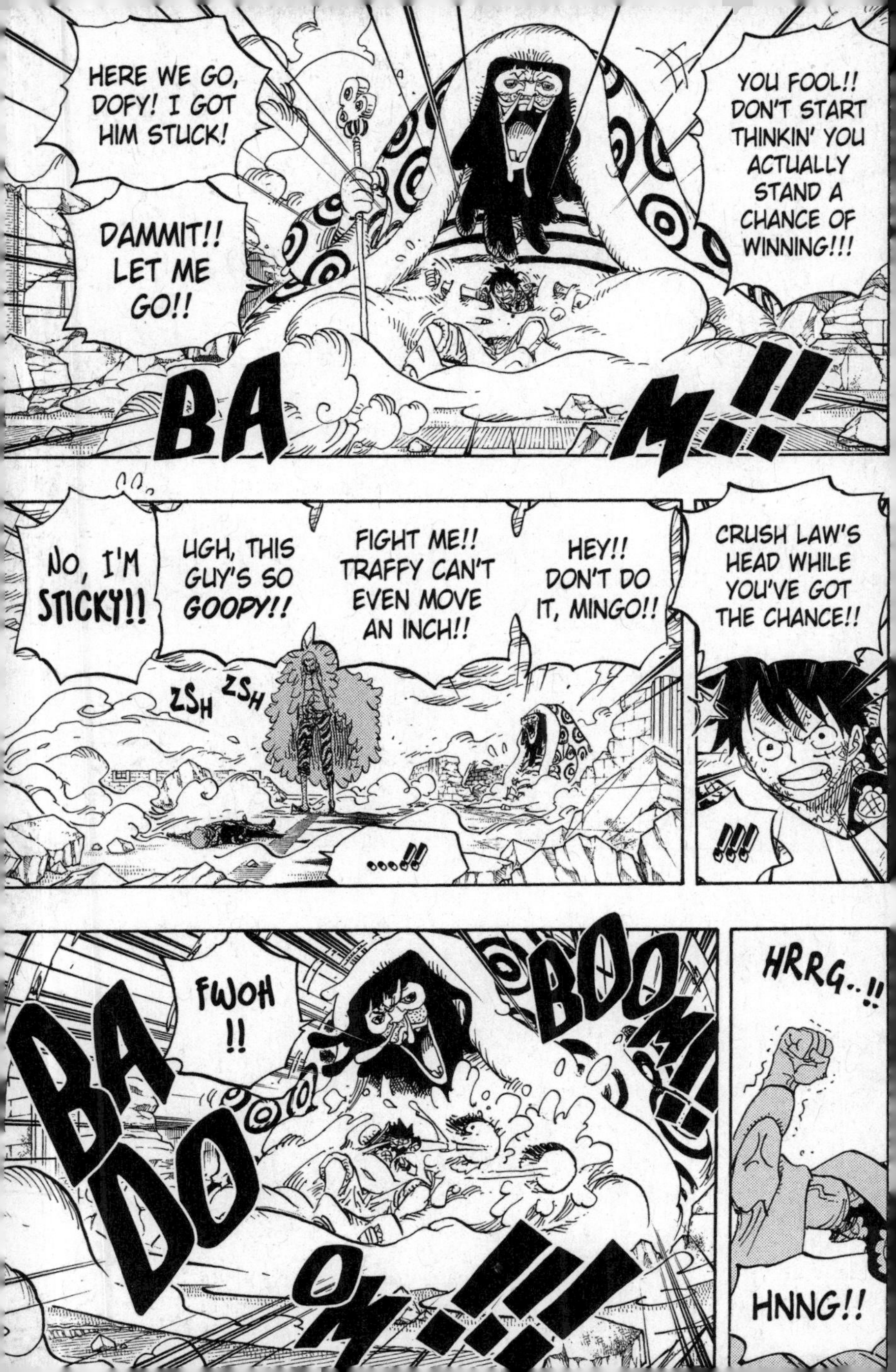
YOU FOOL!! DON'T START THINKIN' YOU ACTUALLY STAND A CHANCE OF WINNING!!!
HERE WE GO, DOFY! I GOT HIM STUCK!
DAMMIT!! LET ME GO!!
BAM!!
CRUSH LAW'S HEAD WHILE YOU'VE GOT THE CHANCE!!
!!!
HEY!! DON'T DO IT, MINGO!!
FIGHT ME!! TRAFFY CAN'T EVEN MOVE AN INCH!!
UGH, THIS GUY'S SO GOOPY!!
NO, I'M STICKY!!
ZSH
ZSH
...!!
HRRG..!!
HNNG!!
BOOM!!
FWOH !!
BADOOM!!!!!

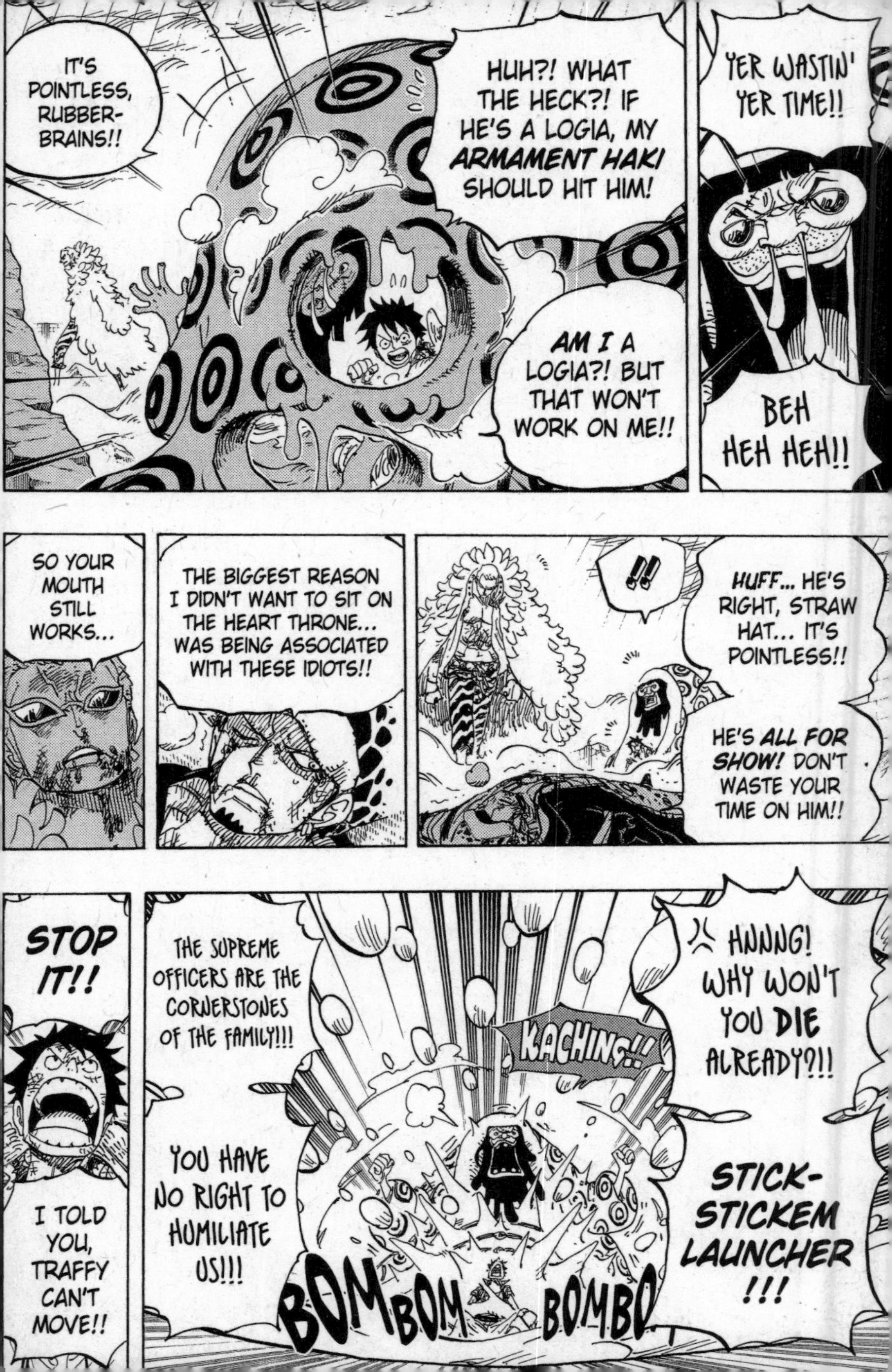
YER WASTIN' YER TIME!!
BEH HEH HEH!!
HUH?! WHAT THE HECK?! IF HE'S A LOGIA, MY ARMAMENT HAKI SHOULD HIT HIM!
AM I A LOGIA?! BUT THAT WON'T WORK ON ME!!
IT'S POINTLESS, RUBBER-BRAINS!!
!!
HUFF... HE'S RIGHT, STRAW HAT... IT'S POINTLESS!!
HE'S ALL FOR SHOW! DON'T WASTE YOUR TIME ON HIM!!
THE BIGGEST REASON I DIDN'T WANT TO SIT ON THE HEART THRONE... WAS BEING ASSOCIATED WITH THESE IDIOTS!!
SO YOUR MOUTH STILL WORKS...
HNNNG! WHY WON'T YOU DIE ALREADY?!!
KACHING!!
THE SUPREME OFFICERS ARE THE CORNERSTONES OF THE FAMILY!!!
STICK-STICKEM LAUNCHER!!!
YOU HAVE NO RIGHT TO HUMILIATE US!!!
BOM BOM BOMBO
STOP IT!!
I TOLD YOU, TRAFFY CAN'T MOVE!!

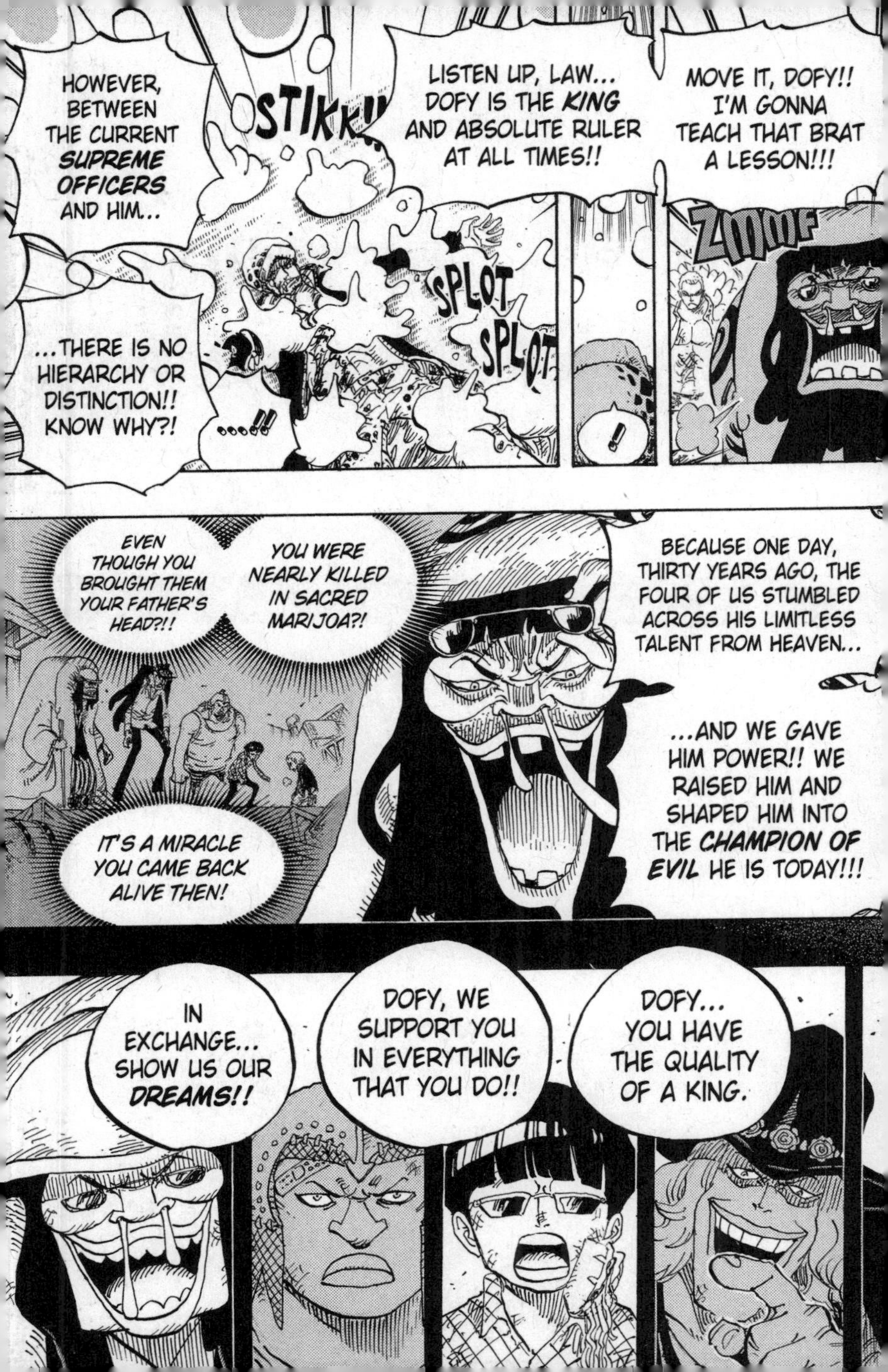
MOVE IT, DOFY!! I'M GONNA TEACH THAT BRAT A LESSON!!!
ZMMF
!
LISTEN UP, LAW... DOFY IS THE KING AND ABSOLUTE RULER AT ALL TIMES!!
HOWEVER, BETWEEN THE CURRENT SUPREME OFFICERS AND HIM...
STIKK!!
SPLOT
SPLOT
...THERE IS NO HIERARCHY OR DISTINCTION!! KNOW WHY?!
....!!
BECAUSE ONE DAY, THIRTY YEARS AGO, THE FOUR OF US STUMBLED ACROSS HIS LIMITLESS TALENT FROM HEAVEN...
...AND WE GAVE HIM POWER!! WE RAISED HIM AND SHAPED HIM INTO THE CHAMPION OF EVIL HE IS TODAY!!!
YOU WERE NEARLY KILLED IN SACRED MARIJOA?!
EVEN THOUGH YOU BROUGHT THEM YOUR FATHER'S HEAD?!!
IT'S A MIRACLE YOU CAME BACK ALIVE THEN!
DOFY... YOU HAVE THE QUALITY OF A KING.
DOFY, WE SUPPORT YOU IN EVERYTHING THAT YOU DO!!
IN EXCHANGE... SHOW US OUR DREAMS!!

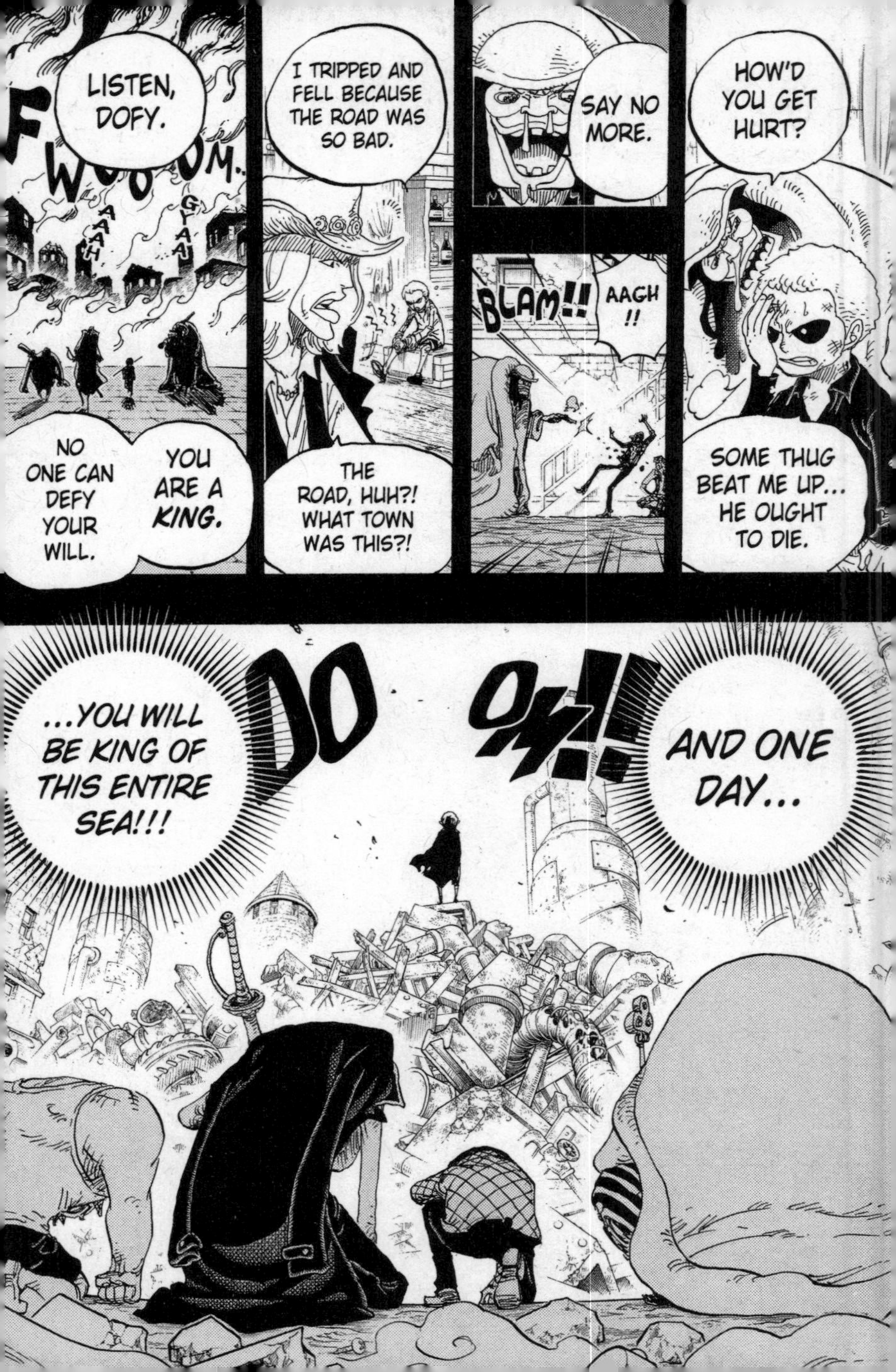
HOW'D YOU GET HURT?
SOME THUG BEAT ME UP... HE OUGHT TO DIE.
SAY NO MORE.
BLAM!!
AAGH !!
I TRIPPED AND FELL BECAUSE THE ROAD WAS SO BAD.
THE ROAD, HUH?! WHAT TOWN WAS THIS?!
LISTEN, DOFY.
FWOOOM..
GYAAA
AAAH
YOU ARE A KING.
NO ONE CAN DEFY YOUR WILL.
AND ONE DAY...
DO ON!!
...YOU WILL BE KING OF THIS ENTIRE SEA!!!

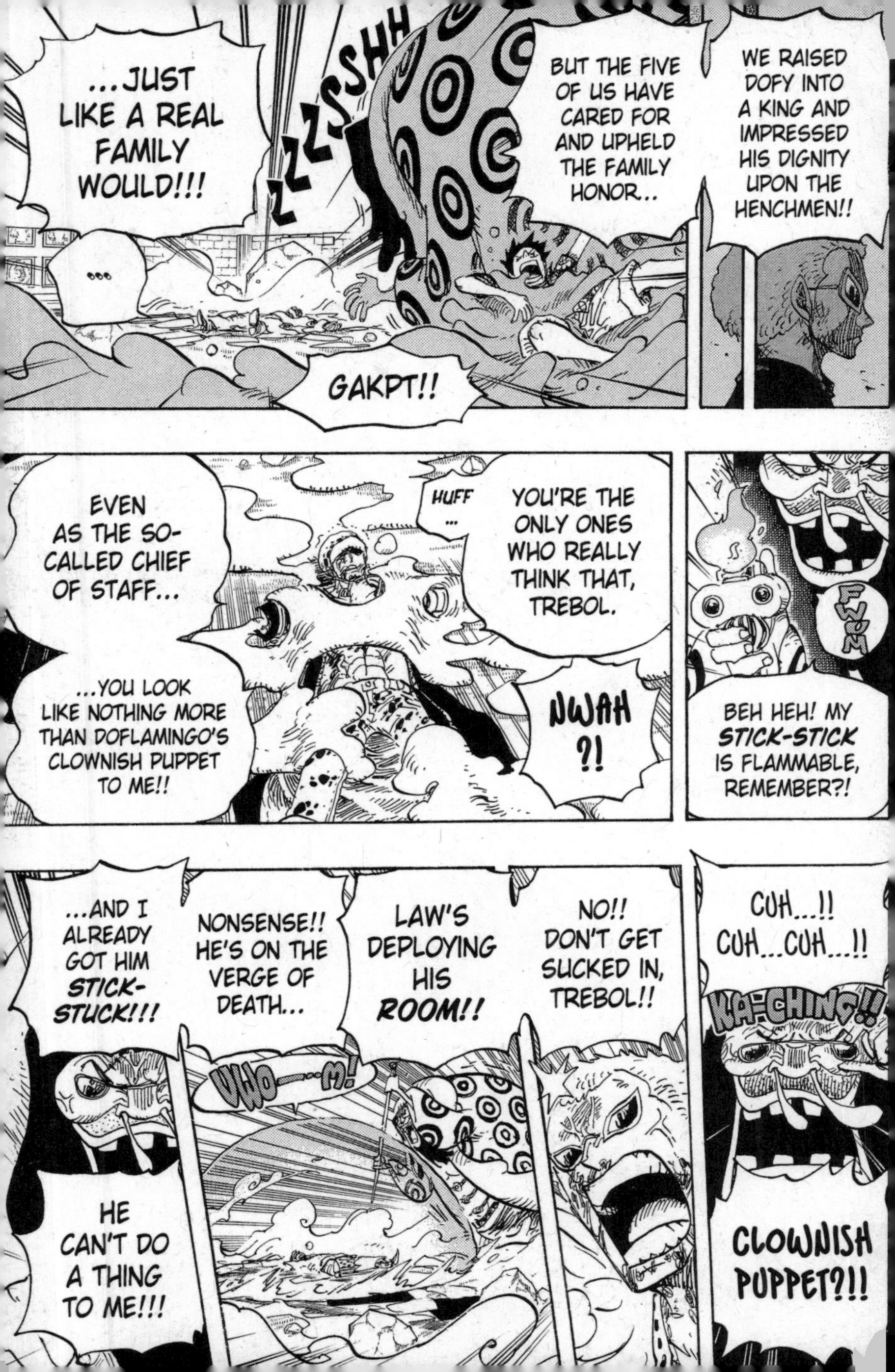
WE RAISED DOFY INTO A KING AND IMPRESSED HIS DIGNITY UPON THE HENCHMEN!!
BUT THE FIVE OF US HAVE CARED FOR AND UPHELD THE FAMILY HONOR...
...JUST LIKE A REAL FAMILY WOULD!!!
ZZZSSHH
...
GAKPT!!
FWOM
BEH HEH! MY *STICK-STICK* IS FLAMMABLE, REMEMBER?!
YOU'RE THE ONLY ONES WHO REALLY THINK THAT, TREBOL.
HUFF ...
NWAH ?!
EVEN AS THE SO-CALLED CHIEF OF STAFF...
...YOU LOOK LIKE NOTHING MORE THAN DOFLAMINGO'S CLOWNISH PUPPET TO ME!!
CUH...!! CUH...CUH...!!
KA-CHING!!
CLOWNISH PUPPET?!!
NO!! DON'T GET SUCKED IN, TREBOL!!
LAW'S DEPLOYING HIS *ROOM!!*
NONSENSE!! HE'S ON THE VERGE OF DEATH...
VHO---M!
...AND I ALREADY GOT HIM *STICK-STUCK!!!*
HE CAN'T DO A THING TO ME!!!

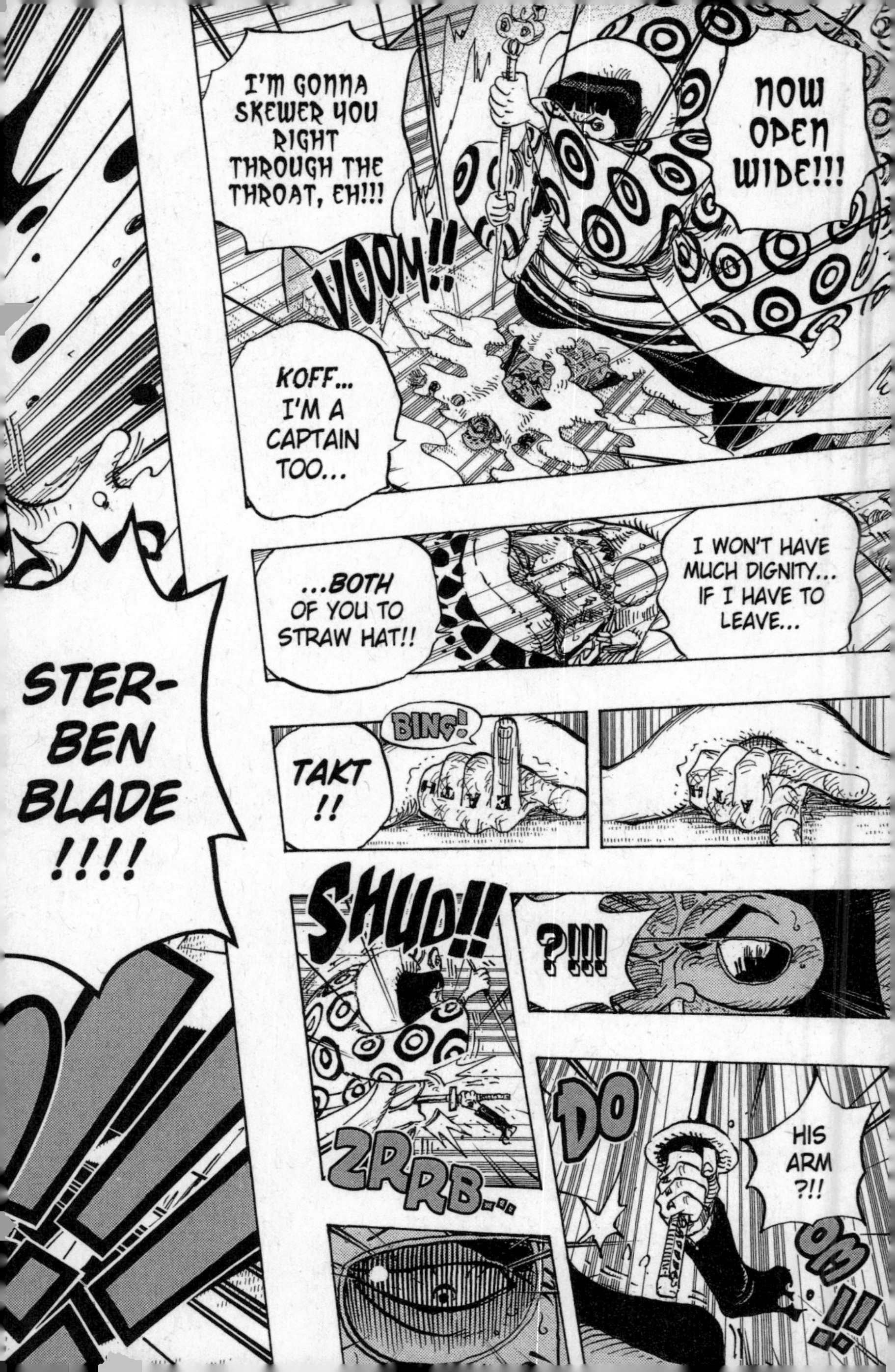
NOW OPEN WIDE!!!
I'M GONNA SKEWER YOU RIGHT THROUGH THE THROAT, EH!!!
VOOM!!
KOFF... I'M A CAPTAIN TOO...
I WON'T HAVE MUCH DIGNITY... IF I HAVE TO LEAVE...
...BOTH OF YOU TO STRAW HAT!!
BING!
TAKT !!
?!!!
SHUD!!
DO
HIS ARM ?!!
OM!!
ZRRB...
STER-BEN BLADE !!!!

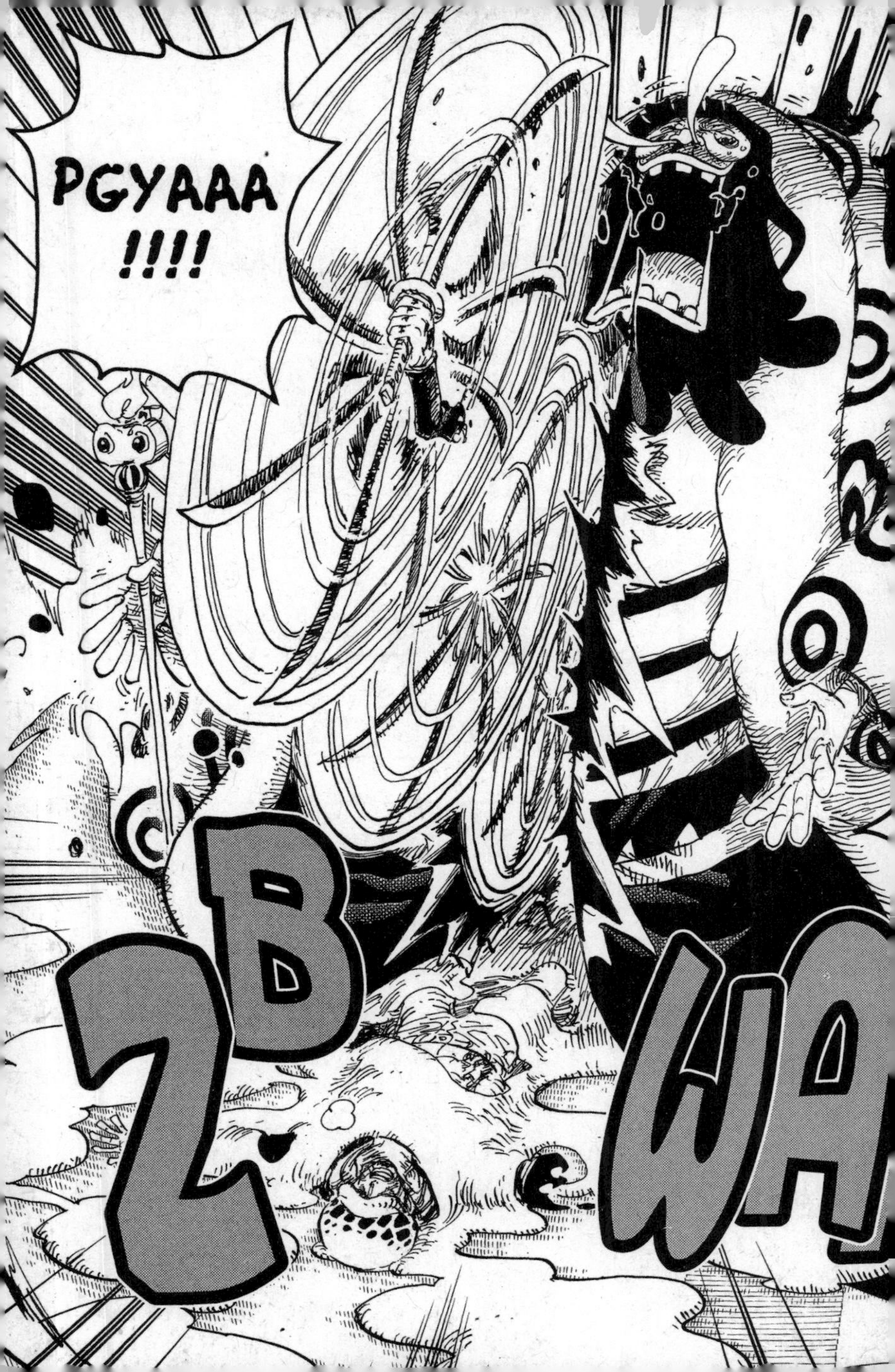
PGYAAA !!!!
ZBWA

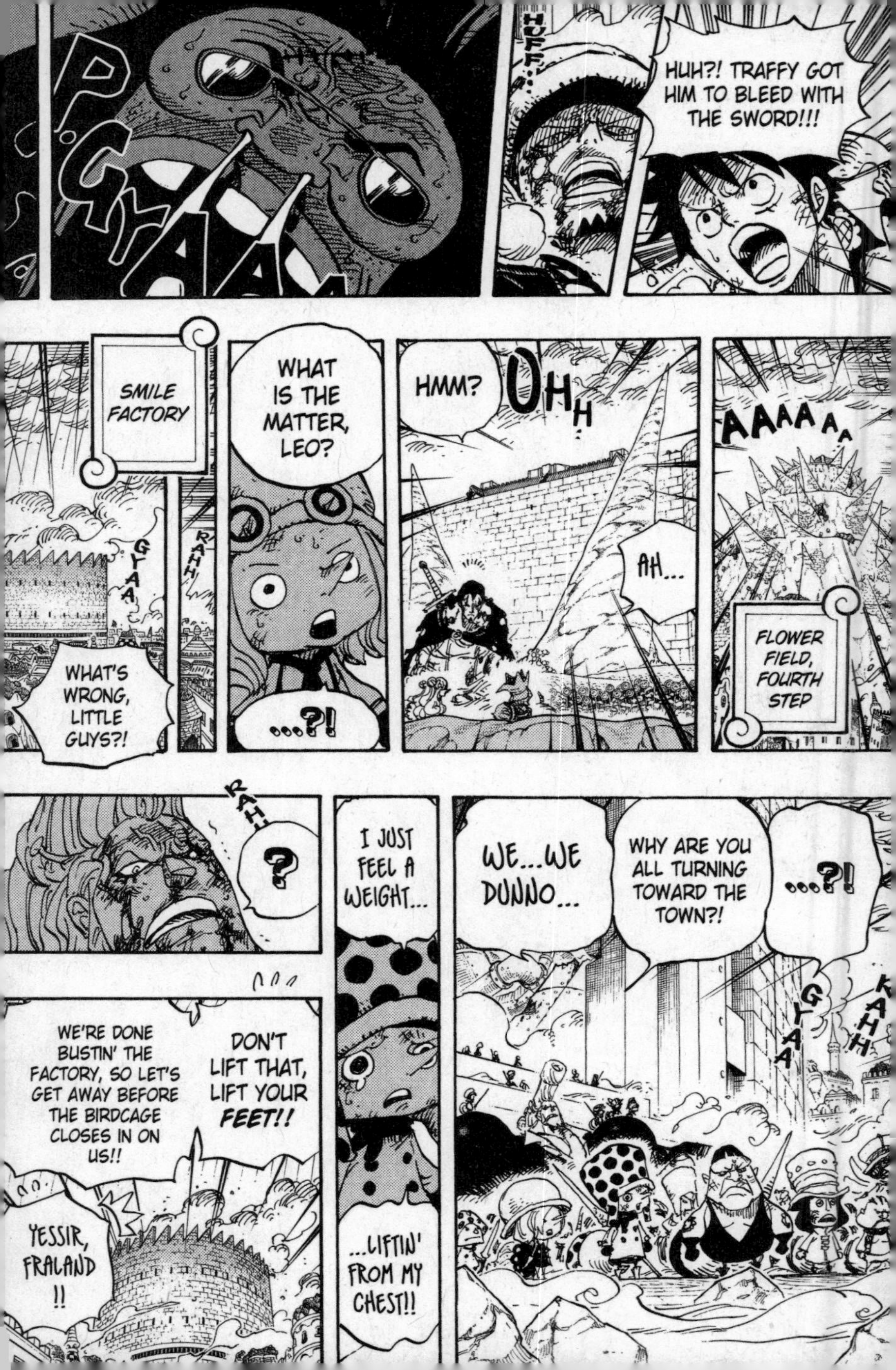
HUFF...
HUH?! TRAFFY GOT HIM TO BLEED WITH THE SWORD!!!
PGYAAA
AAAAAA
FLOWER FIELD, FOURTH STEP
OHHH
HMM?
AH...
WHAT IS THE MATTER, LEO?
...?!
SMILE FACTORY
GYAA
RAHH
WHAT'S WRONG, LITTLE GUYS?!
...?!
WHY ARE YOU ALL TURNING TOWARD THE TOWN?!
WE...WE DUNNO...
KAHH
GYAA
I JUST FEEL A WEIGHT...
...LIFTIN' FROM MY CHEST!!
RAH
?
DON'T LIFT THAT, LIFT YOUR FEET!!
WE'RE DONE BUSTIN' THE FACTORY, SO LET'S GET AWAY BEFORE THE BIRDCAGE CLOSES IN ON US!!
YESSIR, FRALAND!!

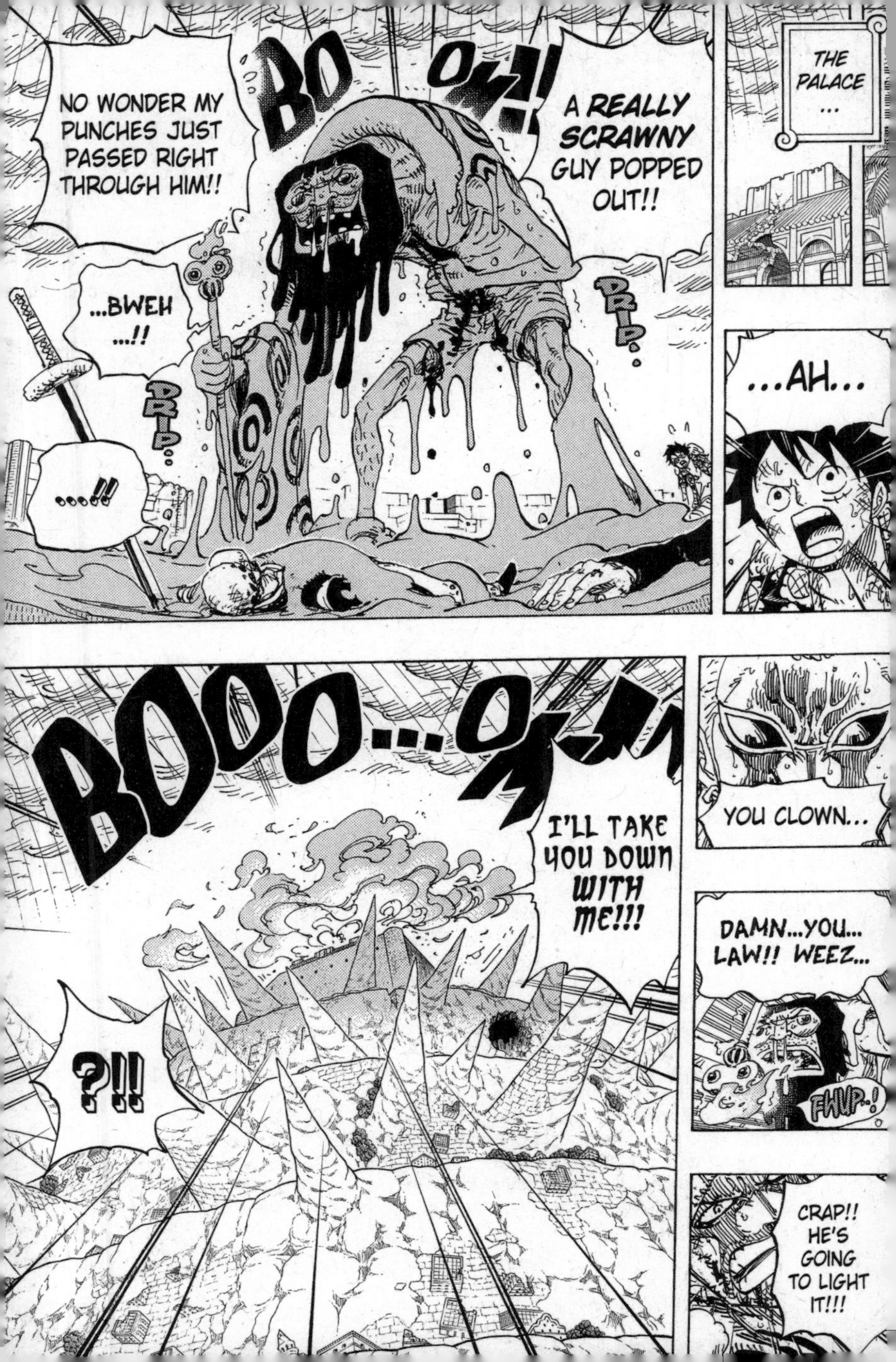

THE PALACE ...
...AH...
A REALLY SCRAWNY GUY POPPED OUT!!
BO OM!!
NO WONDER MY PUNCHES JUST PASSED RIGHT THROUGH HIM!!
DRIP
...BWEH ...!!
DRIP
....!!
YOU CLOWN...
DAMN...YOU... LAW!! WEEZ...
FWIP!
CRAP!! HE'S GOING TO LIGHT IT!!!
I'LL TAKE YOU DOWN WITH ME!!!
BOOO...OM
?!!

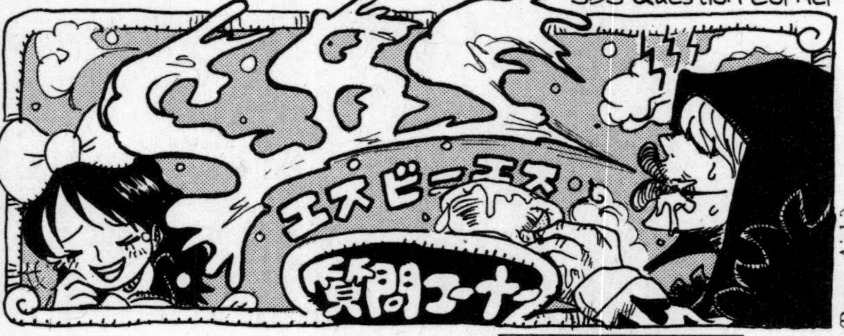
エスビーエス
質問コーナー
(Penae, Aichi)

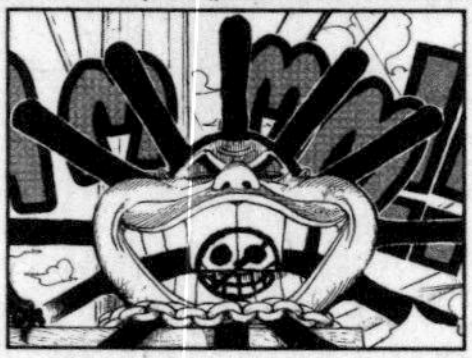

Q: Does Buffalo style that crazy hair himself every morning?
--No. 73

A: It's a cowlick.

Q: The boy named Drie working in the pirate Barrels' crew is actually X. Drake of the Drake Pirates, right?! I figured it out from the X (pronounced "Diez") name, the scar on his chin, and their home in the North Blue. Does that mean Barrels is Drake's father?
--Kazuki from Hyogo

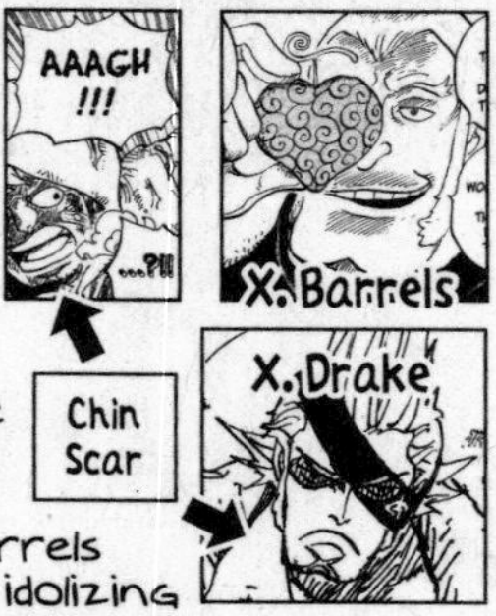
X. Barrels
AAAGH !!!
...?!!
Chin Scar
X. Drake

A: That's right!! Well spotted. X. Drake is one of the "Worst Generation" pirates who are stirring up the world alongside Luffy. His father Barrels was a Naval officer, and he grew up idolizing his pops and dreaming of being in the Navy. But something happened, and Barrels went pirate, turning into a terrible man who abused his son. At this time (13 and a half years ago) Drake was 19, and still following along because he believed in the father he remembered from his youth. He's a bit too big to be considered a "boy," but he looks younger than he is because he's so intimidated by his father. Through his fateful, accidental near miss with Law, he ends up taken in by the Navy, and he becomes a sailor. But through some quirk of fate, Drake moves up the ranks to an officer, and then leaves to become a pirate, just like his father!! What happened to him?! What is he thinking?! What's the big deal, mister?! After his appearance on the cover page story, it really makes you curious what X. Drake is going to do next!!

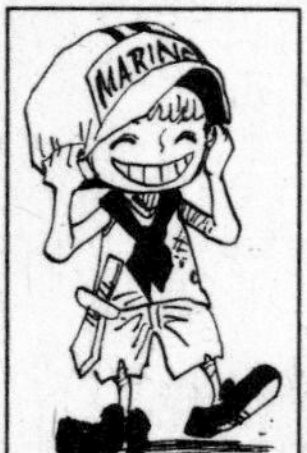

Chapter 783:
IN MY WAY

THE SOLITARY JOURNEY OF JIMBEI, FIRST SON OF THE SEA, VOL. 27: "I WADDA GO WIF YOU"

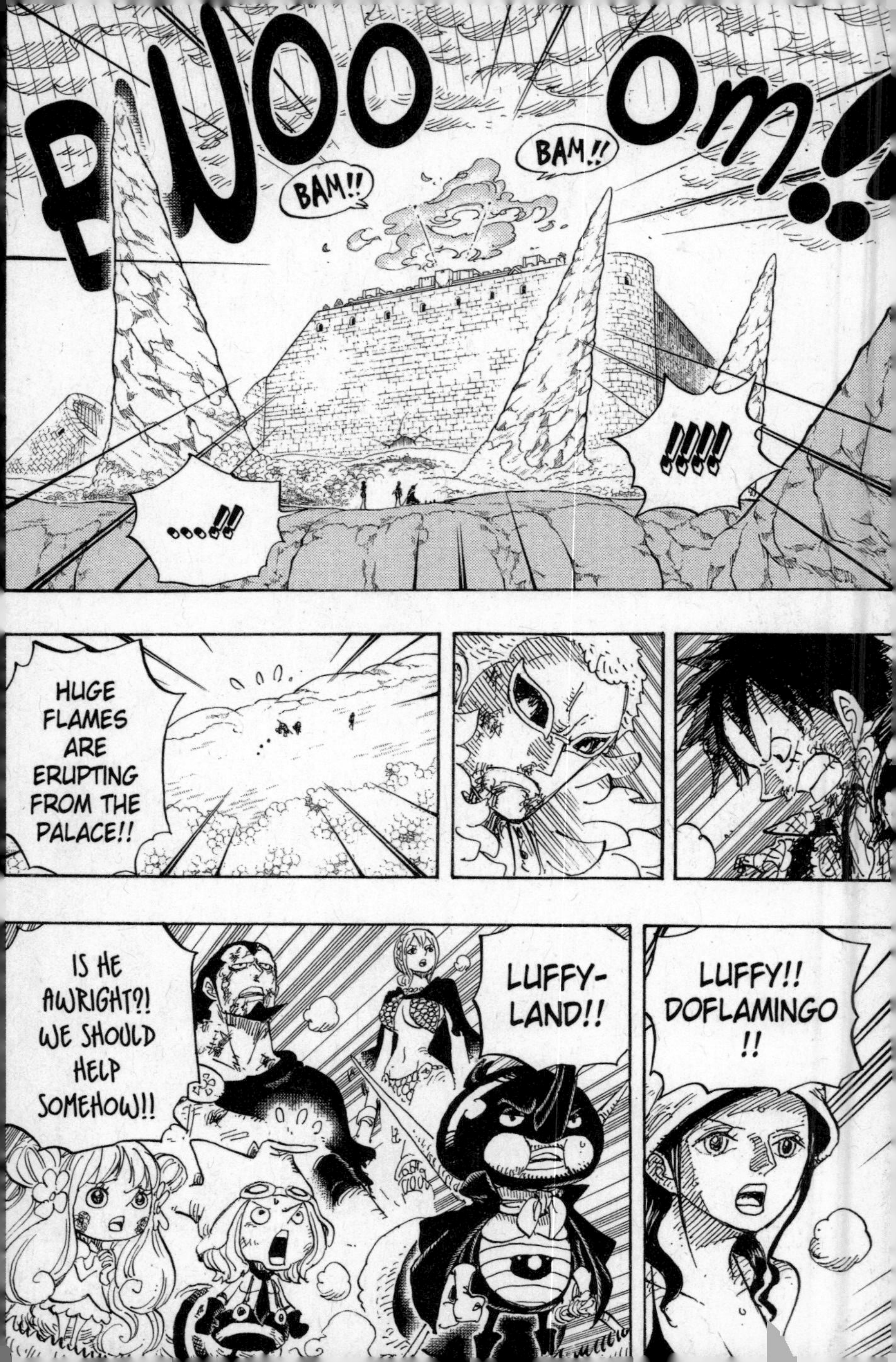
BWOOOM!!
BAM!!
BAM!!
!!!!
....!!
HUGE FLAMES ARE ERUPTING FROM THE PALACE!!
LUFFY!! DOFLAMINGO!!
LUFFY-LAND!!
IS HE AWRIGHT?! WE SHOULD HELP SOMEHOW!!

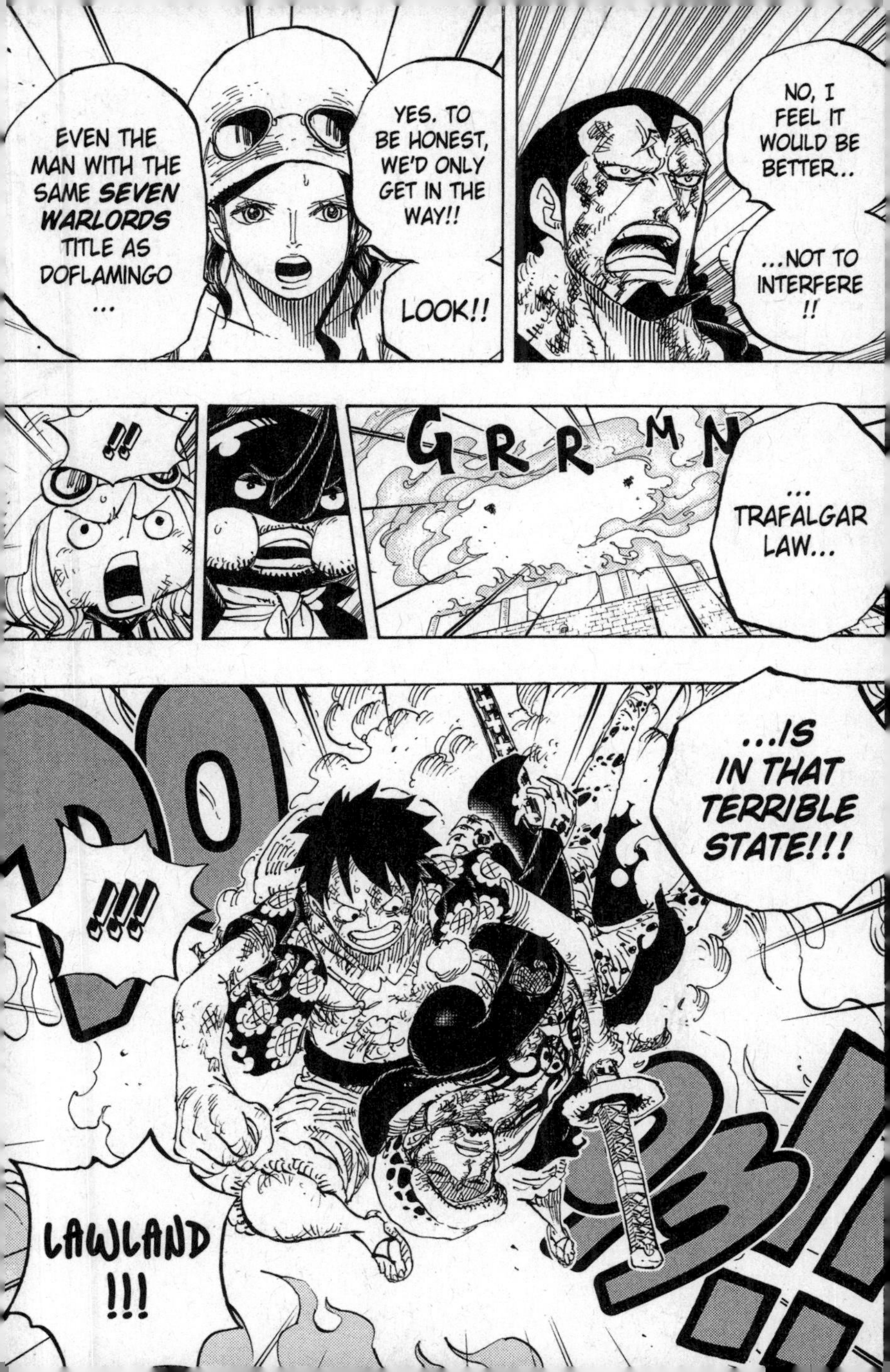

NO, I FEEL IT WOULD BE BETTER...
...NOT TO INTERFERE!!
YES. TO BE HONEST, WE'D ONLY GET IN THE WAY!!
EVEN THE MAN WITH THE SAME **SEVEN WARLORDS** TITLE AS DOFLAMINGO...
LOOK!!
GRRRMN
...TRAFALGAR LAW...
!!
...IS IN THAT TERRIBLE STATE!!!
!!!
LAWLAND!!!

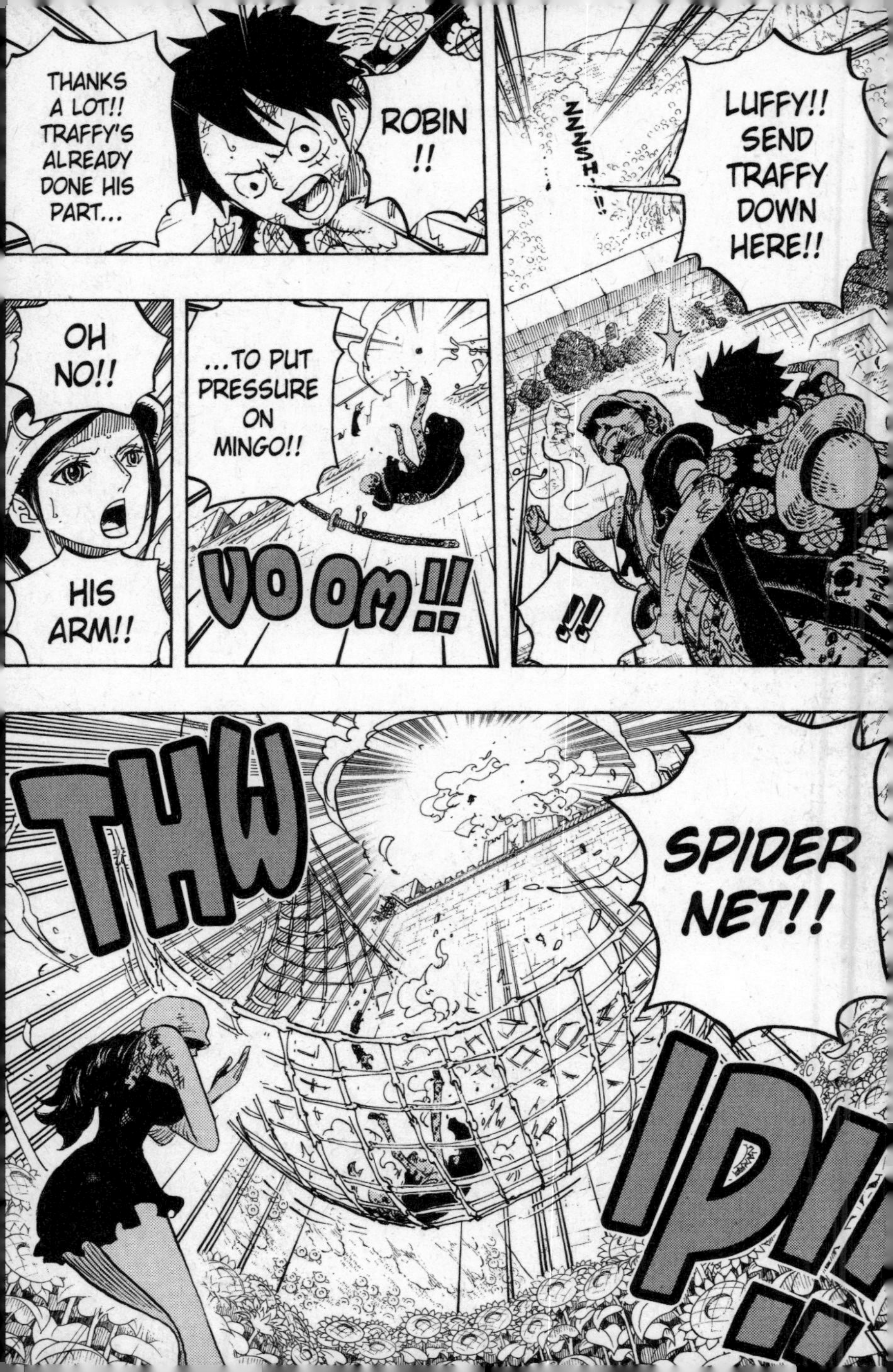

LUFFY!! SEND TRAFFY DOWN HERE!!
ZZZSH!!
!!
ROBIN!!
THANKS A LOT!! TRAFFY'S ALREADY DONE HIS PART...
...TO PUT PRESSURE ON MINGO!!
VOOM!!
OH NO!!
HIS ARM!!
SPIDER NET!!
THW
IP!!

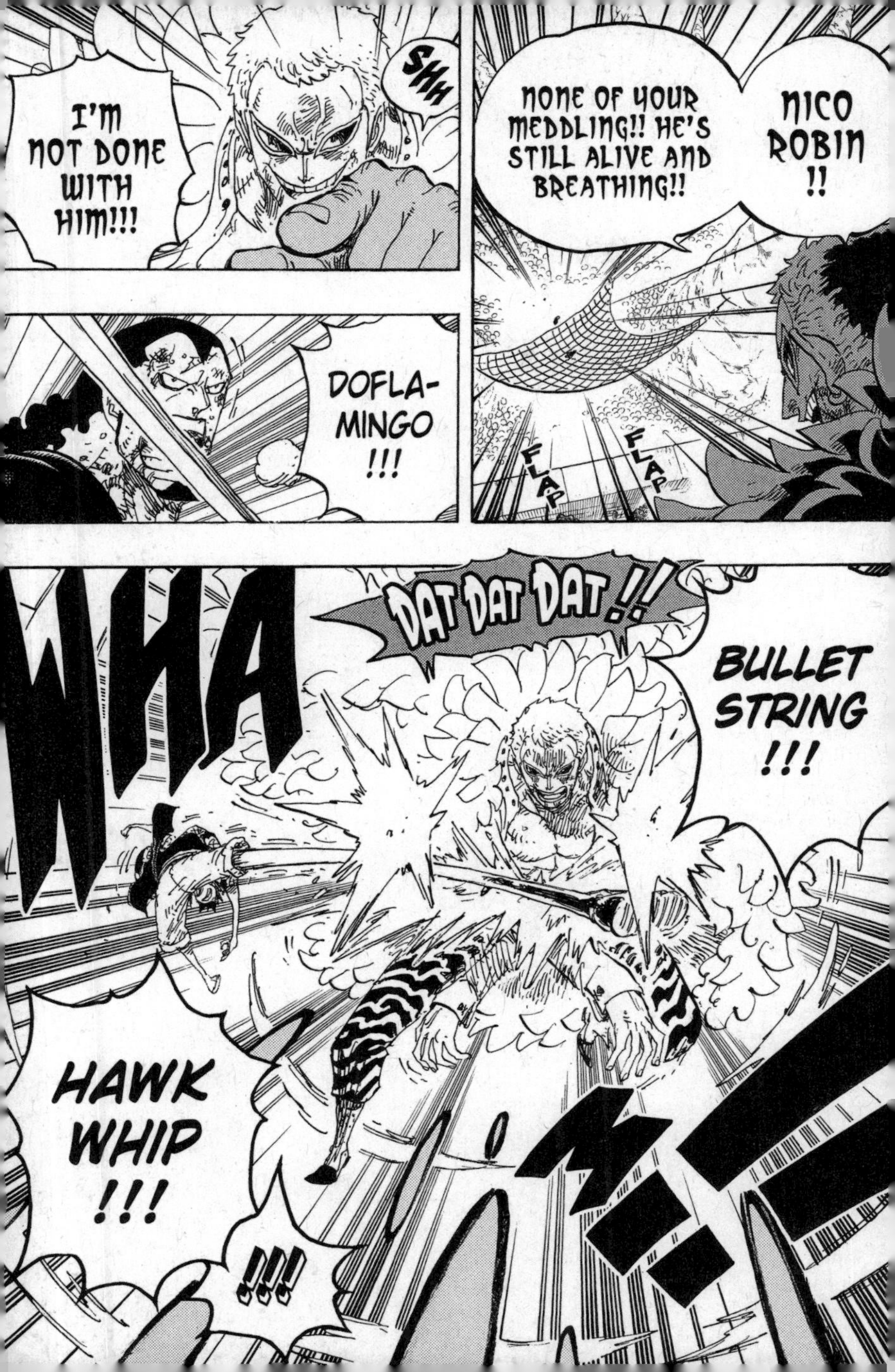
NICO ROBIN!!
NONE OF YOUR MEDDLING!! HE'S STILL ALIVE AND BREATHING!!
FLAP
FLAP
SHH
I'M NOT DONE WITH HIM!!!
DOFLA-MINGO!!!
BULLET STRING!!!
DAT DAT DAT!!
WHA
HAWK WHIP!!!
!!!

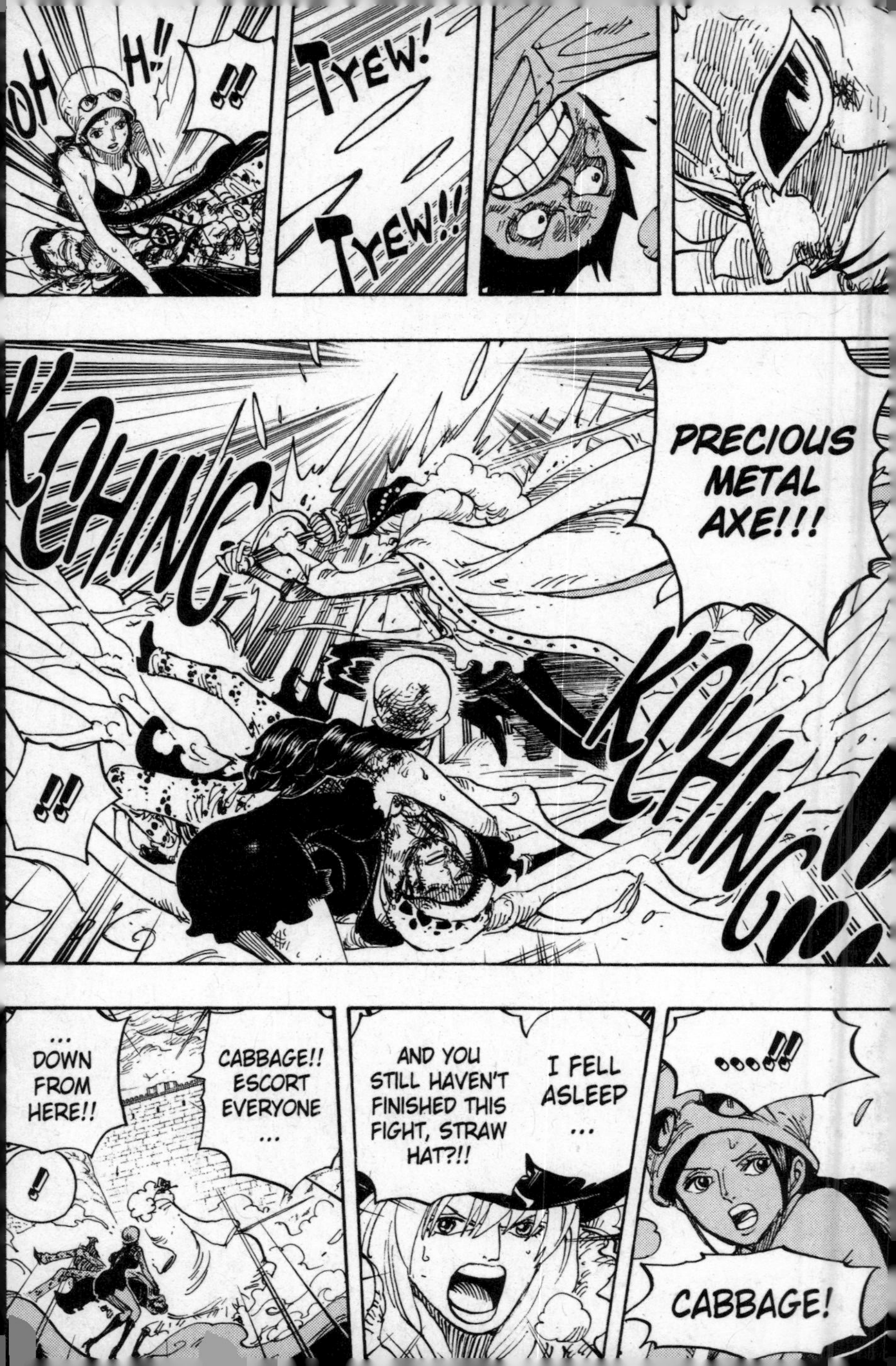
TYEW!
TYEW!!
!!
OH
H!!
PRECIOUS METAL AXE!!!
KCHING
KCHING!!
!!
....!!
CABBAGE!
I FELL ASLEEP ...
AND YOU STILL HAVEN'T FINISHED THIS FIGHT, STRAW HAT?!!
CABBAGE!! ESCORT EVERYONE ...
... DOWN FROM HERE!!
!

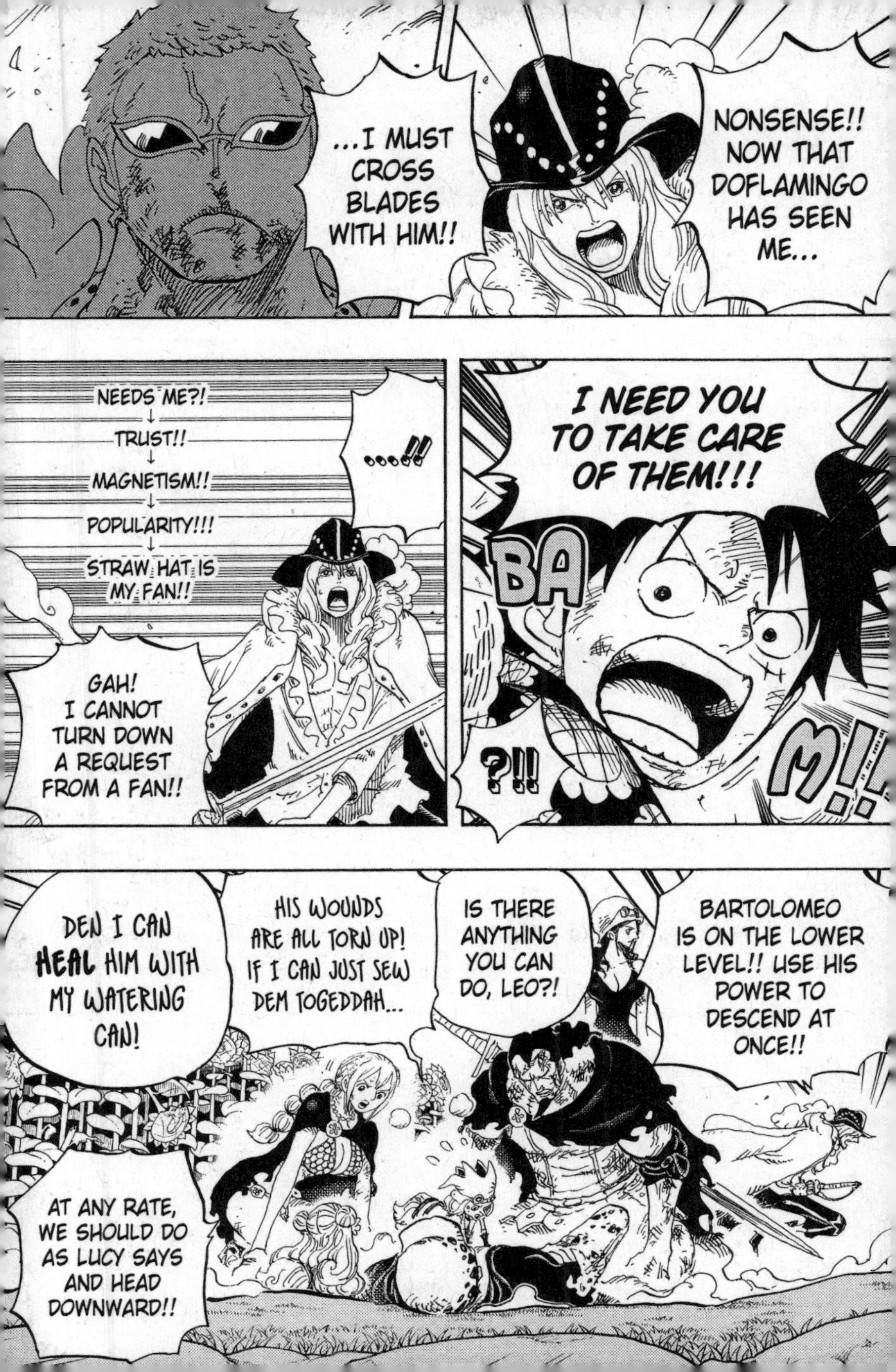

NONSENSE!! NOW THAT DOFLAMINGO HAS SEEN ME...
...I MUST CROSS BLADES WITH HIM!!
I NEED YOU TO TAKE CARE OF THEM!!!
BAM!!
?!!
...!!
NEEDS ME?! ↓ TRUST!! ↓ MAGNETISM!! ↓ POPULARITY!!! ↓ STRAW HAT IS MY FAN!!
GAH! I CANNOT TURN DOWN A REQUEST FROM A FAN!!
BARTOLOMEO IS ON THE LOWER LEVEL!! USE HIS POWER TO DESCEND AT ONCE!!
IS THERE ANYTHING YOU CAN DO, LEO?!
HIS WOUNDS ARE ALL TORN UP! IF I CAN JUST SEW DEM TOGEDDAH...
DEN I CAN HEAL HIM WITH MY WATERING CAN!
AT ANY RATE, WE SHOULD DO AS LUCY SAYS AND HEAD DOWNWARD!!

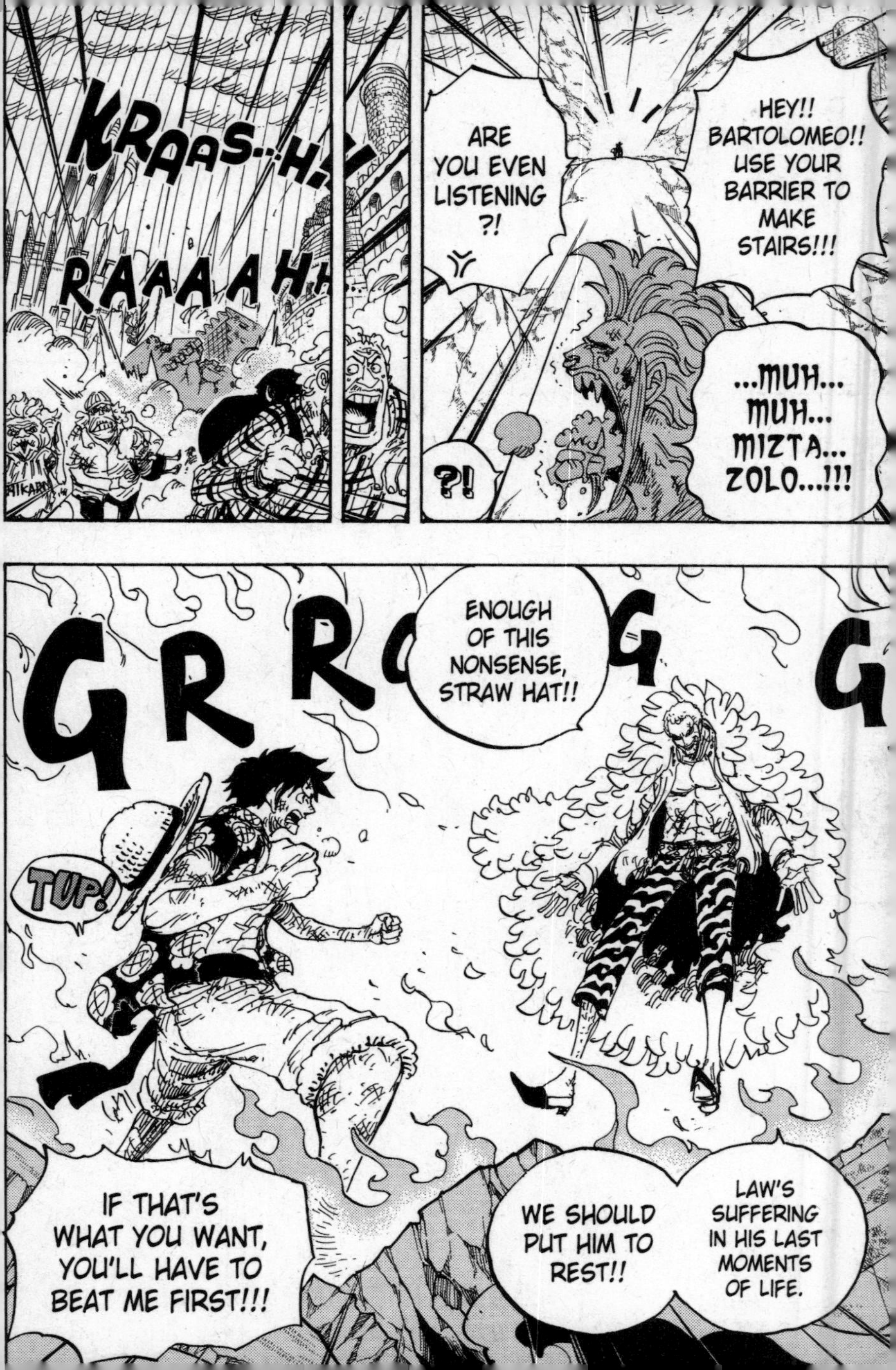
HEY!! BARTOLOMEO!! USE YOUR BARRIER TO MAKE STAIRS!!!
ARE YOU EVEN LISTENING ?!
...MUH... MUH... MIZTA... ZOLO...!!!
?!
KRAAS-H
RAAAAH
GRROGG
ENOUGH OF THIS NONSENSE, STRAW HAT!!
LAW'S SUFFERING IN HIS LAST MOMENTS OF LIFE.
WE SHOULD PUT HIM TO REST!!
TUP!
IF THAT'S WHAT YOU WANT, YOU'LL HAVE TO BEAT ME FIRST!!!

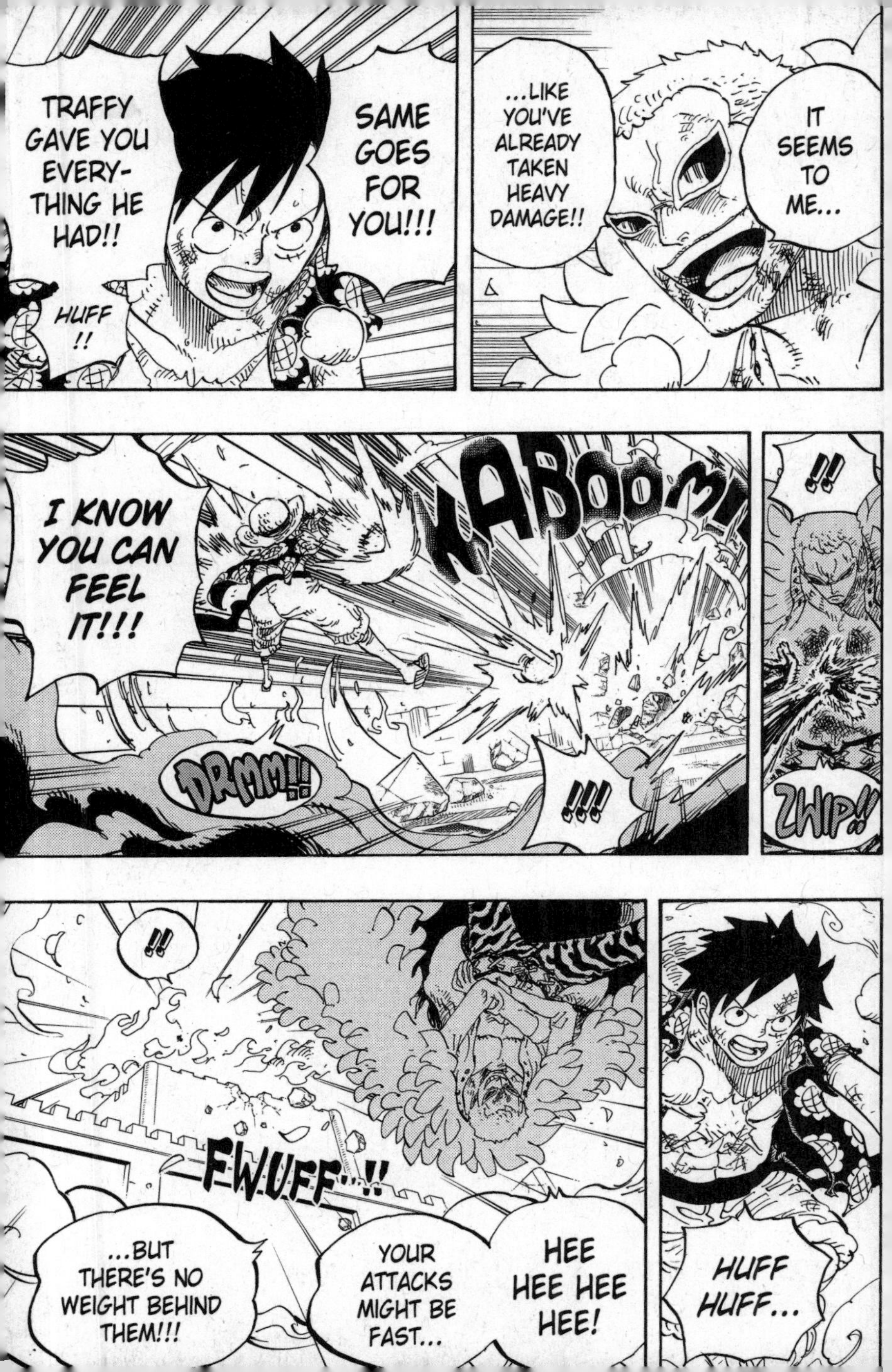
IT SEEMS TO ME...
...LIKE YOU'VE ALREADY TAKEN HEAVY DAMAGE!!
SAME GOES FOR YOU!!!
TRAFFY GAVE YOU EVERY-THING HE HAD!!
HUFF !!
!!
ZWIP!!
KABOOM!!
!!!
I KNOW YOU CAN FEEL IT!!!
DRMM!!
HUFF HUFF...
!!
FWUFF...!!
HEE HEE HEE HEE!
YOUR ATTACKS MIGHT BE FAST...
...BUT THERE'S NO WEIGHT BEHIND THEM!!!

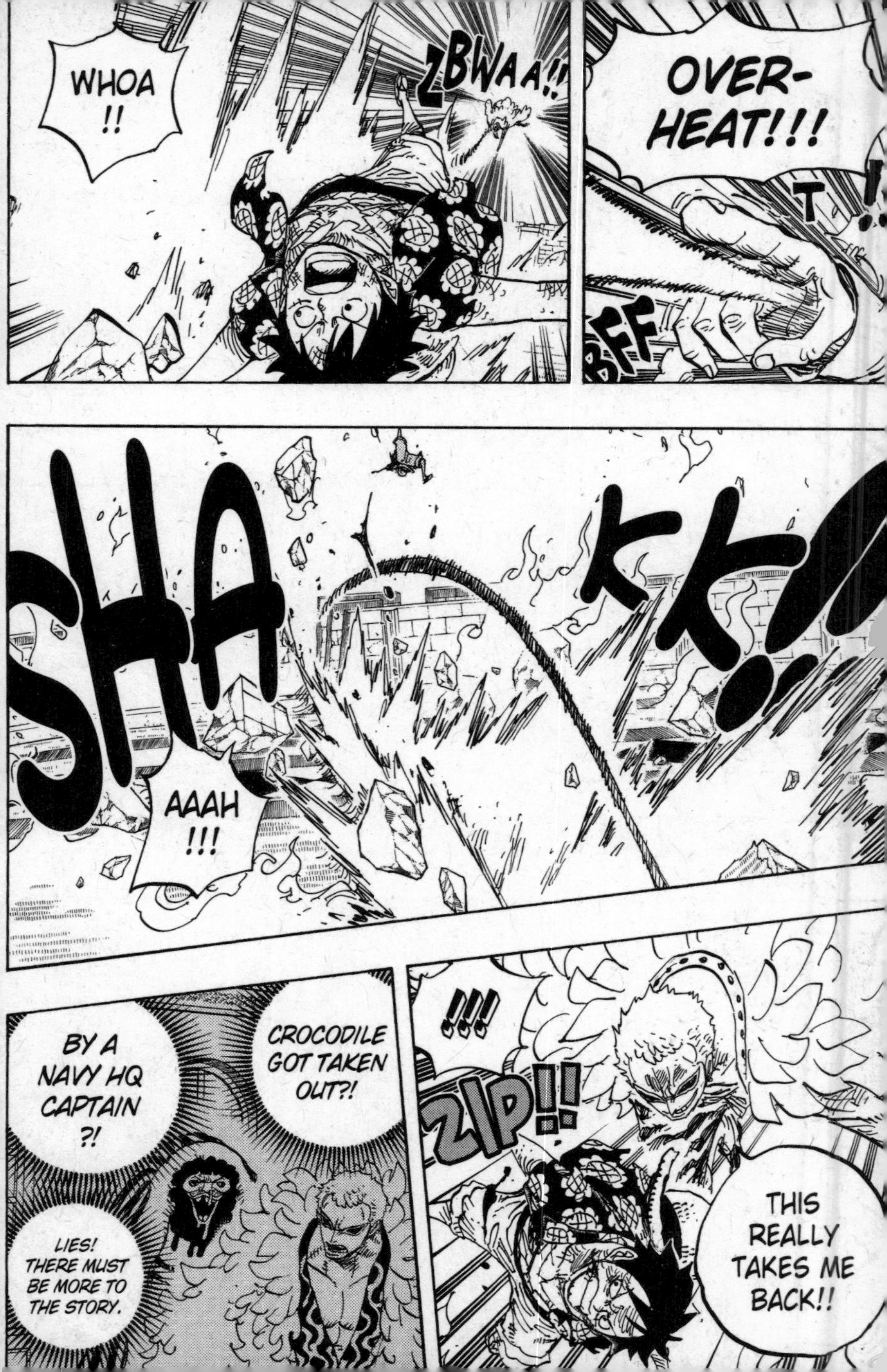
OVER-HEAT!!!
T!!
BFF
ZBWAA!!
WHOA !!
SHAKK!!
AAAH !!!
!!!
ZIP!!!
THIS REALLY TAKES ME BACK!!
CROCODILE GOT TAKEN OUT?!
BY A NAVY HQ CAPTAIN ?!
LIES! THERE MUST BE MORE TO THE STORY.

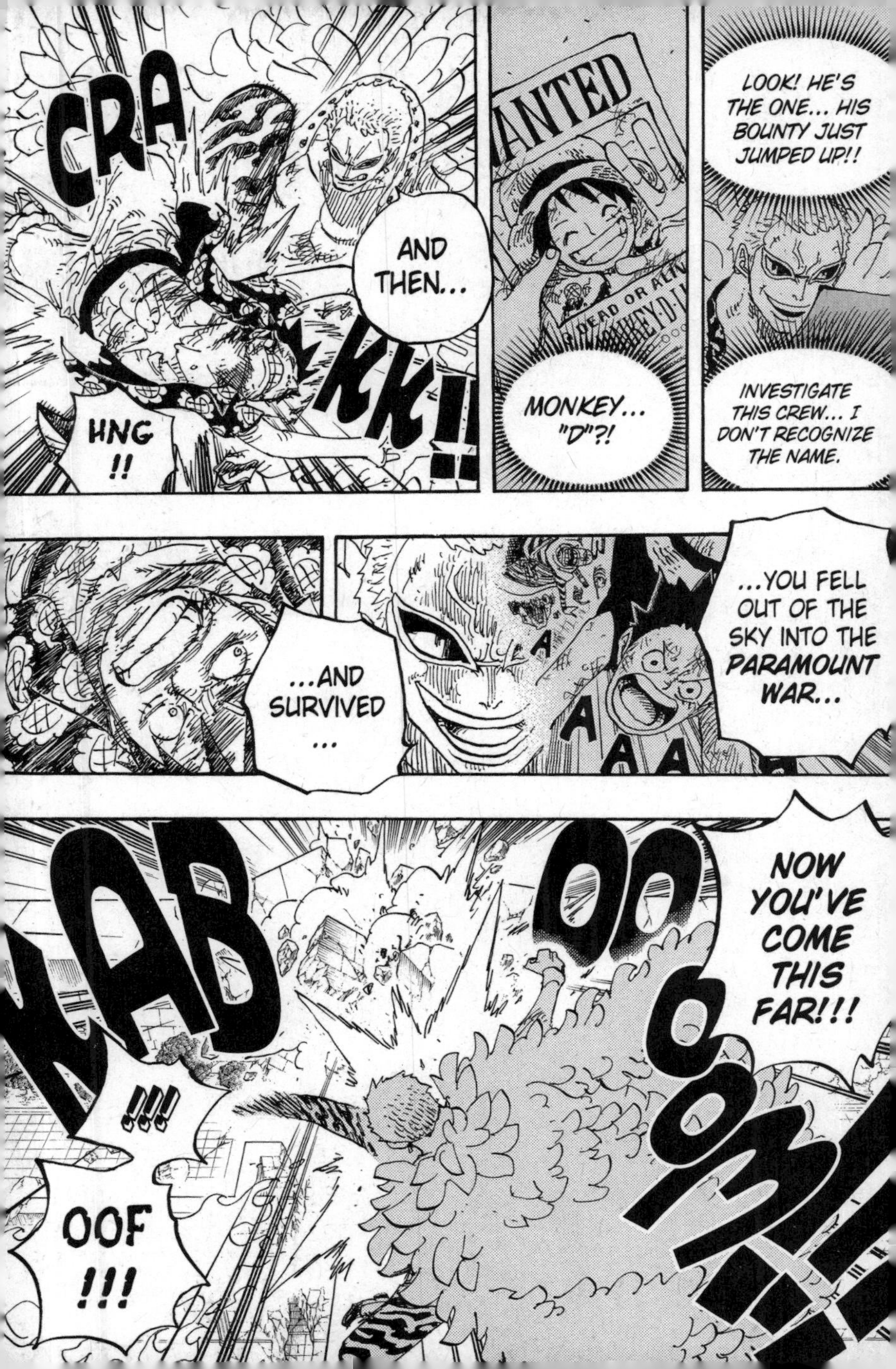
LOOK! HE'S THE ONE... HIS BOUNTY JUST JUMPED UP!!
INVESTIGATE THIS CREW... I DON'T RECOGNIZE THE NAME.
MONKEY... "D"?!
CRA
KK!!
AND THEN...
HNG !!
...YOU FELL OUT OF THE SKY INTO THE PARAMOUNT WAR...
A A A A
...AND SURVIVED ...
NOW YOU'VE COME THIS FAR!!!
OOOM!!
AB
!!!
OOF !!!

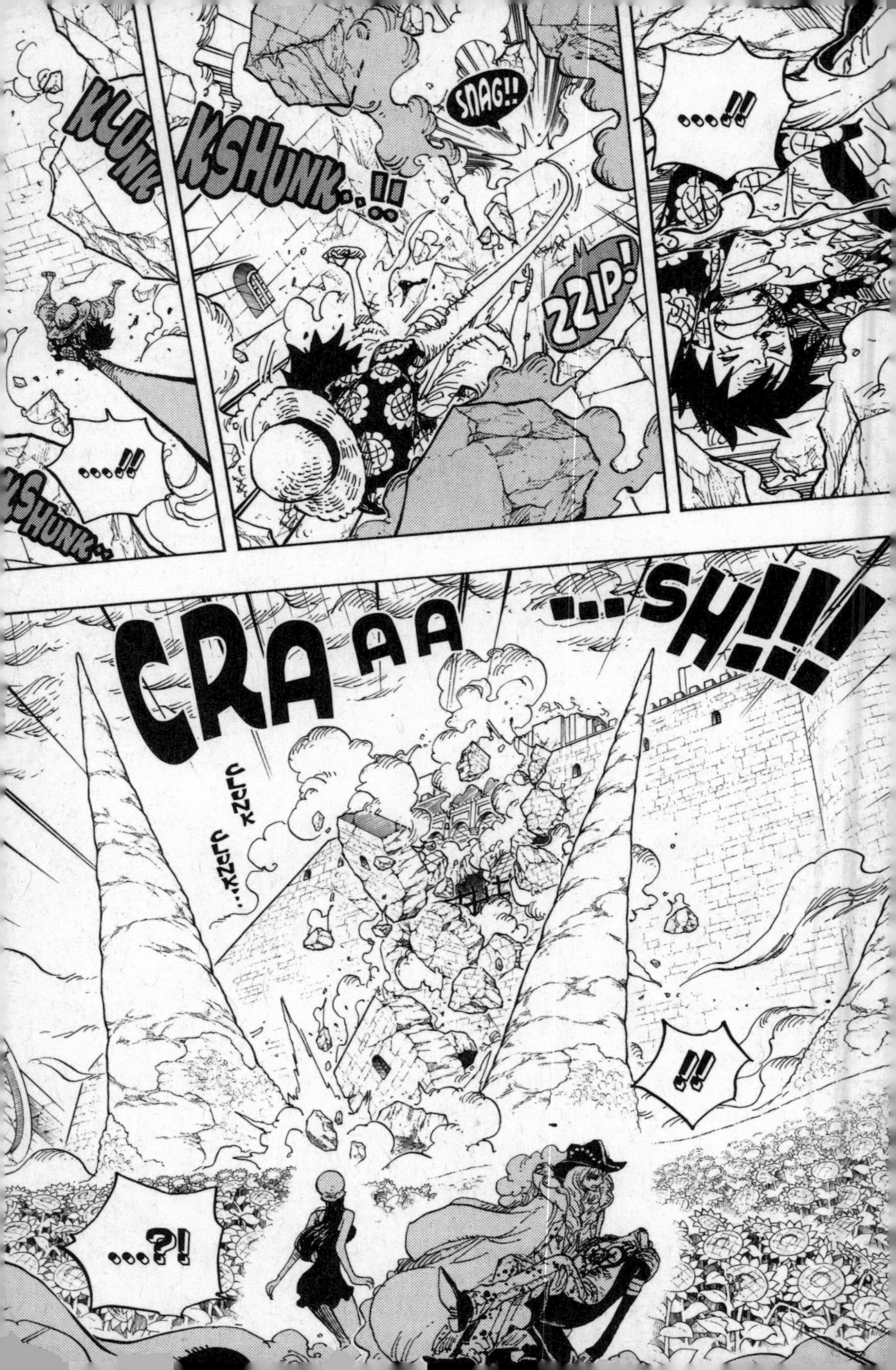

...!!
SNAG!!
KSHUNK..!!
ZZIP!
KLUNK
...!!
KSHUNK..
CRAAA...SH!!!
!!
CLUNK
CLUNK...
...?!

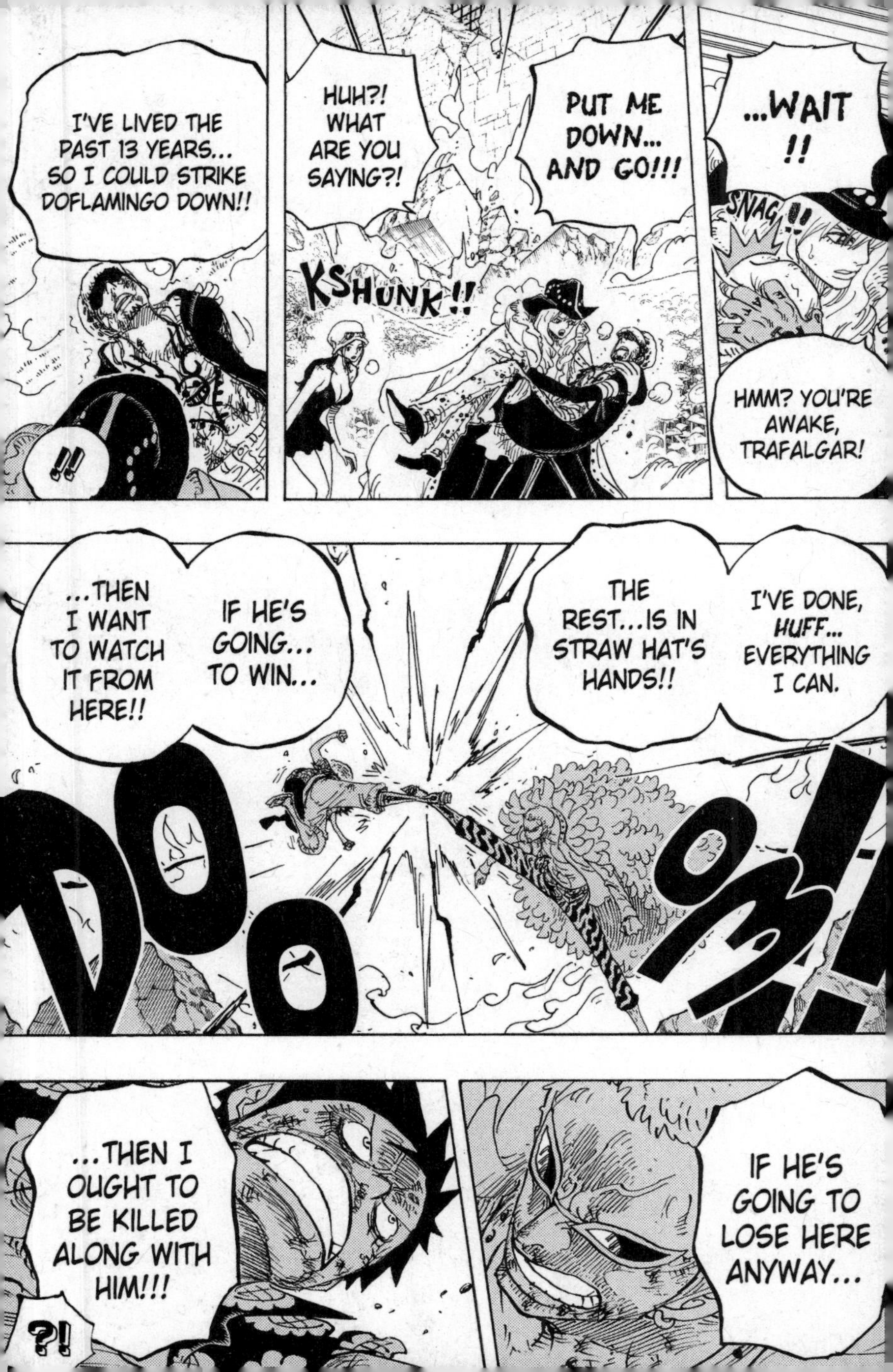
...WAIT !!
SNAG !!
HMM? YOU'RE AWAKE, TRAFALGAR!
PUT ME DOWN... AND GO!!!
HUH?! WHAT ARE YOU SAYING?!
KSHUNK !!
I'VE LIVED THE PAST 13 YEARS... SO I COULD STRIKE DOFLAMINGO DOWN!!
!!
I'VE DONE, HUFF... EVERYTHING I CAN.
THE REST...IS IN STRAW HAT'S HANDS!!
IF HE'S GOING... TO WIN...
...THEN I WANT TO WATCH IT FROM HERE!!
DOOOM!
IF HE'S GOING TO LOSE HERE ANYWAY...
...THEN I OUGHT TO BE KILLED ALONG WITH HIM!!!
?!

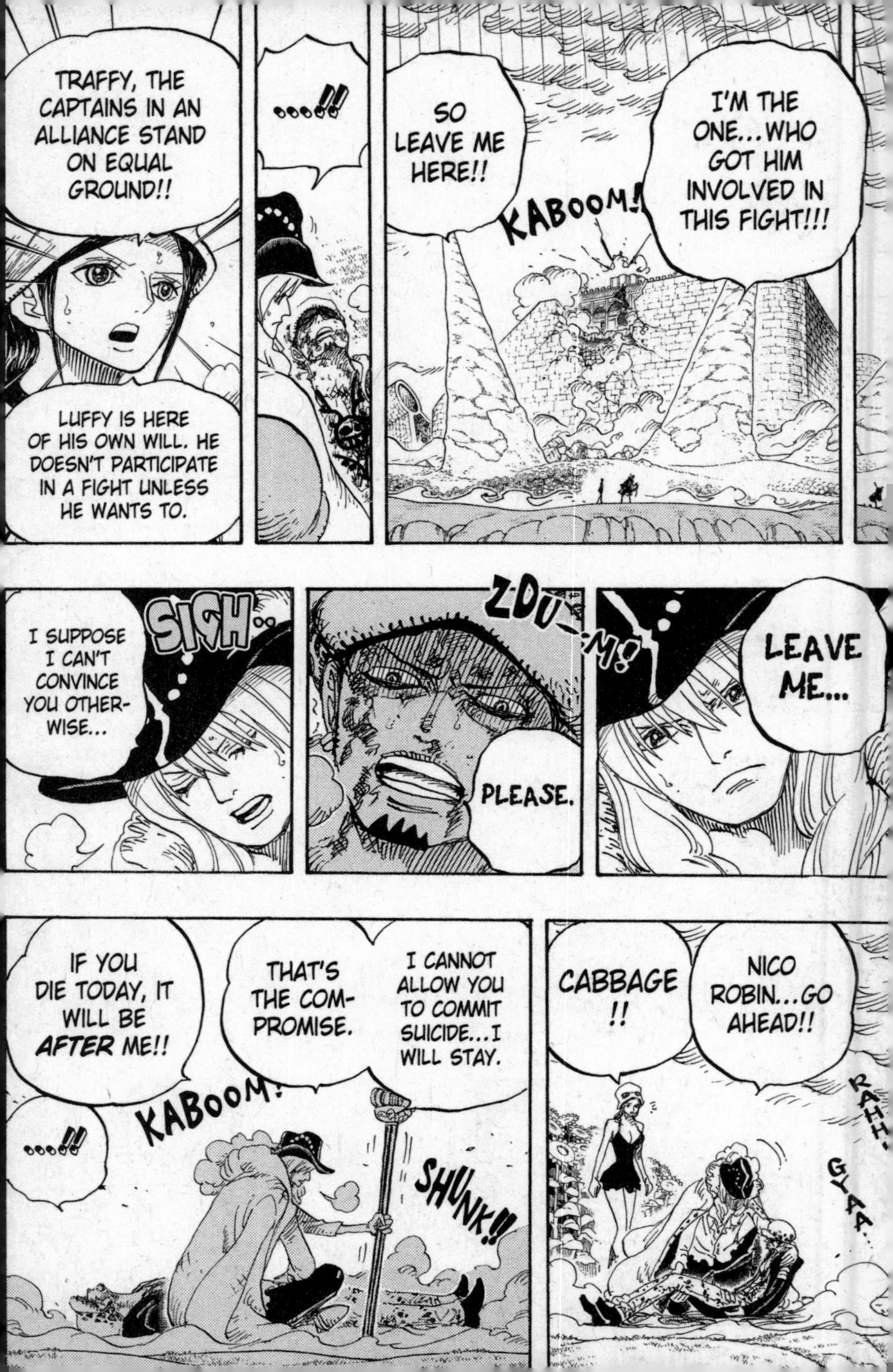
I'M THE ONE...WHO GOT HIM INVOLVED IN THIS FIGHT!!!
SO LEAVE ME HERE!!
KABOOM!
....!!
TRAFFY, THE CAPTAINS IN AN ALLIANCE STAND ON EQUAL GROUND!!
LUFFY IS HERE OF HIS OWN WILL. HE DOESN'T PARTICIPATE IN A FIGHT UNLESS HE WANTS TO.
LEAVE ME...
ZDU-N!
PLEASE.
SIGH..
I SUPPOSE I CAN'T CONVINCE YOU OTHER-WISE...
NICO ROBIN...GO AHEAD!!
CABBAGE !!
RAHH.
GYAA...
I CANNOT ALLOW YOU TO COMMIT SUICIDE...I WILL STAY.
THAT'S THE COM-PROMISE.
IF YOU DIE TODAY, IT WILL BE *AFTER* ME!!
KABOOM!
....!!
SHUNK!!

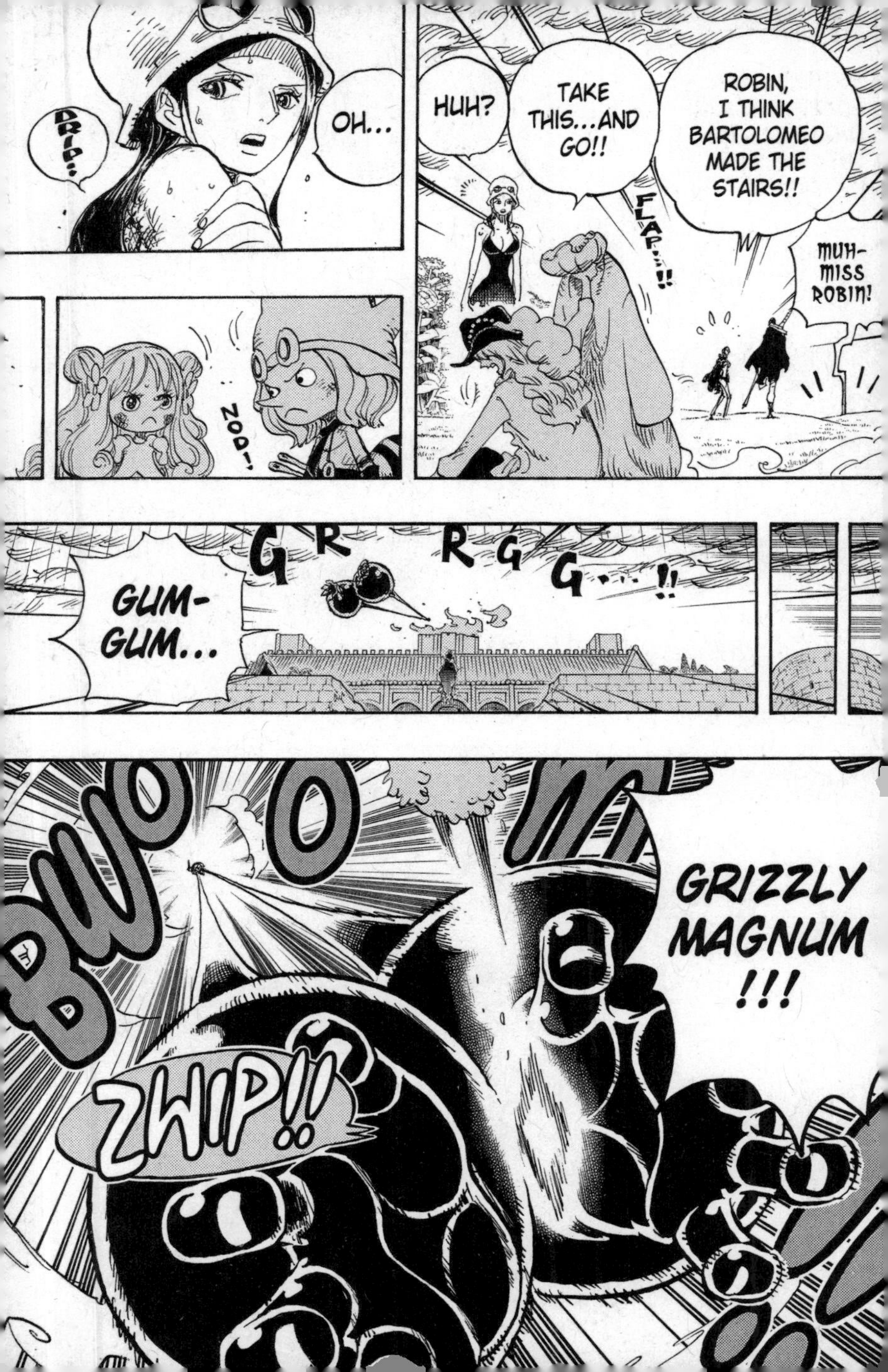
ROBIN, I THINK BARTOLOMEO MADE THE STAIRS!!
MUH-MISS ROBIN!
TAKE THIS...AND GO!!
FLAP...!!
HUH?
OH...
DRIP..
NOD!
GRRGG...!!
GUM-GUM...
GRIZZLY MAGNUM !!!
ZWIP!!

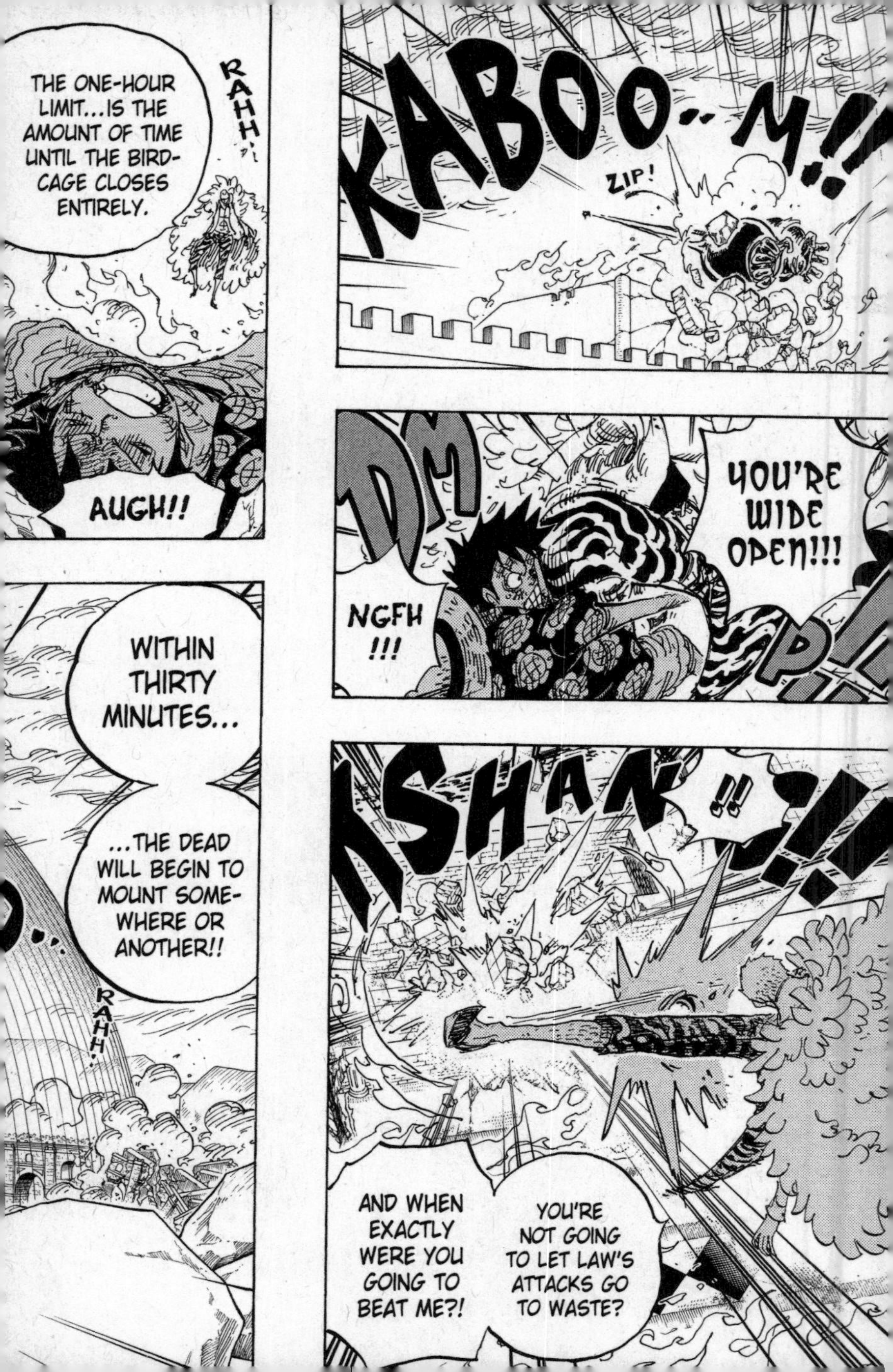

KABOO--M!!
ZIP!
YOU'RE WIDE OPEN!!!
NGFH!!!
YOU'RE NOT GOING TO LET LAW'S ATTACKS GO TO WASTE?
AND WHEN EXACTLY WERE YOU GOING TO BEAT ME?!
THE ONE-HOUR LIMIT...IS THE AMOUNT OF TIME UNTIL THE BIRD-CAGE CLOSES ENTIRELY.
RAHH,
AUGH!!
WITHIN THIRTY MINUTES...
...THE DEAD WILL BEGIN TO MOUNT SOME-WHERE OR ANOTHER!!
RAHH!

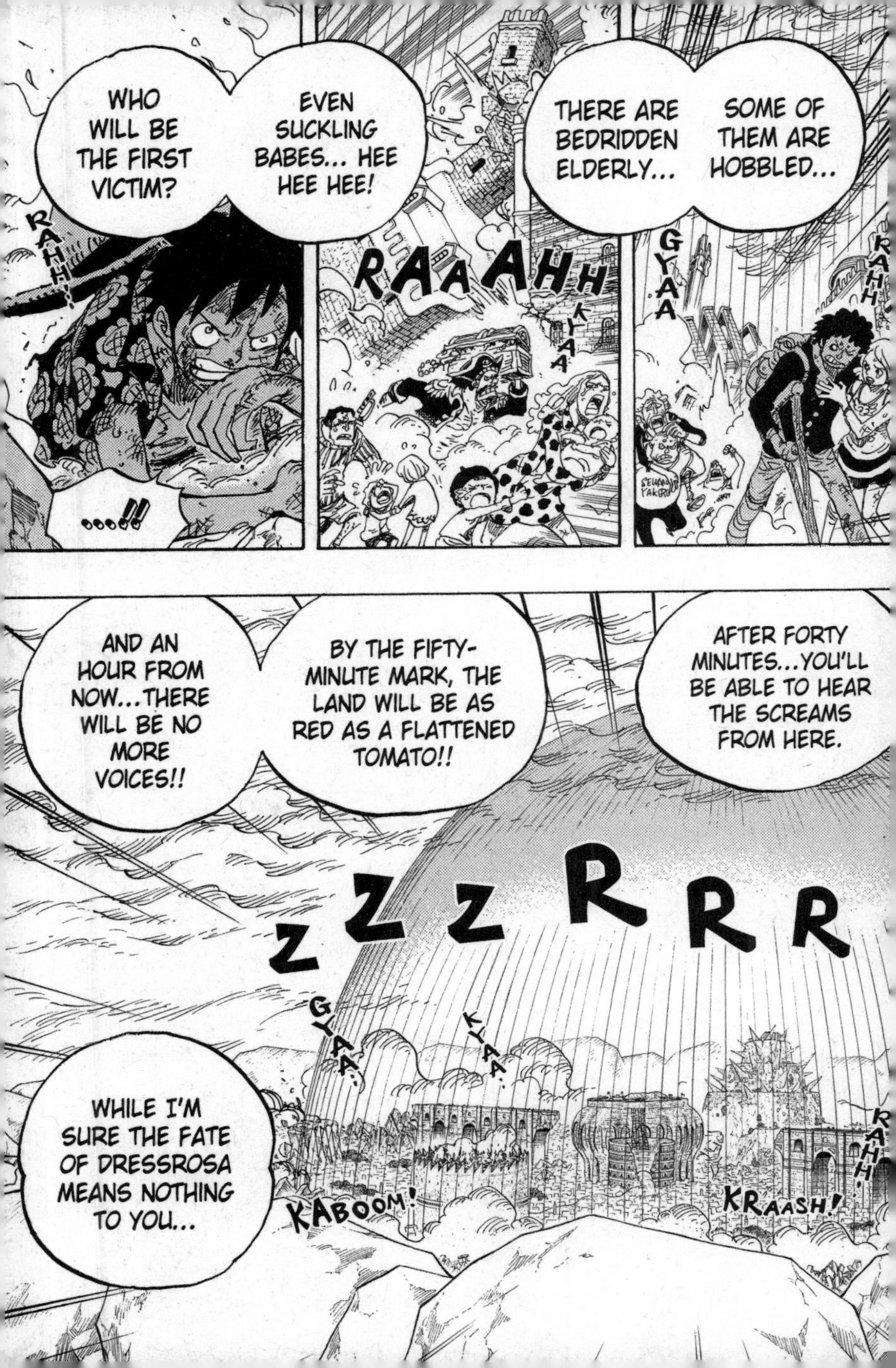
THERE ARE BEDRIDDEN ELDERLY...
SOME OF THEM ARE HOBBLED...
GYAA
RAHH
EVEN SUCKLING BABES... HEE HEE HEE!
WHO WILL BE THE FIRST VICTIM?
RAAAHH
KYAA
RAHH...
.....!!
AFTER FORTY MINUTES...YOU'LL BE ABLE TO HEAR THE SCREAMS FROM HERE.
BY THE FIFTY-MINUTE MARK, THE LAND WILL BE AS RED AS A FLATTENED TOMATO!!
AND AN HOUR FROM NOW...THERE WILL BE NO MORE VOICES!!
ZZZRRRR
KYAA
GYAA
RAHH
KRAASH!
KABOOM!
WHILE I'M SURE THE FATE OF DRESSROSA MEANS NOTHING TO YOU...

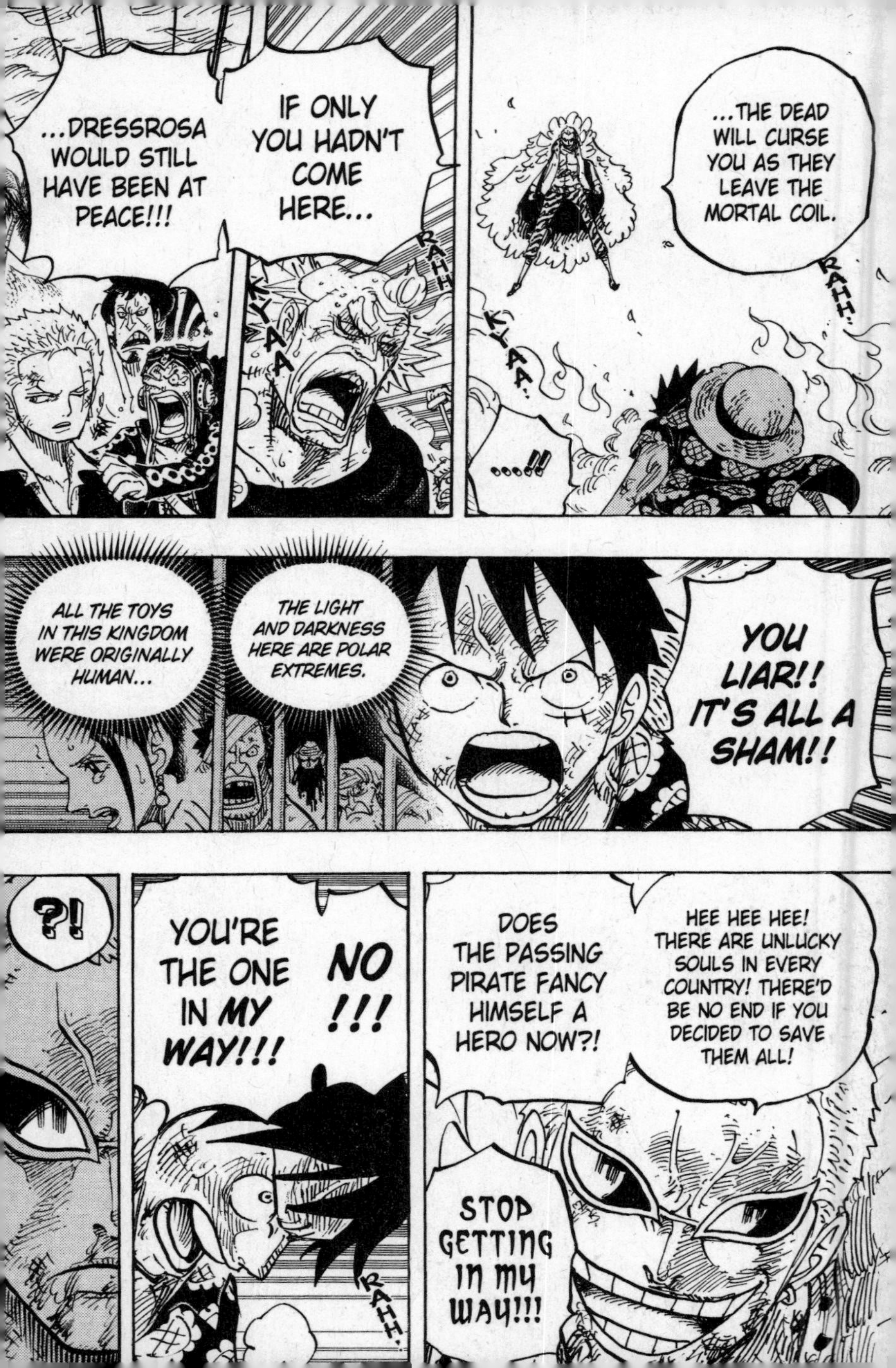

...THE DEAD WILL CURSE YOU AS THEY LEAVE THE MORTAL COIL.
RAHH!
KYAA!
...!!
IF ONLY YOU HADN'T COME HERE...
RAHH
KYAA
...DRESSROSA WOULD STILL HAVE BEEN AT PEACE!!!
YOU LIAR!! IT'S ALL A SHAM!!
THE LIGHT AND DARKNESS HERE ARE POLAR EXTREMES.
ALL THE TOYS IN THIS KINGDOM WERE ORIGINALLY HUMAN...
HEE HEE HEE! THERE ARE UNLUCKY SOULS IN EVERY COUNTRY! THERE'D BE NO END IF YOU DECIDED TO SAVE THEM ALL!
DOES THE PASSING PIRATE FANCY HIMSELF A HERO NOW?!
STOP GETTING IN MY WAY!!!
NO !!!
YOU'RE THE ONE IN MY WAY!!!
RAHH.
?!

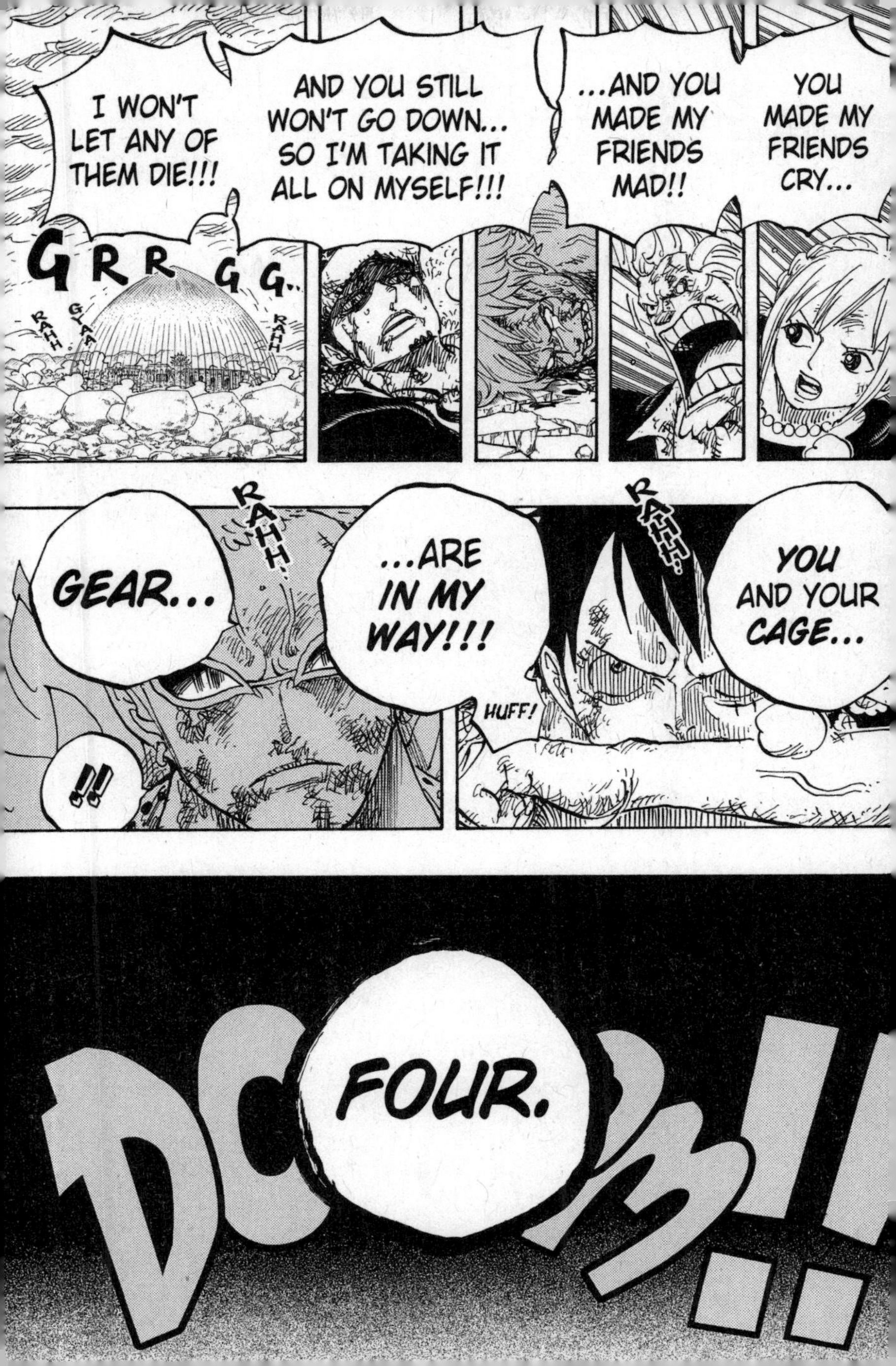

YOU MADE MY FRIENDS CRY...
...AND YOU MADE MY FRIENDS MAD!!
AND YOU STILL WON'T GO DOWN... SO I'M TAKING IT ALL ON MYSELF!!!
I WON'T LET ANY OF THEM DIE!!!
GRRGG..
RAHH
GYAA
RAHH
YOU AND YOUR CAGE...
RAHH
HUFF!
...ARE IN MY WAY!!!
RAHH
GEAR...
!!
FOUR.

Chapter 784: GEAR FOUR

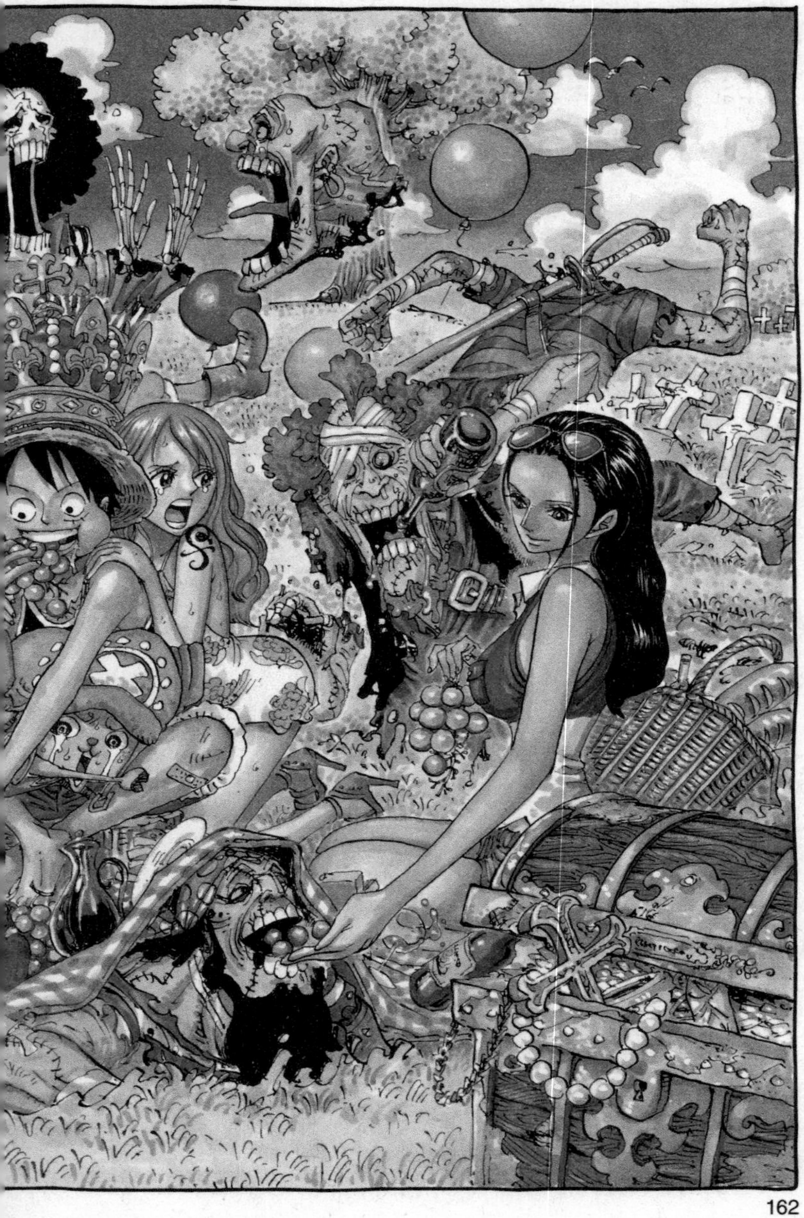

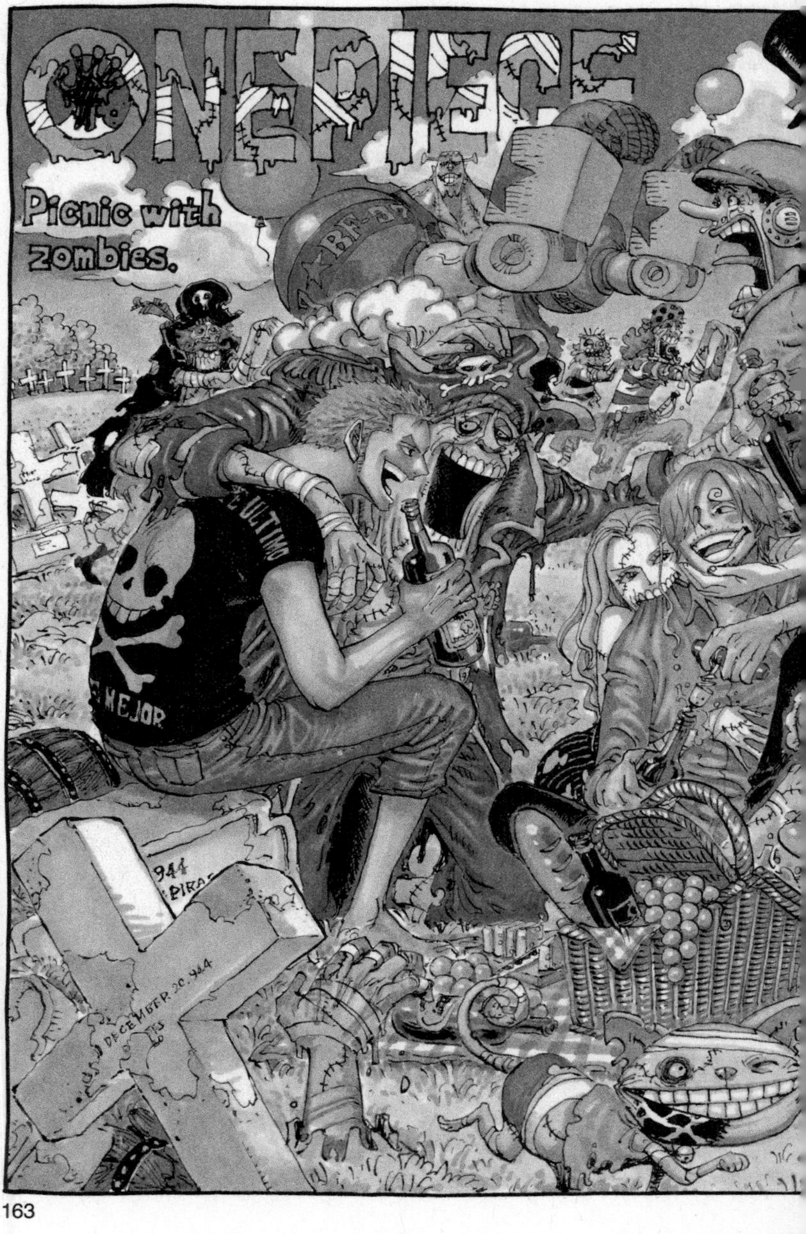
ONE PIECE
Picnic with zombies.

ONE PIECE vol.78

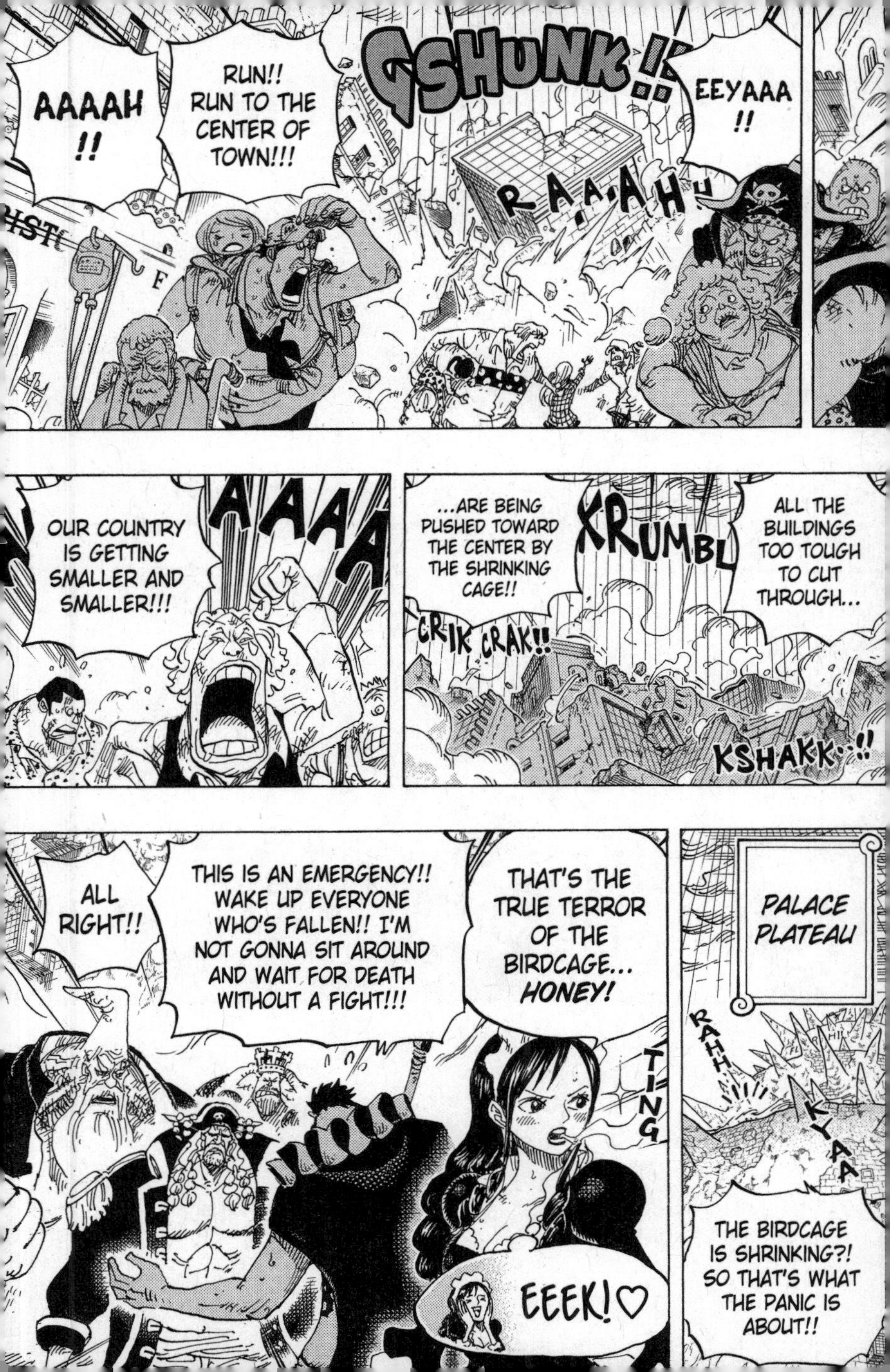
EEYAAA!!
GSHUNK!!
RUN!! RUN TO THE CENTER OF TOWN!!!
AAAAH!!
RAAAHU
ALL THE BUILDINGS TOO TOUGH TO CUT THROUGH...
XRUMBL
...ARE BEING PUSHED TOWARD THE CENTER BY THE SHRINKING CAGE!!
CRIK CRAK!!
KSHAKK!!
AAAA
OUR COUNTRY IS GETTING SMALLER AND SMALLER!!!
PALACE PLATEAU
RAHH!!!
KYAA
THE BIRDCAGE IS SHRINKING?! SO THAT'S WHAT THE PANIC IS ABOUT!!
THAT'S THE TRUE TERROR OF THE BIRDCAGE... *HONEY!*
TING
THIS IS AN EMERGENCY!! WAKE UP EVERYONE WHO'S FALLEN!! I'M NOT GONNA SIT AROUND AND WAIT FOR DEATH WITHOUT A FIGHT!!!
ALL RIGHT!!
EEEK!♡

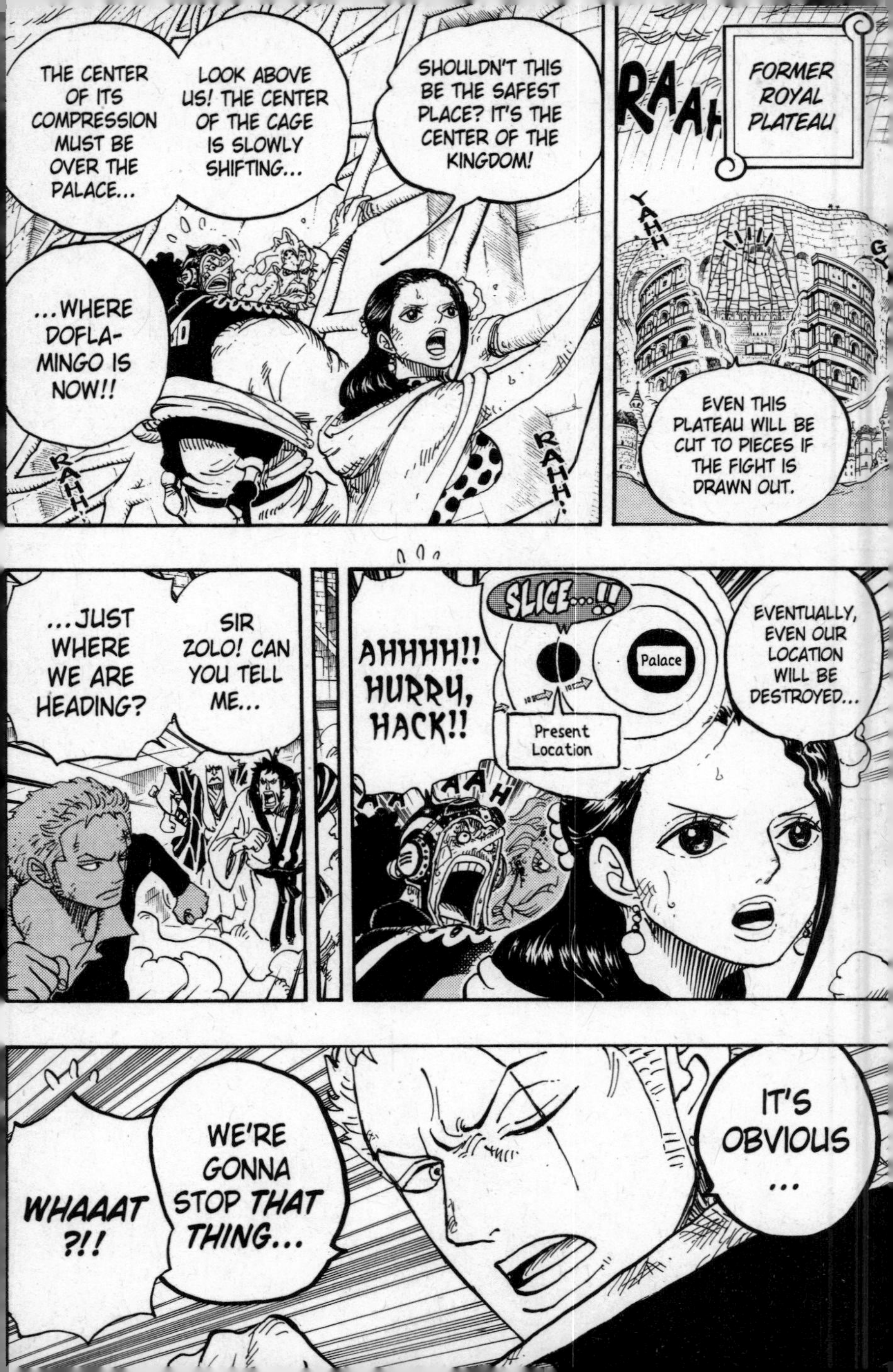
FORMER ROYAL PLATEAU
RAAH
YAHH
EVEN THIS PLATEAU WILL BE CUT TO PIECES IF THE FIGHT IS DRAWN OUT.
SHOULDN'T THIS BE THE SAFEST PLACE? IT'S THE CENTER OF THE KINGDOM!
LOOK ABOVE US! THE CENTER OF THE CAGE IS SLOWLY SHIFTING...
THE CENTER OF ITS COMPRESSION MUST BE OVER THE PALACE...
...WHERE DOFLAMINGO IS NOW!!
RAHH
RAHH
EVENTUALLY, EVEN OUR LOCATION WILL BE DESTROYED...
SLICE...!!
Palace
Present Location
AHHHH!! HURRY, HACK!!
AAH
SIR ZOLO! CAN YOU TELL ME...
...JUST WHERE WE ARE HEADING?
IT'S OBVIOUS...
WE'RE GONNA STOP THAT THING...
WHAAAT?!!

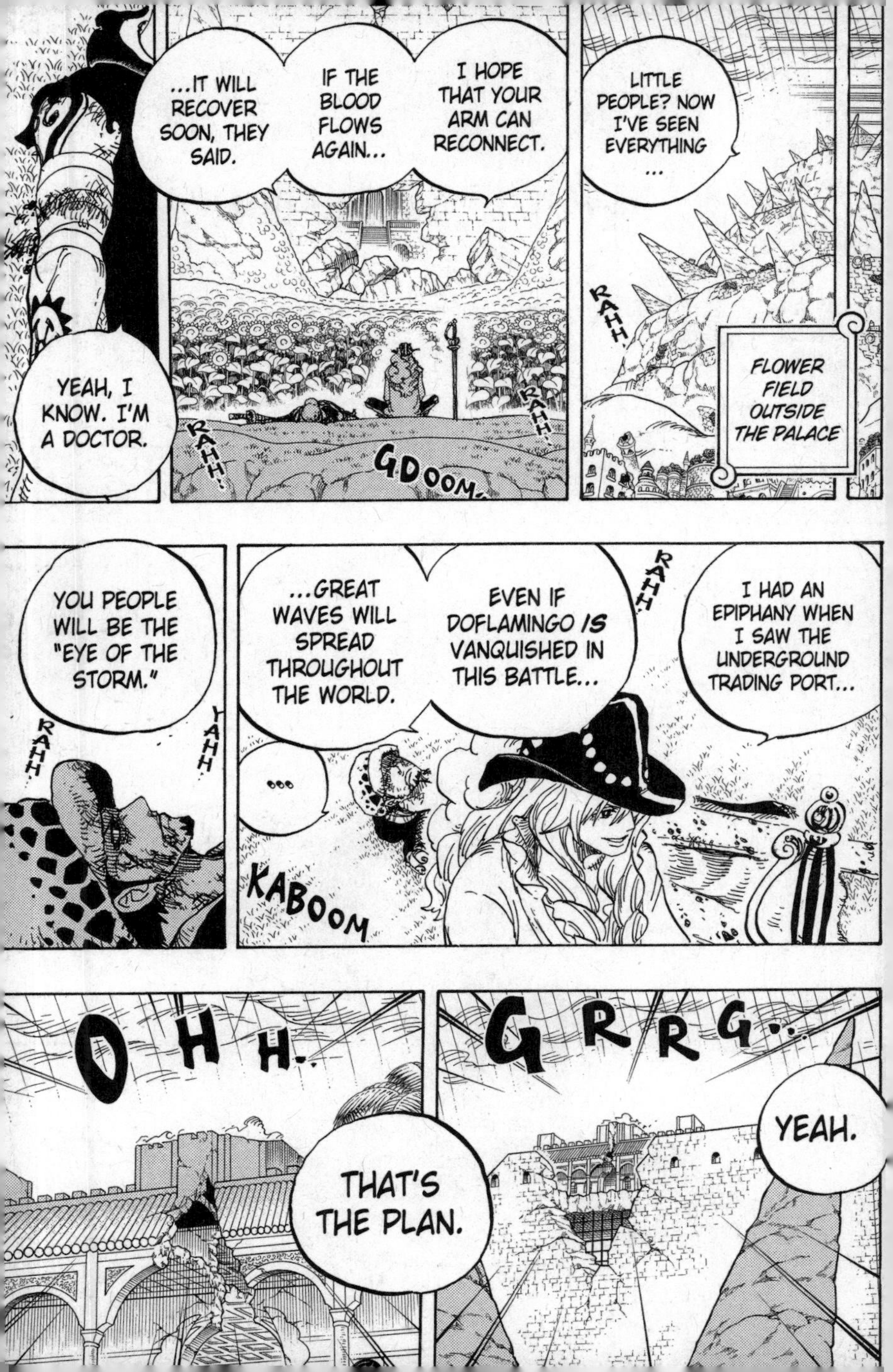
LITTLE PEOPLE? NOW I'VE SEEN EVERYTHING ...
RAHH
FLOWER FIELD OUTSIDE THE PALACE
I HOPE THAT YOUR ARM CAN RECONNECT.
IF THE BLOOD FLOWS AGAIN...
...IT WILL RECOVER SOON, THEY SAID.
RAHH
RAHH
GDOOM
YEAH, I KNOW. I'M A DOCTOR.
I HAD AN EPIPHANY WHEN I SAW THE UNDERGROUND TRADING PORT...
RAHH
EVEN IF DOFLAMINGO *IS* VANQUISHED IN THIS BATTLE...
...GREAT WAVES WILL SPREAD THROUGHOUT THE WORLD.
...
KABOOM
YOU PEOPLE WILL BE THE "EYE OF THE STORM."
YAHH
RAHH
GRRRG..
YEAH.
OHH..
THAT'S THE PLAN.

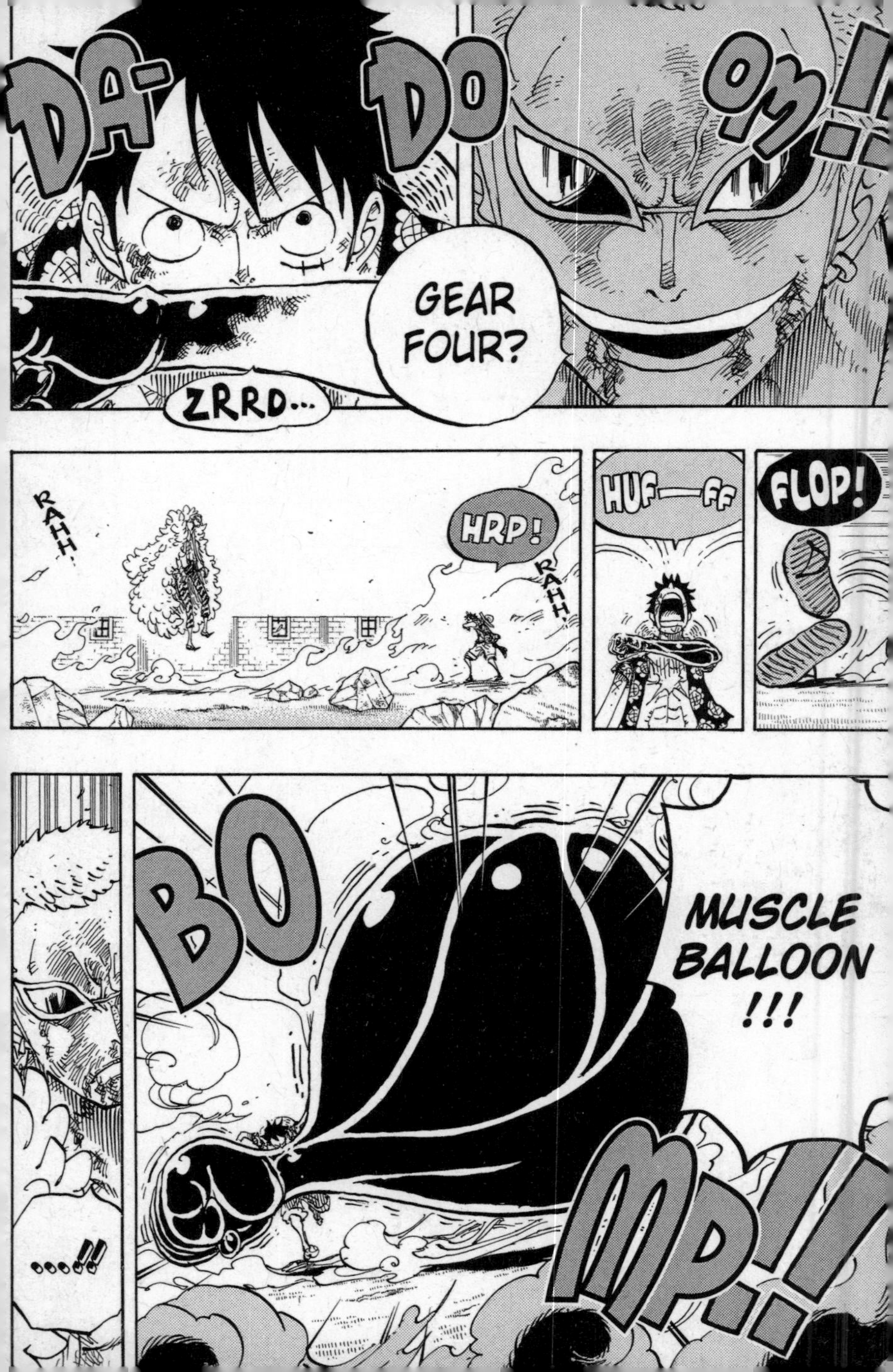

DA-DO-OM!!
GEAR FOUR?
ZRRD...
FLOP!
HUF—FF
HRP!
RAHH
RAHH
BO-MP!!
MUSCLE BALLOON!!!
...!!

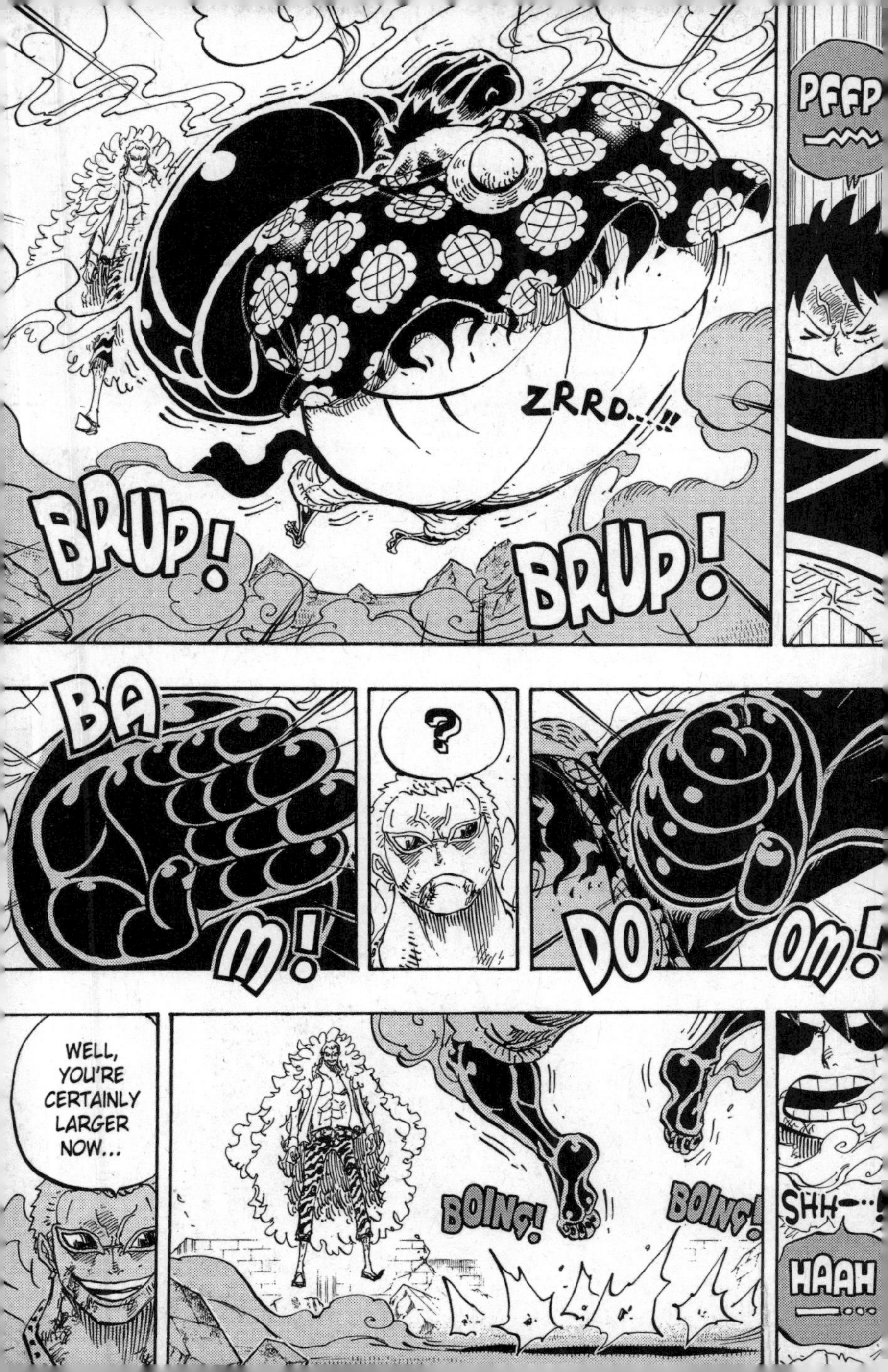
PFFP—
ZRRD...!!
BRUP!
BRUP!
DOOM!
?
BAM!
SHH—!
HAAH—
BOING!
BOING!
WELL, YOU'RE CERTAINLY LARGER NOW...

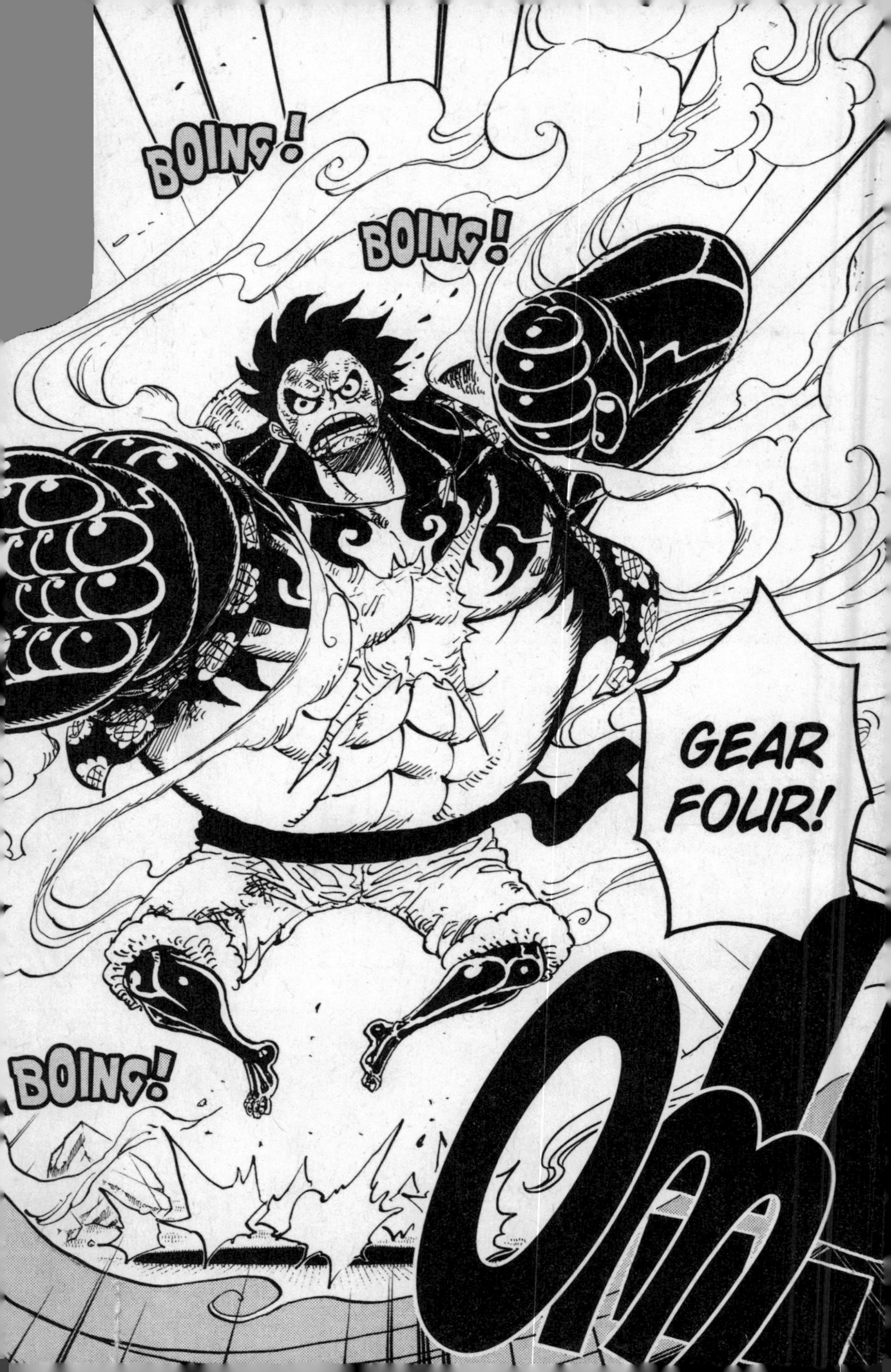
BOING!
BOING!
GEAR FOUR!
BOING!

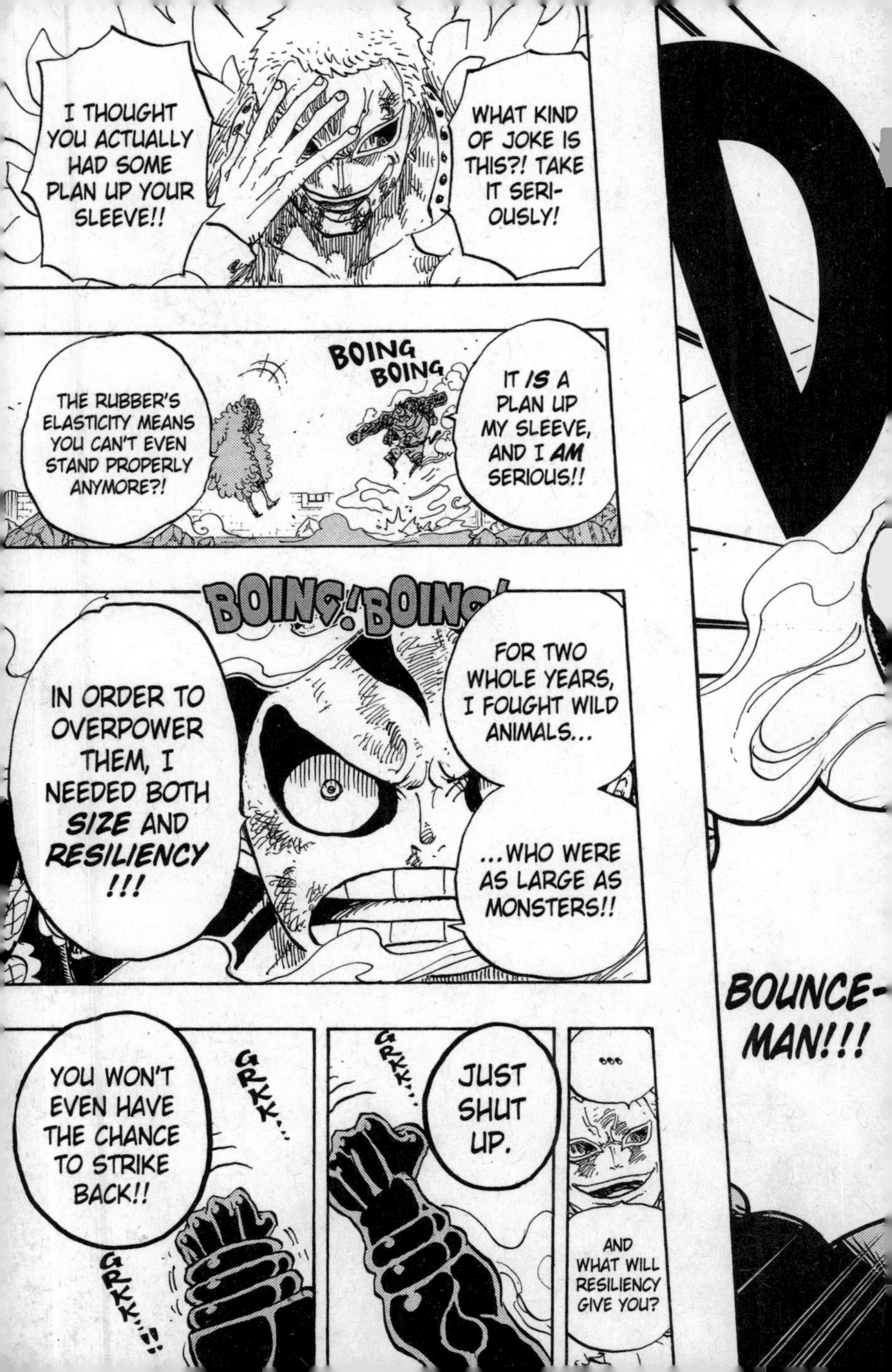
BOUNCE-MAN!!!
WHAT KIND OF JOKE IS THIS?! TAKE IT SERIOUSLY!
I THOUGHT YOU ACTUALLY HAD SOME PLAN UP YOUR SLEEVE!!
BOING BOING
IT *IS* A PLAN UP MY SLEEVE, AND I *AM* SERIOUS!!
THE RUBBER'S ELASTICITY MEANS YOU CAN'T EVEN STAND PROPERLY ANYMORE?!
BOING! BOING!
FOR TWO WHOLE YEARS, I FOUGHT WILD ANIMALS...
...WHO WERE AS LARGE AS MONSTERS!!
IN ORDER TO OVERPOWER THEM, I NEEDED BOTH *SIZE* AND *RESILIENCY*!!!
...
AND WHAT WILL RESILIENCY GIVE YOU?
GRKK...
JUST SHUT UP.
YOU WON'T EVEN HAVE THE CHANCE TO STRIKE BACK!!
GRKK...
GRKK...!!

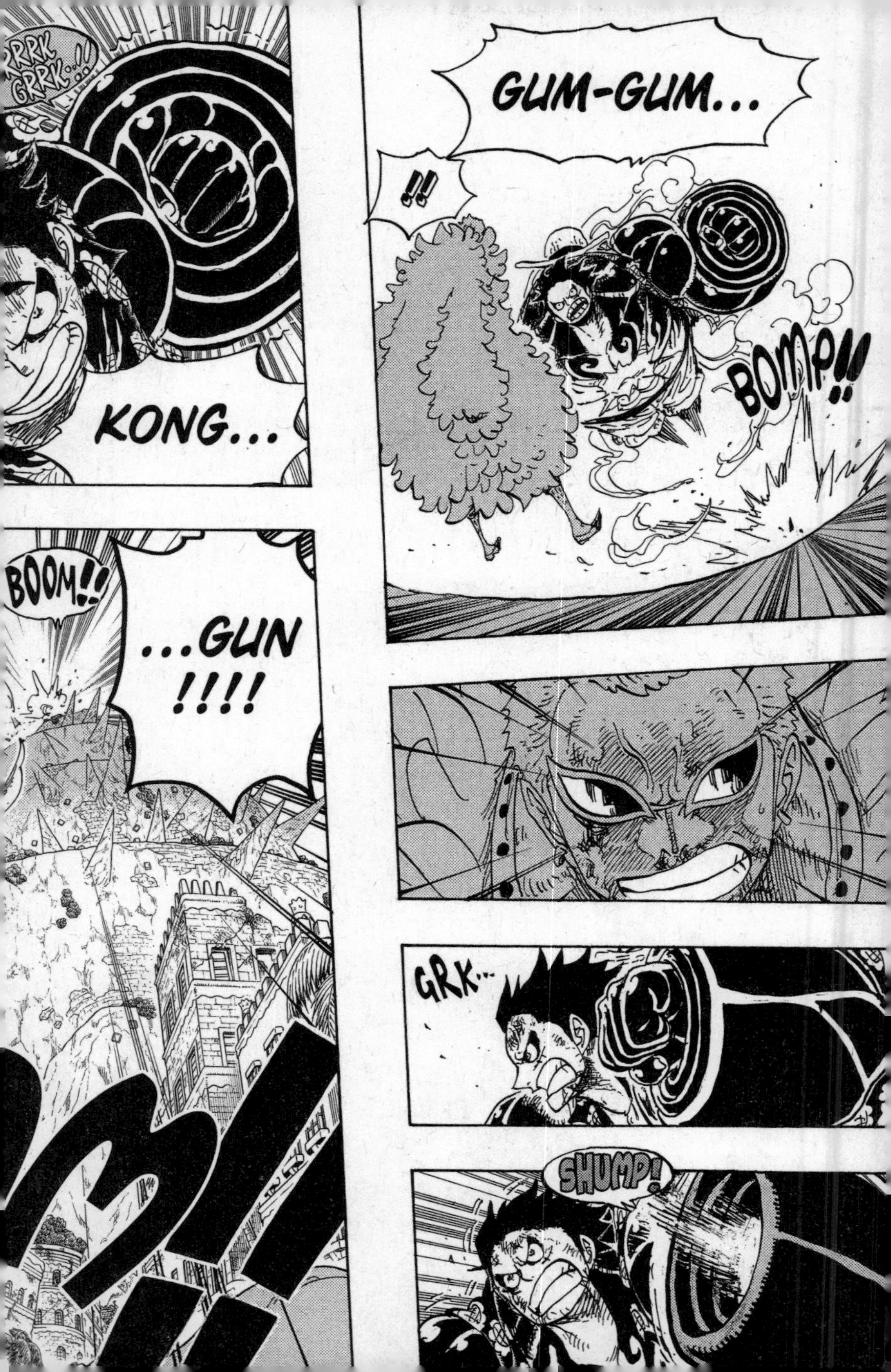
GUM-GUM...
!!
BOMP!!
GRK...
SHUMP!
RRRK GRRK..!!
KONG...
BOOM!!
...GUN !!!!

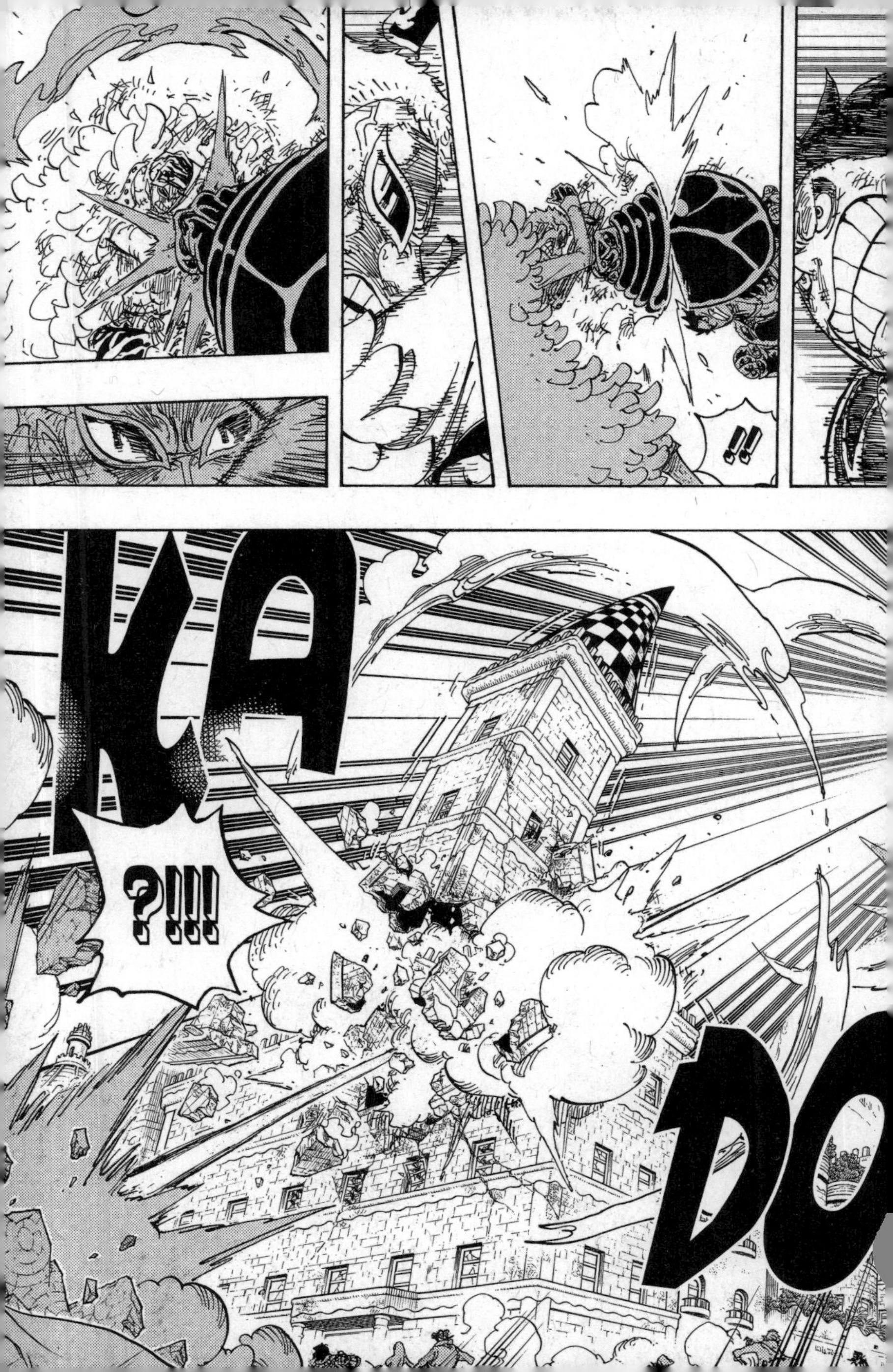
!!
KA
?!!!
DO

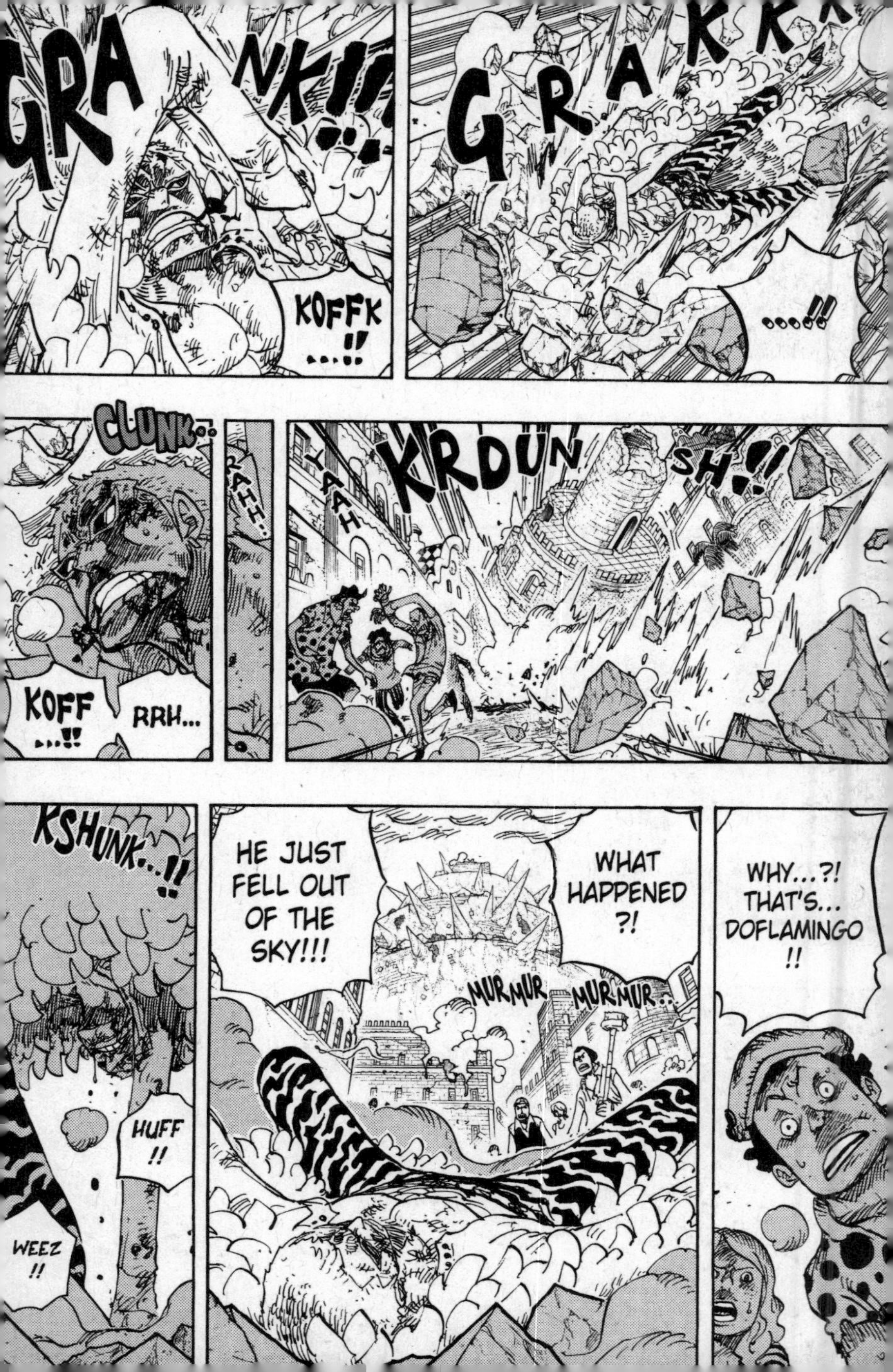
GRAKK
....!!
GRANK!!!..
KOFFK ...!!
KRDUNSH..!!
YAAAH
RAHH...
CLUNK..
KOFF ...!!
RRH...
WHY...?! THAT'S... DOFLAMINGO !!
WHAT HAPPENED ?!
HE JUST FELL OUT OF THE SKY!!!
MURMUR MURMUR...
KSHUNK...!!
HUFF !!
WEEZ !!

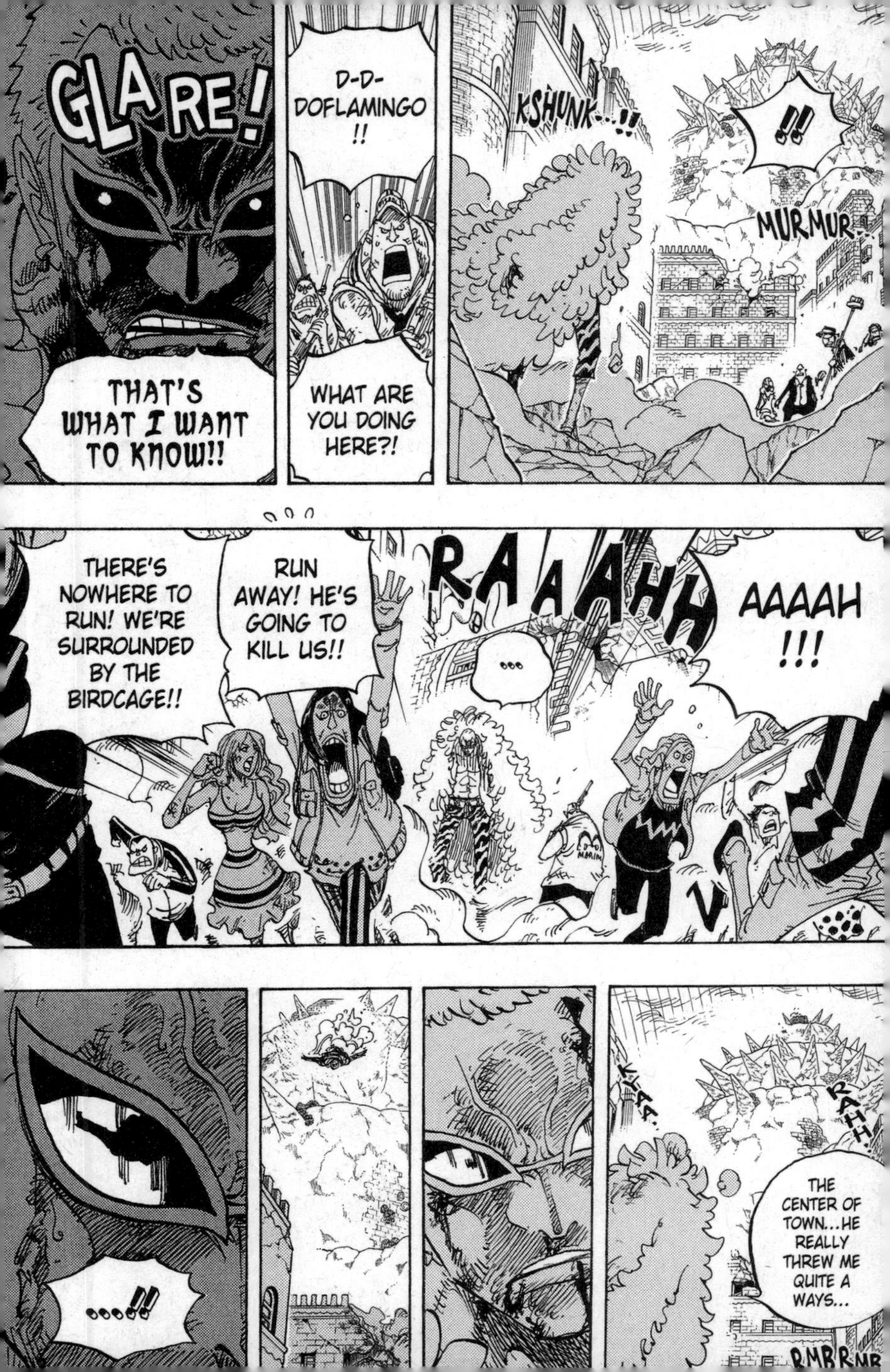
!!
KSHUNK..!!
MURMUR...
D-D-DOFLAMINGO!!
WHAT ARE YOU DOING HERE?!
GLARE!
THAT'S WHAT I WANT TO KNOW!!
AAAAH!!!
RAAAHH
...
RUN AWAY! HE'S GOING TO KILL US!!
THERE'S NOWHERE TO RUN! WE'RE SURROUNDED BY THE BIRDCAGE!!
RAHH..
KYAA..
THE CENTER OF TOWN...HE REALLY THREW ME QUITE A WAYS...
RMBRRMB
....!!

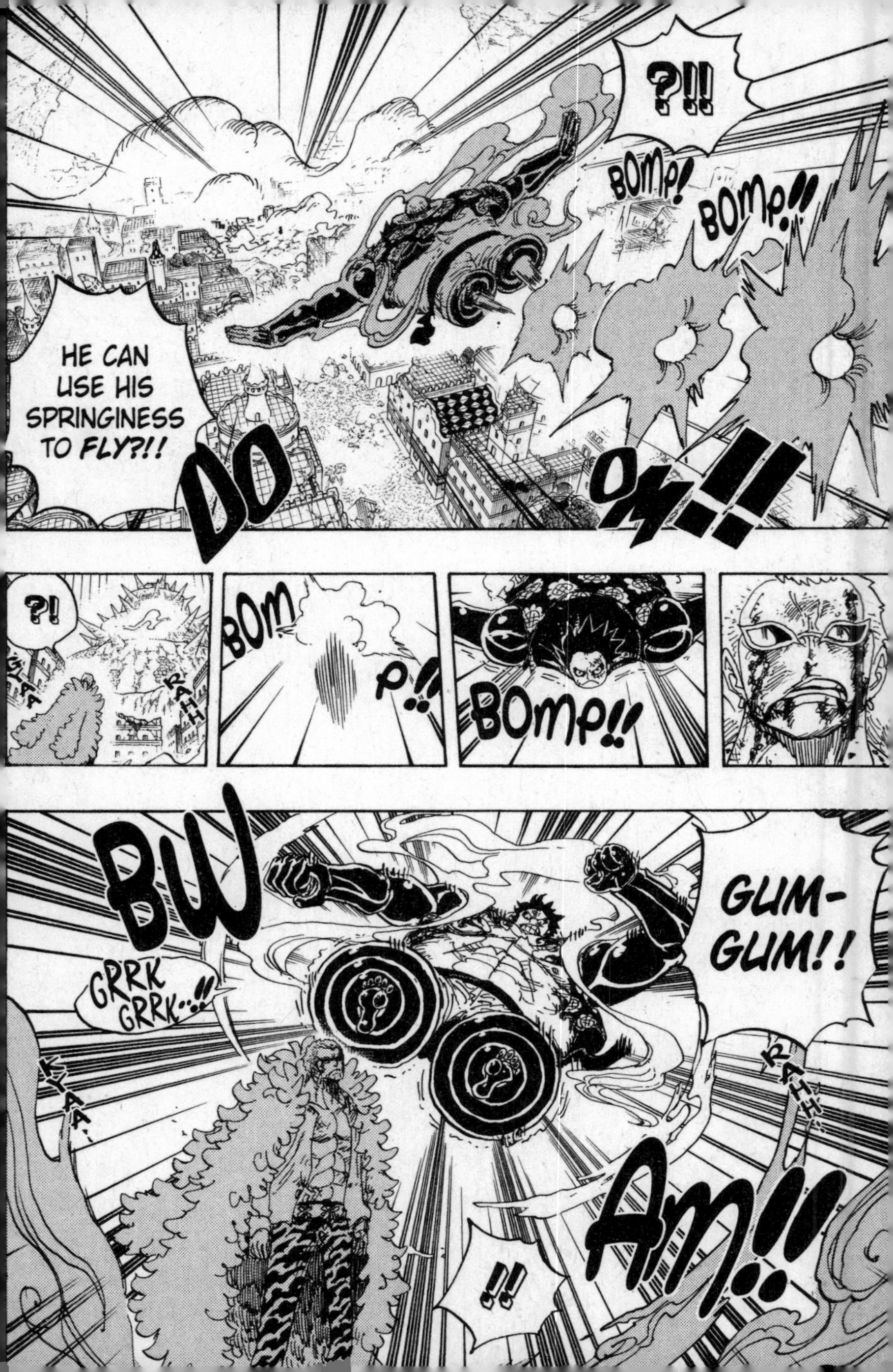
?!!
BOMP!!
BOMP!
HE CAN USE HIS SPRINGINESS TO FLY?!!
DO
OM!!
BOMP!!
BOM
P!!
?!
RAHH
GYAA
GUM-GUM!!
RAHH
BU
GRRK GRRK..!!
AM!!
!!
KYAA

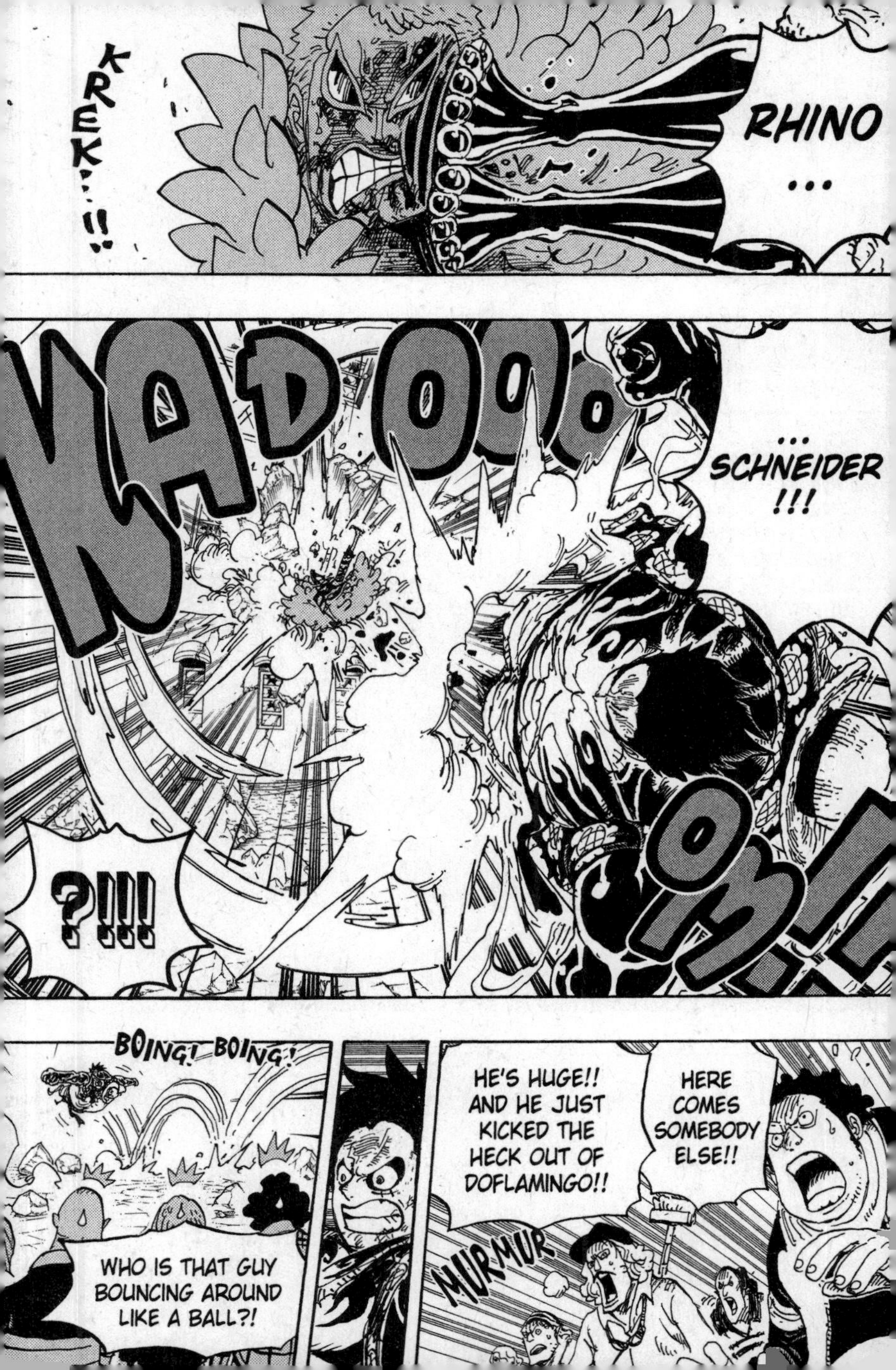
RHINO ...
KREK..!!
... SCHNEIDER !!!
KADOOOOOM!!
?!!!
HERE COMES SOMEBODY ELSE!!
HE'S HUGE!! AND HE JUST KICKED THE HECK OUT OF DOFLAMINGO!!
MURMUR
BOING! BOING!
WHO IS THAT GUY BOUNCING AROUND LIKE A BALL?!

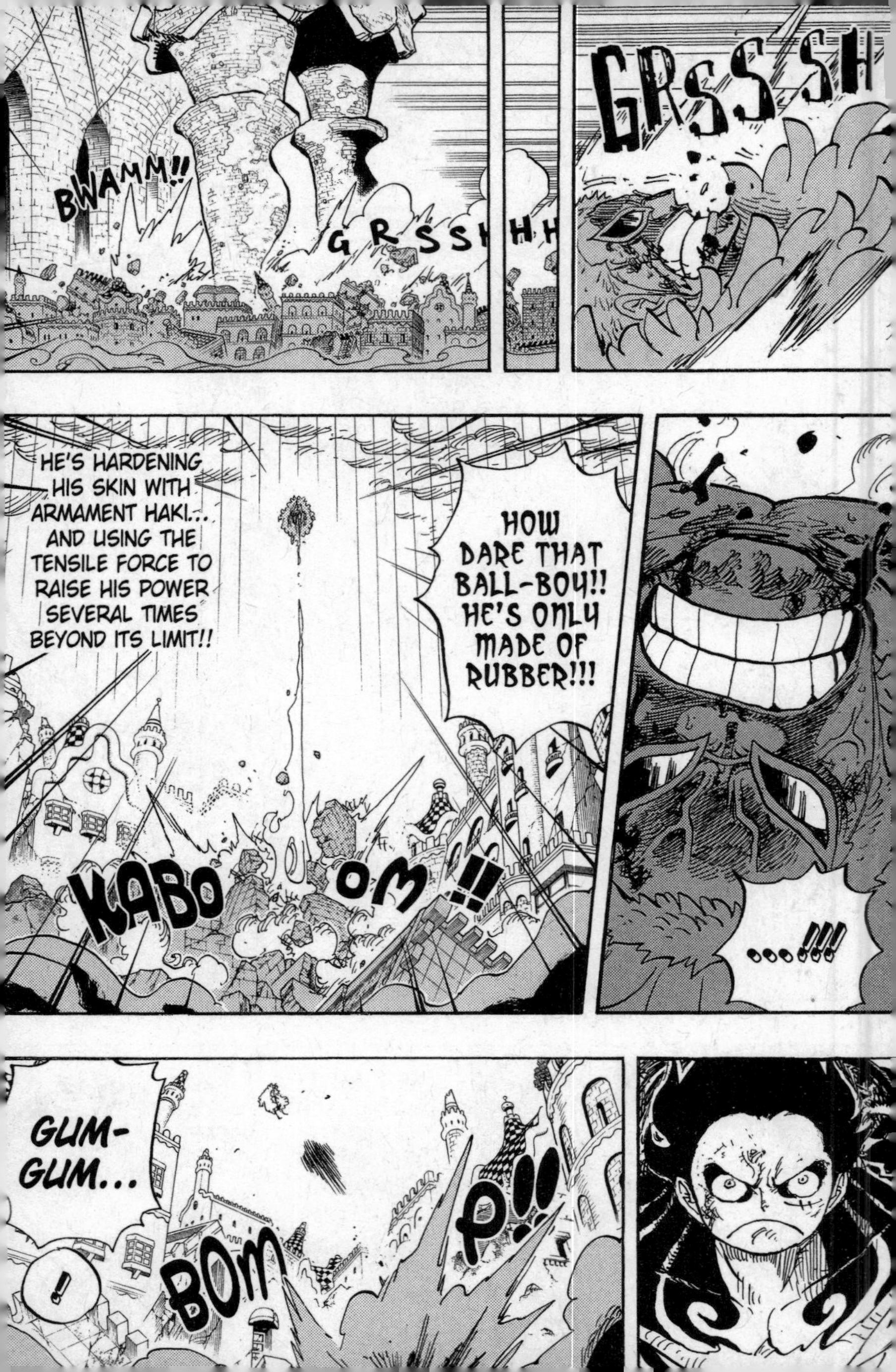
GRSSSH
BWAMM!!
GRSSHHH
...!!!
HOW DARE THAT BALL-BOY!! HE'S ONLY MADE OF RUBBER!!!
HE'S HARDENING HIS SKIN WITH ARMAMENT HAKI... AND USING THE TENSILE FORCE TO RAISE HIS POWER SEVERAL TIMES BEYOND ITS LIMIT!!
KABOOM!!
GUM-GUM...
BOM
P!!
!

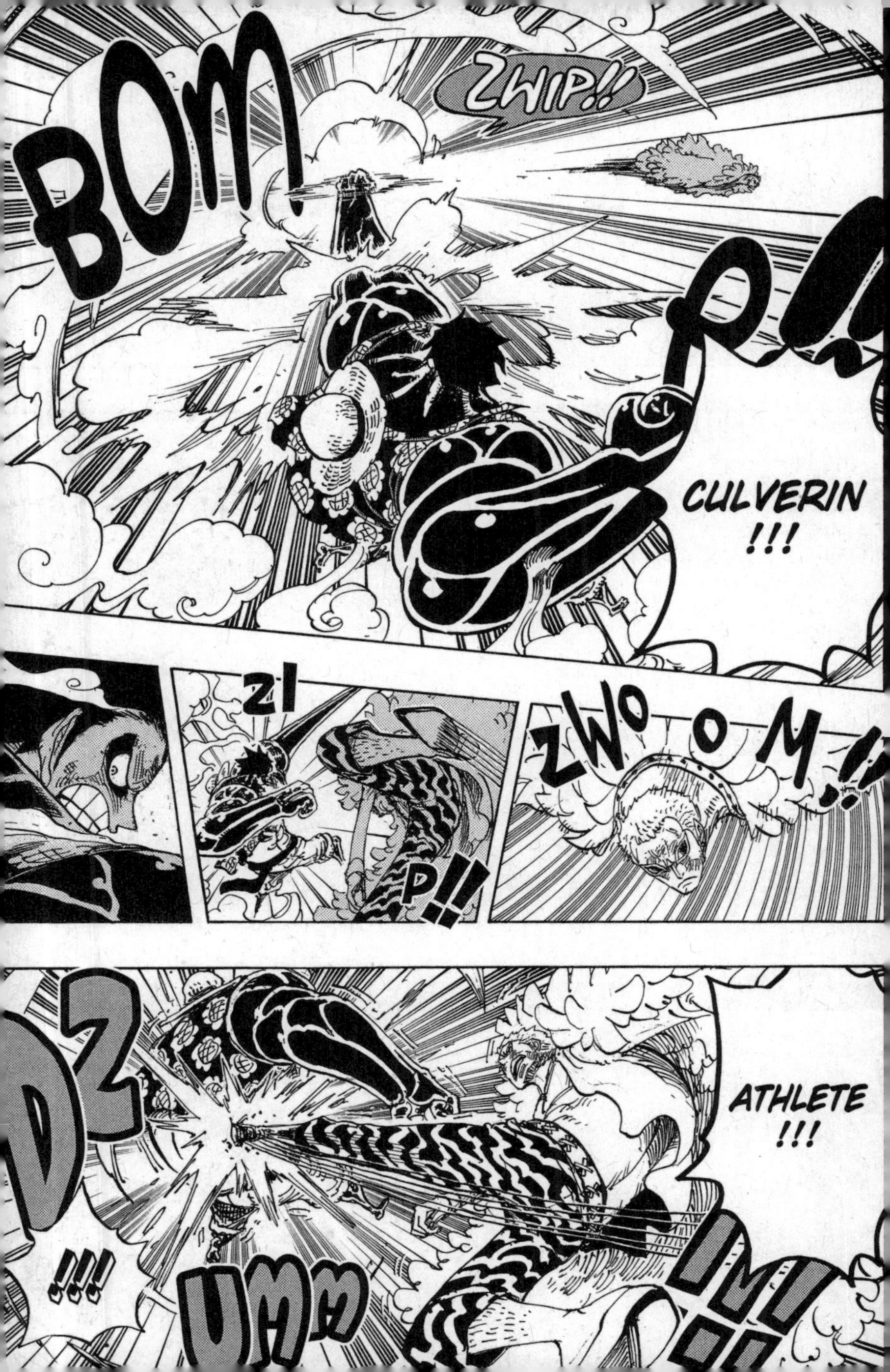

CULVERIN !!!
ZWIP!!
BOM
ZWOOM!!
ZI
P!!
ATHLETE !!!
DZ
UMM
!!!

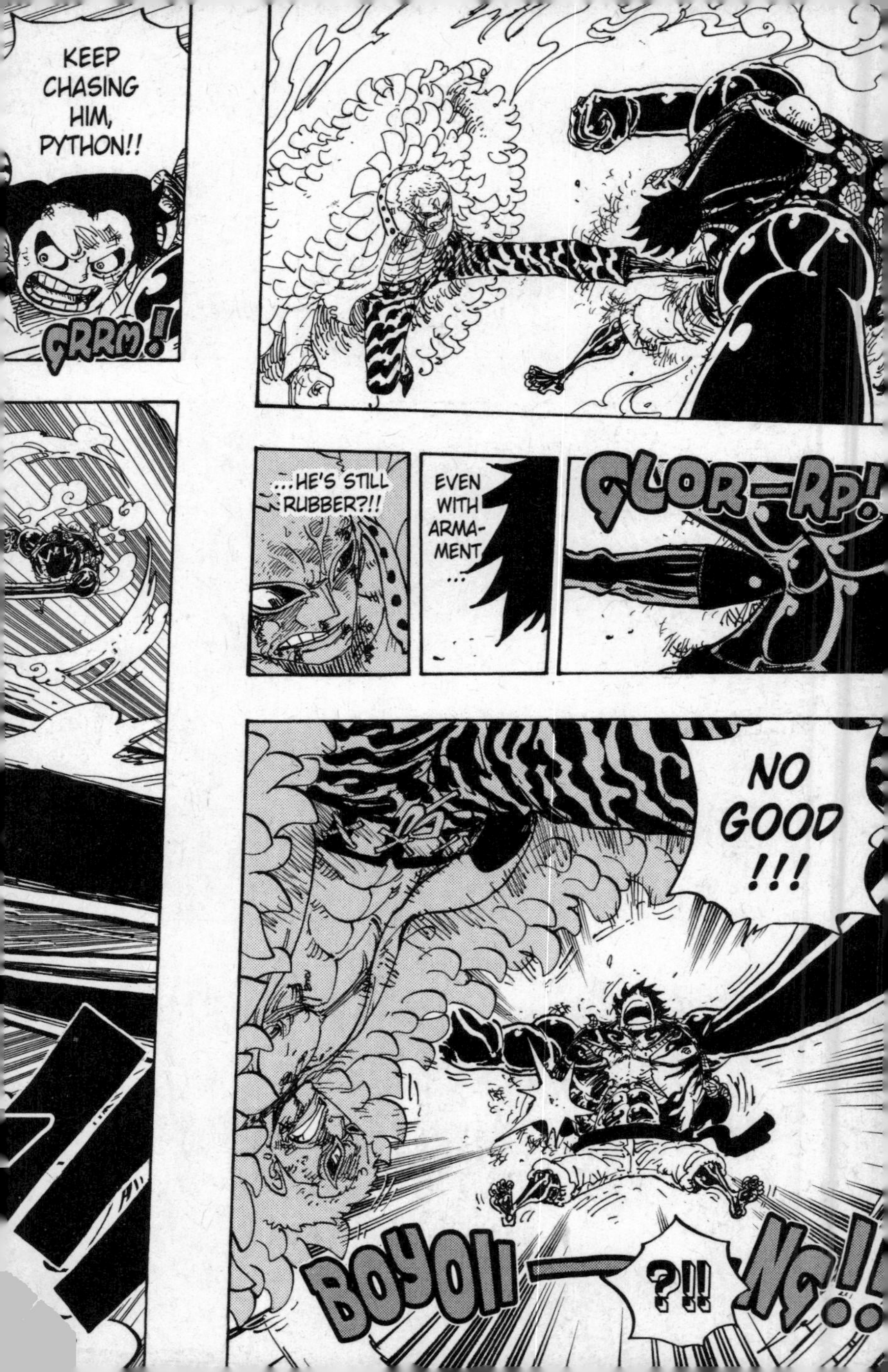
KEEP CHASING HIM, PYTHON!!
GRRM!
GLOR-RP!
EVEN WITH ARMAMENT...
...HE'S STILL RUBBER?!!
NO GOOD!!!
BOYOIII—NG!!
?!!

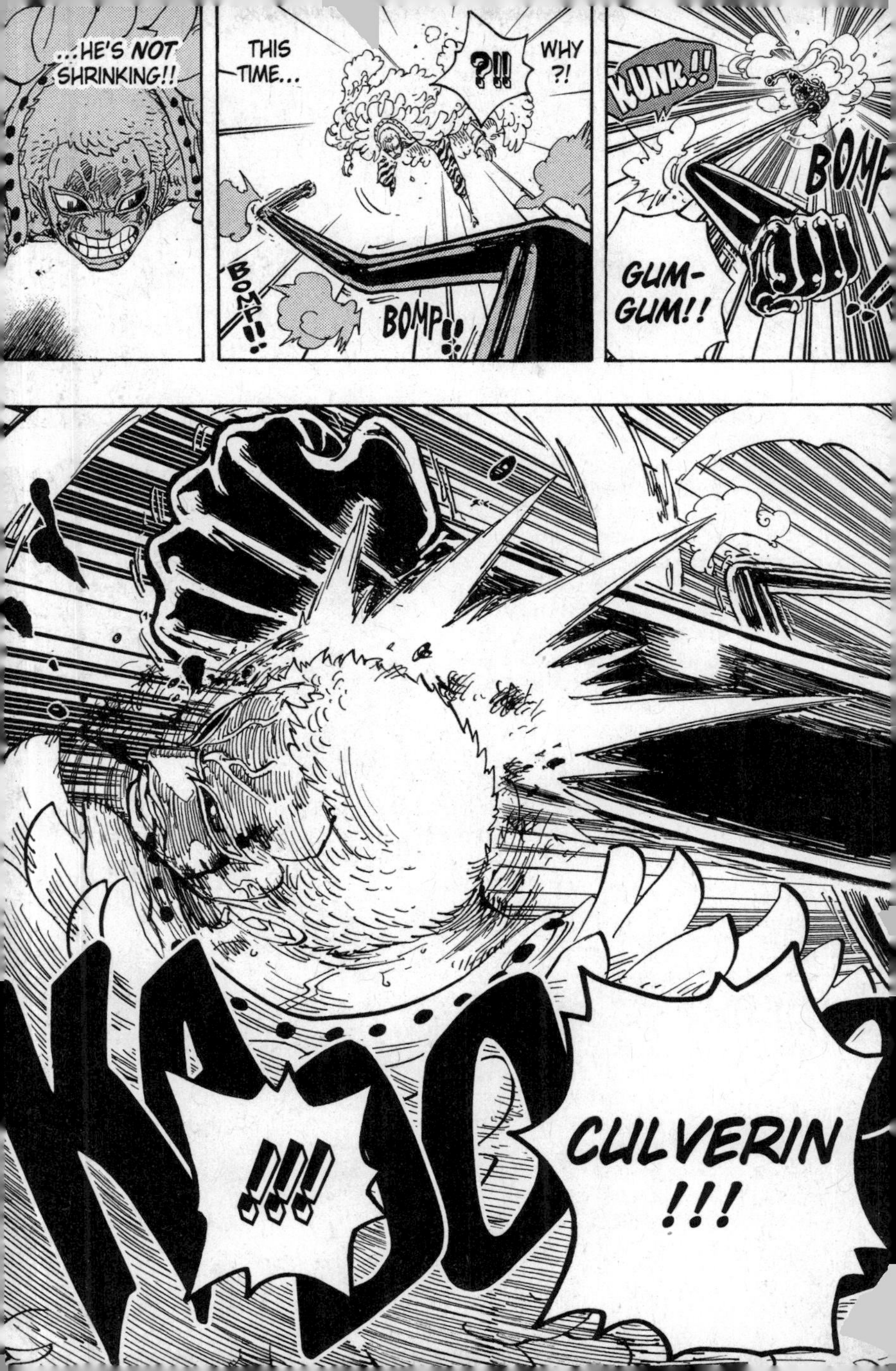
KUNK!!
BOMP!!
GUM-GUM!!
WHY ?!
?!!
THIS TIME...
BOMP!!
BOMP!!
...HE'S NOT SHRINKING!!
CULVERIN !!!
!!!

エス
ビー
エス
質問コーナー

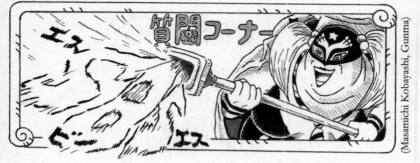

(Masamichi Kobayashi, Gunma)

A: Well, everyone, in the last volume I introduced an old submission to the (Japanese) fan art section, which was sent in by Mr. Horikoshi, who has grown up to draw *My Hero Academia* for *Shonen Jump*. This time, I got a report that one Nozomi Mori, whose fan art recently graced Volume 74, has just made a professional debut with a one-shot under the name Keidai Himuro in the pages of *Monthly Afternoon*. This is totally unrelated to *Jump*, however. Anyways, congrats! I hope you get serialized and make a great name for yourself in the sea of manga! Good luck!! (^ ^)

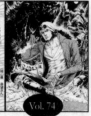

岡山県 森望さん
Vol. 74

岡山県 森望さん
Vol. 45

Q: Hello!! I was watching TV the other day, and learned that the real-life Japanese Navy, when it is out at sea, always serves curry on Fridays to maintain a sense of the days of the week. Does the Navy in *One Piece* have curry too? If that's the case, is Rika's curry super-sweet???

--Kagamin

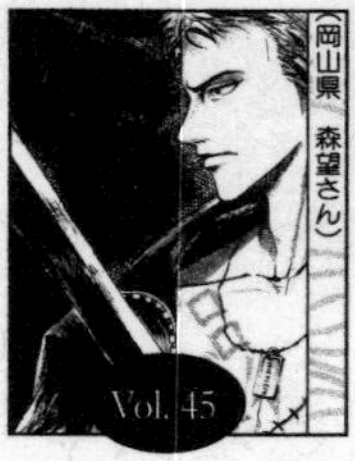

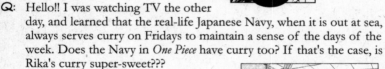

A: Yes, the Navy's curry is quite famous. The Navy in One Piece employs the same custom. Since it serves a purpose of providing extra nutrients that one day a week, I've heard that it's a delicious curry packed full of fresh seafood. It seems that the sweeter curry served at Rika's Naval Branch is quite popular. Well, that's it for this installment of the SBS! See you next volume!!

MARINE
WAN

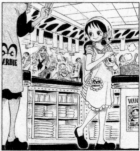

Chapter 785:
ON BROKEN LEGS

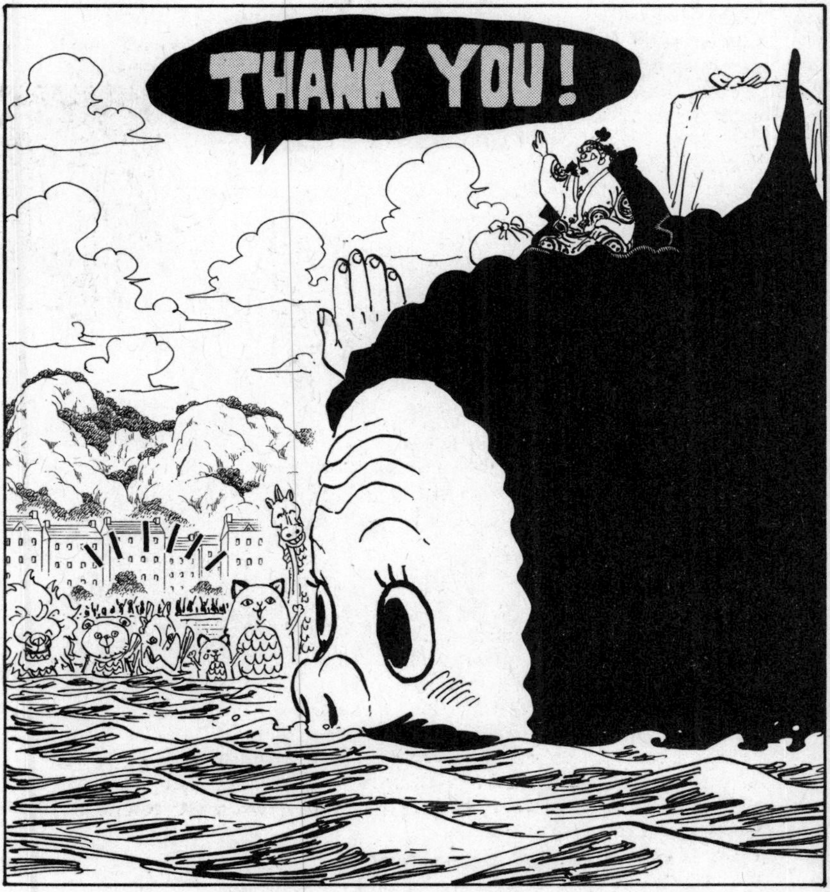
THANK YOU!

THE SOLITARY JOURNEY OF JIMBEI, FIRST SON OF THE SEA, FINAL VOLUME: "SETTING OFF WITH A NEW KIMONO AND SOME GIFTS"

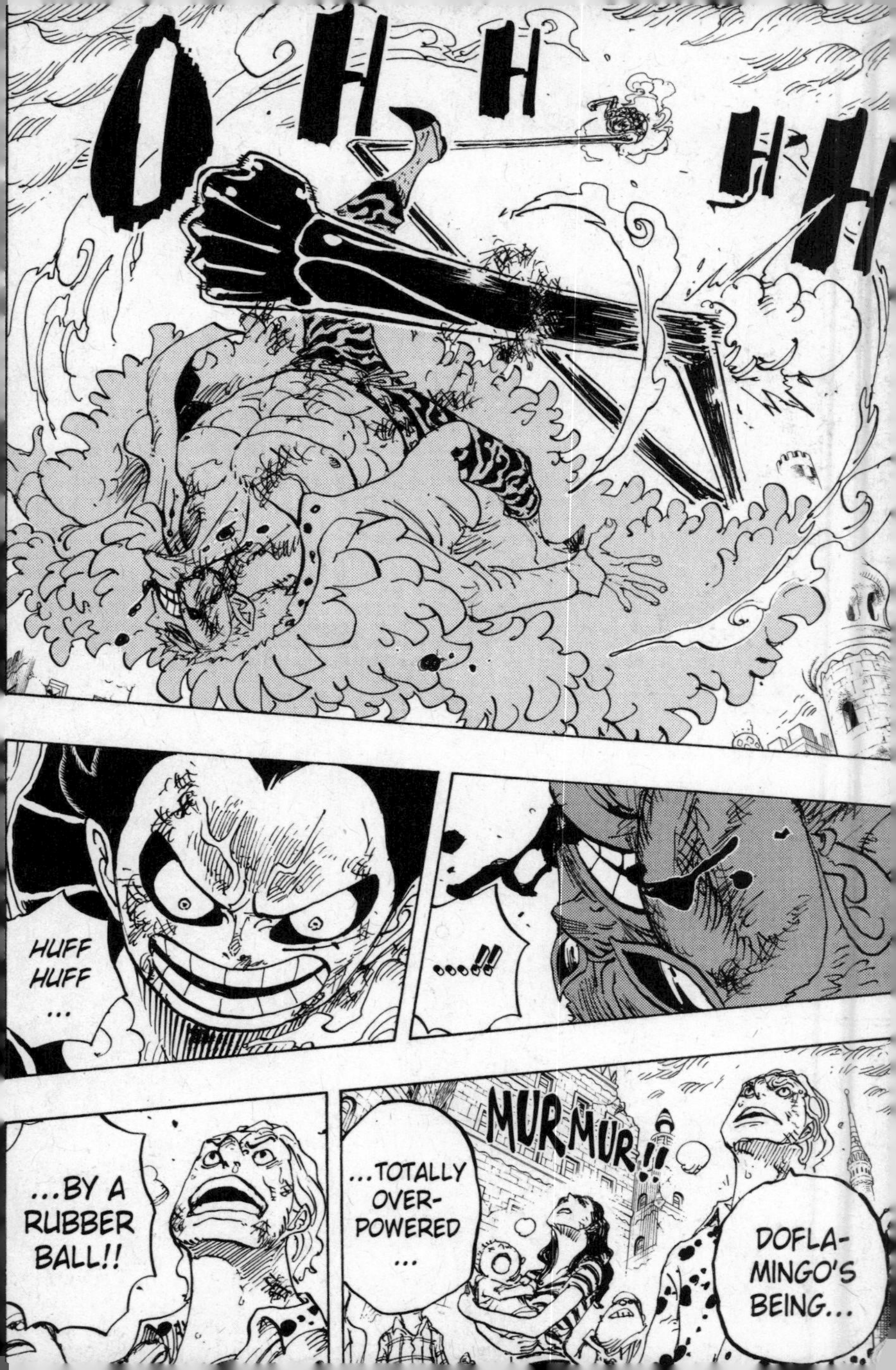
OHHHH
....!!
HUFF HUFF ...
DOFLA-MINGO'S BEING...
MURMUR!!
...TOTALLY OVER-POWERED ...
...BY A RUBBER BALL!!

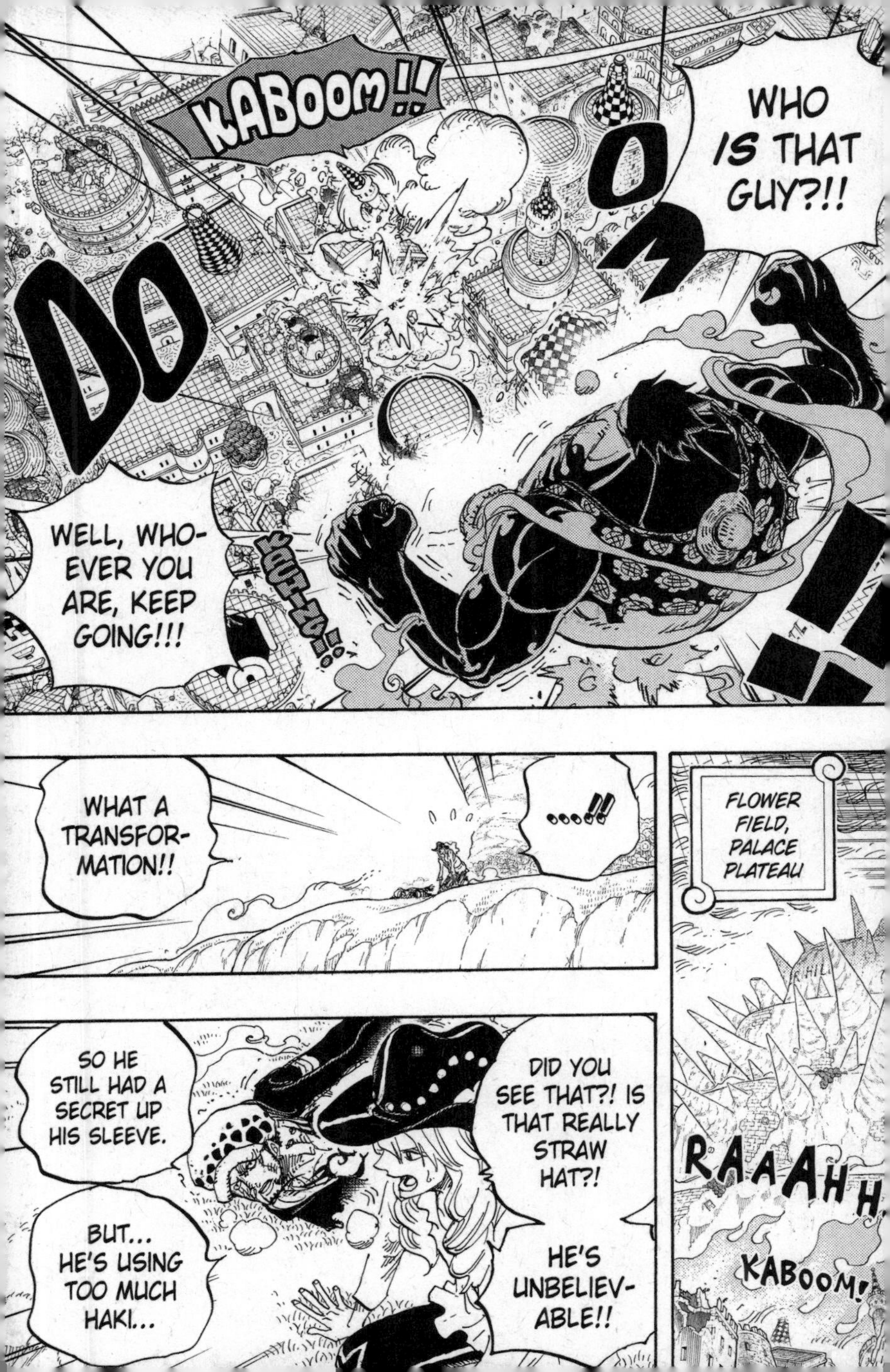
WHO IS THAT GUY?!!
DOOM
KABOOM!!
WELL, WHO-EVER YOU ARE, KEEP GOING!!!
FLOWER FIELD, PALACE PLATEAU
RAAAHH
KABOOM!
....!!
WHAT A TRANSFOR-MATION!!
DID YOU SEE THAT?! IS THAT REALLY STRAW HAT?!
HE'S UNBELIEV-ABLE!!
SO HE STILL HAD A SECRET UP HIS SLEEVE.
BUT... HE'S USING TOO MUCH HAKI...

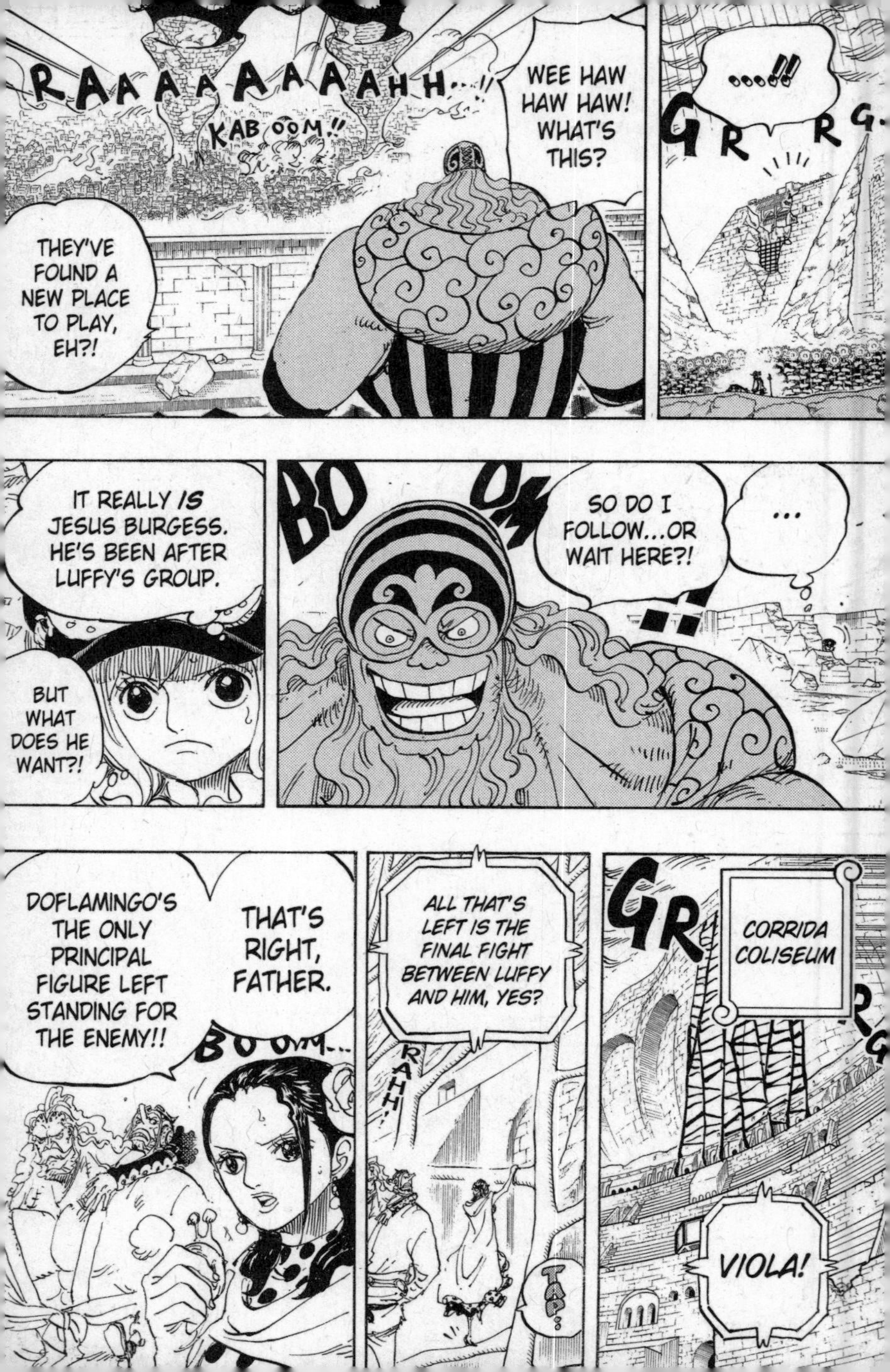
....!!
GRRRG.
WEE HAW HAW HAW! WHAT'S THIS?
RAAAAAAAAAHH...!!
KABOOM!!
THEY'VE FOUND A NEW PLACE TO PLAY, EH?!
...
SO DO I FOLLOW...OR WAIT HERE?!
BOOM
IT REALLY *IS* JESUS BURGESS. HE'S BEEN AFTER LUFFY'S GROUP.
BUT WHAT DOES HE WANT?!
CORRIDA COLISEUM
GR
RG
VIOLA!
ALL THAT'S LEFT IS THE FINAL FIGHT BETWEEN LUFFY AND HIM, YES?
RAHH!
TAP
THAT'S RIGHT, FATHER.
DOFLAMINGO'S THE ONLY PRINCIPAL FIGURE LEFT STANDING FOR THE ENEMY!!
BOOM...

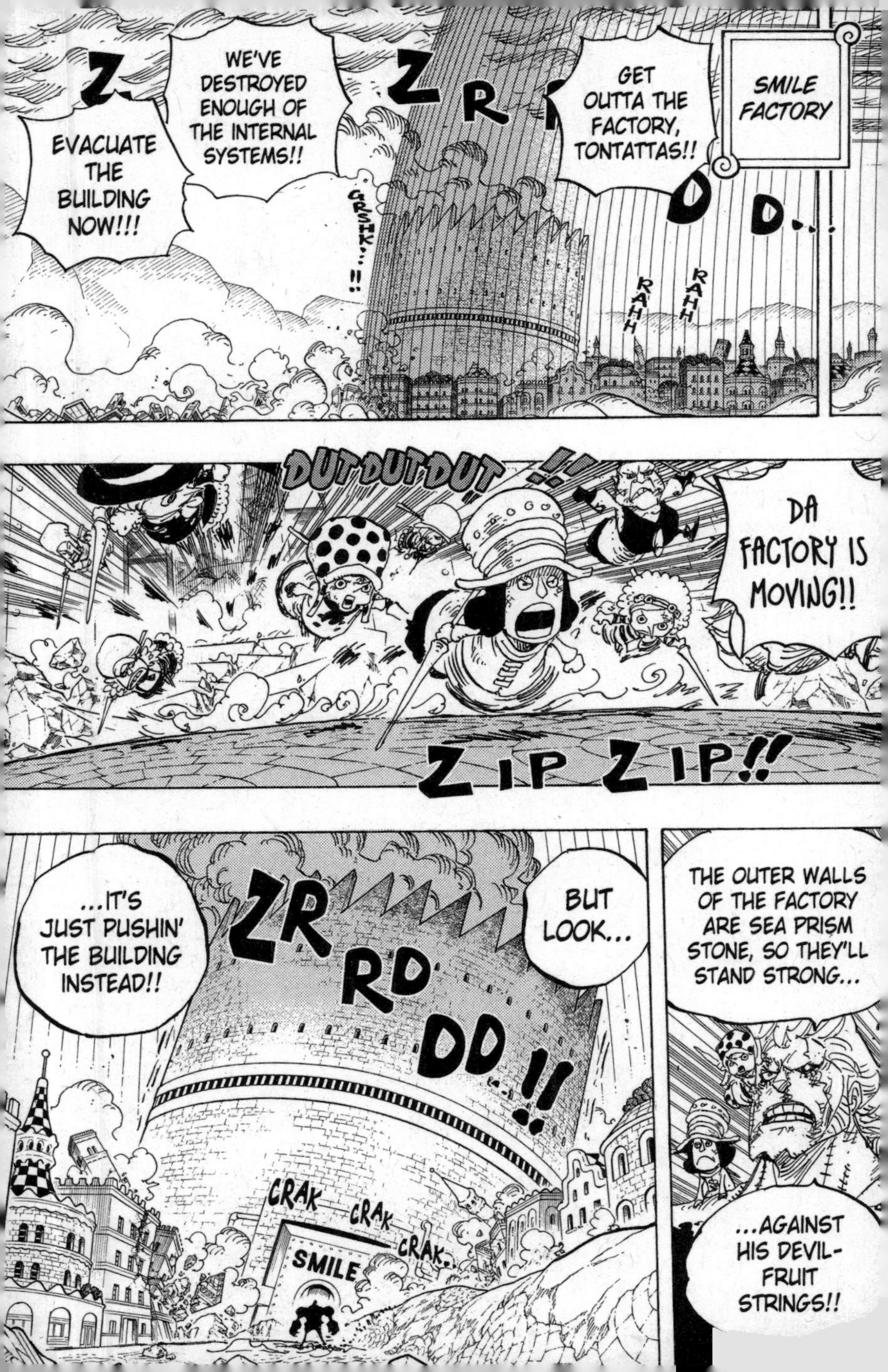
SMILE FACTORY
GET OUTTA THE FACTORY, TONTATTAS!!
Z R D D...
WE'VE DESTROYED ENOUGH OF THE INTERNAL SYSTEMS!!
Z
EVACUATE THE BUILDING NOW!!!
GRSHK...!!
RAHH
RAHH
DA FACTORY IS MOVING!!
!!
DUT DUT DUT
ZIP ZIP!!
THE OUTER WALLS OF THE FACTORY ARE SEA PRISM STONE, SO THEY'LL STAND STRONG...
...AGAINST HIS DEVIL-FRUIT STRINGS!!
BUT LOOK...
...IT'S JUST PUSHIN' THE BUILDING INSTEAD!!
ZR RD DD!!
CRAK
CRAK
CRAK
SMILE

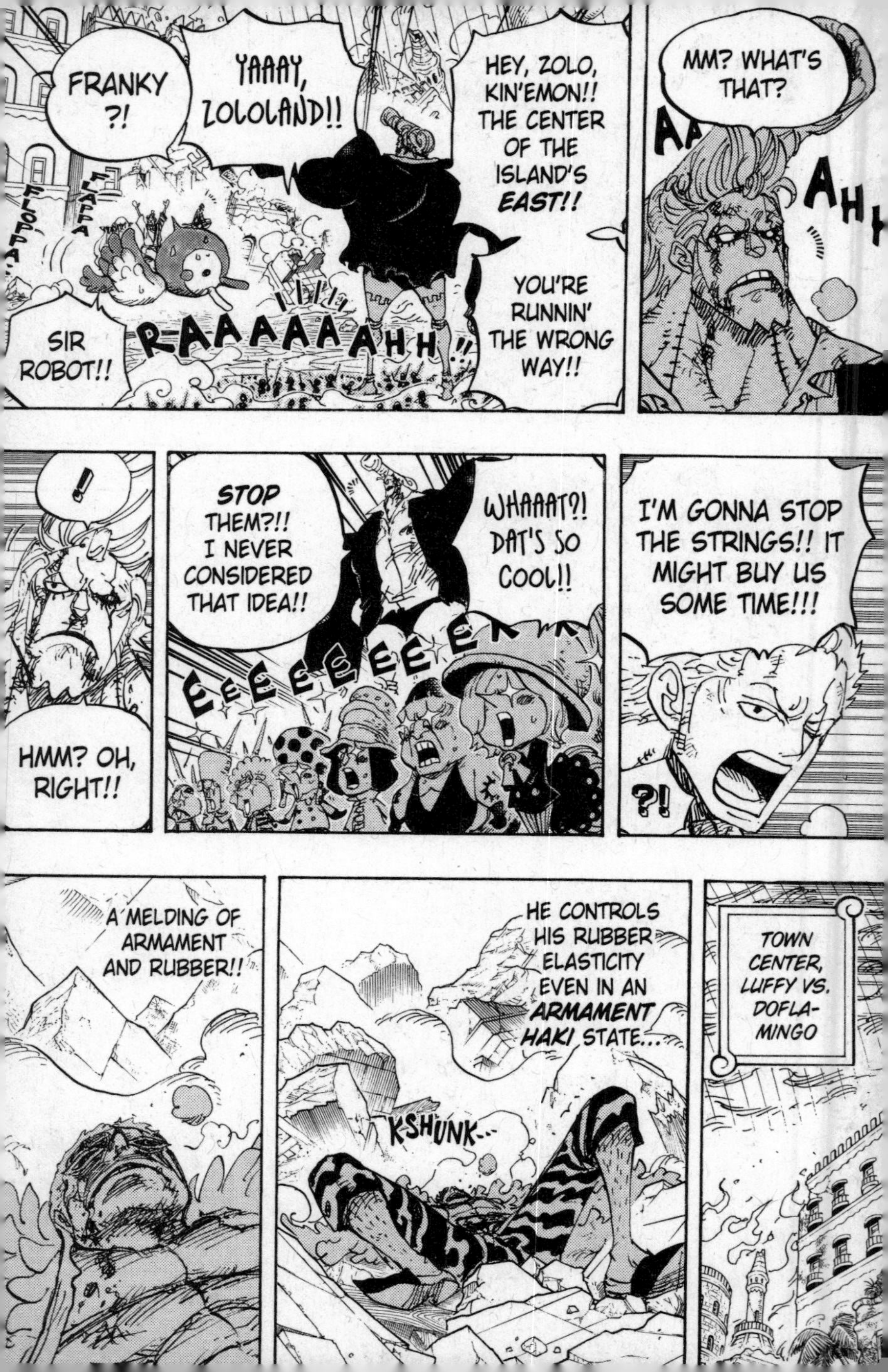
MM? WHAT'S THAT?
AAHH
HEY, ZOLO, KIN'EMON!! THE CENTER OF THE ISLAND'S *EAST!!*
YOU'RE RUNNIN' THE WRONG WAY!!
YAAAY, ZOLOLAND!!
FRANKY ?!
RAAAAAAHH!!
FLAPPA FLAPPA
FLOPPA...
SIR ROBOT!!
I'M GONNA STOP THE STRINGS!! IT MIGHT BUY US SOME TIME!!!
?!
WHAAAT?! DAT'S SO COOL!!
STOP THEM?!! I NEVER CONSIDERED THAT IDEA!!
EEEEEEEEE
!
HMM? OH, RIGHT!!
TOWN CENTER, LUFFY VS. DOFLA-MINGO
HE CONTROLS HIS RUBBER ELASTICITY EVEN IN AN ***ARMAMENT HAKI*** STATE...
KSHUNK...
A MELDING OF ARMAMENT AND RUBBER!!

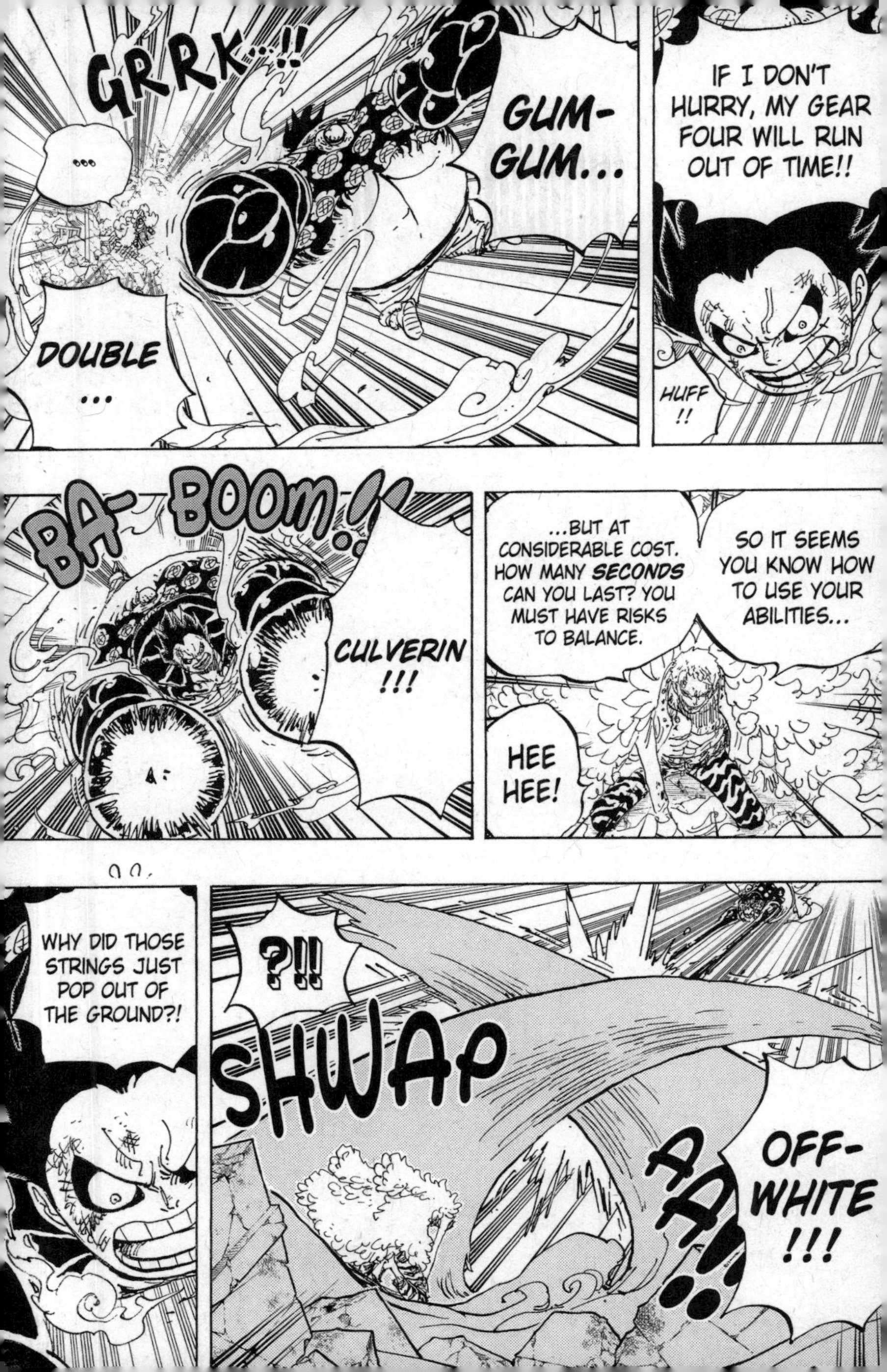
IF I DON'T HURRY, MY GEAR FOUR WILL RUN OUT OF TIME!!
HUFF !!
GUM-GUM...
GRRK...!!
DOUBLE ...
SO IT SEEMS YOU KNOW HOW TO USE YOUR ABILITIES...
...BUT AT CONSIDERABLE COST. HOW MANY **SECONDS** CAN YOU LAST? YOU MUST HAVE RISKS TO BALANCE.
HEE HEE!
BA-BOOM!!
CULVERIN !!!
?!!
SHWAP
OFF-WHITE !!!
AAA
WHY DID THOSE STRINGS JUST POP OUT OF THE GROUND?!

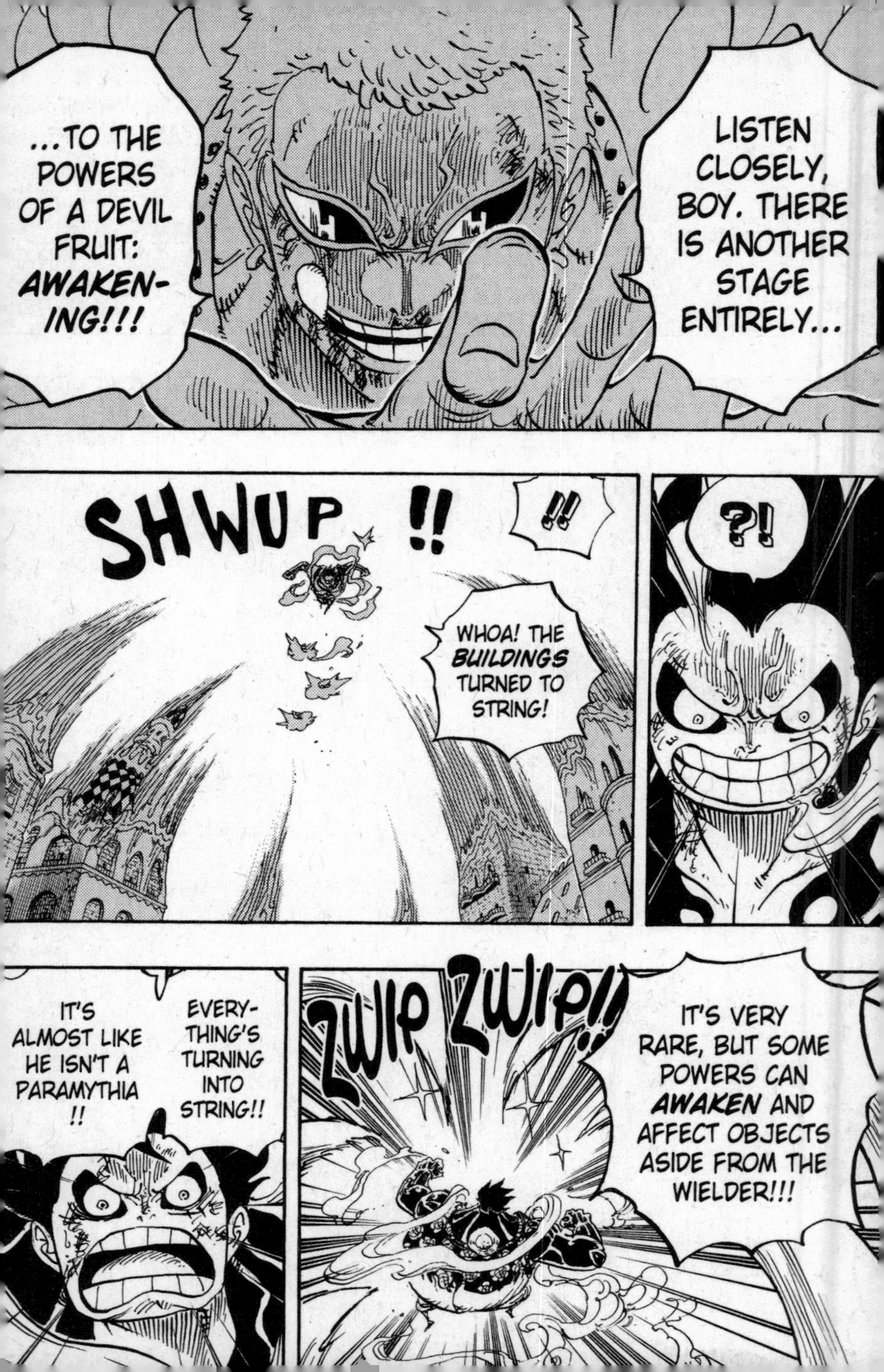
LISTEN CLOSELY, BOY. THERE IS ANOTHER STAGE ENTIRELY...
...TO THE POWERS OF A DEVIL FRUIT: *AWAKENING!!!*
?!
!!
SHWUP!!
WHOA! THE *BUILDINGS* TURNED TO STRING!
IT'S VERY RARE, BUT SOME POWERS CAN *AWAKEN* AND AFFECT OBJECTS ASIDE FROM THE WIELDER!!!
ZWIP ZWIP!!
EVERYTHING'S TURNING INTO STRING!!
IT'S ALMOST LIKE HE ISN'T A PARAMYTHIA !!

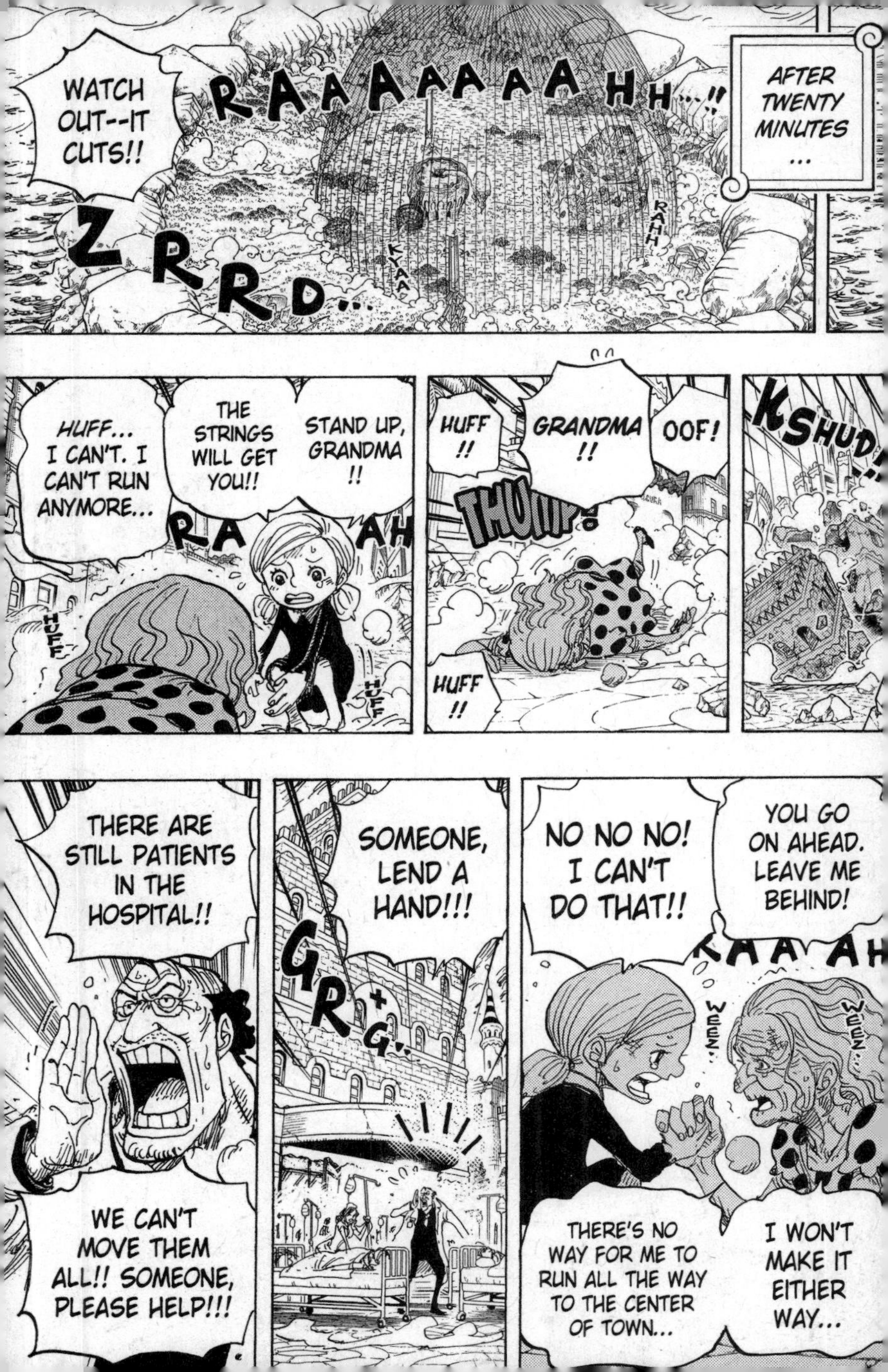
AFTER TWENTY MINUTES ...
RAAAAAAAHH...!!
WATCH OUT--IT CUTS!!
RAHH
KYAA
ZRRRD...
KSHUD
OOF!
GRANDMA !!
HUFF !!
THUMP
HUFF !!
STAND UP, GRANDMA !!
THE STRINGS WILL GET YOU!!
HUFF... I CAN'T. I CAN'T RUN ANYMORE...
RA AH
HUFF
HUFF
YOU GO ON AHEAD. LEAVE ME BEHIND!
NO NO NO! I CAN'T DO THAT!!
RAA AH
WEEZ...
WEEZ...
I WON'T MAKE IT EITHER WAY...
THERE'S NO WAY FOR ME TO RUN ALL THE WAY TO THE CENTER OF TOWN...
SOMEONE, LEND A HAND!!!
GRRG..
THERE ARE STILL PATIENTS IN THE HOSPITAL!!
WE CAN'T MOVE THEM ALL!! SOMEONE, PLEASE HELP!!!

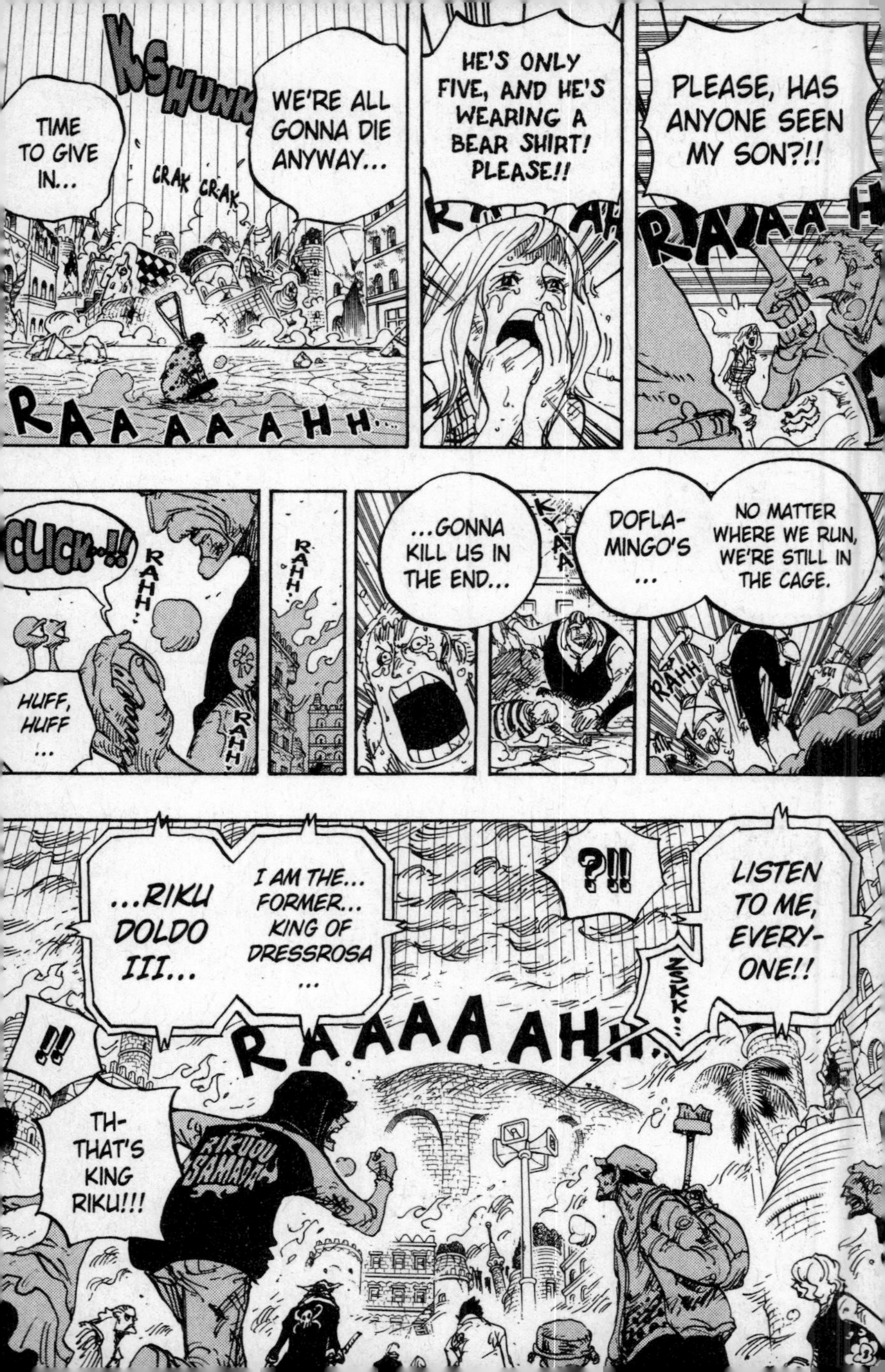
PLEASE, HAS ANYONE SEEN MY SON?!!
RAAAAH
HE'S ONLY FIVE, AND HE'S WEARING A BEAR SHIRT! PLEASE!!
WE'RE ALL GONNA DIE ANYWAY...
KSHUNK
TIME TO GIVE IN...
CRAK CRAK
RAAAAAHH...
NO MATTER WHERE WE RUN, WE'RE STILL IN THE CAGE.
DOFLAMINGO'S ...
...GONNA KILL US IN THE END...
KYAA
RAHH
RAHH...
CLICK..!!
RAHH...
HUFF, HUFF ...
RAHH
LISTEN TO ME, EVERYONE!!
ZSKK...
?!!
I AM THE... FORMER... KING OF DRESSROSA ...
...RIKU DOLDO III...
RAAAAAHH.
!!
TH-THAT'S KING RIKU!!!
RIKUOU SAMA

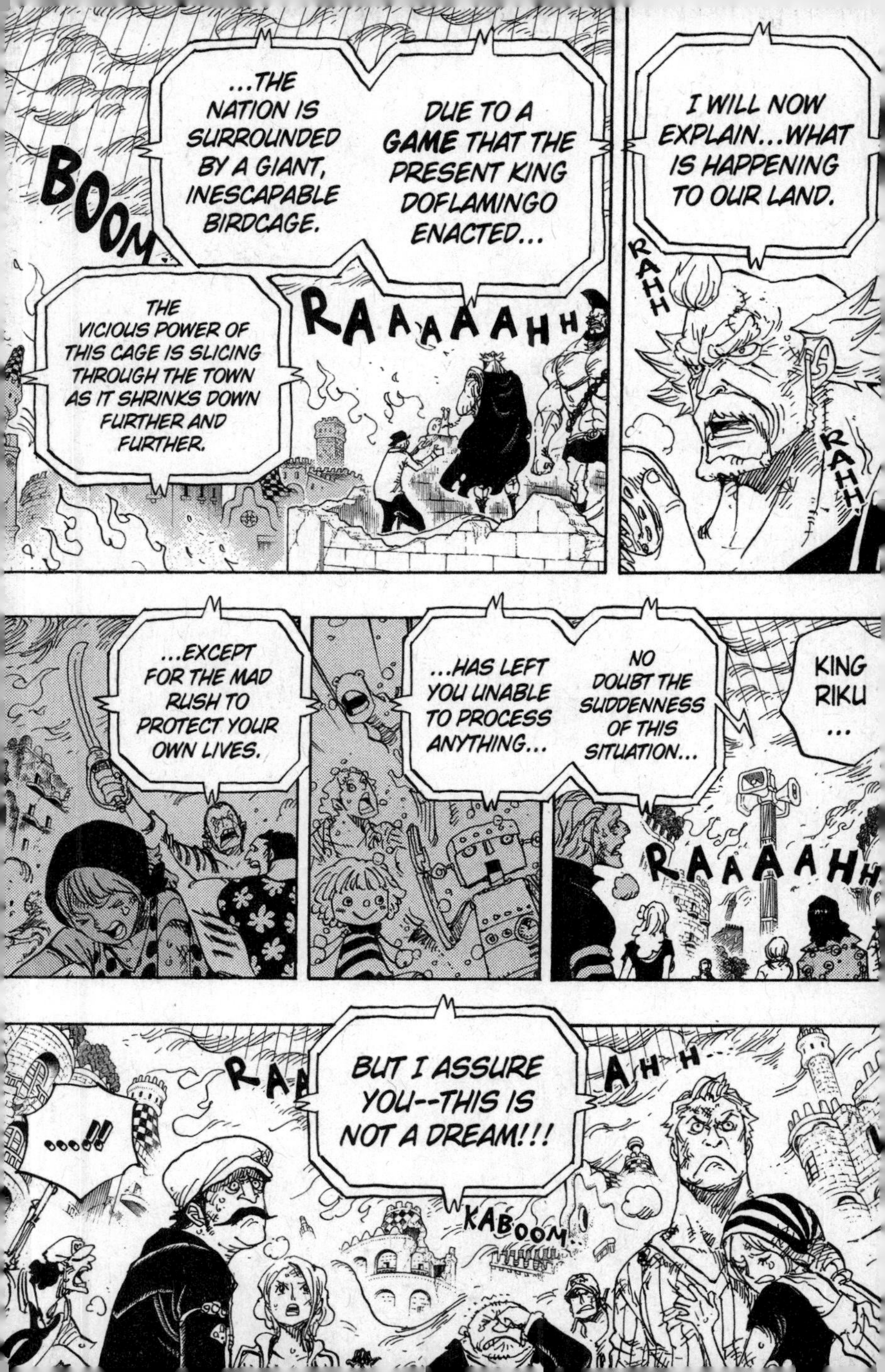
I WILL NOW EXPLAIN...WHAT IS HAPPENING TO OUR LAND.
RAHH
RAHH
DUE TO A GAME THAT THE PRESENT KING DOFLAMINGO ENACTED...
...THE NATION IS SURROUNDED BY A GIANT, INESCAPABLE BIRDCAGE.
BOOM
RAAAAAHH
THE VICIOUS POWER OF THIS CAGE IS SLICING THROUGH THE TOWN AS IT SHRINKS DOWN FURTHER AND FURTHER.
KING RIKU ...
RAAAAHH
NO DOUBT THE SUDDENNESS OF THIS SITUATION...
...HAS LEFT YOU UNABLE TO PROCESS ANYTHING...
...EXCEPT FOR THE MAD RUSH TO PROTECT YOUR OWN LIVES.
RAA AHH
BUT I ASSURE YOU--THIS IS NOT A DREAM!!!
KABOOM
...!!

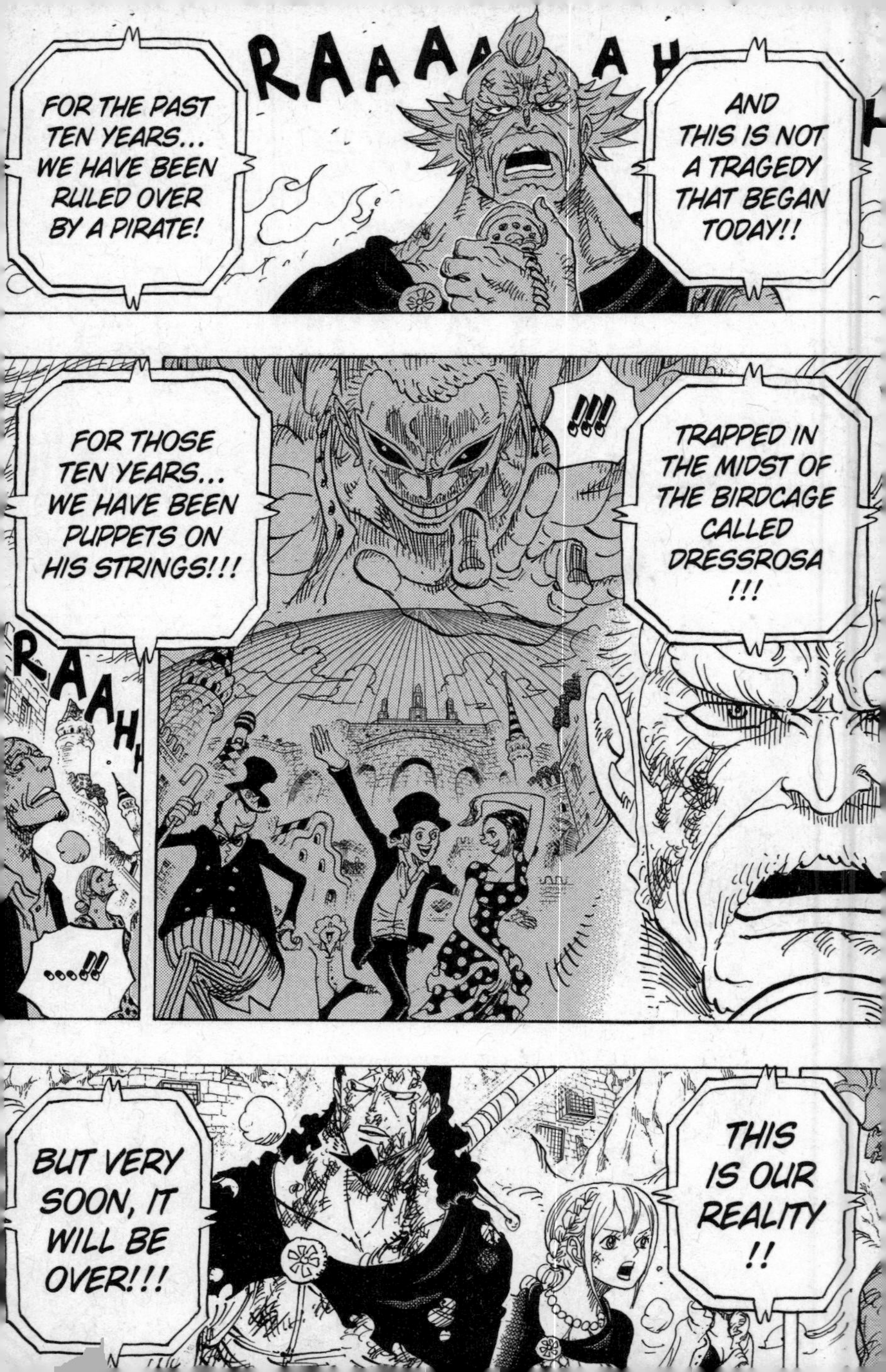
RAAAAAAHH
AND THIS IS NOT A TRAGEDY THAT BEGAN TODAY!!
FOR THE PAST TEN YEARS... WE HAVE BEEN RULED OVER BY A PIRATE!
TRAPPED IN THE MIDST OF THE BIRDCAGE CALLED DRESSROSA!!!
!!!
FOR THOSE TEN YEARS... WE HAVE BEEN PUPPETS ON HIS STRINGS!!!
RAAHH
....!!
THIS IS OUR REALITY!!
BUT VERY SOON, IT WILL BE OVER!!!

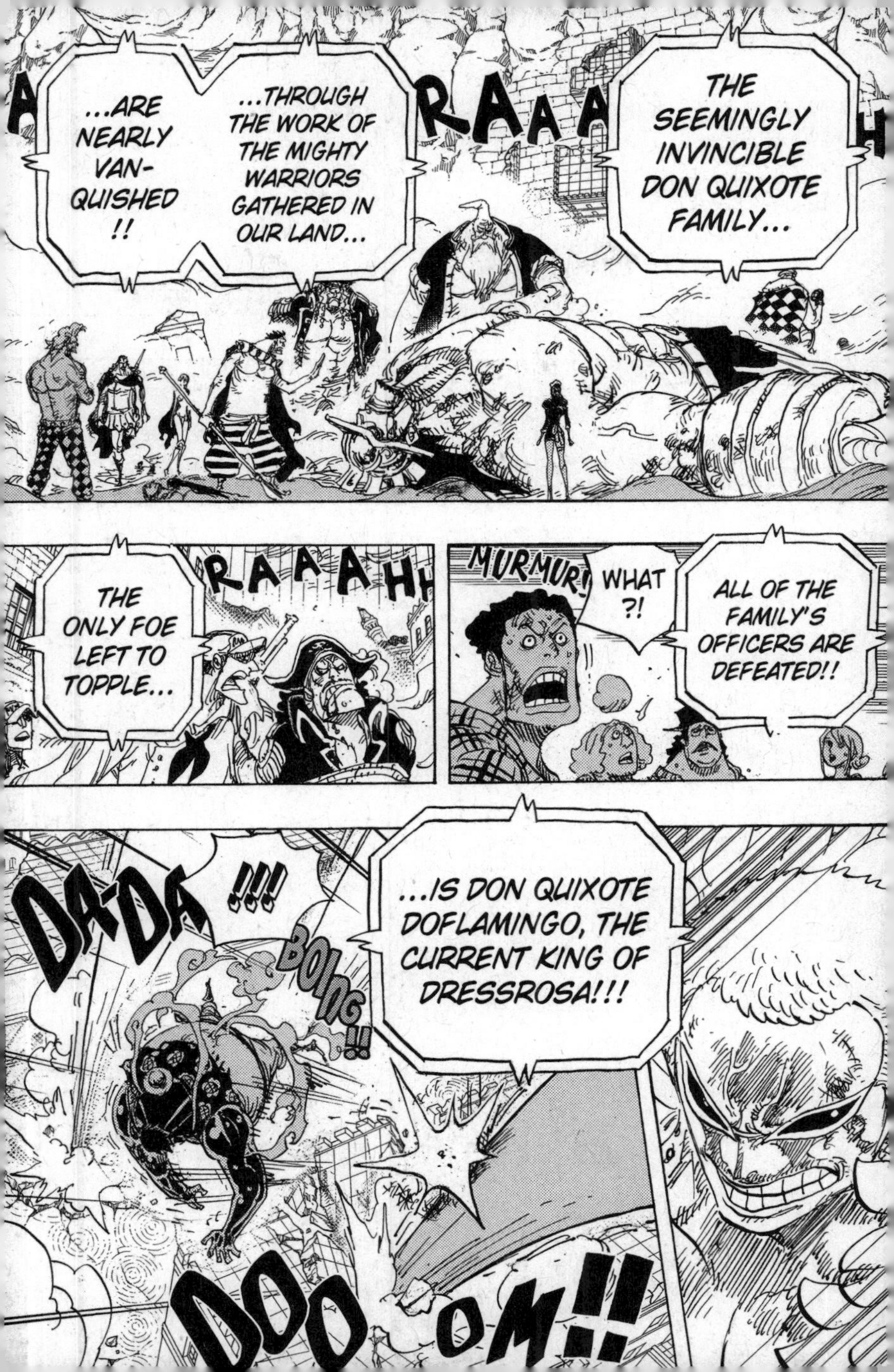
THE SEEMINGLY INVINCIBLE DON QUIXOTE FAMILY...
...THROUGH THE WORK OF THE MIGHTY WARRIORS GATHERED IN OUR LAND...
...ARE NEARLY VAN-QUISHED!!
RAAAH
MURMUR
ALL OF THE FAMILY'S OFFICERS ARE DEFEATED!!
WHAT?!
THE ONLY FOE LEFT TO TOPPLE...
RAAAHH
...IS DON QUIXOTE DOFLAMINGO, THE CURRENT KING OF DRESSROSA!!!
DA-DA!!!
BOING!!
DOOOM!!

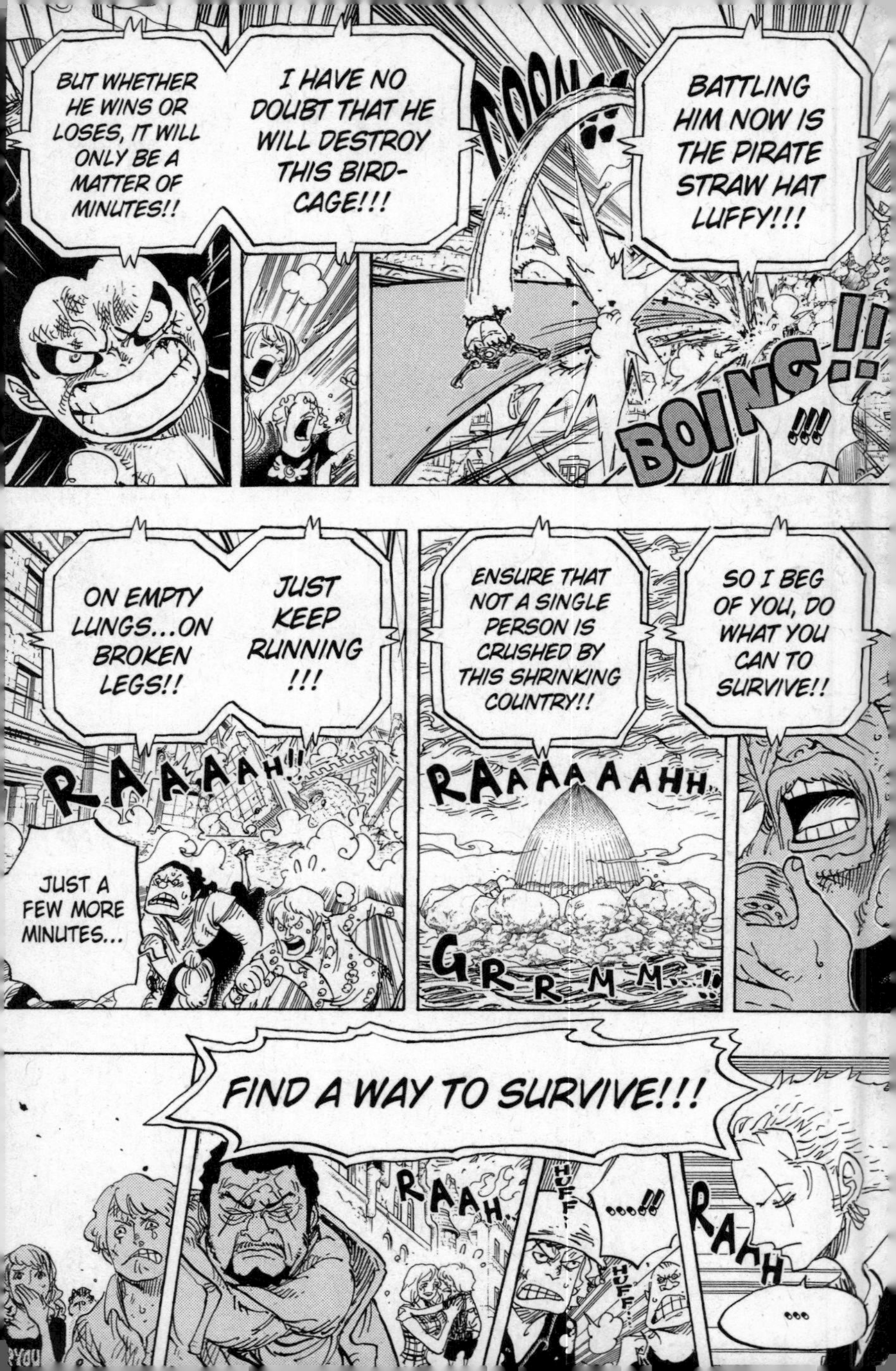
BATTLING HIM NOW IS THE PIRATE STRAW HAT LUFFY!!!
DOON
BOING!!
!!!
I HAVE NO DOUBT THAT HE WILL DESTROY THIS BIRD-CAGE!!!
BUT WHETHER HE WINS OR LOSES, IT WILL ONLY BE A MATTER OF MINUTES!!
SO I BEG OF YOU, DO WHAT YOU CAN TO SURVIVE!!
ENSURE THAT NOT A SINGLE PERSON IS CRUSHED BY THIS SHRINKING COUNTRY!!
RAAAAAAHH..
GRRMM..!!
JUST KEEP RUNNING!!!
ON EMPTY LUNGS...ON BROKEN LEGS!!
RAAAAH!!
JUST A FEW MORE MINUTES...
FIND A WAY TO SURVIVE!!!
RAHH
...!!
HUFF...
HUFF...
RAAH..
...

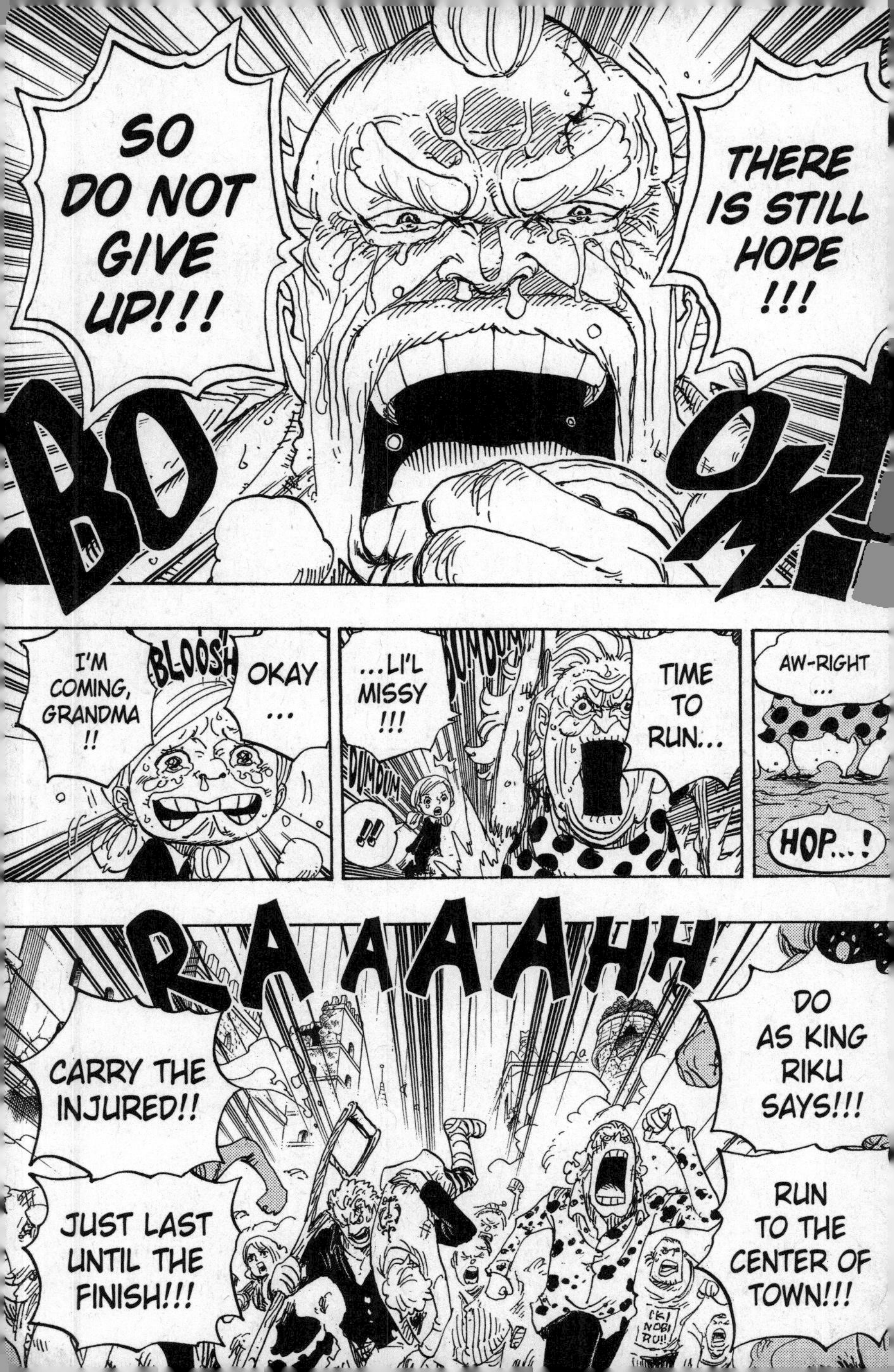
THERE IS STILL HOPE !!!
SO DO NOT GIVE UP!!!
BOOM!
AW-RIGHT ...
HOP...!
TIME TO RUN...
...LI'L MISSY !!!
DUMDUM
DUMDUM
!!
OKAY ...
I'M COMING, GRANDMA !!
BLOOSH
RAAAAHH
DO AS KING RIKU SAYS!!!
RUN TO THE CENTER OF TOWN!!!
CARRY THE INJURED!!
JUST LAST UNTIL THE FINISH!!!
KI NOBI RU!!

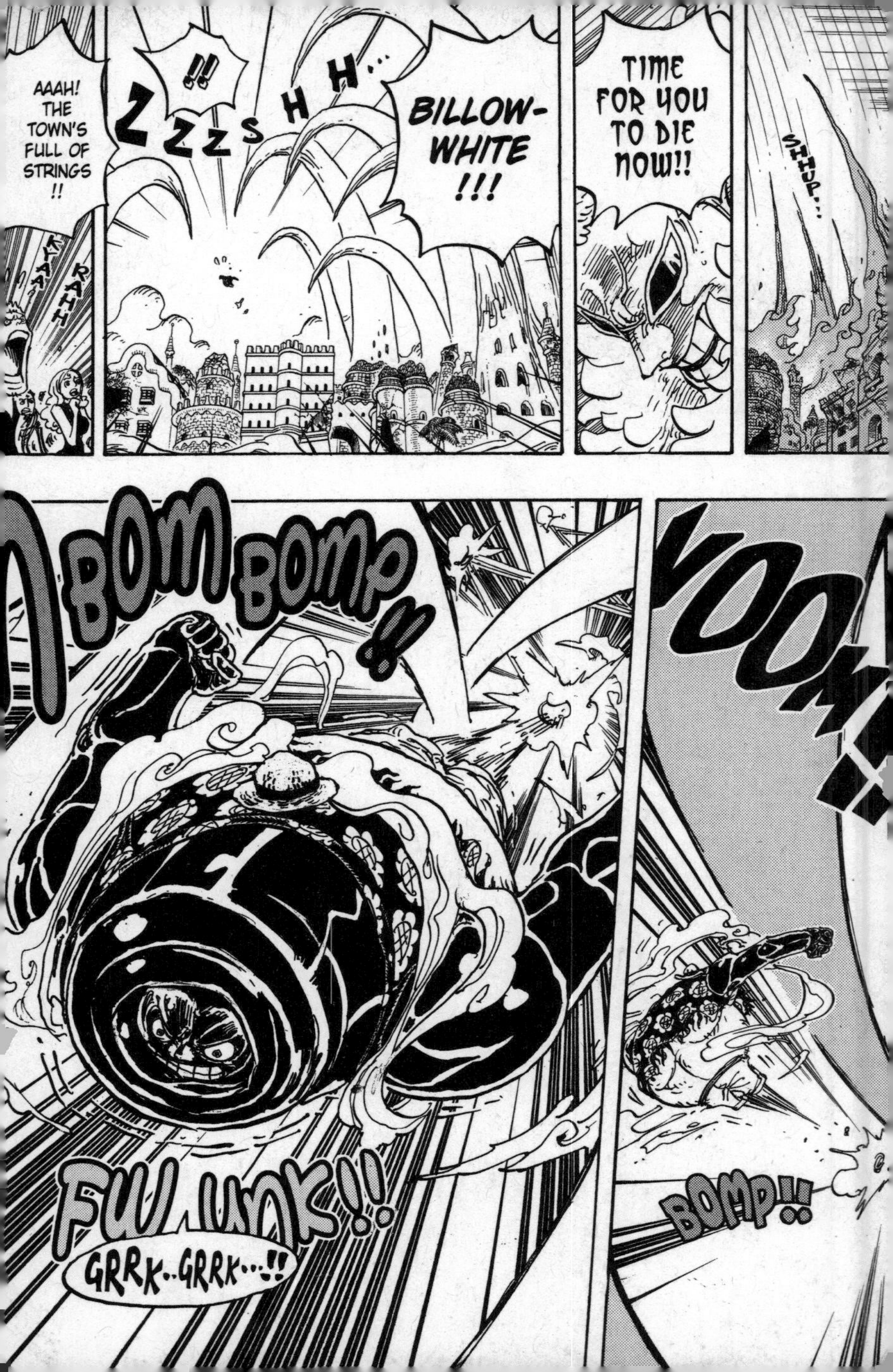
SHHUP!!
TIME FOR YOU TO DIE NOW!!
BILLOW-WHITE!!!
!!
ZZZSHHH...
AAAH! THE TOWN'S FULL OF STRINGS!!
KYAA
RAHH
VOOM!!
BOMP!!
BOM BOMP!!
FWUNK!!
GRRK..GRRK...!!

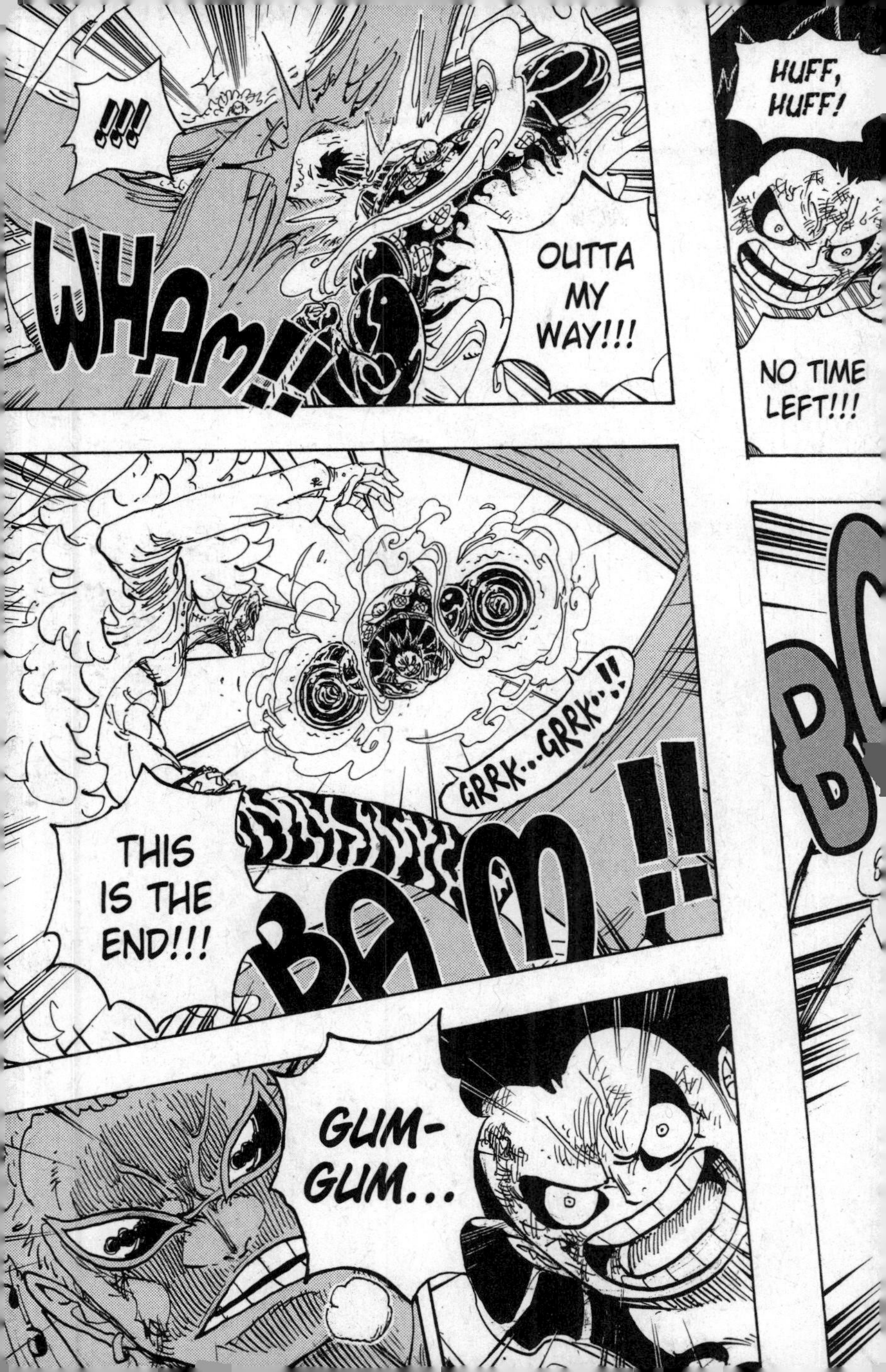

HUFF, HUFF!
NO TIME LEFT!!!
!!!
OUTTA MY WAY!!!
WHAM!!
GRRK...GRRK...!!
BAM!!
THIS IS THE END!!!
GUM-GUM...

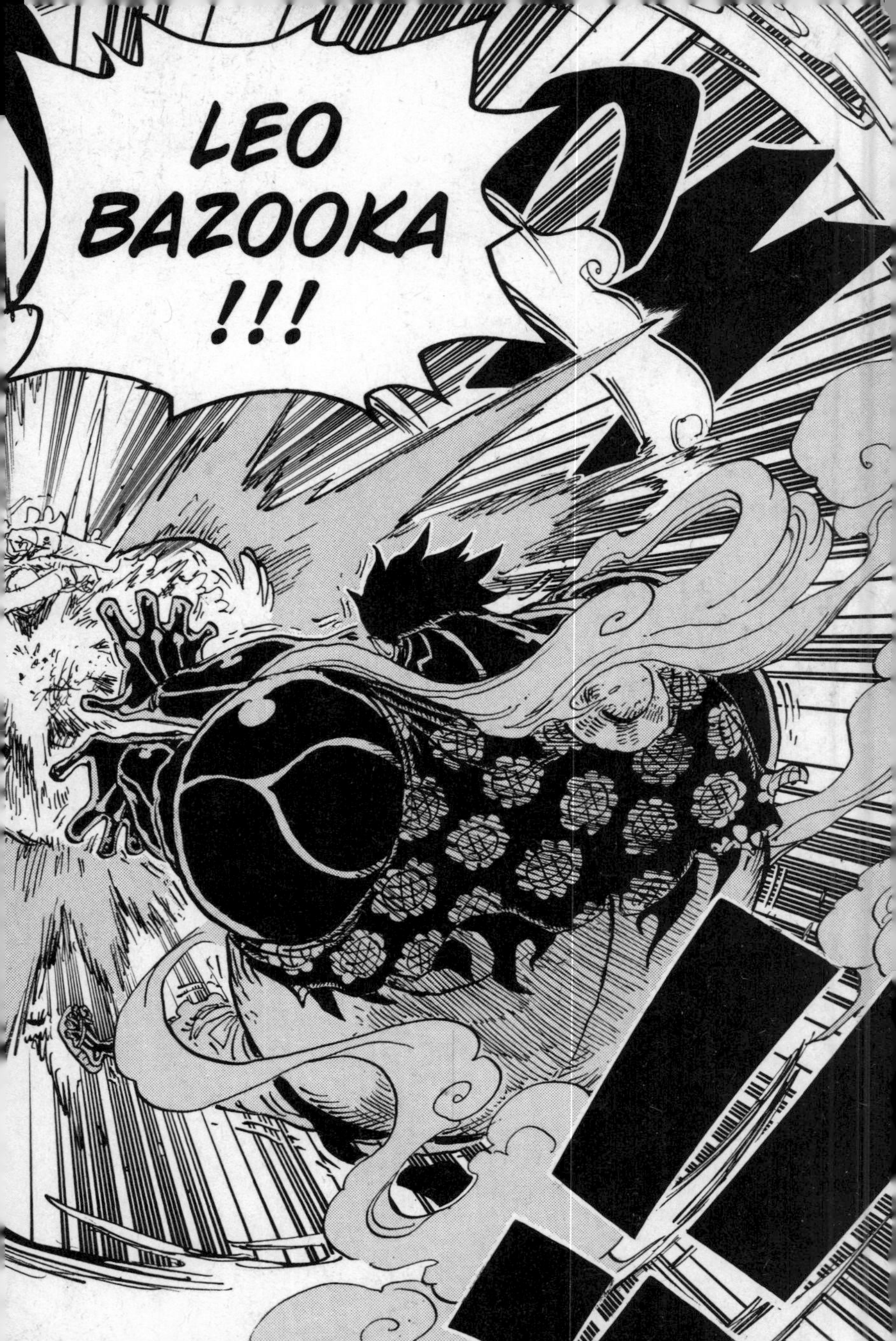
LEO BAZOOKA !!!

TO BE CONTINUED IN *ONE PIECE*, VOL 79!

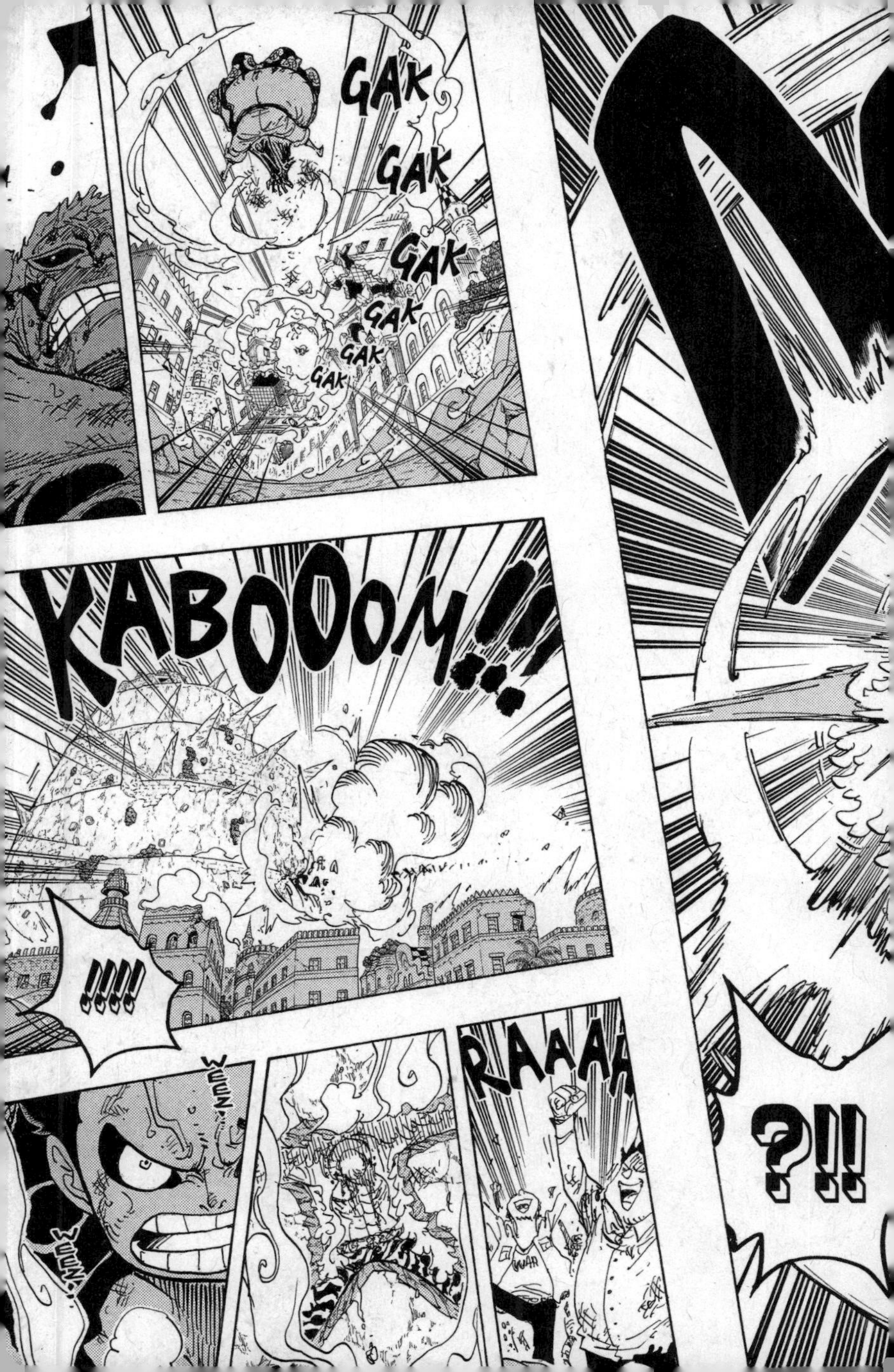
?!!
GAK
GAK
GAK
GAK
GAK
GAK
KABOOOM!!
!!!!
RAAAA
WEEZ
WEEZ

COMING NEXT VOLUME:

YOU'RE OUT OF LINE!!! YOU'VE CAUSED OUR JUSTICE TO LOSE ALL FACE!!!!
IF YOUR FACE IS ALL YOU CARE ABOUT, KEEP IT TUCKED AWAY WHERE IT WON'T GET HURT!!!
IF ADMITTIN' FAULT MEANS YOUR TRUST IS GONE, YOU DIDN'T HAVE NONE IN THE FIRST PLACE!!!

As the Birdcage threatens to destroy Dressrosa and the entire kingdom watches, Luffy and Doflamingo continue their battle. Luffy's Gear Four seems to have given him the upper hand, but what secrets does Doflamingo still hide?

ON SALE AUGUST 2016!

Love triangle!
Comedic antics!!
Gang warfare?!

A laugh-out-loud stor
that features a fake lov
relationship between tw
heirs of rival gangs

Story and Art by
NAOSHI KOMI

NISEKOI
False Love

It's hate at first sight...rather, a knee to the head at first sight when **RAKU ICHIJO** meets **CHITOGE KIRISAKI**! Unfortunately, Raku's gangster father arranges a false love match with their rival's daughter, who just so happens to be Chitoge! Raku's searching for his childhood sweetheart from ten years ago, however, with a pendant around his neck as a memento, but he can't even remember her name or face!

AVAILABLE NOW!

WWW.SHONENJUMP.COM

RATED
T
TEEN
ratings.viz.com

MEDIA
www.viz.

A KILLER COMEDY FROM *WEEKLY SHONEN JUMP*

ASSASSINATION
CLASSROOM

STORY AND ART BY
YUSEI MATSUI

Ever caught yourself screaming, "I could just kill that teacher"?
What would it take to justify such antisocial behavior
and weeks of detention? Especially if he's the best
teacher you've ever had? Giving you an "F" on a quiz?
Mispronouncing your name during roll call...*again*? How about
blowing up the moon and threatening to do the same to
Mother Earth—unless you take him out first?! Plus a reward
of a cool 100 million from the Ministry of Defense!

Okay, now that you're committed... How are you going to
pull this off? What does your pathetic class of misfits have
in their arsenal to combat Teach's alien technology, bizarre
powers and...*tentacles*?!

ASSASSINATION
CLASSROOM

STORY AND ART BY
YUSEI MATSUI
1

SHONEN JUMP ADVANCED